3rd edition

Bankrupt Your Student Loans

And Other

Discharge Strategies

You Can Do It!

By Chuck Stewart, Ph.D.

Learn the inside tips from the author who successfully bankrupted $54,000 in student loans!

SES ● Stewart Education Services

D1205619

AuthorHouse™
1663 Liberty Drive
Bloomington, IN 47403
www.authorhouse.com
Phone: 1-800-839-8640

Bankrupt Your Student Loans and Other Discharge Strategies

Published by Stewart Education Services
www.StewartEducationServices.com

Distributed by Stewart Education Services.
E-mail: info@StewartEducationServices.com

Published by AuthorHouse 9/16/2009, Third edition.

First edition, first printing: September 2005.
Second edition, first printing: January 2006.

ISBN: 978-1-4259-2855-1 (sc)

Library of Congress Control Number: 2006904444

Stewart, Chuck. 1951-
Bankrupt your student loans and other discharge strategies / by Chuck Stewart, Ph.D.
    p. cm.
   Includes index
     1. Bankruptcy—United States—Popular works. I. Stewart, Chuck.

Academic books by Stewart Education Services are available at: www.StewartEducationServices.com

Typeset and printed in the United States of America
Bloomington, Indiana

This book is printed on acid-free paper.

Dedication

To Dean Moffat and James Cabral whose long-time friendships have given me the strength to believe in myself as a writer.

— C.S.

To the readers of this book who had the courage to take the law into their own hands.

Acknowledgments

The author gratefully acknowledges Bonnie Bell for her insightful editing and attention to details in the production of this book; and to Jim Dochterman for his help and support.

About the Author

Chuck Stewart received his Ph.D. in Education from the University of Southern California. Since that time he has written almost 100 academic articles and fifteen academic books including a law dictionary (ABC-CLIO Publications), 3-volume encyclopedia on world culture and politics (Greenwood Publishing), diversity training programs (SAGE Publications), and environmental textbooks on the hazards of lead and mold in residential real estate. He won the David Cameron Legal Research Award in 2001, the President's Award from the Southern California Lambda Medical Association (1999), and multiple grants for academic research and writing by the Institute for the Study of Human Resources (ISHR). He has been responsible for researching and writing a number of teaching curricula and textbooks including some used at the Los Angeles Police Academy. He is a respected author and lecturer.

If you purchase this book, you will gain access to a library of documents, educational videos, and other help from the website– www.BankruptYourStudentLoans.com.

If you have comments or questions about this book, you are welcome to contact Chuck Stewart via E-mail at: info@BankruptYourStudentLoans.com. Please be courteous. Realize that hundreds of E-mails each week come into BankruptYourStudentLoans.com mostly from people asking legal advice. Chuck Stewart is not an attorney and provides legal information, not legal advice. Please don't ask specific questions about your own situation. But, if you have a unique question or slant on the student loan problem and suggested solutions that could benefit others, do write. This book is, in many ways, a community outpouring on the topic since the legal profession and Department of Education actively discourage an honest discussion on the student loan problem.

Chuck Stewart's bankruptcy case is public information and can be found at the California Central Bankruptcy Court case LA04-19681ER, filed August 2004.

July 2009

A PERSONAL LETTER FROM THE AUTHOR,

I want to personally thank you for buying *Bankrupt Your Student Loans and Other Discharge Strategies*. You made a wise choice to educate yourself on this important topic.

You are embarking on a very difficult and personal struggle. I have been there. I was faced with overwhelming financial debt of which student loans seemed an insurmountable problem. I was told it was impossible to bankrupt my student loans. Attorneys actually laughed at me and wanted exorbitant amounts of money to represent me– and then predicted I would lose. When the U.S. Attorney laughed at me for asking how to bankrupt my student loans I felt I had nothing to lose by representing myself. But the problems were daunting. There simply were no books or resources revealing how to go about this.

I wrote this book to help honest debtors, like you, to have the best chance at representing yourself in attempting to bankrupt, or have discharged, your student loans. Not everyone buying this book should consider bankruptcy. There are other means to discharging student loans. The book covers a multitude of options. Perhaps one of them will work for you.

I hope you visited our website– www.BankruptYourStudentLoans.com– and downloaded the Table of Contents and Chapter 1 to help in your decision to buy the book. Not all debtors qualify to attempt to discharge their student loans through the bankruptcy "undue hardship" exemption. However, the book also gives information and strategies for direct negotiations with the Department of Education. Even if you cannot bankrupt your student loans, perhaps you can strongly negotiate with the Department of Education for better loan terms or the discharge of part, or all, of your student loans. The book can help with this negotiation.

Once you complete the process, or decide not to go forward, may I suggest that you donate the book to your local library. If the book is unblemished, they can put it in their reference section. You will be helping future debtors with their problem.

I want to share that during the adversary proceeding process there were times I felt angry, overwhelmed, under attack, like giving up, confused, and more. It is a very emotional journey made difficult by attorneys who are paid not only defend the government, but to attack you. My heart goes out to you.

You are welcome to contact me with questions about the book. <u>I cannot, however, help you with your particular case since I am not an attorney</u>. I would like to hear about your case along with any new insights to add to future editions to the book.

Since the publication of the first issue of this book, hundreds of people have contacted me with their plight. Some common questions have come up that made it necessary to write a third edition. The most common question comes from those who have already been through bankruptcy to only learn that it may have been possible for them to include their student loans. I have heard the pain and anger in their E-mails at being told (or better yet duped into believing) it was impossible to bankrupt their student loans. It may be possible to reopen a bankruptcy and pursue an adversary proceeding. A number of people are trying this approach at this time. I've included a generalized petition they are using. It seems a strategy worth pursuing since tens of millions of people who have been through bankruptcy are still struggling with the burden of student loans. Watch our website for developments on this new strategy. I hope it works. It could open the floodgates of litigation; something I hope happens, as I believe this is the only way to bring this daunting problem to the attention of Congress.

Besides some legal updates, this edition contains:
- Discussion and forms related to reopening a bankruptcy for the purpose of including student loans and filing an adversary proceeding.
- Extended discussion on the Compromise and Write-Off procedures. There seems to be many people who are not considering bankruptcy but live under crushing student loan debt and need to do something to make life more bearable. Here I discuss more the psychology behind these two discharge strategies.

A website– www.BankruptYourStudentLoans.com– has been created specifically on this topic. If you buy this book, you will gain access to the members only section of the website. As a member, you will:
- Gain access to all forms in downloadable format
- Have access to many videos explaining specific aspects of the adversary proceeding including discussions on the overall problem and strategies.
- Be able to share your stories and questions with others in an open Forum.

The website hopes to become a community center where people can come together to help one another on this important topic.

As you read the book, you may come to understand that besides your specific situation, there is need for a complete revision of the student loans discharge options. A national political movement of debtors, attorneys and community activists is needed to address the growing student loan problem. One purpose of the website is to become a center for this political movement. The website contains links to various student loan activists groups. Hopefully attorneys who believe in the cause will join in and help develop a nationwide resource of legal centers and attorneys who are willing to work with debtors on this problem.

Ultimately, I would like to see class action suits attack the inherent unfairness of the adversary proceeding. Student loan debt needs to be reclassified back to being unsecured debt dischargeable through standard bankruptcy process. In the future, there should be no need for this book. Let's work to make this happen.

Best of luck.

Chuck Stewart (*See* About the Author for contact information.)

Table of Contents

CHAPTER 1 You Can Do It! 1

What This Book Covers..2
Why You Should Use This Book 2
Who Qualifies for an Adversary Proceeding, Compromise, or Write-Off and When are they Applied? 3
How to Use this Book 4
Reopening a Bankruptcy 6

CHAPTER 2 Taking Control 9

Postponement and Repayment Options 9
  Deferment 9
  Forbearance 10
  Consolidation...10
Repayment Plans 11
  Standard Repayment Plan..11
  Extended Repayment Plan 11
  Graduated Repayment Plan 11
  Income Contingent Repayment (ICR) Plan..11
Typical Discharge Options 12
Other Discharge or Payment Options 13
  Teaching, State, Professional, Military, Nursing, and National Service 13
  Ask for Relief—Compromise and Write-Off...13
Default and Collections..14
Other Legal Considerations 15
  Federal Benefits...15
  Being Sued...16
  Legal Defenses That Cannot Work 16
Should I Go Forward with an Adversary Proceeding or Compromise or Write-Off? 17
Summary...17

CHAPTER 3 History of the Student Loan Program 19

GSLP 1965 (Stafford Loans)..19
Middle Income Student Assistance Act 1978 19
Media Hype of Abuse...20
Compromise Bill Results in Non-dischargeability of Student Loans 21
1978 Bankruptcy Reform Act Section 523(a)(8)...22
Loan Default Rate Plummets...22
Summary...23

CHAPTER 4 Court Opinions and Tests 25

Bankruptcy Law In U.S. 25
"Undue Hardship" 25
Court Tests for "Undue Hardship" 26
    The Johnson Test...26
    The Bryant Poverty Test..27
    The Totality of the Circumstances Test..28
    The Brunner Test...28
Summary 30

CHAPTER 5 "Undue Hardship" Arguments 33

Characteristics Common to Undue Hardship Tests...33
    Characteristic A—Current Living Condition and the Impact of Repaying Loan on "Minimal Living" Standard 34
    Characteristic B—Prospects for Repaying the Loans...34
    Characteristic C—Good Faith and Loan Repayment 38
Summary 39

CHAPTER 6 Example Court Cases With Analysis 41

Case: In re Cheesman..41
Case: In re Conner...42
Case: In re Courtney 42
Case: In re Ford 43
Case: In re Goulet..43
Case: In re Gravante 44
Case: In re Healey..44
Case: In re Innes 45
Case: In re Kraft 47
Case: In re Lehman 47
Case: In re Myers...48
Case: In re Pena 48
Case: In re Rivers 49
Case: In re Roberson..49
Case: In re Skaggs..49
Case: In re Stebbins-Hopf 50
Case: In re Walcott..50
Case: In re Wetzel..50

CHAPTER 7 Advocacy 53

Rate of Success at Discharging Student Loans 54
Challenges to 11 U.S.C.A. §523(a)(8)... 55
    The Law Is, and Was, Unnecessary 55
    Law Violates Equal Protection Clause of the U.S. Constitution............................. 56
    Unintended Impact on the Poor and Minorities 58
    Violates Bankruptcy's "Fresh Start" Concept.. 59
    Congress Failed to Clearly Define the Law 61
Challenges to Income Contingent Repayment (ICR) Plan 65
2005 Changes to Bankruptcy Code... 66
Chapter 13 Bankruptcies... 66
Summary... 67

CHAPTER 8 Preparing for the Adversary Proceeding................73

The Adversary Proceeding... 73
    PRE-INFO— Undue Hardship Test and Student Loan History 73
    CHARACTERISTIC A— Current Living Condition and the Impact of Repaying Loan on "Minimal Living"
    Standard 74
    CHARACTERISTIC B— Prospects for Repaying the Loans 76
    CHARACTERISTIC C— Good Faith and Loan Repayment 77
    INCOME CONTINGENT REPAYMENT (ICR) PLAN 77
Review.. 78

CHAPTER 9 Step-By-Step Procedures for
The Adversary Proceeding 79

The Adversary Proceeding... 79
    Before Filing the Complaint... 79
    Filing and Serving the Complaint 83
    Status Hearing 85
    Mediation.. 86
    Pretrial Hearing and Trial... 91

CHAPTER 10 Preparing Your Case for
Compromise or *Write-Off* 93

PRE-INFO— Student Loan History 93
CHARACTERISTIC A— Current Living Condition and the Impact of Repaying Loan on "Minimal Living"
Standard 93
CHARACTERISTIC B— Prospects for Repaying the Loans 95
CHARACTERISTIC C— Good Faith and Loan Repayment.. 96
INCOME CONTINGENT REPAYMENT (ICR) PLAN 96
Review.. 97

	CHAPTER 11	Step-By-Step Negotiations for *Compromise* or *Write-Off*	99

CHAPTER 11   Step-By-Step Negotiations for
Compromise or *Write-Off* **99**

Compromise..99
Write-Off...99
Contacting the Agency 100
Writing the Agency..101
Stronger Negotiations..102
Proposing a Settlement..103
Just Who Does the Negotiations at DOE?..103

APPENDIX **105**

APPENDIX A   Department of Education Repayment
Plans and Discharge Options **107**

Postponing Repayments...107
    Deferment 107
    Forbearance...108
    Consolidation..108
Repayment Plans...111
    Standard Repayment Plan...111
    Extended Repayment Plan...112
    Graduated Repayment Plan 112
    Income Contingent Repayment (ICR) Plan...113
    Constant Multiplier and Other Charts..115
Loan Discharge...118
    Direct Loan and FFEL Discharge 118
    Perkins Discharge..119
    Other Discharge Options..120
Loan Default 121
    What is default?..121
    What happens if I default?..121

APPENDIX B Laws and Legal Guidelines 123

Precedent Setting Cases 123
Rules and Regulations 130
   31 U.S.C.A. §3716 — Administrative Offset of Federal Benefits 130
   Standardized Compromise and Write-Off Procedures 133
   Interrogatories— Kentucky 136
   Interrogatories Kentucky—Request for Documents... 141
   IRS Collection Financial Standards 143
Federal Poverty Guideline 153
11 U.S.C.A § 523 (a) (8) 158
Chapter 7 Bankruptcy Forms (California Central District) 163
   Schedule I-Current Income of Individual Debtor (Form B6I) 163
   Schedule J-Current Expenditures of Individual Debtor (Form B6J) 164
   Business Income and Expenses 165
   Chapter 7 Form B6F— Schedule F - Creditors Holding Unsecured Nonpriority Claims (Sample) 166
   Chapter 7 Form B6F— Schedule F - Creditors Holding Unsecured Nonpriority Claims (Blank)........................... 167
Reopening a Bankruptcy 168
   Motion to Reopen Bankruptcy Sample 168
   Motion to Reopen Bankruptcy Sample 2 170
   Amendment to Schedule F Sample 171

APPENDIX D Worksheets 173

Worksheets 173
   Student Loan History 173
   Current Income Status 174
   Current Expenditure Status.. 175
   Work Time Accounting Table... 177
   Income and Student Loan Payment 178
Worksheet Samples 180
   Current Income and Family Status.. 180
   Current Expenditures and Minimalized Living 181
   Work Time Accounting Statement 182
   Personal Limitations Statement.. 183
   Good Faith and Loan Repayment Statement... 185
   Income Contingent Repayment 187

APPENDIX E — Forms for Adversary Proceeding 189

Forms—Instructions 190
    Blue Back 191
    Adversary Proceeding Sheet (Cover) 192
    Adversary Proceeding Complaint 195
    Summons 201
    Proof of Service with Mail Matrix and Cover 203
Forms—Samples 208
    Adversary Proceeding Sheet (Cover) (Sample) 209
    Adversary Proceeding Complaint (Sample) 210
    Summons (Sample) 213
    Proof of Service (Sample) 214
    Mail Matrix (Sample) 215
    Proof of Service Cover (Sample) 216
    Joint Status Report (Sample) 217
    Request for Documents from Department of Education (Sample) 221
    Stipulation (Sample) 224
Forms—Blank 228
    Blank Legal (Pleading) Paper 229
    Adversary Proceeding Sheet (Cover) 230
    Summons and Notice of Status Conference (CA Central District) 231
    Proof of Service 232
    Joint Status Report 233

APPENDIX F — Academic Articles 237

Almost Two-Thirds of All Bankruptcies Due to Medical Bills 238
The Consequences of Age on the Ability to Repay 239
Discrimination Based on Age 241
Discrimination Against the Highly Educated 244
Discrimination Based on Sexual Orientation 246
Reverse Discrimination Based on Gender or Race 247
U.S. Economy (2009) 248
Brunner Test Alternative 251

APPENDIX G — Resources 255

U.S. Bankruptcy Court Contacts 255

Glossary 277

Index 279

Notes 285

CHAPTER 1
You Can Do It!

You have been told that it is impossible to bankrupt your student loans. Attorneys tell you this, the Department of Education tells you this, and it is common knowledge. But it is not true.

You can bankrupt your student loans or discharge your student loans through other means.

However, until now it has been a secret and very difficult. With this book, you will learn that it is, in fact, easy, just emotionally challenging.

Chuck Stewart, Ph.D., author of this book, successfully bankrupted over $54,000 in student loans as part of a Chapter 7 bankruptcy. Like many of you, after receiving his college degree he experienced years of difficulty getting employment. Either the job market was tight, or his degree was in a field that had too many other job seekers, or he lived in the wrong place with few jobs, or the company he worked for downsized and he lost his job, and more. If he tried to get "any" job, including ones well below his education, he was not hired because he was "over-qualified." As he got older, ageism became a real barrier to employment. Years of part-time employment took its financial toll. Credit card debt mounted. He lost his house. He supported his very ill partner who eventually died. After 10-years of struggle, he had large debts, no retirement, no savings, no medical insurance, and little hope of ever finding a decent job. He subsisted at the poverty level.

Many of you have experienced similar problems: loss of job, years of part-time employment, never getting ahead. Many of you have your own medical illnesses— not bad enough to get you permanent disability (for which you could have your student loans discharged) — but bad enough to push you into

Overruled!

Jonathan G, 46, had $100,000 in student loans incurred while earning a degree from the New England Conservatory of Music. He performed with two city orchestras and finally won a position with the Louisiana Philharmonic Orchestra in New Orleans. Even after reaching this high level of professionalism, he taught cello at Tulane University to earn a paltry $20,000 a year. He filed bankruptcy to try and get out from under the crushing debt.

Attorneys from the Department of Education and a guarantee agency that held some of the loans scrutinized his living expenses and argued that he could trim his expenses if he canceled his Internet services ($23.90/m), gym membership ($48.51/m) and got rid of his cat ($20/m). The bankruptcy judge sided with Mr. G saying that the Internet service was needed to look for work, the gym membership to work out the pain in his back caused from playing the cello, and the expenses related to the cat were not "luxuries" considering Mr. G was single and living alone. The judge ruled the loans caused an "undue hardship" and were discharged.

The Education Department appealed and Mr. G lost. The federal appellate court suggested Mr. G find a job as a music-store clerk.

Hechinger, J. (January 6, 2005) U.S. Gets Tough on Failure to Repay Student Loans, *Wall Street Journal*, v.CCXLV n.4,p.1

poverty and keep you there. Or maybe you are taking care of someone with medical needs and that is pushing you over the financial and emotional edge. Medical problems are the number one cause of bankruptcy. It is estimated that two-thirds of all bankruptcies are precipitated by crushing medical bills. For some of you, either you did not finish your education or the training program you paid for was of such low quality or with outdated skills that you never landed a better paying job. In either case, education did not lead to a better life and participation in the American dream. Now you are saddled with student loan debts for an education that did not benefit you. How aggravating!

Of course, the recent decline in the economy is devastating many families. Bankruptcy looms to which student loans add an extra burden.

This book is for you.

What This Book Covers

This book discusses many strategies for discharging your student loans. The focus of the book is to help you discharge your student loans through either bankruptcy OR direct negotiation with the Department of Education (what is termed *Compromise* or *Write-Off*).

Bankruptcy: This book gives the step-by-step procedure for filing, mediating, and arguing an adversary proceeding as part of bankruptcy. *Student loans are not dischargeable in a straightforward bankruptcy.* Student loans are listed as part of the over-all debt in bankruptcy, then, usually within 60 days of the creditor meeting, an adversary proceeding is filed with the bankruptcy court against the U.S. Department of Education to prove that repaying the student loans will create an "undue hardship." If you prevail, the court will discharge all or a portion of your student loans as part of your bankruptcy.

Many people have already been through bankruptcy. Most were told it was impossible to include their student loans in bankruptcy or that it was very very "difficult" and shouldn't be tried. As such, they did not file an adversary proceeding in conjunction with

their bankruptcy filing. Upon publication of this book, some debtors have sought to reopen their previous bankruptcy to attempt an adversary proceeding. This strategy is discussed in detail later in this chapter.

Negotiating a Discharge: If you are not planning a bankruptcy, this book can still provide important information for negotiating a reduction or discharge of your student loans through the *Compromise* or *Write-Off* procedures.

No other book provides the information or guidance needed to help you discharge student loans through bankruptcy or negotiation.

This book provides:

- Step-by-Step process for filing an adversary proceeding or negotiating a Compromise or Write-Off; and, if needed, reopening a bankruptcy
- All forms
- Sample forms
- History and Analysis of the student loan program and its enforcement to help you prepare your own arguments.
- Mediation strategies
- Many more resources

Why You Should Use This Book

When the author of this book first contemplated bankrupting his student loans as part of his Chapter 7 bankruptcy, he sought the advice of a number of attorneys. All of them said it was virtually impossible to win an adversary proceeding but that they would take on the case for $10,000 up front and $450 per hour with court fees. Even still, they said he most likely would not win. The author was broke, down to his last $300, and could not possibly pay the attorney fees. So, he thought he had nothing to lose by representing himself. Being an academic with a number of published books (including a law dictionary), he researched the problem.

First, he discovered that people who represent themselves in an adversary proceeding are more likely to win. Judges are aware that if you can afford a high-priced lawyer, you are obviously not in terrible financial need. Also, you know your situation better than any hired attorney. You can argue your case with greater fervor and conviction.

Second, until the release of this book, there was <u>no concise information that addressed the problem of bankrupting student loans through an adversary proceeding or negotiating a discharge through Compromise or Write-Off</u>. The author researched many law journals, cases, and books to pull together everything that is needed to attack this problem. He also spoke with a number of people who have gone through the process, gleaning from them bits of information that is never written in law journals.

Third, this is a <u>very personal journey</u>. There are many self-help law books that describe the bankruptcy process. When it comes to student loans, they devote less than a page to the problem and refer you to an attorney. These books are well written but very impersonal. An adversary proceeding is very different. The courts will pry deeply into your life, making judgments every step along the way. They will question your purchasing decisions, e.g., did you minimize living expenses by getting rid of your pet to free up $20 more a month to make payments to the government (see the box at the beginning of this chapter describing the ordeal of Mr. Jonathan G). They will question your inability to find work and much more. You will feel besieged and belittled. <u>The author of this book has been through this process</u> and shares his experience about how to minimize the government's efforts to beat you down, and, thus, win your case. No attorney isolated in a glass office, living in the upper levels of income, can possibly understand this.

And **fourth**, <u>there is a track record of success by people who have used this book</u>. Of the people who have corresponded with the author about their experiences, everyone has expressed their gratitude for the help received from the book. Many have either renegotiated their loans for much better terms or have successfully bankrupted all or most of their student loans. The most successful case to date achieved a discharge of $225,000 through bankruptcy in 2009.

Although <u>the author cannot provide legal advice</u>, he would like to hear your stories to improve future updates of this book. See the contact information on the "About the Author" page. Let's make it better for honest debtors to legitimately discharge student loans.

Who Qualifies for an Adversary Proceeding, Compromise, or Write-Off and When are they Applied?

You may qualify to file for an <u>Adversary Proceeding</u>, <u>Compromise</u>, or <u>Write-Off</u> if:

- You have student loans backed or issued by the U.S. Department of Education that you want to have discharged.
- You cannot maintain your current living standard if forced to repay your outstanding debt, including your student loans.
- There are circumstances that will prevent you from obtaining sufficient income in the future to repay your student loans.

Considering Bankruptcy
- You are ready to file, or have filed, a Chapter 7, 11, 12 or 13 Bankruptcy.
- It has not been more than 60 days since your meeting with your creditors.

Previous Bankruptcy
- Have already completed a bankruptcy and want to reopen the bankruptcy for the purpose of including your student loans.

Not considering Bankruptcy
- There are circumstances that will prevent you from obtaining sufficient income in the future to repay your student loans. These include: job market; familia obligations; discriminatory factors such as age, race, sexual orientation, gender; and other circumstances.

The courts have developed a number of comprehensive tests that delve much deeper into your living and financial conditions than the usual bankruptcy courts. These tests have revealed a number of rule-of-thumb guidelines that if you do not meet the conditions, it will be very difficult to explain away. Not that they are impossible to overcome, but it will be very difficult.

These conditions include:

- Your student loans should not make up more than 50% of your total debt.

- You should be living at or near the Federal Poverty Guideline.

- More than 5 years should have passed since obtaining your last student loan.

- You have been diligent in making payments on your student loans. When you were unable to make loan payments, you showed diligence by delaying payment through the proper use of forbearances and deferments, or negotiated alternative repayment plans.

- There should be a sense of "*hopelessness*" with the circumstances of your case.

Even though these are guidelines many courts have adopted, they are not set in stone. It is our hope that with the onslaught of adversary proceedings generated through use of this book, the guidelines will be challenged and changed. Many of the guidelines are not logical and were never specified by Congress. For example, as you will read in this book, the adoption of the Federal Poverty Guideline to determine "undue hardship" was arbitrary. There are other federal measures of poverty. Why was this one– which is the most restrictive and not based on poverty but on survival– adopted by the courts? Easy, the Department of Education used it in one of the earliest cases and it stuck. It is arbitrary and abusive. It needs to be challenged and changed. A few courts have decided that a standard of living below middle-class is an "undue hardship" thereby overruling the accepted practice of using the Federal Poverty Guideline. It will take many more cases ruling for a middle-class standard for it to become adopted practice.

Here is another way to think of your debt situation– If you don't attempt to discharge your student loans, you probably will be stuck with them for the rest of your life, which will prevent you from ever owning a home or achieving the American Dream. So what do you have to lose?

How to Use this Book

If you have filed a Chapter 7 bankruptcy, you have discovered how relatively easy it is. Many free legal clinics can help with the bankruptcy and there are many fill-in-the-blanks books on the topic. Really, it is easy to file a Chapter 7 bankruptcy. Although the recent changes in the bankruptcy laws requires a preliminary step of court oversight, it doesn't change that most people will proceed to the traditional Chapter 7 process. The meeting with the creditors is a non-event. The meeting lasts a few minutes if there are no challenges to the debts of your case. The judicial representative looks over your forms to see that they are complete. That's it. No drama. Usually there are no questions. If you visit the court a few days or hours before your meeting, you will be able to watch the process and be amazed how fast they conduct each case. Maybe one case in thirty has a creditor show up to challenge some aspect of the bankruptcy. So relax. Within 3 months after the meeting of the creditors, your debt will be discharged.

An *Adversary Proceeding* is very different. This is a full-blown lawsuit against the government and its attorneys. They have 20 years of litigating this problem. As such, it is paramount that you educate yourself thoroughly on the topic. You are not expected to be an expert, but you must be able to hold your own. This book is for you.

If you plan to file a *Compromise* or *Write-Off*, this book provides everything you need to prepare your arguments and negotiate with the Department of Education— so much hinges on understanding the psychology of those who work for the Department of Education.

You are strongly advised to read every chapter thoroughly. Not just skim them, but also read them in depth. Take your time. Take a couple of days, and then revisit a chapter. As you begin preparing your case, reread sections that come to mind. You must become fully knowledgeable on this topic if you are to win. It usually takes months between each action in court, so you have time to prepare.

Chapter 2 — Taking Control: Helps you evaluate your student loan situation. Perhaps bankruptcy is not the right action for you to take. There are many other ways to discharge student loans if you qualify. This chapter presents some of the alternatives to bankruptcy.

Chapter 3 — History of Student Loan Program: Gives a historical background to the implementation of student loan programs backed or issued by the U.S. Department of Education. It is important for readers to understand how these programs came about and the concerns the public, and many in Congress, had over the increasing number of students defaulting on their government loans. Congress slowly amended the laws to make it more difficult for debtors to bankrupt their student loans. It is this Congressional debate that molded many court decisions. People planning to defend their adversary proceeding must be familiar with this debate as they, too, will have to use the same language and concepts.

Chapter 4 — Court Opinions and Tests: Briefly examines the U.S. bankruptcy system as related to the concept of "undue hardship." Ultimately, to have student loans discharged, a debtor must present a strong case proving that repaying the student loans would create an undue hardship for them. Unfortunately, Congress failed to define undue hardship leaving it to courts to construct. This chapter describes in great details the four major tests used by a majority of United States courts to determine undue hardship and the dischargeability of student loans.

Chapter 5 — "Undue Hardship" Arguments: Develops a set of characteristics common to all undue hardship tests and reviews some of the arguments you will use to meet the tests.

Chapter 6 — Example Court Cases with Analysis: Presents a number of bankruptcy cases along with an analysis of why they succeeded or failed. You will gain a better understanding of the capricious nature of the courts and the overt aggressiveness displayed by

the Department of Education. You will also learn how to evaluate your own case to increase the possibilities of success.

Chapter 7 — Advocacy: The bankruptcy code that governs the discharge of student loans is bad law. The Department of Education and courts have mostly taken a very narrow interpretation of the law. As a result, few debtors are successful at having their student loans discharged through bankruptcy. This chapter discusses many of the limitations of the law and the poor application by the courts. You may want to engage in advocating for rescinding or overturning this law. If you are successful at having the law rescinded, then your student loan debt becomes just like any other unsecured debt and bankrupted through a standard bankruptcy proceeding.

Chapter 8 — Preparing for the Adversary Proceeding: This chapter helps you gather all the personal and financial information necessary to present a solid case for discharge of your student loan debt. Forms and worksheets were developed and are included in the Appendix.

Chapter 9 — Step-By-Step Procedure for the Adversary Proceeding: This chapter gives the exact steps required to file an adversary proceeding, strategies for effective mediation, and presentation in court (if needed).

Chapter 10 — Preparing Your Case for Compromise or Write-Off: This chapter helps you gather all the documents and personal information needed to prove during a Compromise or Write-Off negotiation that repaying your student loans would be impossible.

Chapter 11 — Step-by-Step Negotiations for Compromise or Write-Off: Provides effective strategies for engaging the Department of Education in tough negotiations to discharge all or part of the student loans during Compromise or Write-Off proceedings.

(If you are not needing to reopen a bankruptcy, you may skip the next section and proceed to Chapter 2).

Reopening a Bankruptcy

Since the publication of the first edition of this book in 2005, the most frequently asked question comes from people who have already completed a bankruptcy. They are interested in knowing if it is possible to still bankrupt their student loans. Their correspondence is usually filled with despair and anger. Bankruptcy relieved them of some personal debt but not their student loans. Upon learning it was possible for them to have included their student loans in their bankruptcy, they feel duped by a system upheld by attorneys and the Department of Education.

A few of these people have recently attempted to reopen their bankruptcy to address their student loans. Some have met with success. They have shared their experiences and documents with the author. None of the cases have proceeded all the way to the final court hearing so we don't know the actual chances for success. The information is presented here as a starting point. If you proceed with this course of action, please keep the author abreast of the case development. We would like to provide accurate information to others needing to take this course of action. Pleases check our website– www.BankruptYourStudentLoans.com– for updates on this strategy.

Recommendation: When other legal self-help books broach the topic of reopening a bankruptcy, they recommend that you seek the advice of an attorney. The author of this book also encourages you to seek the help of an attorney to reopen a bankruptcy.

Bankruptcy Code [Section 11 U.S.C. § 350(b)] authorizes bankruptcy courts to allow for the reopening of bankruptcy cases for a number of reasons. The decision to allow a case to be reopened is at the discretion of the court— meaning that the court is not required to reopen a case.

There are three steps to the process: (1) bring a motion to reopen the case, (2) amend your original petition by modifying Schedule F (this assumes you did not originally list your student loans), and (3) send notice to the creditors, trustee and the U.S. Trustee of the amendment. The fees for reopening and amending the original petition vary according to local law often costing as much as $1,000 and varies depending if you are reopening a Chapter 7, Chapter 11, or Chapter 13. One person who reopened his bankruptcy found that once the court was clear the purpose was to file an adversary proceeding to determine the dischargeability of student loans, the filing fees were waived.

Step 1 — Gather all your bankruptcy documents so that you can pull the necessary information.

Step 2 — Contact the court where your bankruptcy was processed to ask for guidance for filing a motion to reopen your bankruptcy. Forms, fees, timing and exact procedures vary from state to state. Some courts are providing forms that can be filled in and filed through the Internet. The forms and fees vary by court.

Step 3 — Prepare your Motion to Reopen Bankruptcy and file with the court. Two examples and blank form are provided in the Appendix. This shows how they vary depending on location. Remember, these forms are just a suggestion and their exact form may be different at your local court. You must check with your bankruptcy court first to find out what form they use.

Step 4 — Amend Bankruptcy Forms. Most likely, when you filed your original bankruptcy forms, you did not include your student loans under the section for unsecured debt. If this is so, then the forms need to be amended. In a Chapter 7 Bankruptcy, Schedule F is where your student loans should have been listed. Once your Motion to Reopen Bankruptcy is approved, an Amendment to Schedule F needs to be filed with the court. An example and blank form are provided in the Appendix. If you did include your student loans in the original bankruptcy, you do not need to perform this step.

Step 5 — Notify the creditor, trustee and the U.S. Trustee. Here, you notify the creditor (Department of Education) that the bankruptcy has been reopened and the list of creditors modified. Notification details are given in Chapter 9.

It has not been tested, but we believe you will have 30 or 60 days from the date the judge approves the Motion to Reopen Bankruptcy to complete these steps and file the adversary proceeding. Check with your local court to be sure. For details on preparing, filing, and representing yourself in an adversary proceeding, see Chapters 8 and 9.

We hope the best for you. If you have insight on this process, please contact the author so that better information can be provided to future debtors having to engage in this process.

*

Disclaimer

There is no guarantee that by using this book you will achieve a discharge of your student loans.

This book is based on the personal experiences of the author, the experiences of other debtors who have gone through the process and the author's research into the topic. Your experiences may be different.

The author is not an attorney and makes no claims concerning the legal accuracy of this book.

No part of this book should be construed as being legal advice. If in doubt, consult an attorney in your area. Be aware, though, that very few attorneys are knowledgeable in this field. By reading this book, you will be able to better assist any attorney you consult. An attorney or paralegal may be useful in helping you construct the legal document needed to file with the courts.

The author is providing legal information. Legal knowledge is not legal advice.

CHAPTER 2
Taking Control

This book assumes you plan to discharge your student loans through either bankruptcy or a Compromise or Write-Off.

Perhaps bankruptcy is not the best solution for you. Let's evaluate the situation and, by doing so, take control of the problem. Remember, trying to bankrupt your student loan should be viewed as your last possible option. Although the steps are easy, emotionally it is very difficult.

An excellent book for helping you manage your student loans is Robin Leonard and Deanne Loonin, 2001, *Take Control of Your Student Loan Debt*, from NOLO.

Postponement and Repayment Options

If you are struggling to make your student loan payments, one option is to delay or postpone payment until you are in better financial condition. Another option is to change to a different repayment plan. Loan holders and the Department of Education have many different plans to accommodate most debtors. Please see the Appendix A for greater details of these plans, or visit U.S. Department of Education webpage located at: www.studentaid.ed.gov/students/publications/repaying_loans/

Deferment

Deferment is a postponement of repayment of student loans under various and specific circumstances. In some cases, you don't have to pay principal or interest during deferment. In other cases, interest still accrues during the time no payments are made on the loan. In general, you are allowed up to a maximum of 3 deferments (of 1 year each). You must apply for deferments directly though the Department of

If You Ignore It, They Will Come

At one time, students who ignored repaying their student loans often never heard from the government, or if they did, it occurred after the time limit the government had in which to collect. Some students thought that if they stayed out of sight they could get out of repaying their student loans.

Changes in law and an increased effort in debt collection have made such a strategy unworkable. Now, if payments are missed, you probably will hear from the loan holder immediately. Miss a few more and your account will be sent to collection where the government has the right to intercept your federal and state income tax refund check, garnish your wages and social security check, add hefty collection fees, and more. Further, there is no time limitation on how long the government can track you down to get payment!

It is important for you to show diligence by staying current with your loan. In times of financial stress, contact your loan holder and negotiate a delay in repayment, or a new repayment plan, or some other option. Do not ignore your responsibility!

Education. The general status qualifying for deferment is:

- Enrollment in school
- Temporary total disability
- Unemployment
- Economic hardship
- Enrollment in rehabilitation program for the disabled
- Parents with young children

The conditions for deferment change constantly. Contact the Department of Education for requirements concerning deferments. For plan details, see the Appendix A or visit the Department of Education website.

Forbearance

If you're not eligible for a deferment and still need debt relief, you might be granted forbearance for a limited and specified period. During forbearance, your payments are temporarily postponed or reduced, but interest will still be charged. The interest will be capitalized (added to loan amount) if you are unable to pay it during the forbearance period.

You must formally apply for forbearance from your loan holder just as you would for a deferment. The two most common reasons forbearances are granted include:

- inability to pay due to poor health, extended unemployment, or other unforeseen personal problems.
- you are serving in a medical or dental internship or residency serving in a position under the National Community Service Trust Act of 1993

This is not a complete list of conditions that might qualify you for forbearance. As with deferments, you are allowed up to a maximum of 3 forbearances (of 1 year each) on any particular loan.

Contact the Department of Education for requirements concerning forbearances. For plan details, see Appendix A or visit the Department of Education website.

Consolidation

If you have used up all your available deferments and forbearances, consolidation may work for you. Not only can consolidation lower your monthly payments, it restarts the clock for all deferments and forbearances— thus postponing when you must begin repaying your student loans. For example, if you have already used three (3) years of deferments and three years (3) of forbearances for a particular set of loans, by consolidating them into one loan, you can get up to three (3) more years of forbearances.
Consolidation allows you to simplify the repayment process by combining several types of federal education loans into one loan, thereby making just one payment each month. Also, that new monthly payment might be lower than what you're currently paying because interest rates may be lower and repayment time has been extended from 10 to 30 years. Consolidated loans are available from private lenders (Federal Family Education Loan, FFEL) or Direct Consolidation Loan Program offered by the Department of Education.

You may want to consider consolidation if:

- You have used up all your deferments and forbearances, don't qualify for any of the low-payment plans, and cannot afford your monthly payment.
- You want a lower interest rate even though you can afford your current repayment plan.
- Your loans are in default. Under the Direct Consolidation Loan Program, loans that are in default may be consolidated with the government. Loans in default with private lenders may be consolidated, but with greater effort. Often, with private lenders, you must make 3 consecutive months of payments before they will consider allowing your loans to be consolidated.

You may think getting a loan consolidation is a no-brainer since it usually results in a lower interest rate loan with lower payments. However, there are some details that may change your mind.

- First, like all low-payment plans, extending payments over a much longer time results in much more money being paid in interest. Thus, the loan cost more over its lifetime—often times 2 to 3 times greater.
- Second, if you are married, you can consolidate your loans jointly but only if both you and your spouse agree to repayment of the entire loan—even if you divorce. That seems unwise considering most couples divorce within five years of marriage. Further, if you consolidate jointly and one of you dies, the surviving spouse is still responsible for repayment on the entire consolidated loan; unlike if the loans are separate and one person dies, then his or her loans are canceled.

Once made, consolidation loans can't be unmade because the loans that were consolidated have been paid off and no longer exist. Contact the Department of Education for requirements concerning consolidation. For plan details, see the Appendix A or visit the Department of Education website.

Repayment Plans

If you are having difficulty making payments on student loans under a particular repayment plan, perhaps another plan would accommodate your needs and keep you out of default.

There are four repayment plans available when paying Federal Direct Stafford/Ford Loans (Direct Subsidized Loans) and Federal Direct Unsubsidized Stafford /Ford Loans (Direct Unsubsidized Loans):

- Standard Repayment Plan
- Extended Repayment Plan
- Graduated Repayment Plan
- Income Contingent Repayment (ICR) Plan (not available to Direct PLUS loan borrowers)

These plans are described below and in Appendix A. However, if you have more questions, contact the Department of Education or visit the Department of Education website.

Standard Repayment Plan

Under Standard Plan you pay a fixed amount each month until your loans are paid in full. You pay a minimum $50 a month with up to 10 years to completely repay the loans. By setting higher payments, the Standard Plan allows you to repay your loans more quickly and with lower total interest.

Extended Repayment Plan

Under the Extended Repayment Plan, you make minimum monthly payments of at least $50 but for an extended time generally from 12 to 30 years. The length of the repayment period depends on the total amount owed at the point the loans go into repayment. Because the time is extended and payments are lower, you pay more interests.

Graduated Repayment Plan

With this plan, payments begin low and increase every two years for the life of the loan. The repayment period is calculated based on the total amount owed when the loans go into repayment. This plan may be the right choice for you if you anticipate your income increasing steadily over the years.

Income Contingent Repayment (ICR) Plan

The Income Contingent Repayment (ICR) Plan (used by the Department of Education, Direct Consolidation Loan program) or income sensitive plan (used by some private lenders) are plans that base monthly payments on the ability of the debtor to pay. The monthly payment is calculated based upon annual Adjusted Gross Income, family size, loan amount and evaluated against the Federal Poverty Guidelines. To participate in the program, debtors are required to sign a form allowing the IRS to verify income information.

If payments are so low that the interest goes unpaid, the remaining unpaid interest is capitalized (added to your loan) once each year. Capitalization cannot exceed 10 percent of the original amount owed. Therefore, excess unpaid interest continues to accumulate but is no longer capitalized.

The maximum repayment period is 25 years. If the loan has not been fully repaid at the end of 25 years, the unpaid portion is discharged. However, income taxes are due on the amount that is discharged.

—WARNING—
ICR Tax Liability

If you are experiencing dire financial problems, the Department of Education will try to force you into the ICR Plan. They will argue that anyone can make "zero dollar payments" as allowed under the ICR. The tax liability at the end of the program can be huge! Imagine being 65, 70, 80-years old having just finished an IRC Plan and faced with the tax liability on $60,000 income or more? That is definitely an undue hardship. More information is written about the ICR Plan in later chapters.

Typical Discharge Options

Ok, so you've tried to make payments using one of the four-repayment programs but you still can't keep up. Maybe you can discharge (cancel) the loans. There are some very specific situations where you can have student loans discharged. Here are basic discharge options for *Direct Loan* and *FFEL*:

- Borrower's total and permanent disability or death (100% forgiven)
- Full-time teacher for five consecutive years in a designated elementary or secondary school serving students from low-income families (up to $5,000)
- Bankruptcy (in rare cases) (100% forgiven)
- School closure (before student could complete program of study) or false loan certification (100% forgiven)
- School does not make required return of loan funds to the lender (Total amount the school was required to return).

Here are basic discharge options for *Perkins Loans*:

- Borrower's total and permanent disability or death (100% forgiven)
- Full-time teacher in a designated elementary or secondary school serving students from low-income families (up to 100% forgiven)
- Full-time special education teacher (includes teaching children with disabilities in a public or other nonprofit elementary or secondary school—up to 100% forgiven)
- Full-time qualified professional provider of early intervention services for the disabled (up to 100% forgiven)
- Full-time teacher of math, science, foreign languages, bilingual education, or other fields designated as teacher shortage areas (up to 100% forgiven)
- Full-time employee of a public or nonprofit child- or family-services agency providing services to high-risk children and their families from low-income communities (up to 100% forgiven)
- Full-time nurse or medical technician (up to 100% forgiven)
- Full-time law enforcement or corrections officer (up to 100% forgiven)
- Full-time staff member in the education component of a Head Start Program (up to 100% forgiven)
- Vista or Peace Corps volunteer (up to 70% forgiven)
- Service in the U.S. Armed Forces (up to 50% forgiven)
- Bankruptcy (in rare cases—up to 100% forgiven)
- School closure (before student could complete program of study) (up to 100% forgiven)

The details of these discharge options are constantly changing. Contact Direct Loan Servicing Center at 1-800-848-0979 if you have a Direct Loan. For FFEL loans, contact the lender or agency that holds your loan. If you have a Federal Perkins Loan, contact the school that made you the loan. For plan details, see Appendix A or visit the Department of Education website.

Other Discharge or Payment Options

Teaching, State, Professional, Military, Nursing, and National Service

There are a few other options for having loans discharged or paid by someone else. These include:

- Teaching service cancellation/deferment options can be found at www.studentaid.ed.gov. At the site, click on "Repaying," then on "Cancellation and Deferment Options for Teachers."
- Your state might offer programs that cancel or reduce part of your loan for certain types of service you perform (such as teaching or nursing). Contact your state agency for postsecondary education to see what programs are available in your state. For the address and telephone number of your state agency, call the Federal Student Aid Information Center at 1-800-4-FED-AID (1-800-433-3243). You can also find this information at http://www.studentaid.ed.gov. At the site, click on the "Funding" tab, and then go to "State Aid."
- You should also contact professional, religious, or civic organizations to see if any benefits would be available to you for loan repayment.
- Some branches of the military offer loan repayment programs as an incentive for service. Check with your local recruiting office for more information.
- Another type of repayment assistance (again, not a discharge) is available through the Nursing Education Loan Repayment Program (NELRP) to registered nurses in exchange for service in eligible facilities located in areas experiencing a shortage of nurses. For more information, call NELRP, toll-free, at 1-866-813-3753 or visit http://www.bhpr.hrsa.gov/nursing/loanrepay.htm
- The AmeriCorps Program allows participants to earn education awards— including money to repay student loans—in return for national service. For more information, contact the Corporation for National Service, which administers the AmeriCorps Program.

For details, see Appendix A or visit the Department of Education website.

Ask for Relief—Compromise and Write-Off

Ask the government to forgive your guaranteed student loan debt. This may sound crazy, but some debtors have been successful at having their loans reduced or discharged by this method.

Who would do this? — Debtors who do not qualify for any of the discharge plans listed in this chapter, are not planning a bankruptcy, and whose only real debt is their student loan. For example, lets say you live modestly but your student loan payments are so large that they place a severe burden on you and your family. You don't want to file for bankruptcy because you have no real debt except the student loans (i.e., student loans account for more than 70% of your total debt load). There are two conditions under which the Department of Education is authorized to forgive debt. These are: *Compromise* and *Write-Off*.

Compromise Your Loans

The Department of Education regulations allow for a guarantee agency to compromise student loans. That means that they are allowed to accept less than the total amount due to fully satisfy the conditions of the loan (and end a default status). This policy was specified in a regulation the Director of the U.S. Department of Education, Policy Development Division approved on 12/23/93. (*See* Appendix B for *Standardized Compromise and Write-Off Procedures*.)

The collections supervisor at a guarantee agency may reduce ("compromise") your loan under these conditions:

- If you agree to pay the full amount of the loan— principal and interests owed on defaulted loans— then all collection costs, including the standard 25% collection fee, may be waived.

- If you agree to pay the remaining principal and interest owed on a defaulted loan, then up to 30% of the principal and interest may be waived.

- If you are in dire conditions and it looks like you won't be able to service your loans in the future, the agency's director has the authority to waive even more than 30% of the principal and interest of your defaulted loans.

- If you agree to pay off the entire principal (with certified check) of your defaulted loans within 30 days of negotiating the compromise, then all interests charges may be waived.

The letter authorizing *Compromise* is included in the Appendix B of this book because few people in the Department of Education even know the existence of these options. If you can afford to pay a substantial lump sum to pay off your student loan debt, then contact the guarantee agency and ask about a Compromise. Most likely, you will be directed to the head of the collections department.

The agency determines if the compromise represents the best interest of the government. Obviously this is very subjective open to the judgment of the agency director. If you can show that you have very limited income and that it will not change in the future, they may accept your request. The only alternative for the government is to sue, which is a fairly expensive process for the government.

Strategy Tip

Compromise works best for old loans where most of the principal has been paid and has been in default for a while. If you can afford to pay the remaining principal in one lump sum, they are most likely to cancel the interest and collection fees.

Write-Off Your Loans

Another idea is to ask the guarantee agency of the Department of Education to *Write-Off* your loans. This works only if you are in dire financial straits, do not believe you will ever be able to repay your loans, and you don't qualify for Discharge or Compromise.

The three conditions most likely to be written-off include:

- The balance on your principal is $100 or less.

- The total balance of your loans does not exceed $1000.

- The balance of your loans is for interest, court fees, collection costs, and costs other than the principal, regardless the total loan amount.

If you can convince the Department of Education that your situation is hopeless, it can write-off much larger loans and end collection efforts. *If you receive a Write-Off, you may never again seek a federal school loan. If you do go back to school and seek education loans, your old loans will be revived and you will be responsible for paying them back.*

Convincing the Department of Education that your situation is hopeless is similar to proving "undue hardship" (discussed at length in this book). We suggest that if you attempt to obtain a Write-Off of your loans, to read this book carefully and use Chapters 10 and 11 to help prepare and guide your negotiations with the Department of Education.

We hope you the best in your negotiations.

Default and Collections

Default occurs with *Federal Perkins Loan* when you don't make an installment payment when due or don't comply with the promissory note's other terms. Default for a *FFEL* or *Direct Loan* occurs if you become 270 days delinquent (if you're making monthly payments) or 330 days delinquent if payments are made less than monthly.

The consequences of default are severe:
- Your entire loan balance (principal and interest) can be immediately due and payable.
- You'll lose your deferment options.
- You won't be eligible for additional federal student aid.
- Your account might be turned over to a collection agency. If so, you'll have to pay

---

additional interest charges, late fees, collection costs, and possibly court costs and attorney fees.

- Your account will be reported to national credit bureaus resulting in your credit rating being damaged. You might find it very difficult to receive other types of credit, such as credit cards, car loans, or mortgages. Many landlords do credit checks and a negative student loan report may make it difficult to even rent an apartment. Similarly, some employers check to see if you're "responsible" by looking at your credit rating and a negative one may affect your getting a job. Additionally, your default will remain on your credit report for up to seven years.
- Without having to go to court, the government can seize your federal income tax refunds (and in some states, your state income tax refunds as well).
- Without having to go to court, your wages may be withheld (garnished).
- You might be unable to obtain a professional license in some states.

These are serious consequences; so, don't fall into default. Make sure to contact your lender as soon as you think you might have trouble making payments. Don't ignore calls or letters from your lender or servicer, either. Putting things off is never the answer because these loans won't go away. Talk to your lender and discuss all the options for making payment easier. Get the details from your lender/servicer on how you can benefit from the various options. Contact the Department of Education before you default. For details, see Appendix A or visit the Department of Education website.

Other Legal Considerations

Federal Benefits

If you receive federal benefits, read this section closely.

The 1996 Debt Collection Improvement Act[1] (DCIA) allows federal agencies (including the Department of Education) to take certain federal benefits to pay federal non-tax debts. Taking some of your federal

benefits to satisfy government debt is called "*offset*." This means that instead of receiving your full benefit check, a portion of it is kept ("offset") by the government to pay toward your student loan debt.

The government <u>may offset</u> benefits originating from:
- Social Security Retirement
- Social Security Disability (SSDI)
- Black Lung (part B only)
- Railroad Retirement Benefits (other than tier 2 benefits)

Benefits that <u>may not be offset</u> include:
- Supplemental Security Income (SSI)
- Black Lung (other than part B)
- Railroad Retirement Benefits (tier 2 benefits)
(*See* Appendix B for 31 USCA 3716 at (c)(3)(a)(i) for details.)

The government did not begin using offset until March 2001. What is still unclear is how to challenge an offset when it occurs. If you are subject to an offset of your federal benefits, and you believe the offset is incorrect or misplaced, contact the agency listed on the offset letter. You may need to contact a consumer protection agency for help.

Student Loans Less Than 10-Years Old

For persons receiving income from which offset may be applied, and with student loans that are <u>less</u> than 10-years old, <u>the first $9,000 (or $750 per month) cannot be seized</u>. If you have federal benefits greater than this amount, the government cannot take more than 15% of that income. For example, if your federal benefit income is $950 per month, the government is allowed take the <u>lesser</u> of 15% of that income (15% of $950 is $142.90) or the amount over $750 per month ($950-$750 is $200). In this example the lesser amount, and the most the government could offset from your federal benefits, would be $142.90. (*See* Appendix B for 31 USCA 3716 at (c)(3)(a)(ii).)

Student Loans More Than 10-Years Old

~~If your government guaranteed student loans are more than 10-years old, the federal government may not apply offset against your federal benefits [31 U.S.C.~~

We have left the above language in this book but as "strikeout" so you can see what use to be true in case someone mentions this issue to you. The U.S. Supreme Court in December 2005 declared that the government may seize a person's Social Security benefits to pay old student loans. Justice Scalia wrote that Congress "unambiguously authorized, without exception, the collection of 10-year-old student loan debt . . ." In doing so, it flatly contracted and thereby effectively repealed part of the Social Security Act. Thus, the claim that student loan debt more than 10-years-old cannot be collected from Social Security no longer is valid. See *Lockhart v. U.S., 04-881.*

Remember, if you have other assets or other sources of income not related to federal benefits, the government may sue you to recover on the student loan debt, regardless of the protected status of your federal benefits.

Being Sued

At one time there was a statute of limitations that applied to student loans. On April 9, 1991, President Bush signed into law the Higher Education Technical Amendments that did away with the limitation retroactively, back to 1965 when student loans were first issued. Thus, there is no statute of limitation preventing the government from finding default debtors and suing them.

Legal Defenses That Cannot Work

Over the years, debtors have tried raising certain legal arguments in the hope of having their student loans discharged. In case you hire an attorney to represent you, here are the arguments that cannot succeed, so you don't waste time and money trying these legal defenses:
- Statute of Limitations
- Laches
- Infancy
- Truth-in-Lending

Statute of Limitation

In general, the government has up to six years to sue someone for breach of contract or default on government loans (such as Federal Housing or Small Business Administration loans). As noted above, President Bush specifically rescinded the statute of limitations for student loans in 1991, and extended it back to the very first student loans issued by the government in 1965. Thus, you cannot raise the statute of limitation argument to have your student loans discharged.

Laches

Since statute of limitation arguments are no longer valid, some debtors have tried to argue that the government was unreasonably delayed in initiating a lawsuit and it would be prejudicial to the debtor being sued to defend the case. This is the legal concept of laches. In general, the laches argument cannot be used against the government and almost every court that has considered this argument in relation to student loans has concluded that the laches defense may not be raised.

However, in one extreme case, the court ruled in favor of laches. Here the government did not attempt to sue the student debtor until 17 years after the loans came due. In the intervening years, the school closed and the student could not obtain his records. Further, the borrower had evidence that he did, indeed, pay back the loan. The court allowed the laches defense simply because the case was so extreme (*United States v. Rhodes*, 788 F. Supp. 339 (E.D. Mich. 1992)). Just one year later, this same court was faced with a much more ordinary case and disallowed the laches defense (*United States v. Robbins*, 819 F. Supp. 672 (E.D. Mich. 1993)).

Infancy

Some debtors have tried to argue that, since they were under age 18 when they signed the loan documents, they were not competent to enter into a contract. Although this defense, called *infancy*, can be used with consumer contracts, it was eliminated in 1991 at the same time the statute of limitations was repealed.

Truth-in-Lending

The federal Truth in Lending Act (15 U.S.C. § 1638) requires lenders to disclose the terms of the loan including the interest rate, payment schedule and more. Failure to provide this information is grounds for having the loan canceled. Although the defense is applicable in consumer contracts, federal law specifically states that it is not a defense in cases of student loan default.

Should I Go Forward with an Adversary Proceeding or Compromise or Write-Off?

Hopefully the information in this chapter helped you to better evaluate your situation. Perhaps simply delaying payment on your loans will give you the time to catch up and begin repayment at a later time. Possibly, one of the other repayment plans would work for you; or, you qualify to have your loans discharged through one of the discharge options. With almost two-thirds of all bankruptcies related to medical illness and the resulting unemployment and medical bills, perhaps you qualify for a medical disability discharge.

If none of these standard discharge options work for you, then you may choose to file a bankruptcy with an *Adversary Proceeding* or to pursue a *Compromise* or *Write-Off*. Proceed to the next chapter.

Summary

- Payment for student loans may be delayed by:
  - Deferment
  - Forbearance
- Consolidation
  - May yield lower payments and interest but higher overall costs
  - Restarts clock for deferments and forbearances
- Repayment plans include:
  - Standard Repayment Plan
  - Extended Repayment Plan
  - Graduated Repayment Plan
  - Income Contingent Repayment (ICR) Plan (not

available to Direct PLUS loan borrowers)
- Student loans may be discharge (in general):
  - Borrower death
  - Borrower total and permanent disability
  - <u>Bankruptcy</u> (very difficult)
  - School closure or false loan certification
  - Very specific conditions of service (teaching, law enforcement, armed forces, and others)
  - Student loans may be paid off under some very specific conditions
  - Ask to relieve the debt through <u>Compromise</u> or <u>Write-Off</u>
- Default on loans may result in
  - Entire loan balance coming due and payable
  - Loss of deferment options
  - No longer eligible for additional student loans
  - Collection agency with additional expenses
  - Credit standing impacted
  - Without court order, the seizure of federal income tax refunds, wages garnished and more.
- Other arguments
  - In general, receiving various federal benefits that do not exceed $9,000 a year make student loans uncollectible.
  - ~~If student loans are more than 10-years old, most federal benefits cannot be "off-set" to pay for them.~~
  - Statute of limitations no longer apply to student loans
  - Laches defense generally do not apply to student loans
  - Infancy defense exempted from student loans
  - Truth-in-Lending arguments exempted from student loans

---

[1] 31 U.S.C. § 3720D.

CHAPTER 3
History of the Student Loan Program

Unlike a Chapter 7 bankruptcy in which you fill out forms and file with the bankruptcy court, to bankrupt student loans you must first file a Chapter 7 bankruptcy and then sue the U.S. government, and successfully argue your case. To do so, it is important to know the history of the student loan program including legislative language and court challenges. It is highly recommended that you read these next few chapters and become thoroughly familiar with the concepts and language.

A great debate over the state of American higher education occurred after the successful launch of the first unmanned space vehicle, Sputnik, in 1957 by the USSR. In response, Congress passed the National Defense Education Act (NDEA) in 1958 to address perceived deficits in the national defense and educational systems. Among other provisions, NDEA established the National Defense Student Loan (NDSL) to provide low interest (5%) loans to qualified students. NDSL loans (also known as Perkins Loans) were the first federally funded higher education loan program, which continues to the present.

Stafford Loans are primarily funded by private lenders and ultimately guaranteed by the U.S. government. Initially, only the most needy students qualified for a loan. To qualify, "borrowers [had to] demonstrate financial need in excess of other financial aid sources and family contributions."[1] Forbearance and deferment options allowed students to delay repayment of the loans. A number of repayment plans help accommodate fluctuations in student income. (*See* Appendix A for details on these options and repayment plans.) Today, the financial requirements have been significantly relaxed and most students qualify for government financed or guaranteed loans.

Before the adoption of the Bankruptcy Reform Act in 1978, student loans were treated as any other unsecured debt and could be directly discharged through bankruptcy. Very few students attempted to eliminate their student loan debt through bankruptcy. In 1968-70, there were only 760 bankruptcies nationwide that involved student loans. By 1976, these numbers jumped to 8,641 bankruptcies involving student loans for a total of $33.1 million in unpaid loans.

GSLP 1965 (Stafford Loans)

The success of the NDSL program led to enactment of the Guaranteed Student Loan Program (GSLP) in 1965 as part of the Higher Education Act. The GSLP (later renamed the Stafford Loan Program) was aimed to help reduce financial barriers to postsecondary education for the poorest students. The program was based on the core principle that students without adequate financial resources should still be able to obtain higher education even though they may be viewed as an unacceptable credit risk.

Middle Income Student Assistance Act 1978

The success of the Higher Education Act of 1965 for the poorest students did little to help middle income Americans. The cost of education increased by 75% between 1965 and 1975. Middle class students who did not qualify for student loans were hard-pressed to pay for increased education costs. In 1978, Congress made federal loans available to virtually all students regardless of need through the Middle Income Student Assistance Act. Student borrowing increased rapidly and federal loan expenditures skyrocketed. Between

1975 and 1979, new federal student loan volume increased by $2 billion. Ironically, as federal spending for higher education increased, state funding for higher education decreased in all fifty states.[2] As a consequence, students took on more and more debt.

The Department of Health, Education, and Welfare reported that in 1976, $500 million was paid to banks for nearly 350,000 student loan defaults. Congress became concerned about the high numbers of student loan defaults. The student loan programs responded to the increased level of loan defaults by tightening up requirements and implementing stricter collection procedures. The default rate plummeted. Yet, the media fixated on a handful of stories of student loan fraud and default that gave the impression that the student loan program was on the verge of collapse through massive abuse. The public believed loopholes in the student loan programs enabled substantial abuse by students defrauding the taxpayers.

Media Hype of Abuse

The media played up reports of students discharging their student loan debts immediately upon graduation, never once having made any payments, and subsequently accepting high-paying jobs. Two cases illustrate the problem. In 1973, a former New Jersey student filed for bankruptcy fourteen days after graduating from Stanford Law School for the sole purpose of discharging $17,272 of his student loans. He had already earned a business degree and a master's degree in engineering.[3] Similarly, a Massachusetts couple was successful at discharging $20,000 worth of student loans through bankruptcy immediately after graduation. The husband held a law degree while the wife held a graduate degree. They never made a payment on the loans.[4]

Many in Congress found such actions reprehensible, unethical, and "tantamount to fraud."[5] Debate in Congress focused on this abuse of the liberal discharge provisions of the Bankruptcy Code. Representative Allen Ertel (D-Pa) observed that federal student loan defaults increased by more than 300% between 1972 and 1976. He explained, "These bankruptcies could easily destroy the federal student

loan programs . . . This problem cannot be permitted to spread nationwide, because destruction of the student loan programs would operate to deny the benefits of higher education to many would-be students who are otherwise qualified for post-high school education or training . . . This destruction of student loan programs would represent a tremendous waste of one of this nation's greatest assets, the minds and skills of American youth."[6] Rep. Ertel later introduced the amendment that eventually became 11 U.S.C.A. Section 523 (a)(8).

The facts are very different. Very few students abused the Bankruptcy Code in discharging their student loans. The 1973 Bankruptcy Review Commission acknowledged that student loan abuse was "more perception than reality."[7] A 1976 General Accounting Office study concluded that only 1/2 to 3/4 of 1% of all matured educational loans had been discharged through bankruptcy[8]. Similarly, The House Report on the Bankruptcy Law Revision (1977) stated, "a high default rate has been confused with a high bankruptcy rate, and has mistakenly led to calls for changes in bankruptcy laws."[9] Further, the House Report on the Bankruptcy Law Revision noted that the "rise [in student loan defaults] appears not to be disproportionate to the rise in the amount of loans becoming due or to the default rate generally on educational loans."[10] It can be concluded that most people who resorted to bankruptcy did so because they needed to, not because they were attempting to defraud the government.

Yet the media frenzy[11] created the impression that students habitually received discharges of their loans through bankruptcy immediately after graduation.

Some in Congress saw past the media hype. For example, Rep. Cornell stated, "We can all agree that the intent of [§523(a)(8)] is to prevent abuse of our student loan program by those who would use bankruptcy simply to avoid repayment of their student loans."[12] *Fraud and abuse of the student loan program is what concerned many in Congress, not that some people had a legitimate need to seek bankruptcy.*

Some thought implementing a waiting period for filing bankruptcy after graduation would stem most student loan defaults and bankruptcies. As one academic noted to Congress, the average time between the last student loan and filing for bankruptcy ranged between "thirty months and forty-one months."[13] Thus, implementing a waiting period from the time the last student loan is used and filing bankruptcy should eliminate most fraud. Sheldon Steinbach, Assistant Director of Government Relations of the American Council on Education stated, "[b]aring educational debts from discharge during the in-school period and first 5 years of repayment will erect a necessary barrier to graduates

and dropouts who deliberately seek to dissolve their repayment obligations at a time when their assets are at a minimum."[14] Similarly, Judge Edward York testified, ""[o]ur purpose in proposing an amendment [§523(a)(b)] to the bankruptcy laws [was] to terminate the growing propensity of student loan borrowers to resort to bankruptcy immediately upon graduation."[15]

Rep. Ertel stated, "if a [student debtor] has a hardship he can go to the court and say: 'I have a difficulty' and ask for a discharge," or "[a]fter the five-year period, if he has not been able to accumulate assets, he can go into bankruptcy."[16]

History of Bankruptcy Reform Act

1976
Congress modifies the Higher Education Act of 1965 (codified as 20 U.S.C.A §§ 1097-3) to include §439A, which states:
(a) such loan, benefit, scholarship, or stipend overpayment first became due more than 5 years (exclusive of any applicable suspension of the repayment period) before the date of the filing of the petition; or
(b) excepting such debt from discharge under this paragraph will impose an undue hardship on the debtor and the debtor's dependents;"

1978
§439A is repealed and similar nondischargeability provisions language placed within the 1978 Bankruptcy Reform Act §523(a)(8)[1].

1990
5-year wait period extended to 7-years, and made the law apply to both Chapter 7 and Chapter 13 bankruptcies.

1998
Removed the number of years completely and implemented the Income Contingent Repayment (ICR) Plan. This is the current law.

Compromise Bill Results in Non-dischargeability of Student Loans

The non-dischargeability of student loans was not originally included in the House bankruptcy bill. The House Judiciary Committee did not find adequate evidence of abuse to warrant making student loans non-dischargeable. The House bill made no distinction between student loans and other dischargeable debt. The Senate bill, on the other hand, made student loans non-dischargeable with only two exceptions. Eventually, the final bill that passed in 1976 adopted the Senate version without change. This was word-for-word the same draft bill recommended by the Bankruptcy Review Commission in its 1973 report to Congress.

Instead of a blanket non-dischargeability of student loan debt, Congress decided to include both a 5-year waiting time and "undue hardship" exceptions. The five-year exception was intended to close the loophole by preventing abusive discharges. The "undue hardship" exception was intended to provide "the honest, financially-troubled debtor the opportunity for a fresh start."[17] The language of Section 523(a)(8) was taken directly from 439(A) of the Higher Education Act of 1965. Student loans were listed in Section 523 along with other non-dischargeable debts including: taxes; fraudulent income tax returns or invoices; money owed for negligent or unlawful acts such as drunk driving (resulting in manslaughter); money or assets fraudulently or unlawfully attained (e.g., embezzlement); debts provided for in any final judgment against the debtor; penalties and fines owed

---

to the government; debts not listed by the debtor; and child support and alimony. As one congressman explained as to the type of debtor Section 523 was aimed, "we only define groups of people or different statuses for three types of people who are exempted from discharging their claims under bankruptcy"[18]— felons, those convicted of a fraud, and those who are indebted in alimony payments.

The Report of the Committee on the Judiciary in 1977 provided what ultimately became Section 523 and "retains the provisions of current law governing when a discharge is granted and when it is denied. Most of the grounds for denial of discharge concern misconduct by the debtor in the events leading up to the bankruptcy or during the conduct of the case."[19]

The concern about fraud influenced the Senate to include non-dischargeability of student loans in Section 523 along with other crimes of moral turpitude. However, it was recognized that not all debtors seeking bankruptcy engaged in fraud. As such, the undue hardship exception was created as an appropriate safeguard.

1978 Bankruptcy Reform Act Section 523(a)(8)

In 1976, Congress modified the Higher Education Act of 1965 (codified as 20 U.S.C.A §§ 1097-3) to enact §439A[20] which made student loans non-dischargeable in bankruptcy unless: (a) the debt first became due more than 5 years before the date of filing of the bankruptcy, or, (b) failure to discharge the debt would cause "undue hardship" to the debtor or to dependents of the debtor. Later, Congress repealed §439A of the Higher Education Act and placed the non-dischargeability provisions and language within the 1978 Bankruptcy Reform Act Section 523(a)(8)[21]. This is the Act that guides the discussion of this book.

Most bankruptcy cases decided under §523(a)(8) involved the undue hardship exception. This is a difficult endeavor since the drafters of the Bankruptcy Code did not define "undue hardship."[22] The drafters explicitly stated that the bankruptcy courts must decide undue hardship on a case-by-case basis, considering all the debtor's circumstances.

By 1981, 3.5 million students borrowed $7.7 billion from the Guaranteed Student Loan Program (GSL) program. This represented a 52% increase in the number of students and 60% increase in the amount of money borrowed by students over the previous year. Year by year, more and more money was being borrowed by students for college education— an education that cost more each year.

In 1990, Congress extended the original five-year exception for discharging student loans to seven years[23]. At the same time, the law was extended to apply to both Chapter 7 and Chapter 13 bankruptcy cases when previously it had applied only to Chapter 7 cases.

Congress became concerned about the solvency of the federal loan program and wanted to protect it from bankruptcy challenges. The Reagan administration proposed reductions in federal aid to postsecondary education. This prompted a bitter and protracted political debate in Congress about the role of the federal government in educational loans. Yet, legislation was passed in 1992 that made it even easier for middle-class students to borrow federal money for higher education.[24] Borrowing increased by 57% between 1992 and 1996 with federal expenditures reaching an all-new high of $23.1 billion annually.[25]

By the late 1990s, the federal government was guaranteeing almost $50 billion a year of student loans. Loans were (and still are) easy to get. Students who would otherwise be deemed poor credit risks are able, if not encouraged, to borrow money for college. As expected, mounting student indebtedness has led to an increase in the number of discharges sought based on undue hardship.

Loan Default Rate Plummets

In light of all the indebtedness, the loan default rates have been steadily declining. From a high of 22.4% in 1990, the number of student loan defaults has dropped to 5.4% in 2001. Yet, in 1998, Congress eliminated the time limitation of §523(a)(8) altogether[26]. *The only avenue debtors have to discharge student loan debt issued or backed by the government is to demonstrate their hopeless financial situation and prove that repayment would subject them and their dependents to "undue hardship."* For many student loan debtors, this is virtually impossible to do.[27] (The next Chapter discusses in depth the judicial construction of "undue hardship.")

Today, the average undergraduate borrows about $16,000 during school. The average graduate student ends up owing about $25,000 by graduation. The typical borrower who attends professional school typically owes about $50,000. It is not uncommon for medical students to owe hundreds of thousands of dollars. It is estimated that half of all students who attend law or medical school have student loans far in excess of their expected annual salary. In fiscal year 2002, eight million postsecondary students borrowed almost $56.5 billion for college. Approximately 8%[28] of all Americans owe money on their student loans totaling more than $287 billion[29]. It is expected these numbers will continue to grow.

Many people have attempted to bankrupt their student loans. As stated above, the law requires the debtor to prove "undue hardship." This was not defined by Congress but left up to the courts to determine on a case-by-case basis. The next section of this book examines some of the approaches used by courts to determine "undue hardship." This will help guide you in your efforts to develop your own bankruptcy case.

Summary

- Student loans were initially treated as any other unsecured loan and discharged through bankruptcy.
- The student loan default rose significantly in the 1970s causing great alarm in Congress about the solvency of the student loan programs.
- A few high-profile cases made media headlines involving students using bankruptcy to obtain a discharge of their student loans immediately or soon after graduation.
- The Congressional discussion leading up to the implementation of §523(a)(8) of the 1978 Bankruptcy Reform Act shows:
  - o Congress was most concerned about student loan abuse. They wanted to prevent dishonest borrowers from procuring a free college education by filing for bankruptcy shortly before or immediately after graduation.
  - o Congress was very aware that some form of bankruptcy relief was necessary for honest debtors who found themselves unable to service their student loan debt.
  - o Implementing a 5-year waiting time from the assumption of the last student loan to the use of bankruptcy to discharge the loans was thought to weed out most attempts at abuse. This was later increased to 7-years but eliminated altogether in 1998.
  - o Implementing the "undue hardship" clause gave another avenue to students in financial difficulties to discharge the loans.
- By 1998, only the "undue hardship" exception could be used to discharge student loan debt.

---

[1] Zackerman, Jeffrey L. (1997). (Note) Discharging Student Loans in Bankruptcy: The Need for a Uniform "undue hardship" Test. *U. CIN. L. REV.* (691). 65.

[2] The Mortenson Report (2001). The sorry state of the States: State Tax Fund Appropriations for Higher Education, FY 2001. *Postsecondary Education Opportunity*, (103), 12-16.

[3] *See* Bankruptcy Act Revision: Hearings on H.R. 31 and H.R. 32 before the Subcomm. On civil and Constitutional Rights of House Comm. On the Judiciary, 94th Cong. 1078 (1976) (testimony of Hon. Edward York, U.S. Deputy Commissioner, U.S. Office of Education).

[4] *See* Bankruptcy Reform Act: Hearings on S. 235 and S. 236 before the Subcomm. On Improvements n Judicial Machinery of the Senate Comm. On the Judiciary, 94th Cong. 220-21 (1975).

[5] *In re Pelkowski*, 990 F.2d 737, 742 (3rd Cir. 2993), quoting 124 CONG. REC. 1793.

[6] Representative Allen Ertel (D-Pa). H.R. No. 95-595, 95 Cong. 1st Session (1997), U.S. Code Cong. And Adm in. News, 1978. pp. 5759, 5963.

[7] National Bankruptcy Review Commission Report, Pub. L. No. 103-394, at 197 (established pursuant to the Bankruptcy Reform Act of 1994) (Oct. 20, 1997) (recommending in its final report that Congress eliminates §523(a)(8)).

[8] H.R. REP. NO. 595, 95th Cong., 1st Sess. 133 (1977). See infra note 23 and accompanying text.

[9] H.R. Rep. No. 95-595, at 133 (1977), reprinted in 1978 U.S.C.C.A.N 5963, 6094.

[10] H.R. Rep. No. 95-595, at 133 (1977), reprinted in 1978 U.S.C.C.A.N. 5963, 6094. See also A&P 124 Cong. Rec. 1794 (daily ed. Feb 1, 1978).

[11] The popular press argued that student loan default and bankruptcy rates were unacceptably high. *See:* Time of reckoning for student deadbeats. (July 18, 1977) *U.S. News & World Report*, 21; Study now, pay never. (March 7, 1977). *Newsweek*, 95; Student loan mess. (Dec. 8, 1975). *Time* 8.

[12] A&B 124 Cong. Rec. 1794 (daily ed. Feb. 1, 1978) (statement of Rep. Cornell).

[13] Kosel, Janice E. (1981). Running the gauntlet of "undue hardship"; The discharge of student loans in bankruptcy. Golden Gate U. L. Rev., (11), 457, 465. (citing statistics from H.R. Rep No. 595, at 142 (1977), reprinted in 1978 U.S.C.C.A.N 6103).

[14] Bankruptcy Reform Act: Hearings on S. 235 & 236 before the Subcommittee On Improvements in Judicial Machinery of the Senate Comm. On the Judiciary U.S. Senate, 94th Cong. 217 (1975) (statement of Sheldon Steinbach).

[15] *See* supra notes 48-49; Bankruptcy Act Revision: Hearings on H.R. 31 and H.R. 32 before the Subcomm. On Civil and Constitutional Rights of the House Comm. On the Judiciary, 94th Cong. 1078 (1976) (testimony of Hon. Edward York, U.S. Deputy Commissioner, U.S. Office of Education)

[16] A&B 123 Cong. Rec. H457, H469 (daily ed. Feb. 1, 1978) statement of Rep. Ertel).

[17] Collins, Thad. (1990). Forging middle ground: Revision of student loan debts in bankruptcy as an impetus to Amend 11 U.S.C.A. § 523(a)8. *Iowa L. Rev.* (75), 742 (Note 67).

[18] A&P 123 Cong. Rec. H457, H467 (daily ed. Feb. 1, 1978) (statement of Rep. Dodd).

[19] H.R. Rep. No. 95-595, at 128 (1977), reprinted in 1978 U.S.C.C.A.N. 5963, 6089 (emphasis added). The "provisions of current law" being referred to in this quote are 14, and 17, as discussed above.

[20] Section 439A of the Education Amendments provided: A debt which is a loan insured or guaranteed under the authority of this part may be released by a discharge in bankruptcy under the Bankruptcy Act only if such discharge is granted after the five-years period (exclusive of any applicable suspension of the repayment period) beginning on the date of commencement of the repayment period of such loan, except that prior to the expiration of that five-years period, such loan may be released only if the court in which the proceeding is pending determines that payment from future income or other wealth will not impose an undue hardship on the debtor of his dependents.

[21] Bankruptcy Reform Act of 1978, Pub. Law No. 95-598, 92 Stat. 2549, 2591 (1978).

[22] *See* Report of the Commission on the Bankruptcy Law of the United States, H.R. DOC. NO. 137, 93d Cong., 1st Sess., Pt. II, 140 (1973).

[23] 11 U.S.C.A. Section 3007 (b), 104 Stat. At 1388-28 (1990).

[24] William, Ian. (Sept. 20, 1996). The indentured class: Student loans are robbing us of our future. Providence Phoenix, 8. Quote, "Colleges suddenly saw the government as this giant wobbling teat just waiting to be sucked and started a spastic race towards who could charge the most ludicrous tuition for four years. . . ."

[25] William, Ian, id.

[26] Higher Education Amendments of 1998, Pub. Law No. 105-244, 112 Stat. 1837 (1998).

[27] Huey, B.J. (2002). Undue hardship or undue burden: Has the time finally arrived for Congress to discharge Section 523(a)(8) of the Bankruptcy Code? *Texas Tech Law Review*, (34), 89.

[28] Discharging Student Loans in Bankruptcy. (September 1996). *LRP Publications*.

[29] U.S. Department of Education . Briefing on the National Default Rates. September 16, 2003. www.ed.gov/offices/OSFAP/defaultmanagement/cdr.html.

CHAPTER 4
Court Opinions and Tests

This chapter reviews the basic tenants of U.S. bankruptcy law, the designation of "undue hardship" and the relevant court tests.

Bankruptcy Law In U.S.

The U.S. Constitution authorized Congress to "establish . . . uniform laws on the subject of bankruptcies throughout the United States."[1] The bankruptcy of debts serves important social and economic purposes. It frees hopeless debtors to become responsible consumers and producing members of society[2]. Congress enacted the Bankruptcy Code along with a separate judiciary to administer the Code.

The Bankruptcy Act of 1898 was the first bankruptcy legislation enacted by Congress. It had two major goals: (1) to provide honest, hard-working debtors with a "fresh start" in which they are free of oppressive debt, and (2) to obtain fair and equitable treatment for debtors and creditors alike.[3] Congress made a concerted effort to ensure a balance between the interests of creditors and needs of debtors. Congress recognized that "[a] bankruptcy system that does not balance the interests of creditors and the interests of debtors will have neither their confidence nor, of even greater importance, the confidence of the American people."[4]

In the 1970s, Congress began discussion about revamping the bankruptcy code. Student loan default and bankruptcies became major controversies in the Congressional debate. Eventually, the Act of 1898 was replaced with the Bankruptcy Reform Act of 1978[5]. It provided two avenues for debtors to file bankruptcy and obtain a fresh start. The Reform Act allowed debtors to file under Chapter 13 or Chapter 7 of the Bankruptcy Code.

Born during the Great Depression, Chapter 13 bankruptcy was enacted in 1938 to better represent the needs of creditors. Debtors choosing Chapter 13 bankruptcy submit a repayment plan and reorganize their finances to eventually pay off some or all of their debt under court supervision within 3 to 5 years. Chapter 13 debtors agree to commit all of their disposable income to the repayment plan in exchange for keeping their possessions and paying the debt agreed by the court. Chapter 13 bankruptcy results in better long-term credit worthiness for debtors and collects more money for creditors.

Debtors filing under Chapter 7 obtain a quick and full discharge of debts. It is designed to offer rapid debt relief for honest, but over-burdened debtors. Nonexempt assets are relinquished to the trustee who then sells the assets. Proceeds from the bankruptcy sale are distributed among the creditors. As such, the debtor receives an immediate "fresh start" as all remaining debt is discharged. Because of the automatic and expeditious discharge of debt, Chapter 7 bankruptcy is the preferred method of bankruptcy for many debtors.

Student loans are no longer discharged in a Chapter 7 bankruptcy. Instead, the debts are listed in the Chapter 7 bankruptcy and a subsequent adversary proceeding is initiated. Here, a separate court decision specifically rules on the dischargeability of student loans. The 11 U.S.C.A. Bankruptcy Reform Act (1998) §523(a)(8) requires debtors to prove "undue hardship" in order to have their student loans discharged as part of a bankruptcy.

"Undue Hardship"

Congress did not clarify in §523(a)(8) the meaning of "undue hardship." Considering all the debate over the dischargeability of student loans, it is surprising that

Congress left it up to the courts to define what the phrase meant.[6] Legislative history provides little help in defining the undue hardship exception. Congress left it up to the various bankruptcy courts to "utilize their discretion in defining what [the] term means after an analysis of the statue and a review of applicable legislative history."[7] As noted in other court cases, "Congress wanted to save the student loan programs and bar the undeserving student borrower from abusing the bankruptcy process [but did] not directly identify how Congress intended the discharge to be granted in cases of undue hardship."[8]

Over the past quarter-century, courts have developed many tests to determine the existence of undue hardship. Although courts have made a concerted effort to accurately reflect and enforce Congressional policy and intent, there are significant differences between the tests and their outcomes. It is often said, "that there are as many tests for undue hardship as there are bankruptcy courts."[9] Each test reflects a particular court and its goal of balancing congressional intent to limit loan discharges with bankruptcy debt relief. "While these tests have received varying degrees of acceptance, no particular test authoritatively guides or governs the undue hardship determination."[10] There is, however, a general agreement among courts that undue hardship means more than just temporary financial adversity.[11]

Currently, there are 4 tests that most courts use to determine the dischargeability of student loans under the undue hardship provision. These are:
- **"Johnson Test"**
  — Pa. Higher Educ. Assistance Agency v. Johnson (In re Johnson), 5 Bankr. Ct. Dec. 532 (Bankr. E.D. Pa. 1979)
- **"Bryant Poverty Test"**
  — Bryant v. Pa. Higher Educ. Assistance Agency (In re Bryant), 72 B.R. 913 (Bankr. E.D. Pa. 1987)
- **"Totality of the Circumstances Test"**
  — Andrews v. South Dakota Student Loan Assistance Corporation, 661 F.2d702 (8th Cir. 1981).
- **"Brunner Test"**
  — Brunner v. N.Y. State Higher Educ. Servs. Corp. (In re Brunner), 831 F.2d 395 (2d Cir. 1987), aff'g 46 B.R. 752 (Bankr. S.D.N.Y. 1985)

It should be noted that even in courts that use the same test, the "subtleties" by which the tests are applied often produce inconsistent results.[12]

Many courts have harshly and narrowly ruled that debtors cannot discharge educational loans unless they can demonstrate "a certainty of hopelessness" about their long-term financial condition. Some academic writers have noted that "certainty of hopelessness" has become the unofficial standard[13] and common thread for these kinds of bankruptcies.

Below are discussed some of the tests used by bankruptcy courts in deciding student loan discharges. In each case, the specific District Courts where the test is applicable are noted.

Court Tests for "Undue Hardship"

The tests are presented in their historical context.

The Johnson Test

One of the first tests developed to determine the existence of undue hardship came from Pennsylvania Higher Education Assistance Agency v. Johnson. This 1970 case developed a 3-prong test that has been adopted by many courts, but rejected by many other courts as being too "intricate." The **first prong** is a "mechanical analysis" of the debtor's current and future ability to repay the loan. This prong looks at the debtors' present employment and income, future employment and income, educational level and skills, marketability of skills, personal health, and dependents. Future expenses are evaluated by estimating the expenses of a comparably situated debtor plus any extraordinary expenses the debtor may have to pay in the future (such as medical expenses, tax liabilities, child support, alimony, etc.). These factors are compared against the official Federal Poverty Guideline to determine if the debtor can maintain a "subsistence or poverty standard of living"[14] while repaying the loan. If repaying the loans pushes the debtor to or below the poverty level, then the second prong of the test is evaluated. If the debtor can maintain a minimal standard of living while repaying the loan, the analysis stops and the case is dismissed without discharge of the debt.

The **second prong** of the test is known as the "good faith" analysis. Here, debtors must demonstrate that a good faith attempt was made to repay the student loan debt. The court measures the debtor's attempt to obtain employment, maximize income, and minimize expenses. Interestingly, the Johnson court held that making minimal payments on the loan was not, in and of itself, evidence of good faith. While making this analysis, the court also tries to determine if the debtor was culpable in causing his or her own poor financial condition. If the court determines that the debtor's irresponsible or negligent acts cause the debtor to fall below the poverty level while repaying the loan, there is a presumption against discharge and the case will be dismissed without discharge of the debt. However, the debtor may challenge this presumption by the third prong test.

A "policy analysis" makes up the **third prong** of the Johnson test. First the court compares the debtor's total indebtedness against the student loan amount while estimating the probability of future employment. Next, the court asks two questions: (1) Did the debtor file bankruptcy for the primary purpose to discharge his or her student loans? (2) Did the debtor benefit financially from the education that was financed, in its entirety or partially, through the government loans seeking to be bankrupted? The Johnson court emphasized that debtors who gained financially from their education have a special responsibility to repay their debt. If the answer to both questions is "no" then the debt is normally discharged. If answers to either of the questions are "yes," then the debt is not discharged.

The Johnson Test is <u>sequential</u>. If the debtor qualifies under the first prong, then the second prong is evaluated and so on to the third prong. <u>If the debtor fails to meet any of the prongs, the test is stopped and the debt is not discharged</u>. Some courts that adopted the Johnson Test did not follow these procedures and subjected debtors to all three prongs even if they failed a lower level prong. As such, there was much subjectivity associated with the Johnson Test.

To many people, the Johnson test seemed harsh. Yet, it influenced other courts to adopt its principles. Primarily, it suggested that "undue hardship" was to be measured against the official Federal Poverty Guidelines.

The Bryant Poverty Test

Eight years after the Johnson decision, the same court decided the Bryant v. Pennsylvania Higher Education Assistance Agency in 1987. The court acknowledged that its original test was too complicated and sought a more "objective" test— now known as the Bryant Poverty Test. Here, <u>only debtors with after-tax net income near or below the federal poverty level are eligible for undue hardship discharge</u>. Student loans were presumed to be dischargeable if the debtor's income was not "significantly greater than the poverty level."[15] The court explained that it had discretionary authority to grant discharges when debtor income was close to the poverty level but failed to define the term "significantly greater." Lenders challenged this finding, e.g., by showing that the debtor failed to maximize resources or had apparent signs of increased future income.

If a debtor's income was above the poverty level, then the debtor must prove "unique" or "extraordinary"

Bryant Poverty Test Example

A law student graduated with $11,000 in student loan debt. He failed to pass the state bar exam five different times. Subsequently, he became certified as a substitute teacher and had a net annual income that exceeded the Federal Poverty Guidelines level for a single person by only $200. He sought to have his student loans discharged. The debtor suffered from diabetes and faced $700 in "unique" and "extraordinary" expenses for medical supplies (insulin and needles). The lender argued against discharging the loan emphasizing that the debtor would eventually pass the bar exam and become an attorney. The court decided otherwise believing the debtor's chances of becoming an attorney were highly unlikely.

circumstances before the loan could be discharged. The court interpreted "unique" and "extraordinary" as situations where the debtor would experience more than mere "unpleasantness" if forced to repay the loans.

Most importantly, the Bryant Poverty Test formally established the Federal Poverty Guidelines as the primary means test for undue hardship. Although few courts rely solely on the Federal Poverty Guidelines for determining undue hardship, most courts include some consideration of the poverty level in their overall analysis. [16]

The Totality of the Circumstances Test
(Currently used in 8th Circuit Court.)

The Eighth Circuit Court in Andrews v. South Dakota Student Loan Assistance Corp (1981) took a different approach. The court was influenced by *In re Wegfehrt*[17], which held that each undue hardship determination must be examined on the specific set of facts and circumstances involved in that particular bankruptcy. The Eighth Circuit developed the "Totality of the Circumstances Test," which requires an analysis of: (1) the debtor's past, present, and reasonably reliable future financial resources; (2) calculation of the debtor's and his or her dependents' reasonable living expenses; and (3) any other relevant facts and circumstances related to that specific case. By examining all the circumstances on a case-by-case basis, the court believed it could better balance the need to determine undue hardship as specified in Section 523(a)(8) in light of the fresh start goal delineated in the Bankruptcy Code. As such, the Totality of Circumstances Test is viewed by many to be more equitable and fair than other undue hardship tests.

Some courts apply the Totality of the Circumstances Test from their own unique perspective. For example, the Seventh Circuit Court also considers whether a "certainty of hopelessness" exists regarding a debtor's financial future.[18] Some of the factors other courts have examined during the Totality of the Circumstances Tests include: whether or not the debtor is permanently or temporarily disabled; the ratio of the student loan debt to the debtor's total

indebtedness; determining if the debtor's hardship is long-term; whether or not the debtor made payments on the student loans or sought other relief such as deferment or forbearance; and other conditions. As court observer Jennifer Frattini observed, "the subjectivity inherent with this method, combined with numerous and varying factors different courts consider, can lead to unpredictable and inconsistent standards of undue hardship."[19]

The Brunner Test
(Currently adopted and used in 2nd, 3rd, 6th, 7th, and 9th Circuit Courts. Not formally adopted, but has been used in the 5th, 10th, and 11th Circuit Courts.)

The Brunner Test was developed in 1985 in a Second Circuit Court case of Brunner v. New York State Higher Education Services Corp. Although the debtor lost the case and was required to make payments on her student loans, the Brunner Test became the most widely used legal instrument for determining undue hardship. The Brunner Test was formally adopted on appeal by all courts of the Second Circuit in 1987.

In determining if Brunner was entitled to a debt discharge, the court explored the purpose and meaning of undue hardship. First, the court articulated the belief that student loans are different from other unsecured debt because there is little or no consideration given to the borrower's credit status. Further, student loans require no co-signers or collateral. For access to this easy money through federal loan programs, the government demands quid pro quo. In return for obtaining a government loan, students are denied access to bankruptcy and discharge of their student loans in all but the most hopeless of circumstances. The court concluded that student borrowers must decide for themselves whether the risk of future hardship outweighs the potential rewards in accepting the education loan.

To discharge student loans under the undue hardship rule as specified by Brunner, it must be shown: (1) that the debtor cannot maintain, based on current income and expenses, a "minimal" standard of living . . . if forced to repay the loans; (2) that additional circumstances exist indicating that this state of affairs is likely to persist for a significant portion of the repayment period of the student loans; and (3) that the debtor has made good faith efforts to repay the loans. *All three prongs must be satisfied for a student loan debt to be discharged.*

The **first prong** analyses contains two steps: (1) observe the debtor's "lifestyle attributes" to determine his or her current standard of living, and (2) determine if forcing the debtor to make loan repayments will prevent him or her from maintaining a minimal living standard. This standard does not require showing that making minimum loan payments would force the debtor to live at or below the poverty level, but does require showing that the debtor is more than simply strapped for cash. The debtor is expected to make personal and financial sacrifices to repay the student loan. If the debtor is successful at proving the first prong, then the second prong is evaluated, otherwise the process is stopped and the loan is not discharged.

The Brunner Test

Brunner obtained a Master's degree in social work and owed $9,000 in student loan debt. Seven months after receiving her degree, she filed for bankruptcy and her outstanding debts were discharged, but not her student loans. Prior to the hearing, she was unemployed and supported with the help of food stamps and Medicaid. She testified that she sent out over 100 resumes without any success in obtaining employment in her field of study. She was under the care of a therapist for treatment of anxiety and depression related to her unemployment. She testified that she was capable of working.

The Court agreed that she met the first prong of the Brunner Test showing that her student loan debt accounted for 80% of her total debt load and that she was on public welfare. But she failed to give any evidence indicating a total foreclosure of job prospects in her area of training, and thus failed the 2nd Brunner Test prong. Also, she failed the 3rd Brunner Test prong because she filed for bankruptcy too soon after obtaining her degree, failed to make any loan repayments and demonstrated a lack of "good faith."

The **second prong** is the most difficult of the three prongs to prove. In essence, the debtor must convince the court that there is no hope for improvement in future income. The court recognized that this prong is similar to a finding of "certainty of hopelessness" accepted by other courts. However, as the Brunner court itself conceded, "[p]redicting future income is . . . problematic." Courts who have used the Brunner Test have looked for "unique" or "exceptional" circumstances that impact future employment and earnings. These circumstances include: "illness, lack of usable job skills, the existence of a large number of dependents, or a combination of [the three]."[20] The second prong takes into account any possibility that a debtor's financial situation could improve in the future, and as the Second Circuit noted on appeal, "more reliably guarantees that the hardship presented is 'undue'."[21]

The **third prong** of the test was created "in accordance with the legislative intent behind §523(a)(8) of preventing intentional abusers from filing [for] bankruptcy immediately after graduation and making no effort to find employment and to make payments on their student loans." [22] Here, the debtor must show a "good faith" effort was made to repay the loan. Factors considered by the court include, "the number of payments the debtor made, attempts to negotiate with the lender, proportion of loans to total debt, and possible abuse of the bankruptcy system."[23]

The Brunner Test has been adopted or used by a majority of courts. Although courts view Brunner as an appropriate test for determining undue hardship, in reality, it often causes harsh consequences for debtors and fails to further the core goal of the Bankruptcy Code, which is to facilitate a "fresh start" for honest but unfortunate debtors.

Summary

- The U.S. Constitution provides for uniform laws on the subject of bankruptcies.
- The Bankruptcy Act of 1898 had two goals:
  - to provide honest, hard-working debtors with a "fresh start" in which they are free of oppressive debt
  - to obtain fair and equitable treatment for debtors and creditors alike
- Student loans were initially treated as any other unsecured loan and could be discharged in Chapter 7 bankruptcy.
- §523(a)(8) of the 1998 Bankruptcy Reform Act allows student loans to be discharged only incases of "undue hardship."
- "Undue hardship" was not defined by Congress
- courts have had to construct tests to determine when undue hardship exists
- There are 4 major tests used by a majority of courts to determine undue hardship:
  - **Johnson Test** — 3 prongs
    - Prong 1— "Mechanical Analysis" evaluates debtor's current and future ability to repay the loan.
    - Prong 2 — "Good Faith Analysis" requires debtors to demonstrate they made a good faith attempt to repay the loans.
    - Prong 3 — "Policy Analysis" tries to determine if the primary purpose of the bankruptcy is to discharge the loans and evaluate whether or not the debtor benefited from the education obtained through the loans.
  - **Bryant Poverty Test** was developed by the same court that created the Johnson Test and tried to make it simpler.
    - Debtors must have after-tax net incomes near the Federal Poverty Guidelines to be considered for discharging their loans.
    - This case established the Federal Poverty Guidelines as the criteria all courts would use to measure undue hardship.
  - **Totality of the Circumstances** Test — By examining all the circumstances on a case-by-case basis, the court believed it could better balance the need to determine undue hardship as specified in Section 523(a)(8) in light of the fresh start goal delineated in the Bankruptcy Code.
    - the debtor's past, present, and reasonably reliable future financial resources
    - calculation of the debtor's and his or her dependents' reasonable living expenses
    - any other relevant facts and circumstances related to that specific case.
  - **Brunner Test** — The test used by a majority of U.S. courts has 3 prongs.
    - Prong 1 — that the debtor cannot maintain, based on current income and expenses, a "minimal" standard of living . . . if forced to repay the loans
    - Prong 2 — that additional circumstances exist indicating that this state of affairs is likely to persist for a significant portion of the repayment period of the student loans
    - Prong 3 — that the debtor has made good faith efforts to repay the loans.
    - ***All three prongs must be satisfied for a student loan debt to be discharged.***

---

[1] United States Constitution, Article 1, Section 8, cl. 4.
[2] Jackson, Thomas H. (1985). The fresh start policy in bankruptcy law. *Harvard Law Rev.* (98), 1393, 1420.
[3] King, Lawrence & Cook, Michael. (1996). *Creditors' rights, debtors' protection, and bankruptcy* (3rd Edition). New York, NY: Matthew Bender and Col., Inc.
[4] See *Bankruptcy: The next Twenty years: National Bankruptcy Review Commission Final Report.* (October 20, 1997). National Bankruptcy Review Commission. Ch 1.4.5.
[5] Bankruptcy Reform Act of 1978, Pub. Law No. 95-598, 92 Stat. 2549, 2591 (1978).
[6] *See* Taylor v. United Student Aid Funds, Inc. (*In re Taylor*), 223 B.R. 747, 754 (B.A.P. 9th Cir. 1998); § 523(a)(8); Brunner v. N.Y. State Higher Educ. Servs. Corp. (*In re Brunner*), 831 F.2d 395, 396 (2d Cir. 1987), aff'g 46 B.R. 752 (Bankr. S.D.N.Y. 1985).
[7] Fox v. Pa. Higher Educ. Assistance Agency (*In re Fox*), 163 B.R. 975, 978 (Bankr. M.D. Pa. 1993); See also *In re Kapinos*, 243 B.R. at 274 (stating that Congress preferred leaving the construction of undue hardship to the courts).

[8] See *In re Andersen*, 232 B.R. at 130 ("[T]he legislative history offers little to define the nature of the exception (undue hardship) to he exception (nondischargeability).")

[9] Salvin, Robert F. (1996). Student loans, bankruptcy, and the fresh start policy: Must debtors be impoverished to discharge educational loans? *Tul. L. Rev.* (*71*), 149 Supra note 73, at 149.

[10] Collins, Thad. (1990). Forging middle ground: Revision of student loan debts in bankruptcy as an impetus to Amend 11 U.S.C.A. § 523(a)8. *Iowa L. Rev.* (75), 733, 744.

[11] *In re Brunner*, 831 F.2d 395, 396 [42 E. Law Rep. [535]] (2d Cir. 1987); Douglas v. Great Lakes Higher Education Servicing Corp. (*In re Douglas*), 237 B.R. 652, 654 (Bankr. N.D. Ohio 1999).

[12] Salvin, Robert F. (1996). Student loans, bankruptcy, and the fresh start policy: Must debtors be impoverished to discharge educational loans? *Tul. L. Rev.* (*71*), 149 Supra note 73, at 150.

[13] Fossey, Richard (1997). The certainty of hopelessness: Are courts too harsh toward bankrupt student loan debtors? *Journal of Law and Education*, (*26*), 29, 36. According to Fossey, the term "certainty of hopelessness" is mentioned in more than 30 federal cases and has become the "unofficial standard" for granting discharges to student loans.

[14] 5 Bankr. Ct. Dec. 532 (Bankr. E.D. Pa. 1979) at 544.

[15] Bryant v. Pennsylvania Higher Education Assistance Agency, at 917.

[16] Salvin, Robert F. (1996). Student loans, bankruptcy, and the fresh start policy: Must debtors be impoverished to discharge educational loans? *Tul. L. Rev.* (*71*), 149 Supra note 73, at 162.

[17] *In re Wegfehrt*, 10 B.R. 826, 830 (Bankr. N.D. Ohio 1981).

[18] *See* Roberson v. Ill. Student Assistance Comm'n (*In re Roberson*), 999 F.2d 1132, 1136 (7th Cir. 1993).

[19] Frattini, Jennifer. (2001). The dischargeability of student loans: An undue burden? (Note and Comment). *Bankr. Dev. J.* (*17*), 537, 556 supra note 144, at 565.

[20] Briscoe v. N.Y. State Higher Educ. Servs. Corp. (*In re Brisco*), 16 B.R. 128, 131 (Bankr. S.D.N.Y. 1981) at 755.

[21] Brunner v. N.Y. State Higher Educ. Servs. Corp. (*In re Brunner*), 831 F.2d 395, 396 (2d Cir. 1987), aff'g 46 B.R. 752 (Bankr. S.D.N.Y. 1985).

[22] Frattini, Jennifer. (2001). The dischargeability of student loans: An undue burden? (Note and Comment). *Bankr. Dev. J.* (*17*), 537, 556 supra note 144, at 563.

[23] United States Dept. of Educ. V. Wallace (*In re Wallace*), 259 B.R. 170, 185 (Bankr. C.D. Cal. 2000).

CHAPTER 5
"Undue Hardship" Arguments

UNBELIEVEABLE

Ms. Carol Ann Race borrowed $20,000 to study theology and philosophy in the 1980s. She made $300 monthly payments for 2 ½ years before losing her job as a religious educator in 1994. During this time she married and began to have children. Two of her five children are autistic requiring her to devote full-time to being an at-home mother.

Her husband works as a nursing-home aid and earns $18,000 annually. The family of seven lives in Minnesota on $28,000, including government disability payments for the autistic children.

Ms. Race filed for bankruptcy in the hopes of canceling the student loans — which are the family's only debt. The bankruptcy judge ruled against her since he was sure an appellate judge would overrule him. The bankruptcy judge did not believe he could erase the debt unless it was determined that repayment of the loans would strip the family of "all that is worth living."

In the end, Ms. Race debt increased to $34,000 at 7% interest. She has been placed on an income sensitive plan linked to the family's net income.

Hechinger, J. (January 6, 2005) U.S. Gets Tough on Failure to Repay Student Loans, *Wall Street Journal*, v.CCXLV n.4,p.1

In the previous chapter, we examined the major tests developed by the courts to determine "undue hardship" under Section 523(a)(8). Here, a general list of salient characteristics extracted from these tests is developed, then a wide-range of arguments are presented that could be used to meet these characteristics. Some of the arguments are presented in greater depth as academic articles in the Appendix F. *If you decide to use an article from Appendix F, do not copy it since courts will recognize where it comes from (this book) and this may prejudice the court. Instead, present it in your own words but use the footnotes to make it look authoritative.*

Characteristics Common to Undue Hardship Tests

The Brunner test is used by a majority of bankruptcy courts in the United States. It embodies much of the Johnson test. Here we review the court finding for the Brunner, Johnson, Bryant Poverty and the Totality of the Circumstances Test, and summarize 3 broad conditions common to every test.

Every undue hardship claim is reviewed in three areas:

Characteristic A — Current Living Condition and the Impact of Repaying Loan on "Minimal Living" Standard

Characteristic B — Prospects for Repaying the Loans

Characteristic C — Good Faith and Loan Repayment

Characteristic A—Current Living Condition and the Impact of Repaying Loan on "Minimal Living" Standard

Characteristic A explores two conditions: (1) the debtor's current living condition, and (2) whether repaying the student loans will push the debtor to, or below, the poverty level.

Condition 1: Every court reviews the debtor's <u>current living condition</u> and evaluates it against the Federal Poverty Guidelines. Rightly or wrongly, debtors with incomes above poverty will be scrutinized by the courts to assure all expenses are "minimized." The court will challenge expenditures for gym or video membership, Internet service, pet expenses, child or adult care, beauty salon, and more. Expenditures will be compared to an "idealized" debtor of similar situation but at the official poverty level. Expenditures that deviate from this ideal must be explained in terms of being necessary and extraordinary (e.g., needles and insulin for debtors or dependents who are diabetic), related to finding work (e.g., need for the Internet service), or related to keeping work (e.g., buying tools required for work or gym membership to relieve pain). (See Chapter 8—Preparing Your Case, for details about creating a Financial Status.)

Condition 2: Once the court is satisfied the debtor has minimized living expenses, the court evaluates whether repaying the student loans will push the debtor down to or below the poverty level. If the debtor's net income drops below the poverty level, the debt may be discharged. Some courts have granted "partial discharges" in situations where repaying the entire loans would be too severe. Partial discharges are controversial and may not be legal under certain circumstances (see discussion in Chapter 7—Advocacy).

The Department of Education and courts have a long history of evaluating debtors' lifestyle against the Federal Poverty Guidelines (formally established in the Bryant Poverty Test). We believe this is incorrect and describe our objections in the Chapter 7—Advocacy. Regardless, you must develop your personal case around this federal measure.

Characteristic B—Prospects for Repaying the Loans

Courts evaluate debtors' prospect for improved future income. Even though courts recognize that predicting future income is problematic, it hasn't stopped the practice. In general, the debtor must show there are "unique" or "exceptional" circumstances that impact future employment and earnings. We divide these circumstances into two categories: (1) Personal Limitations, and (2) Social Factors.

Category 1—Personal Limitations

Debtors need to address in detail any <u>personal limitations</u> that may impact the ability to obtain appropriate employment. Courts have enumerated three instances (or combination thereof) of unique or exceptional personal circumstances and includes: (a) medical limitations, (b) support of dependents (and their medical conditions, if applicable), and (c) lack of useable job skills. These need to be described in detail and with supporting documents.

Strategy Tip
<u>Account for Your Time</u>

In so many cases, debtors make a strong showing for their situation only to have the court reject the claim and tell the debtor to get a part-time minimum-wage job and use that money to make loan payments. Regardless of how laughable or tragic this may seem, it happens frequently. Thus, the debtor needs to <u>account for his or her time working or providing dependent care, or both</u>. Debtors need to clearly point out to the court that asking the debtor to take on any more work would push him or her over a standard workweek, and that would be an undue hardship.

(a) Medical Problems

If you have medical problems that contributed to your bankruptcy, there are three things you will want to show the court:

1. Your medical condition contributed to your bankruptcy. Here you need to give a complete history of your medical condition and subsequent loss of work and income.
2. The costs related to the medical condition are the primary cause of bankruptcy. Courts are often unaware how devastating medical bills can be and how medical conditions can push people into bankruptcy and continued poverty. Appendix F contains an article on the effect medical bill has on bankruptcy
3. Finally, that your medical condition will continue into the future, most likely become worse, and that it will be impossible to make payments on the student loans.

Most debtors make a good showing on the first two items above. The real problem is convincing the court that the medical problems will persist for at least 10 years, thereby impacting the debtor's ability to make student loan payments. This is a fuzzy area in which courts are inconsistent when interpreting the law.

(b) Dependents

Courts are aware that dependents cause time constraints for debtors who otherwise could use the time for employment. Thus, the larger the number of dependents and the time involved in their care directly impacts the debtor's ability to repay student loans.

Children: Courts make the assumption that children will leave home at 18 years of age. Thus, courts will calculate when the youngest child is expected to leave home and try to determine if the debtor would be capable of resuming payments on his or her student loans at that time. Extenuating circumstances would include a disabled child who continues to reside with the parent.

Many cases are lost because courts decide that once the children leave, the debtor can resume loan payments. This is often not true. The debtor will be 10- to 30-years older once children leave home. Ageism becomes a real issue for debtors over 50 years

---

Strategy Tip
Medical Strategy 1

The clearest and easiest way to discharge student loans is to be declared, "permanently disabled." If you are declared permanently disabled due to severe medical conditions, then a disability discharge is filed and you won't even need to go through the aggravation of an adversary proceeding. If you have a physician who will not declare you permanently disabled, look for a different physician. If necessary, find one who will declare you partially disabled and who will give documentation showing that this will last the rest of your life. Too many court cases have fallen apart at this step because it is difficult to prove the future.

Strategy Tip
Medical Strategy 2

Let's say you are partially disabled and that it will continue into the foreseeable future but won't necessarily get worse. How do you convince the court that you will not be able to repay your loans? One approach is to combine this problem with another, e.g., ageism. Once you are over 50 years old, it becomes virtually impossible to obtain employment (*see* Appendix F). Argue with the court that your medical disability and age will preclude you from finding appropriate work in the future.

of age. Thus, combining the problem of dependent children with getting older and being out of the workplace for so many years, might actually work to your advantage.

<u>Spouse, Civil Union, or Domestic Partner</u>: Courts are sensitive to the situation where debtors provide financial and emotional support for medically ill spouses (whether by marriage, Civil Union, or Domestic Partnership). Unlike with children, there is no assumption the spouse will leave. Even still, we encourage you to combine the care of a medically ill spouse with other factors that will impact your future ability to make income.

<u>Elderly or Medically Ill Parents or Siblings</u>: There have been a number of cases where courts have shown themselves insensitive to debtors who take care of elderly or medically ill parents or siblings. The courts question why the debtor is taking care of these people. It may seem obvious to the debtor, but not to the court. Thus, debtors need to make a strong case as to why it is they, and not their siblings, parents, or government taking care of these people. If this is your situation, you may want to discuss your moral or religious convictions that have influenced you to be the caretaker of these persons. Too often courts take the position that the debtor should not take on this responsibility and, instead, focus on paying back student loans. We encourage you to combine the care of a medically ill parents or siblings with other factors that will impact your future ability to make income.

(c) Lack of Useable Job Skills

Many debtors filing bankruptcy have student loans from training programs they either did not complete, or the program was of such dubious value that the debtor gained no improved job skills. Courts have been sensitive to debtors who lack useable job skills. They are aware that without proper job skills, it is very difficult for debtors to obtain high-paying employment and, subsequently, be able to make student loan payments.

Quite the opposite problem is highly educated debtors who also find they are unable to find work. It is not uncommon to find unemployed M.A.s and Ph.D.s. There is a social and court bias that believes highly educated people are guaranteed employment. Nothing could be further from the truth (*see* Appendix F). If you belong to this class of debtors, we encourage you to combine this problem with other factors you believe will impact your future ability to make income.

> ***Strategy Tip***
> **<u>Lack of Useable</u>**
> **<u>Job Skills</u>**
>
> Even though the court may agree with you that your lack of useable job skills is hurting your employment prospects, they may come back to you and ask why you don't educate yourself further to get a better job. A good answer is to explain the lack of time for furthering your education is due to the responsibilities of working and dependent care.

Category 2—External Factors Impacting Employability

Most debtors have had the challenge of showing "unique" or "exceptional" circumstances that prevent them from repaying their student loans. By focusing on unique or exceptional circumstances, courts end up evaluating personal limitations such as medical illness, dependents or lack of useable job skill (described above). But there are also many external factors that affect employment opportunities. For example, if the economy is doing poorly, jobs are often scarce. If the debtor has been terminated from many jobs or was a whistleblower, future job interviewers may see him or her as a problem or troublemaker and not offer the job. Having a bankruptcy closes certain job opportunities. And, finally, discrimination plays a significant role in our society placing many job environments out of reach of millions.

Certain cases evaluated by the Totality of the Circumstances Test have looked at some of the external factors. Courts have been hesitant to include these factors since it would require them to accept the fact that not all employment doors are open to all workers, i.e., the American dream is a myth. Let's get real. When was the last time you saw a TV announcer who was under 4 feet tall, or with Cerebral Palsy, or with extensive physical deformities? Our society has preferences and discriminates by age, race, ethnicity, religion, gender, sexual orientation, disability, height, weight, general attractiveness, and many more. All these factors impact a debtor's chances for employment.

There are many societal factors that impact particular debtors in their search for work. We present only a few of the major ones below:

- U.S. Economy
- Discrimination Based on Age
- Discrimination Against the Highly Educated
- Discrimination Based on Sexual Orientation
- Discrimination Based on Race, Gender, Ethnicity, Disability, Physical Characteristics, Religion, and other.
- Past Terminations or Whistleblower

We encourage you to look over some of the factors and determine if they apply to you. If so, include a discussion of them in your case. In general, we suggest that you first develop your argument with academic research of the societal problem, and then make it specific with examples out of your own life story.

Can you think of other factors that are applicable to your situation?

U.S. Economy

Since the crash of 2008, the U.S. economy has lost millions of jobs, which impacts debtors' chances to find work. This is particularly true if the kind of work you are trained for has been subjected to "downsizing" and "outsourcing," you can make a strong case about the difficulty in finding work in the future. See Appendix F for an article on this topic. Combine the statistics of the article with your personal experiences to build your case.

Discrimination Based on Age

Ageism is such a problem in the United States that federal and state laws have been passed to protect workers based upon age. Every state and most major cities have departments of ageing. Bottom line: as you get older it is harder to find employment. After 50-years of age, it is next to impossible to find work.

If this factor applies to you, two articles in Appendix F will help you formulate your writing. Then, make the research real by using examples from your own life. For example, if comments were made to you about your age while applying for a job, cite the details of the interview.

Discrimination Against the Highly Educated

Most educated workers can tell stories of being told he or she was "over-qualified" for a particular position. Appendix F contains an article giving the research on this problem. Personalize the research by telling your own experiences.

Discrimination Based on Sexual Orientation

If you are lesbian or gay, surely you have many experiences to call upon to demonstrate discrimination. Appendix F contains an article that gives the empirical data proving discrimination. Cite the evidence and give your personal story detailing how sexual orientation discrimination has impacted your ability to gain employment.

Discrimination Based on Race, Gender, Ethnicity, Disability, Physical Characteristics, Religion, and other

The United States is not supportive of many classes of people. If you have direct experience with employment discrimination due to any of these factors, include them in your report to the court. Visit the government website for the Equal Employment Opportunity Commission (EEOC) at www.eeoc.gov. There are many articles and statistics showing rampant discrimination in the United States. Put together the information you need to show the court the extent of the problem, and then personalize the statistics by presenting your own personal experiences of discrimination. Emphasize how this will affect your future. If these problems are not explained to the court, they will not consider them to be important.

Reverse discrimination can also present a problem for certain debtors. See Appendix F for ideas of how to write your own case.

Past Terminations or Whistleblower

Many job applications ask if you ever have been terminated or forced to resign. Of course this must be answered truthfully. If the later discovers that you were terminated or forced to resign, they may legally terminate you for lying on the application. That poses a problem for those who have been discriminated against. Your termination may not have been ethical or legal, but placing it on the application opens you to prying eyes of interviewers who probably will not believe or accept your answer without prejudice.

In your adversary proceeding, you will need to tell the court about the effect prior terminations or being a whistleblower has had on your job searches. If possible, use statements made by interviewers who brought up the problem. Being viewed as a "pariah"

Strategy Tip
Combine Factors!

One strategy to combat the court's belief your situation will improve in the future is to combine factors that show they will, in fact, make your situation worse in the future. This really is how life is, not how the courts want it to be. Most medical conditions worsen with time, not get better. Dependents may come and go, but all the while you were caring for them you were getting older; and it becomes more and more difficult to obtain employment when you are old. Many forms of discrimination exist that directly impact your ability to find work. These need to be brought to the attention of the court.

impacts all future efforts to obtain employment. In general, tell the court about the factors that impact your ability to obtain employment. You must emphasize how this impacts your future.

Characteristic C—Good Faith and Loan Repayment

Congress was most concerned with debtors who seemingly "defrauded" the government by bankrupting their student loans soon after graduation. To reinforce that concern, courts want debtors to demonstrate "good faith" attempts to repay student loans. This is shown by answering a few questions:

- Did the debtor make payments when he or she could? There is an expectation that any time the debtor's net income exceeds the Federal Poverty Guidelines, payments would be made on the student loans. It is suggested that debtors make a table showing their yearly net income and payments, if any, made on the student loans. If payments were not made, an explanation is required.

- If the debtor was in financial trouble, did he or she contact the Department of Education to arrange for restructuring the loan or delaying the payments? Debtors are expected to show diligence in maintaining their loans and keeping them out of default. Whenever there were times of financial difficulty, debtors must show that they worked with the lender to resolve the issue instead of letting loans fall in arrears.

- What is the ratio of the student loan debt to the total debt being bankrupted? If the student loans exceed approximately 50% of the debtor's total debt load, courts will be suspicious that the primary purpose of the bankruptcy is to discharge the student loans. In these cases, debtors must give a strong showing regarding the other common characteristics developed above.

- How soon after receiving the last student loan is the debtor trying to bankrupt the debt? Debtors who bankrupted their student loans months or days after finishing college are the ones that alarmed Congress, enough for them to pass the Bankruptcy Reform Act of 1978. Courts are still sensitive to the timing of bankruptcy filings. In general, at least 5 or more years should have passed since obtaining the last student loan. Otherwise, there is a presumption of fraud, which the debtor must overcome.

debtor received his or her last student loan and filing bankruptcy

Summary

Characteristics Common to Undue Hardship Tests

To discharge student loans, debtors must show:

- Current Living Condition and the Impact of Repaying Loan on "Minimal Living" Standard
  - Debtor's current living condition is not above Federal Poverty Guidelines
  - Repaying the student loan will push debtor into Poverty
- Prospects for Repaying the Loans
  - Debtor is already working and/or taking care of dependents full-time
  - Debtor has personal limitations that impact the ability to work in the future. These include:
    - Medical illness (of self and/or dependents)
    - Taking care of dependents
    - Lack of useable job skills
    - There are societal factors impacting the debtor's chances for future work. These include:
    - U.S. economy and lack of jobs
    - Ageism
    - Discrimination against the highly educated
    - Discrimination based on sexual orientation
    - Discrimination based on race, gender, ethnicity, disability, physical characteristics, religion, and others.
    - Past terminations and whistleblower
    - Other
- Good Faith and Loan Repayment
  - Made student loan payments when he or she could
  - When in financial trouble, contacted the Department of Education to arrange for restructuring the loan or delay in payments
  - Ratio of the student loan debt to the total debt being bankrupted is less than 50%
  - 5 years have passed between the time the

CHAPTER 6
Example Court Cases
With Analysis

This chapter presents many examples of court cases where debtors attempted to have their student loans discharged through bankruptcy. In each case, the details are given, court ruling, and a brief analysis of the deficits of the case. Even if you are not planning a bankruptcy but are pursuing a Compromise or Write-Off, this chapter will help you understand the Department of Education's defense logic.

We suggest you read through each case as each one presents a different resolution. They may give you ideas for your own case.

Case: In re Cheesman

Cheesman v. Tennessee Student Assistance Corp., 25 F.3d 356 (6th Cir. 1994)

Details: Dallas and Margaret Cheesman filed a Chapter 7 bankruptcy in 1991. Of their approximately $30,000 in outstanding debt, $14,267 was attributed to student loans guaranteed by the Tennessee Student Assistance Corporation (TSAC). Margaret Cheesman took out approximately $5,000 in student loans and received a bachelor of arts in English in 1984. After a six-month grace period and five-month extension she made two payments toward her student loan debt. She worked as a teacher's aid from 1989 to 1991 with a gross monthly salary of $651. She took a maternity leave in 1991 during which her position at the school was eliminated. She began to receive unemployment compensation of $53 a week.

Dallas Cheesman earned a bachelor degree from Austin Peay State University. He took out $3,500 in student loans in 1985 to study educational psychology. He withdrew from college in 1985 to

take a second job. He made two $50 payments on his student loans. From October 1986 through October 1987, he earned a gross salary of $1,538 a month as director of Giles County Alternative School. From 1988 to 1990, he worked as a family worker in a residential treatment program for emotionally disturbed children for a gross salary of $1,632 a month. At the time of the bankruptcy filing, he worked a similar job but at the reduced pay of $1,123 a month.

In 1991, the Cheesman household has a net income of $13,720 a year. They had monthly expenses of $1,594 (or $19,128 a year) that included $100 monthly tuition to send their 7-year old daughter to private school; they also had a 14-month old son. Cheesmans explained that they sent their daughter to private school because they disapproved of corporal punishment used in public schools. The daughter also had asthma and required medical treatment. The Cheesmans owned a 1988 Chevrolet Nova worth approximately $3,000, which they made monthly payments of $350.

Court Decision: Discharge granted. Appeal court affirmed. Bankruptcy court stated that the Cheesmans were "in a downward spiral and will continue to go deeper in debt." The court recognized that the Cheesmans had a monthly deficit of approximately $400 and that there was no indication that their financial situation would improve in the foreseeable future. The bankruptcy court decided to place the case on its docket to be reviewed in 18 months to see if the family financial status had improved before fully discharging the student loan debt. The court held that section 105(a) [bankruptcy equitable powers] authorized the bankruptcy court to impose the eighteen-month stay.

Analysis: Delaying the final decision of this case for 18 months through use of equitable powers caused much controversy. The Cheesmans prevailed, but they had to take the case through appeal.

Case: In re Conner

Conner v. Illinois State Scholarship Comm'n, 89 B.R. 744, 744-46 (Bankr. N.D. Ill. 1988)

Details: Ruth Conner was a fifty-one-year-old divorcee with debts of approximately $65,000 including $36,000 in student loan debt. All of her debts were past due and in default. She held a managerial position in a small company where she earned $25,000 annually. She supported two children in college and received no child support from her former husband. She lived with her youngest daughter in a one-bedroom apartment and drove an eleven-year-old car. She needed glasses and dental work but delayed both because she could not afford the cost. She had been evicted from several apartments for non-payment of rent.

Court Decision: Discharge denied. Court reasoned that after her children finished college she would be able to pay her student loans over 25 years using a graduated monthly payment schedule. The court ordered a four-year deferment on repayment and ordered the parties to renegotiate the loan for payments over twenty-five years.

Analysis: The court did not have evidence about the debtor's future ability to service her loan. Ms. Conner may have prevailed by showing that her income most likely would drop or be insufficient in the future. At age fifty-one, the debtor could have made a strong case for age related restrictions on future employment. A 25-year repayment plan that did not start until her 55th birthday would last until she reached age 80. She could have argued against any repayment plan past age 65, as the taxes on the discharged portion would have been an undue hardship. See Appendix F for two articles on age, and Chapter 7 for discussion on the ICR.

Case: In re Courtney

Courtney v. Gainer Bank, 79 B.R. 1004, 1010-11 (Bankr. N.D. Ind. 1987)

Details: Thirty-one-year-old male attempted to discharge through bankruptcy $2,500 in student loans which were incurred when taking courses at vocational school. The debtor did not have a high school diploma and failed to complete the vocational training program. The debtor was induced to file for bankruptcy after he received a $300,000 judgment against him attributed to a car accident for which he had no insurance. The debtor supported his wife and three young children on an annual income of $21,000. He worked intermittently and his income fluctuated accordingly. His incomes for the four years prior to filing for bankruptcy in 1987 were $10,000, $14,600, $14,000, and $21,800 respectively. At the time of the bankruptcy, the debtor stated his monthly take-home pay at $1,200 and claimed monthly expenses of $1,545. In his expense account, he failed to quantify medical bills not covered by insurance for treatment he received for his eye injury, or for the medication his wife took to control epilepsy. He failed to list another student loan of $2,500. Also absent from the family's budget was anything for medical insurance, savings, car insurance, or entertainment. The debtors assets included two old automobiles valued less than $500 each, a recreational vehicle valued at $3,000, $750 in household goods, and a boat valued at $750. All these assets were exempted under section 522 of the Bankruptcy Code.

Court Decision: Discharge denied. The court purported to use two prongs of the Johnson test— the mechanical and good faith tests— while rejecting the policy test. The court decided the debtor could raise money to pay the student loans if he liquidated his recreational vehicle and boat. Although these items were exempt and, thus, protected from creditors, the court believed these items were not essential and could be sold. Moreover, the court found the debtor's list of expenses not credible since in a prior court filing he listed his expenses at $894 a month instead of the $1,545 claimed at trial. The court decided this discrepancy amounted to fraud and that the debtor's income must be greater than listed.

Analysis: This case shows the importance of the facts and figures listed in a bankruptcy matching those listed in the adversary proceeding. The court, in this case, did not believe the debtor's income or expenses; they just did not add up. Furthermore, the debtor failed to include <u>all expenses</u> and missed listing another outstanding student loan debt. The court might not have gone after his RV or boat, but they did; demonstrating the capricious nature of courts in these kinds of legal proceedings. He also needed to make a strong case for his family's marginal living for many years to come because of having small children and an ill wife.

Case: In re Ford

Ford v. Tennessee Student Assistance Corp., 151 B.R. 135, 138-39 (Bankr. M.D. Tenn. 1993)

Details: Ms. Ford was a partially disabled woman in her fifties. She had co-signed on her daughter's educational loan that she (the mother) attempted to bankrupt. Ms. Ford was trained as a nurse's assistant and employed for sixteen years from 1972 until 1988, when she suffered a back injury and had to quit working. She was considered to be fifty-percent disabled and received Social Security Disability payments along with food stamps and mortgage assistance from the Department of Housing and Urban Development. Her low income qualified her for free legal services through the local bar association.

Court Decision: Discharge denied. Using the Totality of the Circumstances Test, the court decided that Ms. Ford failed to maximize her income by finding appropriate part-time work. The court believed that if she had done so, she would have been able to make payments on the loans. Also, the state appellate court had previously turned down her request for unemployment compensation because she placed greater restrictions on work than were medically necessary. Finally, the student loans represented the bulk of her total unsecured debt, demonstrating that she filed the case primarily to have the student loans discharged.

Analysis: Ms. Ford could have benefited by finding a physician who would declare her permanently disabled and have the loans discharged that way. Barring that, she could have made major issues about her age and the ability to find work and the inappropriateness of the ICR. See Appendix F for two articles on age and Chapter 7 for discussion on the ICR.

Case: In re Goulet

Goulet v. Educational Credit Management Corp., 284 F.3d 773 (7th Cir. 2002).

Details: At the time of his bankruptcy filing, John P. Goulet was 55 years old and lived with his mother in Eau Claire, Wisconsin. He worked occasionally and helped his mother around the house. He had an 11 year-old son for whom he did not have custody and owed $228 per month in child support. His mother did not charge him rent or lodging expenses and paid half of the child support. Goulet did not receive any form of public assistance.

Goulet graduate from high school in 1963. In 1972, he earned a bachelor's degree in history. Between 1972 and 1983 he worked various jobs including bartending and restaurant management. In 1984, he returned to Eau Claire and worked as a life insurance agent living comfortably on $20,000 to $30,000 a year. In 1989, he was charged with insurance fraud and lost his insurance license. He was also arrested for felony cocaine possession with intent to deliver. From 1988 to 1990 he attended outpatient counseling and worked as a bouncer and bartender. From 1991 to 1995, he returned to school and completed most of the coursework for a master's in psychology. He received 21 student loans totaling $76,000. He failed to obtain his degree because he did not complete a statistics course. He also decided against continuing schooling toward a counseling license since it required 3,000 additional hours of post-degree experience and he was concerned his felony conviction would prevent him from securing a state certificate needed for employment as a counselor. After quitting school, he was not hired for the counseling positions for which he applied and returned to bartending. He attempted to work in real estate but without success. He delayed making payments on this student loans through the use of forbearances. He never made a single payment on his student loans.

Goulet testified that he suffered from alcoholism for 30-years and attended Alcoholics Anonymous; although witnesses claimed not to see a problem with his drinking. At the time of his bankruptcy filing he earned $1,490 a year and had yearly expenses of approximately $5,904, without factoring in the student loan payments.

Court Decision: Discharge granted but the Appeals court reversed the decision affirming that the student loans were not dischargeable. The Brunner test was used. The bankruptcy court accepted Goulet's contention that his age, the enormous amount of his debt, his substance and alcohol abuse, and his felony conviction created significant barriers to future, well-paying employment. As such, his ability to repay his loans was impacted. However, the circuit court concluded that Goulet's circumstances failed to rise to the level of "additional, exceptional circumstances" necessary to satisfy Brunner's second prong. Further, the court noted that even if his prospects in the mental health field and insurance industry are closed, he presented no evidence to conclude that he was unemployable in other fields. As such, the court concluded that Goulet's situation did not reach the "certainty of hopelessness" required by the second prong of the Brunner test for undue hardship.

Analysis: The bankruptcy court was correct in its handling of this case. There is no way a 55-year old man with a 20-year history of earning below the poverty level would be able to make $600 a month payments on student loans. The appeals court raised the bar so that it was impossible to prevail. In retrospect, Goulet could have made a stronger case about his age impacting future employment. He could have better documented his alcoholism and related it to other medical conditions. Also, he could have argued that being placed on the ICR would create an undue burden. In his case, when the ICR plan finished up after 25 years, he would be 80 years old living on social security with no discretionary income. Thus, the tax liability on the loan discharge amount

would be a severe burden.

Case: In re Gravante

In re Correll, 105 B.R. 302 (W.D. Bankr. Pa 1989), at 309.

Details: Jimilene Gravante took out student loans to finance training in medical office assistant. When she enrolled, she was a single mother with two children. She did not finish the training program because one of her children became ill, and later she remarried and had two more children. Her husband was employed as a field engineer and earned a "substantial" income. There was a history of family illness that placed their finances on a tight budget. She claimed she received no benefit from the education.

Court Decision: Discharge granted. The court concluded that if she were required to pay back the student loan, the family's finances would become unstable and place all six family members on the public welfare rolls. As such, the court believed forcing Gravante to repay her student loans would violate the Bankruptcy Code's fresh start policy.

Analysis: Showing that the large family was at risk of being thrown onto the public welfare rolls convinced the court to discharge the loans.

Case: In re Healey

Healey v. Massachusetts Higher Education, 161 B.R. 389, 394 (E.D. Mich. 1993)

Details: Ms. Healey graduated in 1990 with a Masters degree in education. She was unable to find full-time employment and settled for substitute teaching that paid $35-$50 per day. That summer she took a job at McDonald's to pay the bills. Later that year, she received a full-time teaching position for the teaching year 1991-1992 that paid $1,000 per month for ten months. Renewal of her teaching contract in 1992 resulted in a $50/month raise. Her net annual income at the time of filing totaled $9,064 year. She shared an apartment to cut expenses. She estimated her monthly expenses to total $764 for food, rent, clothing, transportation, and medical costs. Her telephone expenses included $35 a month in long-distance charges attributed to phone calls to her family that lived out of state. She claimed it was impossible for her to pay the minimum $219 a month in student loan payments.

Court Decision: Discharge denied. Court used the Brunner test. The court was very suspect of her expenses. They believed she was spending a "fairly sizeable amount" for a single person, but, without explanation, agreed that she was minimizing her expenses (contradictory conclusions). However, the court claimed that she failed part two of the first Brunner test— that the debtor must maximize his or her personal income. The court asked Ms. Healey why she did not look for work outside the teaching field. She responded that it took considerable time and money to go to college to get a teaching credential and that she really wanted to stay in the field and teach. The court did not approve of her response and concluded that she was not maximizing her personal resources. Further, the court concluded that she failed the second prong of the Brunner test for undue hardship. They claimed that to pass this test, the debtor is required to show "additional circumstances" indicating her state of affairs would persist for a significant portion of the repayment period. Ms. Healey failed to do so.

Analysis: Her expenses of $764 a month was not a sizeable amount as the court claimed. What we don't know from the details of the case is the debtor's age. If she were under 50-years-of-age, her best bet would have been to delay repaying the loans through the use of deferments or forbearances until her income improved or decreased. If her income improved, she could have serviced her loan. If it decreased, she would have had a stronger case since more time would have passed after college graduation. Finally, perhaps if she had emphatically argued that the value of the education (see Chapter 7 under Judicial Lawmaking— "Discrediting the Value of Education") should have been considered, the court may have not made the outrageous contention that she needed to look for work outside her field.

Case: In re Innes

Innes v. Kansas State Univ., 207 B.R. 953, 957 (Bankr. D. Kan. 1997).

Details: The Innes filed a Chapter 7 bankruptcy petition in 1995, but converted the case to Chapter 13 soon thereafter because they found that they would be unable to retain their two vehicles in a Chapter 7 case. They proposed a Chapter 13 plan under which they would pay $130 per month to the Chapter 13 trustee for fifty-seven months, an amount that would pay debts secured by their vehicles and their washer and dryer, and also pay their attorney's fees and the costs of administering the plan. They continued paying for their home outside the plan.

Over a number of years before the debtors filed for bankruptcy, Mr. Innes borrowed more than $45,000 in student loans towards a bachelor's degree in history. He did not finish his master's degree, thereby failing to qualify to teach history at the secondary school level. By April 2000, interest added another $17,000 to his debt increasing his total to $61,184.68. Mrs. Innes has no legal liability on the student loans. Other than student loans, the debtors listed almost $30,000 in unsecured debts, most of which were owed on credit cards.

When they initially filed for bankruptcy, the Innes were in their mid-thirties. She worked at Wal Mart. Mr. Innes was unemployed for 18 months, then got a job as a locksmith and general maintenance worker with a contractor at Fort Riley military base. Since their income varied during the early years of the Chapter 13 bankruptcy, they supplemented their income with public assistance (when they qualified) in the form of medical cards, food stamps, a school lunch program, and the Women, Infants, and Children program. Their vehicles then had 150,000 and 160,000 miles on them.

By the year 2000, Mrs. Innes had become a department manager for Wal Mart, earning $13.44 per hour for an annual income of $28,149. Mr. Innes earned $14.74 per hour, and grossed an annual income of $30,690.32. Both figures included some overtime. Their combined annual gross income was $58,839.32, yielding a monthly gross approximately $4,900. The debtors had no reasonable expectations of receiving anything more than cost-of-living wage increases. Both debtors' employment histories indicated they were not likely to move into substantially better-paying jobs in the foreseeable future. Mrs. Innes had a retirement fund at work that was worth about $26,000 in 1995.

The Innes had six children ranging in age from one to seventeen. A four-year-old and fifteen-month-old were not yet in school and the other children were in second, sixth, tenth, and eleventh grades. The Innes' combined gross income exceeded the federal Department of Health and Human Services annual income poverty guideline for a family of eight by about 100%. [*See Annual Update of the HHS Poverty Guidelines*, 65 Fed. Reg. 7555, 7555 (2000) (poverty level for family of eight is $28,650)]. Eligibility for some public assistance programs, for example, Kansas Legal Services, Inc., is set at 185% of the HHS poverty guidelines. The debtors' income was about $5,000 above this threshold. Neither of the debtors had any inheritance expectancy. One of their children worked part-time for Wal Mart in 1999 and earned $4,951.28 before deductions for taxes and social security. From the net, the child paid some of his expenses for clothing, auto (including gasoline), and school (except lunches). During their Chapter 13 case, the debtors paid off their vehicles but also wore them out and replaced them with used ones. Mr. Innes made a one-hundred-mile round trip to and from work every day in a 1985 Honda with 225,000 miles on it. Mrs. Innes drove a 1995 Ford Winstar that had 60,000 miles on it when they purchased it. She drove about 30,000 miles per year, mostly to and from work. The debtors were making monthly payments on the Winstar.

The Innes lived in the country in order to have lower house payments than they could have in town. During the Chapter 13 case, they were allowed to use part of a tax refund to help them pay to convert their garage into a third bedroom. They got permission to use a portion of another tax refund to help pay for repairs to their septic field, which had been draining raw sewage into their yard. Nevertheless, as indicated by the testimony, their home still needed substantial repairs.

They set up a method of borrowing small amounts to accomplish some repairs and it was obvious that it would be a continuing process because they did not have the ability to pay for all the needed repairs at the same time. The debtors used much of their 1999 tax refund for a family vacation to Colorado. According to the testimony, the family rarely ate out during the vacation in order to save money. For their meals, the family economized by eating canned rather than fresh fruit and vegetables; for meat, they ate hamburger.

The family had health insurance through Mrs. Innes's job. The policy had a $1,000 deductible and a 20% co-pay requirement for covered services beyond that amount. The co-pay requirement appeared to set a maximum annual obligation of $4,450 with 100% coverage over that amount.

Of the family, only Mr. Innes had any ongoing medical problems. He has a below-the-knee amputation of his left leg and usually wears a prosthesis, although he sometimes uses a wheelchair; and, a bone spur on the leg-stump that needed to be surgically removed. His prosthesis must be replaced on an irregular basis at a cost of $5,000 and its use requires disposable sleeves that cost about $1,500 per year. He has been diagnosed as having bipolar disorder, for which Prozac has been prescribed.

Based on a student loan debt of $61,184.68 and an adjusted gross income of $58,856, three payment plans were considered to be available to Mr. Innes. Under the plans, he would could pay: (1) $459.66 per month for thirty years; (2) $514.60 per month for a maximum of 25 years, with any remaining balance being discharged and treated as taxable debt forgiveness; or (3) $750.45 per month for 10 years. Also possible was the graduated repayment plan for people who expect their income to steadily increase under which payments would increase every two years to a maximum of one-and-one-half times the standard repayment amount. Since Mr. Innes had no reason to expect his income to increase, he chose not to participate in this plan. The debtors' net take-home pay was $3,842.04 per month with monthly expenses totaling $4,327.47, meaning the family faced an almost $500 net under funding each month.

Court Decision: Discharge granted. The Brunner test was used. Creditors took exception to the expenses listed by the debtors. In general, there was the feeling that since the Innes had a net income exceeding the Federal Poverty Guidelines, then discretionary income should have been available to pay creditors, including the student loans. The court analyzed item-by-item and determined that the expenses were not excessive, but, in fact, actually lower than expected for such a large family. The court stated, "Families are not required to live at a poverty level or to obtain public assistance in order to service student loans; a modest budget without frivolous expenditures is sufficient to establish that student loans should be discharged."

The state of Kansas fought the discharge of its student loans to the Innes claiming that they were not bound by a decision made by a federal bankruptcy court. The district court determined that when a state enters into agreement with the U.S. Department of Education for lending money for education loans, then all the federal rules and legislation regulating the loans apply. Thus, the federal bankruptcy court had the legal power to discharge the loans even though the loans originated through the state of Kansas.

Analysis: This is an example where student loans were discharged through a Chapter 13 bankruptcy.

Case: In re Kraft

Kraft v. New York State Higher Educ. Servs. Corp., 161 B.R. 82, 84 (Bankr. W.D.N.Y. 1993)

Details: Kraft, a thirty-eight-year-old divorced female attempted to have $18,000 in student loans discharged. She currently worked as a school bus driver and earned approximately $800 a month. The previous sixteen years, she worked for a fast food restaurant at minimum wage and raised three children. She enrolled in a trade-school program for tourism and travel management. After completing the program, she looked for work in a number of states near her immediate area. She found employment opportunities slim and discovered that she had been trained on an obsolete computer ticketing system that few travel agencies used. After eighteen months of looking for appropriate work, she accepted a job as a school bus driver although it did not provide year-round work. She lived a frugal life consuming only the essentials—shelter, food, and transportation. She made no allowances for clothing, health care, or health insurance. She paid $200 a month for a one-room apartment, requiring her children to live with their paternal grandparents.

Court Decision: Discharge denied. The court applied the Brunner test and concluded the debtor made a poor educational decision to pursue a course of study that was neither high paying nor opportunity laden. The court decided that she failed the second prong test since she could not prove she was doomed to a life of low-income jobs. Further, she failed the third prong of the test because she filed within eighteen months of accepting the final student loan. Thus, the court found no exceptional circumstances and a lack of good faith.

Analysis: The decision in this case shows the absurdity by some courts to punish poor debtors. Regardless, Ms. Kraft could have waited almost five years before filing for bankruptcy and delayed repaying her loans with deferments and forbearances in the meantime. Proving that she was doomed to low-paying jobs for the rest of her life is next-to-impossible at age 38. She may have been successful by aggressively attacking the legality of the bankruptcy code as discussed in Chapter 7.

Case: In re Lehman

Lehman v. New York Higher Educ. Servs. Corp., 226 B.R. 805, 809 (Bankr. D. Vt. 1998).

Details: A 34-year-old single male who attended Oxford University in England applied to have his student loans discharged. He had no dependents nor physical disability or illness. He taught for three years immediately after graduation at an annual income of $28,000. He quit his job to open a pottery studio. Never once did he make a payment toward his student loan debt.

Court Decision: Discharge denied. Court concluded that the debtor's conduct failed to meet the good faith (third prong) requirement of the Brunner test.

Analysis: This case demonstrates the importance for debtors to stay in the good graces of the lender. Lehman should have made loan payments during the three years his income was $28,000, unless he had significant medical or other qualified expenses that took most of his income. He demonstrated bad faith in repaying the loans. He may have achieved a discharge if he attacked the legitimacy of the bankruptcy code itself. *See* Chapter 7 for various arguments.

Case: In re Myers

Myers v. Pennsylvania Higher Education Assistance Agency, 150 B.R. 139 (Bankr. W.D. Pa. 1993).

Details: A fifty-year-old woman took out student loans to acquire a Bachelor of Science degree in Public Administration from Slippery Rock University. The woman had previously been trained, and worked, as a nurse. Unfortunately, she was unable to find a job in public administration and returned to nursing. Her monthly expenses included mental health treatment and telephone calls to her daughter.

Court Decision: Discharge denied. Court was not convinced that she had done enough to minimize her expenses. It is this case that the court stated, undue hardship analysis entailed more than "mere unpleasantness" or "garden variety" hardship.

Analysis: Unfortunately, not much more is known about this case. It is often cited because of its use of the terms "mere unpleasantness" or "garden variety" to indicate the level of undue hardship needed to convince the court.

Case: In re Pena

Pena v. United Student Aid Funds, 155 F.3d 1108, 1110 (9th Cir.1998).

Details: Ernest and Julie Pena filed for Chapter 7 bankruptcy in 1994. Besides other debts, the Pena's sought relief from federally guaranteed student loans used by Ernest to attend ITT Technical Institute (ITT) in Phoenix, Arizona. The student loans totaled $9,399.60. Ernest discovered the certificate he earned at ITT was useless, not accepted by other colleges, and did not lead to increased employment. He made several payments on the loan before loosing his job. He ceased making payments on the student loans. Later, he found employment in the wafer fabrication room of a technical company for which he earned $22,600 per year. Ernest Pena is 40 years old. Julie Pena has suffered from serious mental disability (bi-polar disorder) for most her life. In 1992, she became psychotic and was hospitalized. She has never been able to hold a job longer than 6 months. In August 1995, Julie received a lump-sum payment of approximately $8,000 as an award for past-due disability benefits attributed to her mental condition. The Pena's used the lump sum to buy a 20-year old car and to pay other bills. Julie received $378 per month in disability payments. At the time of the bankruptcy filing, the Pena's claimed a monthly income of $1,748 and monthly expenses of $1,803. The Pena's also had a 9-year-old dependent son.

Court Decision: Discharge granted. Affirmed by the 9th Circuit Court. The court used the Brunner test and found for the Pena's. USAF appealed claiming that, besides other reasons, the bankruptcy court erred by considering evidence regarding the value of the IT education. The district court concluded, "We agree that consideration of educational value as a separate factor in analyzing undue hardship would improperly place too much emphasis on this evidence. However, as part of the second prong analysis, the value of Ernest's education is relevant to this future ability to pay off the student loans. The bankruptcy court did not err in considering that Ernest's income was not likely to increase as a result of his ITT education."

Analysis: The important finding of this case is that undue hardship was determined by taking into consideration the Pena's present marketable skills, extent of his education, and the prospects of increased education or skill training at his age and economic status. The debtors were <u>not</u> required to prove that "exceptional circumstances" existed to block improvements in their future financial status.

Case: In re Rivers

Rivers v. United Student Aid Funds, 213 B.R. 616, 620 (Bankr. S.D. Ga. 1997).

Details: Ms. Rivers earned a master's degree in social work and held a job typical for someone with her credential in that career. Her $30,000 a year salary supported her and her son in an austere lifestyle. She owed approximately $55,000 in student loans at the time of her bankruptcy filing. If she were to make payments over 30 years, the loan payment would have been $427 a month. She claimed making such payments would have prevented her from maintaining a minimal standard of living.

Court Decision: Partial discharge granted. The court used the Brunner test but was critical of the second prong. The court stated, "projecting income over a period of years is a very difficult undertaking for a finder of fact. Such projections rest as much on evidence of future income prospects, which in this case is scant to nonexistent, as on common sense and experience, which are both highly subjective." Further, the court referred to the equitable nature of bankruptcy and stated that a "court should not read and apply a statute in a manner which leads to an 'absurd' result." The court decided that a partial discharge was the most equitable legal path to take.

Analysis: This is an example of a lower-middle class debtor being successful at having her student loans partially discharged. She could have challenged the court's use of a partial discharge; however, if she challenged the use of partial discharge she could have run the risk of the court denying the discharge completely.

Case: In re Roberson

Roberson, 999 F.2d 1132, 1135 (7th Cir. 1993)

Details: Mr. Roberson was 35 years old and accumulated approximately $10,000 in student loan debt. He obtained a degree in industrial technology in 1986. He was laid off from his job at an automobile assembly plan. At the time of his bankruptcy filing, he was unemployed, occupied a one-room apartment that lacked a toilet or kitchen, and was divorced. He had child support obligations and two drunken driving convictions.

Court Decision: Discharge granted but reversed by Seventh Circuit that reinstated the debt. The court used the Brunner test. According to the Seventh Circuit, Mr. Roberson failed to show a "certainty of hopelessness" in his future employment opportunities as required under the second prong test. The court stated, "Mr. Roberson has not indicated his road to recovery is obstructed by the type of barrier that would lead us to believe he will lack the ability to repay for several years." Further, the court found that it was immaterial whether or not he received any value from his college education.

Analysis: It is this case that the term and measure "certainty of hopelessness" came about. It raised the level to which debtors must prove financial adversity. At age 35 and with a technical degree, Mr. Roberson's best bet would have been to obtain delays in repaying his loans through the use of deferments and forbearances. After 6 years of deferments or forbearances, he could have refinanced (consolidated) his loans to restart the clock. Without medical illness, it would be impossible for him to show a bleak employment future. Another approach would be to aggressively attack the validity of the bankruptcy code (see Chapter 7).

Case: In re Skaggs

Skaggs v. Great Lakes Higher Educ. Corp., 196 B.R. 865, 867-68 (Bankr. W.D. Okla. 1996).

Details: Mr. Skaggs owed approximately $47,000 in student loans originating from a Bachelor of Arts degree in history and a Masters degree in education. He made a "vigorous and good faith effort" to find employment but resorted to working as an insurance agent for $20,000 a year. He lived with his wife and three children in a mobile home. They owned three high-mileage automobiles. The family used discount coupons extensively to purchase food, and clothing was acquired at discount stores and garage sales.

Court Decision: Discharge granted. The courts stated, "The common sense approach to whether or not repayment of a student loan under the facts in a particular case amounts to an undue hardship is, in itself, a sufficient guide to the exercise of judicial discretion under 523(a)(8)." It is from this case we have the quote, "there are as many factors and tests which have been used to determine undue hardship as there are courts to decide the issue."

Analysis: Finally, a court that used reason to treat honest debtors fairly.

Case: In re Stebbins-Hopf

Stebbins-Hopf v. Texas Guaranteed Student Loan Corp., 176 B.R. 784, 785 (Bankr. W.D. Tex. 1994)

Details: Catherine Stebbins-Hopf suffered from arthritis, bronchitis and nerve damage in her foot. Her daughter was epileptic and her mother had cancer. A couple of her grandchildren were asthmatic. Debtor used her limited financial resources to help her daughter, mother and grandchildren.

Court Decision: Discharge denied. "She intentionally chose to help her family financially even though these individuals were not legally her dependents ... Her moral obligation to family members ... does not take priority over her legal obligation to repay her educational loans," concluded the court.

Analysis: Unfortunately, not much is known about this case except that the court denied her request because she spent much of her income to help people the court did not accept as her dependents (mother and grandchildren). The lesson learned here is that debtors need to be clear that "dependents" are legal dependents.

Case: In re Walcott

Walcott v. USA Funds, Inc., 185 B.R. 721 (Bankr. E.D.N.C. 1995)

Details: Stephanie Walcott graduated with a Bachelor of Arts degree in English in 1991. She accumulated $14,000 in student loans. Upon graduation she searched for professional positions but was told that she was under-qualified. Out of desperation, she widened her search to include salesperson, restaurant hostess, secretary, child-care provide, hotel desk clerk, and temporary worker to only be told that she was over-qualified or inexperienced. During the three-year period 1991 to 1994, she worked various minimum-wage paying jobs. These included vacuum cleaner salesperson, soliciting pledges, cleaning condominiums, stockroom clerk at J.C. Penny, distributing flyers at apartment complexes, answering phone and aiding a blind man– none of these jobs ever exceeded $5.50 an hour. She also took computer courses to improve her marketability. She continued to search for better jobs. She minimized her expenses by living at home with her parents. While her bankruptcy case was pending, she applied for 38 more jobs and finally acquired one that paid $9.00 per hour teaching literacy classes. This was her highest salary ever.

Court Decision: Discharge denied. Brunner test was used. The court recognized that she had made substantial effort to find work and minimized expenses, thus complying with the first prong of the Brunner test. However, the court noticed that she found a new job with increased monthly income. They concluded that she did not demonstrate that her future prospects for employment and increased income were "hopeless" as required by the second prong of the Brunner test.

Analysis: Ms. Walcott made the mistake of trying to bankrupt her student loans too soon. Because only 4 years had gone by since graduating from college, she really had no track record for the courts to determine if she experienced more than "garden variety" hardship and the predictability of her future employment prospects. She could have used deferments and forbearances to delay the on-set of repayment.

Case: In re Wetzel

Wetzel v. New York State Higher Educ. Servs. Corp., 213 B.R. 220, 223 (Bankr. N.D.N.Y. 1996)

Details: Genevieve Wetzel was a fifty-four-year-old

divorced woman in 1996, suffering from Meniere's disease, degenerative disc disease, and fibrocystic breast disease. She lived with her dependent nineteen year-old autistic son in a two-bedroom apartment. She owed $17,567 in student loans— a combination of four student loans used to attend business school. After graduation, she was unable to procure employment. She landed one job only to have the position eliminated soon after being hired. Subsequently, she was able to find part-time work for only two days a week at $6.50 an hour. The job did not provide health insurance. She had difficulty finding appropriate work since she needed to stay home to take care of her son. She sought bankruptcy relief from the student loans since she claimed she could not simultaneously repay the student loans and maintain a minimal lifestyle for herself and son.

Court Decision: Discharge denied. The court decided that she was not entitled to an undue hardship discharge of her entire student loan obligation because she failed to demonstrate "a showing of exigent or exceptional long-term circumstances which [were] beyond [her] control."

Analysis: This case is cited by many academic papers to illustrate the absolute wrong-headedness of courts in their analysis of undue hardship. At age fifty-four, she could have made a strong case for age impact on her ability to find work. See Appendix F for two articles on age and Chapter 7 for discussion on the ICR.

CHAPTER 7
Advocacy

United States Code Chapter 11, Section 523(a)(8) as specified in the 1998 Bankruptcy Reform Act is bad law. The language specifying "undue hardship" is vague, misleading, and unworkable. As seen in previous chapters, court interpretations of the Act has led to a virtual block to anyone seeking relief from student loan debt. Congress did not intend that to happen.

The Department of Education has extreme power over debt collection and its employees and attorneys often abuse this power. The Department may seize or garnish part of a borrowers paycheck, social security benefits, or tax refund without a court order. Only the IRS has as much power to collect on debts; such power is difficult to moderate.

Often the Department of Education threatens borrowers, instead of counseling them on their rights to debt reorganizing or having debt discharged. Many consumer credit organizations have tracked and reported such abuses. For example, as stated in an earlier chapter, *persons who are supported through certain government benefit programs (disability, SSI, etc.), cannot be forced to repay government debt (including student loans).* Yet, there are continued

---

Disability Check Garnished to Pay Loans!

When Clay S., 39, returned from the hospital after a lengthy stay to combat a viral infection related to AIDS, he received a distressing phone call from a private collection agency acting on behalf of the U.S. Department of Education. They demanded that he pay $69 a month on a long-forgotten student loan. The bill collector claimed that if he did not make the payment, a larger sum of $189 per month would be taken from his Social Security disability checks.

Mr. S took out $3,700 in student loans twenty years ago to attend community college in Hot Springs, Arkansas. He did not complete school since he had to go to work to support himself. For the next 20 years, he worked many jobs including as a clerk in a hospital, a toy-store manager, bartender, and blackjack dealer, never earning more than $7 per hour.

He was diagnosed with AIDS about 10 years earlier and completely depends upon Social Security disability checks for his income. He is 6 feet 2 inches tall but weighs only 106 pounds. Rubber bands help hold a ring on his finger. He cannot hold a job and takes 16 pills a day to stay alive. He shares an apartment to help reduce rental costs.

His monthly income from Social Security was $696. His monthly expenses included $225 to pay for an old car he used primarily to drive to a medical clinic located many miles away in the next major city. The bill collector suggested he get rid of the car in order to make student loan payments!

His loans could be discharged if his doctor declared him permanently disabled. But, for some reason, his doctor would not sign the forms.

Early in 2005, Mr. S's Social Security disability check rose to $785 per month. He immediately received a letter from the Department of Education saying it had directed the Treasury Department to make automatic deductions from his disability checks toward his delinquent loan. The letter said the government was permitted to take up to 15% of his check providing the monthly benefit did not fall below $750.

Hechinger, J. (January 6, 2005) U.S. Gets Tough on Failure to Repay Student Loans, *Wall Street Journal*, v.CCXLV n.4,p.1

---

reports of the Department of Education going after borrowers with such loans. These kinds of debts are legally uncollectible but that has not stopped the Department of Education from making harassing phone calls, sending threatening letters, or from attaching disability checks. These are abusive collection methods that need to stop!

Similarly, the Department of Education has been overly aggressive in defending against bankruptcy challenges. The law allows discharge in cases of "undue hardship." Because of aggressive tactics by Department attorneys the courts have interpreted this to mean "certainty of hopelessness." *This is not what Congress intended*. The Department of Education is to blame for the development of the four major court tests, and the resultant harsh court decisions.

Many consumer groups have called upon the Department of Education to stop abusing its power and give accurate information to debtors. Most legal experts and writers on the topic of §523(a)(8) agree that it needs to be rescinded or overturned and replaced with law that better balances the needs to keep the student loan program viable while at the same time allowing honest debtors a fresh start. You can be part of this process by advocating changes to the law through your own bankruptcy and adversary proceeding.

Rate of Success at Discharging Student Loans

How many people each year are successful at having their student loans discharged under the 1998 Bankruptcy Reform Act? Unfortunately, the Department of Education keeps no statistics on this topic. It is unknown how many people file an adversary proceeding as part of their Chapter 7 Bankruptcy. Nor is it known the outcome of those proceedings. From informal conversations the author had with attorneys at the Department of Education, it is estimated that less than 200 people nationwide file adversary proceedings each year. A handful of debtors, maybe 20, are successful at winning their cases and have their student loan debt discharged. This is amazing considering approximately 1.6 million

people filed for bankruptcy each year and almost half of them have student loan debts.

Which brings us to the point of this chapter. We believe that it will strengthen your case to include arguments asking the court to mitigate or overturn 11 U.S.C.A. §523(a)(8). This is a long shot at best. Most judges are cautious and do not want to establish legal precedent. However, if your judge agrees with your arguments and repeals or overturns §523(a)(8), then your student loans will be treated as any other unsecured debt and be discharged as part of your Chapter 7 Bankruptcy. In one fell swoop; the debt will be discharged without having to go through the rigors of the court tests described in previous chapters. And you will be helping thousands more honest debtors who deserve to have their student loans discharged as part of their Chapter 7 Bankruptcy.

Strategy Tip
Mediation is Where You Win

You will learn in the Step-By-Step chapters that mediation and negotiation is where student loans can be rewritten or forgiven. We believe a large number of adversary proceedings are resolved this way. It is unknown how many people succeed at bankrupting their student loans through mediation or negotiation, but it is definitely more than those who go all the way to trial. The author of this book was successful at bankrupting 90% of his student loans during the mediation process.

Although we suggest advocating for overturning the law, a fairer, yet more complicated alternative test to the Brunner Test is given in the Appendix F. You may want the court to consider this *Brunner Test Alternative*.

The Step-By-Step plan given later in this book asks you not only to advocate overturning §523(a)(8), but also to fully prepare arguments for the various court tests. This way you will be ready for the intense scrutiny of the court.

Challenges to 11 U.S.C.A. §523(a)(8)

Chapter 11, Section 523(a)(8) of the 1998 U.S.C.A. Bankruptcy Reform Act should be rescinded. Some of the arguments against the law are discussed below.

The Law Is, and Was, Unnecessary

As discussed in earlier chapters, "a few serious abuses of the bankruptcy laws by debtors with large amounts of educational loans, few other debts, and well-paying jobs, who filed bankruptcy shortly after leaving school and before any loans became due, generated the movement for an exception to discharge."[1] Until 1978, student loans were processed through bankruptcy courts the same as any other unsecured debt.

How threatening was student bankruptcy to the educational loan program?   In 1976, the General Accounting Office (GAO) (GAO) was directed to conduct a study to "determine how bad the abuse, if any, there was so that"[2] Congress could consider the facts during discussion on revising the bankruptcy system. The GAO found the problems with the student loan program stemmed from a high default rate that was <u>not</u> caused by bankruptcy. At that time, approximately 18% of all student loans were in default, yet only 3-4% of these were through bankruptcy. The study[3] concluded that:

- only 1/2 to 3/4 of 1% of all matured educational loans [were] discharged in bankruptcy
- only 20% of bankruptcy filers had student loan debt exceeding 80% of their total debt load
- the average individual earnings for the year prior to filing the bankruptcy were at or below the Federal Poverty Guideline.

The majority of people filing for bankruptcy were poor, and for whom their educational loans represented a contributing factor to their financial woes. Even still, these debtors represented a minuscule fraction of the borrowers defaulting on student loans. This fact is very different than the hype, which surrounded the Congressional discussion to change the bankruptcy laws.

The House Report on the Bankruptcy Law was concerned with the overall increase in student loan bankruptcies, but realized the "rise appears not to be disproportionate to the rise in the amount of loans becoming due or to the default rate generally on educational loans."[4] This pattern held true in later years. The National Bankruptcy Review Commission Report of 1997 recognized that bankruptcy rates rise and fall with the economy and other factors "irrespective of [the] dischargeability [of student loans in] bankruptcy."[5]

So what caused the financial problems with the educational loan programs in the 1970s to 1990s? The default rate peaked in 1990 at 22.4%. But by 2001, this rate dropped to 5.4%. Was this because it became more difficult to bankrupt student loans? No! *As one bankruptcy judge commented, "it appears to be primarily the program itself and the manner in which it is administered that is causing the difficulty and not that of bankruptcy abuses."*[6]

Loan defaults plummeted and increases in loan repayments came about because of better debt collection techniques by the Department of Education. Restricting student loan bankruptcies with §523(a)(8) played a negligible part in the improvements in overall loan collection.

The Department of Education implemented a number of programs and initiatives designed to improve recovery of student loans. These included simple things such as notifying borrowers if they fell behind in payments (which surprisingly was not done in the early years), tracking borrowers after college so as to keep in communication with them, verifying that borrowers who claimed disability discharge or death discharge were really disabled or dead, and more. Once defaulters were identified and located, actions such as change in payment plan, intercepting IRS tax refunds, wage garnishing, and other techniques helped reduce the loan losses.

Schools were also scrutinized. Schools would be evaluated annually to determine the number of their students who defaulted on student loans. If the school's Cohort Default Rate was above a certain level, then the school would forfeit eligibility to participate in the student loan program. This alone eliminated more than 1,000 schools nationwide (mostly trade proprietary schools) which were often loan mills providing very little real education or training.

The frequency of bankruptcies of student loans, which were done in bad faith, is not known. Richard Fossey reported on research conducted from 1990 to 1993 in which bankruptcy cases were evaluated for bad faith. Of the cases reviewed, he found "little evidence" of bad faith, but rather "most of the cases involved individuals who encountered difficult life circumstances and whose economic situations were made more precarious by the burden created by their educational loans."[7] Indeed, only a handful of published cases involved the kind of abuse Congress was concerned about when it passed §523(a)(8). In most cases, debtors experienced true hardship that made repaying student loans virtually impossible. Most people seeking bankruptcy were unemployed or under-employed, single parents trying to get by on too small an income and often in poor health. Many debtors received little value for the education they so dearly paid for with debt, time and effort.

The research indicates that only a handful of debtors used the bankruptcy process to defraud the government out of repaying student loans. Most (and we mean virtually all) debtors using bankruptcy do so in good faith. Making student loans dischargeable in bankruptcy, as they previously were as common unsecured debt, will not result in massive defaults. *The drop in default rates is related to better collection methods, not making student loans virtually impossible to discharge through bankruptcy.* There was no actual need for §523(a)(8) and it should be rescinded or overturned.

Law Violates Equal Protection Clause of the U.S. Constitution

The U.S. Constitution requires laws to be fairly applied to all citizens. The question to ask is, "Have the courts applied the undue hardship clause of §523(a)(8) equally to all debtors?" In the only known research on this question, Andrew M. Campbell reported in *American Law Reports* (ALR) his findings on how courts have applied undue hardship.

The table below *(Success Rate for "Undue Hardship" Discharges)* shows that low-income debtors with chronic medical conditions and dependents have the highest rate of success at proving undue hardship (77%). For these same categories of debtors (low-income and having medical conditions), not having dependents drops the success rate by almost a third (to 55%). We see a similar pattern for low-income debtors with no medical condition. Simply not having dependents drops the success rate by almost two-thirds (from 48% to 17%). Thus, the courts have shown an overwhelming bias towards debtors with dependents over single debtors seeking the same debt relief.

Some could argue that the courts are recognizing the fact that debtors with dependents have a greater responsibility and greater need for debt relief. But, the low-income level from which the analysis is made is higher for those with dependents ($10,000 before 1990 and $15,000 in subsequent years) than those without ($7,000 before 1990 and $10,000 in subsequent years). In a sense, these are similar to the Federal Poverty Guidelines and the differences in income levels for those with dependents versus those without is reflected in the guidelines. Since the Guidelines adjust for the presence of dependents, courts should treat single debtors without dependents exactly the same as those with dependents– taking in account that the income level cut-offs already accommodates for the difference. *Since the courts favor those with dependents, it means that either there is bias in the court toward debtors with dependents, or the court, indirectly, does not believe the validity of the Federal Poverty Guidelines. Either way, the court is violating the U.S. Constitution by treating different classes of debtors differently.*

Rates of success at discharging student loans
through court finding of "undue hardship"[1]

	Depen-dents	Overall Discharge Rate	Have Medical Condition?		
			Overall	No College Degree	College Degree
Low income[1]	Yes		Yes — 77% No — 48%	Yes — 80% No — 64%	Yes — 78% No — 25%
Low income[2]	No	36%	Yes — 55% No — 17%		
Higher income[3]	No	13%	Yes — 21% No — 7%		

1 Low income <u>with</u> dependents is defined as under $10,000 before 1990 and below $15,000 in subsequent years.
2 Low income <u>without</u> dependents is defined as under $7,000 before 1990 and below $10,000 in subsequent years.
3 Higher income is defined as being above the low-income cut-offs.

<u>Medical condition</u> also influences court decisions. Low-income debtors with medical conditions and dependents are one and one-half times more likely to achieve success at discharging their debt than similar debtors without medical conditions (77% vs. 48%). This effect is even more pronounced for low-income debtors without dependents where having a medical condition results in three times the success rate over similar debtors without a medical condition (55% vs. 17%). *Courts have shown an overwhelming bias toward debtors with medical conditions over those without.*

It may be argued that having a medical condition is strong evidence that a borrower will have little success with future employment and even less ability to repay student loans. This is often true, but there are many other factors equally important than medical condition related to a person's ability to find work. We live in an ageist society where it is next-to-impossible for older workers to find full employment at good wages. Expecting someone over 65 years of age to find a new job is ludicrous. There are many other social factors that impact just as severely the ability of healthy workers to find employment, as does a medical disability. A list of these factors is discussed in the previous chapters and in Appendix F.

Courts seem to ignore factors other than medical conditions that impact debtors in their ability to secure employment. Courts seem to believe that if a debtor is healthy, then he or she should be able to get work, and, if he or she doesn't, it is the debtor's fault and the court denies the student loan discharge. Courts have shown a bias against factors other than medical conditions that present equal challenges to finding employment.

Having earned a <u>college degree</u> also seems to impact court decisions. For low-income debtors with dependents and medical conditions, there is little difference in the success rates for those with or without a college degree. But for similar debtors who do not have a medical condition, lower-educated debtors have two and one-half better successes at discharging student loans than those who have a college degree (64% vs. 25%).

Courts act as though a college degree guarantees full-time employment at an income sufficient to service even the largest student loan debt. This is not automatically true, and was discussed in the previous chapter and in Appendix F. The value of a college education has fallen, but court decisions have not reflected that change. Courts show bias when they discharge student loans of debtors without college degrees at a rate that is two and one-half times greater than those with a college degree.

Finally, having <u>income</u> above the minimal levels has a significant impact on court decisions. For single debtors with no dependents, those with low-income are almost 3 times more successful at discharging their loans than those with higher income (36% vs. 13%). Again, we see the influence that medical conditions has on courts where higher income single debtors with medical conditions are 3 times more likely to succeed at achieving a debt discharge than similar debtors with no medical conditions (21% vs. 7%).

In reality, this is an issue of courts accepting the Federal Poverty Guidelines as the correct criteria to evaluate a debtor's undue hardship. <u>Neither the Bankruptcy Code nor the Department of Education Regulations requires debtors to be evaluated by the Federal Poverty Guidelines.</u> There are other federal measures that are considered more accurate. A complete discussion regarding this topic is included later in this chapter. Courts show bias against those whose incomes may be near but above the income level specified by the Federal Poverty Guidelines.

In conclusion, we see courts have a demonstrable bias in finding undue hardship for debtors who are low-income with dependants and who have a medical condition. Debtors who are single or without medical condition are treated less equitably by the courts. Having a college degree severely impacts the success of debt relief for low-income debtors who do not have a medical condition. Single debtors, without medical conditions, particularly those with incomes above the poverty level, are the least successful at obtaining a student loan discharge.

Chapter 11 U.S.C.A. §523(a)(8) of the U.S. Bankruptcy Code is not applied equally to all persons, violates the equal protection clause of the U.S. Constitution, and should be overturned.

Unintended Impact on the Poor and Minorities

The media and Congressional frenzy in the 1970s concerning student loan defaults painted a picture of the typical defaulter as a "middle-class college graduate who obtained good value from [his or her] education then refused to pay for it."[8] This is the debtor to whom Congress aimed §523(a)(8) to impact, and the stereotype that the courts and the Department of Education envisioned in their harsh interpretation of the law. Many studies have shown the reality to be very different.

Logic tells us that students most needing help to finance college or trade school would be poor— minorities, single parents, independent students (those not receiving support from home), and partially disabled. That is, in fact, what the research confirms. The typical student loan borrower is not a middle-class man or woman attending a 4-year college. For example, during the 1989-1990 academic year, students coming from families with less than $10,000 annual income represented 32% of all student loan borrowers, whereas students coming from families with $100,000 annual income represented only 3.1% of all student loan borrowers.[9] In the same time frame, African American students accounted for 29% of all borrowers compared to 17.7% of the white population. Also, short-term programs (primarily operated by proprietary schools) offered specific job training that attracted poor workers as a path to a more lucrative job placement. Approximately 46.5% of students attending short-term programs borrow government money to finance their education, whereas only 25% of students attending a 4-year college incur similar debt.

Again, logic would suggest that the class of debtors most likely to <u>default</u> on student loans would be the poor— minorities, single parents, independent students, and those partially disabled. Again, the facts[10] affirm this position. Students who attended short-term programs are three times more likely to default on student loans than those who attended four-year institutions. The poorer or more marginalized the family, the greater the likelihood of default. The GAO summarized in their 1988 report, "Many defaulters are poor, attended proprietary school, dropped out of their course of instruction, and have little or no means to repay."[11]

Probably the two most disturbing findings from the 1988 GAO report were:

- recognizing that African Americans and American Indians who came from families with very little education had default rates from 30% to 60%[12] — higher than any other category of borrowers.
- many of the proprietary students who defaulted on their educational loans, "were 'pressured' to enroll by unscrupulous recruiters. Moreover, many of these students received poor-quality education that resulted in 'dismal employment prospects'."[13]

Hearings were conduced by the Senate Permanent Subcommittee on Investigations in 1993 and confirmed many of the GAO's observations. Proprietary schools often existed for the sole purpose of collecting student aid money. Representative Maxine Waters[14] of California has said that these kinds of scams are common when the poor are victimized by trade schools that take their student loan money while offering worthless courses, producing no job leads, and leaving them with the repayment of loans they cannot afford.

One court, in particular, voiced its belief that the majority of courts err by applying rules (such as the Brunner or Johnston Tests) to low-income wage earners but which were designed for well-educated, upper income professions:

> It is apparent that judicially developed rules defining circumstances, which indicate "abuse" of the bankruptcy system, were developed to apply to high-income professionals, but have come in recent years to be applied to poverty line wage earners. We conclude that the key word in the legislative history is "abuse" and that [it] is inappropriate to apply the same standards to poverty line wage earners as is applied to high income professionals and other college graduates.[15]

Our culture promotes education as the key to a better future. Mostly the poor (minority, single parents, partially disabled, and others) have heeded the call and taken out student loans often with disastrous results. The passage of §523(a)(8) was aimed at college-educated middle-class debtors but had the unintended impact of blocking large numbers of poor debtors from obtaining a fresh start through bankruptcy. Debtors faced with bankruptcy should encourage courts to rescind or overturn §523(a)(8) because it has a disproportionate impact on poor, mostly minority, debtors.

Violates Bankruptcy's "Fresh Start" Concept

As described in Chapter 4, the bankruptcy of debts serves important social and economic purposes. It frees hopeless debtors to become responsible and productive members of society[16]. The Bankruptcy Act of 1898 stated two major goals: (1) to provide honest, hard-working debtors with a "fresh start" in which they are free of oppressive debt, and (2) to obtain fair and equitable treatment for debtors and creditors alike.[17]

Thirty years of litigation surrounding §523(a)(8) reveals that the Department of Education and bankruptcy courts distinctly favor the repayment of student loans over providing a fresh start for debtors.

The goal of the fresh start policy is to help debtors restore financial health through bankruptcy. Without bankruptcy, citizens could be saddled with a lifetime of debts that depresses their participation in society. When creditors are calling, wages garnished, and more, debtors are likely to stop working and become public charges. Unmanageable debt impacts families, increases divorce, and, in extreme cases, leads to crime and suicide. All these conditions have significant costs for society. The fresh start policy helps to minimize these costs and bring the debtor back to economic productivity.[18]

Although §523(a)(8) renders student loans presumptively non-dischargeable, a review of the entire Bankruptcy Code reveals that the fresh start provision takes precedent over §523(a)(8).

Here are the reasons:

- Congress stated in Section 507 of the Code which debts are given priority during liquidation or reorganization. Included are tax liabilities, debts owed to employees of bankrupt businesses, and others.19 Congress perceived these debts to be more important than other kinds of debt and gave them priority status. Student loan claims are absent from Section 507, indicating Congress did not consider student loans to be among the most important kinds of debts considered during bankruptcy proceedings. The Bankruptcy Court in Fox v. Pennsylvania Higher Education Assistance Agency came to this same conclusion when it attempted to assess the priority repayment of student loans.20
- The structure of §523(a)(8) shows <u>that student loans are not required to be repaid, but rather, are prohibited from discharge</u>. This is a significant distinction because if Congress desired repayment of student loans over all other bankruptcy objectives, it would have done so by enacting specific legislation to that effect. It did not.
- The inclusion of the undue hardship exception to §523(a)(8) indicates, by definition, that the repayment policy is limited in scope and superceded by other objectives deemed by Congress to be more important.
- The undue hardship exception is included in §523(a)(8) to protect debtors, not creditors. As such, it functions to *preserve the fresh start policy* of the Bankruptcy Code.[21]

The Bankruptcy Code gives priority to repayment of student loans up to the point of impinging upon a debtor's fresh start. At that point, the fresh start policy predominates in the undue hardship analysis and allows for the discharge of student loans.

Now we must consider what constitutes *fresh start.*

The purpose of a fresh start policy is to allow debtors to afford the necessities of life at a quality and quantity expected within the mainstream American culture. It is consistent within the Bankruptcy Code and the fresh start policy for all debtors, including debtors with student loans, to have lifestyles approximating the middle class. The Bankruptcy Code legislative history supports this position. This is obvious if you review the impact bankruptcy has on debtors. *Neither Chapter 13 nor Chapter 7 debtors are forced into poverty to achieve discharge of their loans.*

But the history of debtors with student loans is different. With very few exceptions, debtors with student loans are unable to discharge their student loan debt unless they are at, or below, the Poverty Guidelines. The Bankruptcy Commission suggested that the undue hardship criterion meant debtors must observe a "minimal standard of living" during repayment.[22] This does not require poverty levels of living! *Poverty[23] denotes "subminimal."* When Congress and the Bankruptcy Commission spoke of minimal standard of living, they meant a level of living that brings debtors back into society at the lower ends of the middle class.

> It is far preferable to free debtors from coercive collection techniques so they have incentive to become employed, and consequently pay taxes, rather than be a drain on society's resources. Society will gain more in the long run by releasing low-income debtors from liability on student loans they are unlikely to repay. This reasoning reflects the essence of the fresh start policy.[24]

The undue hardship analysis must include the fresh start policy and that is to be evaluated at a middle-class lifestyle, not at a subminimal poverty level. <u>Debtors filing an adversary proceeding should not allow courts to evaluate their financial and living conditions against the Federal Poverty Guidelines (see full discussion below). When courts do this, they are violating the fresh start policy of the Bankruptcy Code. Debtors need to challenge courts that violate the fresh start policy during undue hardship analysis.</u>

Congress Failed to Clearly Define the Law

Congress failed to define "undue hardship" in §523(a)(8). The aggressive defense mounted by the Department of Education in adversary proceedings has led to severe interpretation of the law. Courts, in desperation to deal with the oversight, have engaged in judicial lawmaking to clear up the meaning of undue hardship. Both of these court actions violate Congress' intent for the law.

Certainty of Hopelessness

Courts universally recognize that the repayment of debt, any debt, represents a certain degree of hardship.[25] Many courts have evaluated undue hardship to mean more than temporary financial adversity[26] and something more than "garden variety"[27] hardship.

A large number of courts have viewed very negatively those debtors attempting to discharge their student loans. As one court stated to justify its harsh ruling, "[o]f all the many supplicants for financial relief who come before this and other bankruptcy courts, few, as a class, inspire less sympathy than the well-educated beneficiaries of student loans seeking to avoid those debts on the ground of undue hardship."[28] These courts have ruled that the discharge of student loans requires debtors to be living in dire conditions; that the undue hardship analysis requires "unique and extraordinary circumstances" or "a certainty of hopelessness."[29]

However, courts diverge greatly as to the <u>degree of hardship</u> necessary to meet undue hardship. A minority of courts has ruled less harshly. For example, in *Correll v. Union National Bank of Pittsburgh* (1989) the court stated:

> We do not believe, however, that Congress intended a fresh start under the Bankruptcy Code to mean that families must live at poverty level in order to repay educational loans. Where a family earns a modest income and the family budget, which shows no unnecessary or frivolous expenditures, is still unbalanced,

> a hardship exists from which a debtor may be discharged of his student loan obligations. Use by the Bankruptcy Court of poverty level or minimal standard of living guidelines are not necessary to meet the congressional purpose of correcting [the abuse Congress perceived].[30]

The Bankruptcy Commission (1978) suggested debtors observe a "minimal standard of living" to meet the undue hardship rule. The Johnson court substituted the phrase "subsistence or poverty level"[31] for "minimal standard of living." No explanation was given for this substitution but it helped establish the undue hardship analysis at the poverty level. Later, the Bryant court would formalize the adoption of the Federal Poverty Guidelines into the undue hardship analysis.

In the previous section analyzing the *fresh start* concept of bankruptcy, we discovered that *undue hardship* should be evaluated within the bounds of middle class income and lifestyle. *Poverty is a subminimal level of living rejected by the bankruptcy courts. Yet, during adversary proceedings a majority of courts have adopted the Poverty Guidelines as the level of analysis for debtors with student loans.*

So, at what level is *undue hardship* evaluated? Is it at the middle class, modest income, poverty, *minimal standard of living, subsistence or poverty level*, with *unique and extraordinary circumstances, with a certainty of hopelessness*, or what? That is the entire point of this section. Congress failed to clearly define *undue hardship*. Aggressive defense by the Department of Education has influenced many bankruptcy courts to take a very narrow, harsh reading for the term requiring debtors to live hopelessly at, or below, the poverty level. Yet other courts have seen through this and understood the intent of Congress and blended it with the core concept of bankruptcy for a fresh start, allowing debtors to live above the poverty level and still discharge student loans. This wide reading of *undue hardship* is evidence §523(a)(8) is bad law and should be rejected by courts. Debtors engaged in an adversary proceeding need to help courts understand how the undue hardship analysis is unworkable and encourage that the law be rejected.

Judicial Lawmaking

Only the legislative branch of the government has the power to make laws. Courts interpret law and discuss and settle discrepancies between laws but are not authorized to make law. Judges that make law engage in what is known as *judicial lawmaking*.

Laws enacted by Congress take on meaning when they are tested in court. When laws are vague, courts look to the recorded Congressional discussions to help find meaning for the law. *When there is wide variance in the application of a law, courts are considered to have engaged in judicial lawmaking — something they are professedly prohibited from doing.*

In review of court interpretations of the undue hardship provision, it is apparent that courts have overstepped their bounds in constructing meaning for the phrase. The evidence supporting the contention that courts have engaged in judicial lawmaking includes: partial discharges and modified repayment plans, wide variance in hardship tests, arbitrary use of Federal Poverty Guidelines, and discrediting the value of the education.

A. Partial Discharges and Modified Repayment Plans

Because so many courts have ruled harshly against debtors with student loans as a result of the undue hardship test, some courts have modified repayment plans and/or allowed a partial discharge of the student loans in order to "promote fairness by affording some relief to the debtor, while ensuring that the government is not unjustly deprived by a complete discharge of student loans that could be repaid in part without imposing 'undue hardship'."[32]

The concept of partial discharges originates from *Littell v. State of Oregon Board of Higher Education (In re Littell)*, 6 B.R. 85, 89 (Bankr. D. Or. 1980). Here, the court ruled (without giving legal justification), "[I]nstead of the all-or-nothing approach [prevailing in nearly every case to date], the courts

should consider whether only part of the debt should be dischargeable and what monthly payment the debtor could afford." As a result of this case, the number of courts granting partial discharges or other equitable relief under section 523(a)(8) increased considerably.

Courts that favor partial discharges infer their authority from the equitable powers as codified in section 105(a) of the Bankruptcy Code. It states:

> (a) The court may issue any order, process, or judgment that is necessary or appropriate to carry out the provisions of this title. No provision of this title providing for the raising of an issue by a party in interest shall be construed to preclude the court from, *sua sponte*, taking any action or making any determination necessary or appropriate to enforce or implement court orders or rules, or to prevent an abuse of process. [33]

The equitable powers allows bankruptcy courts to fashion solutions to problem cases "as are necessary to further the purposes of the substantive provisions of the Bankruptcy Code."[34] But the defects in §523(a)(8) are so great, as evidenced by the wide range of rulings, that courts are necessarily engaging in judicial lawmaking. "*The courts are not granted power to remedy perceived defects in legislation by the failure of Congress to legislate precisely or equitably.*"[35] The language of §523(a)(8) is clear and unambiguous concerning the discharge of the entire loan. *Only Congress has the power to modify the law to allow for partial discharges.*

For similar reasons discussed above, some courts have modified student loan repayment plans to lessen the harsh outcomes of the undue hardship analysis and/or obtain greater repayment than would otherwise be realized if the loans were completely discharged. These legal approaches are controversial. In *Hawkins v. Buena Vista College (In re Hawkins)*, 187 B.R. 294, 300-01 (Bankr. N.D. Iowa 1995), the court noted that it only had the authority under §523(a)(8) to determine dischargeability of student loans.

"Congress has not given bankruptcy courts the authority to rewrite student loans," noted the court. "Congress could have provided that student loans will be dischargeable 'to the extent' excepting such debt will impose undue hardship upon a debtor and her dependents" but did not explicitly state that. Further, the Hawkins court observed, "the bankruptcy court's power under section 105 is not a limitless authorization to do whatever seems equitable."

The Bankruptcy Code provides for the discharge of student loans but grants no authority to modify student loan repayment. Putting debtors on a court-imposed payment schedule resembles a mandatory Chapter 13 proceeding, which is rejected by the Bankruptcy Code.[36]

Conclusion: Courts do not have the power to partially discharge student loans or modify the payment schedules of student loans during bankruptcy proceedings. Either the loans are discharged in total or not. Any other decision represents judicial lawmaking, which is prohibited by law.

B. Wide Variance in Hardship Tests

In order for the undue hardship test to be valid, there needs to be consistency in the application and outcome of the test. Research indicates the contrary. Courts and judges have differed dramatically in the application of the undue hardship analysis. Besides the four major tests previously detailed in this book, there have been many other tests developed and used. Even courts using one of the standard tests often give vastly different interpretations of the law and modify the tests at will. As a result, similarly situated debtors often receive wildly different results.

There is strong disagreement, if not animosity, between courts in interpreting the law. For example, a Georgia bankruptcy court allowed a partial discharge when applying the Brunner test even though the debtor did not satisfy all prongs of the test. The court believed the Brunner test was "inequitable"[37] and chose to give a partial discharge.

Lack of Congressional guidance has led to this appalling situation of courts applying many different tests in determining undue hardship, restructuring loans, and allowing partial discharges. Judges have been given unbridled discretion to use their own personal values and sensitivities to determine the meaning of undue hardship. As the Johnson court so succinctly stated, "there are as many factors and tests which have been used to determine undue hardship as there are courts to decide the issue."[38]

The lack of uniformity by the courts in the interpretation of undue hardship tests has resulted in several cases of *forum shopping* by debtors attempting to get the best deal for their situation. Forum shopping adds to the public's perception that the bankruptcy system is unfairly administered and leaves debtors confused. The *principle of uniformity* within the legal system requires debtors to be treated consistently under the Bankruptcy Code. Debtors with similar situations should be treated similarly. By making student loans dischargeable like other forms of unsecured debt, courts would no longer have to conduct adversary proceedings to evaluate debtors under the undue hardship exception. Debtors filing an adversary proceeding should encourage courts to reject all undue hardship analysis, rescind or overturn §523(a)(8), and ask to have their student loan debts treated like other forms of unsecured debt.

C. Arbitrary use of Federal Poverty Guidelines

Undue hardship needs to be measured against some financial and lifestyle guidelines. Aggressive tactics by attorneys from the Department of Education influenced courts to use the Federal Poverty Guidelines (hereinafter, referred to as Poverty Guidelines) as their unit of measure. As you will read, this was unfortunate, since no other poverty measures produce such low cut-off points.

The Poverty Guidelines was used in many of the early court cases and formally adopted in *Bryant v. Pennsylvania Higher Education Assistance Agency* (otherwise known as the Bryant Poverty Test). Subsequent tests, such as Brunner, included use of the Poverty Guidelines. It was often claimed, as it was in Bryant, that using the Poverty Guidelines brought "objectivity" to the test.[39] But, the Poverty Guidelines are anything but objective. The Social Security

Administration developed the guidelines in 1964 by guessing[40] the average family's total expenditure for food and multiplying it by a factor of three. This number is updated yearly, but the basic definition has never been changed. The Social Security Administration's determination for a food budget was based on the temporary or emergency dietary needs of a family, and not the cost for an adequate, sustainable diet.[41] Further, food no longer represents 1/3 of the average American household budget, but closer to 1/4[42], meaning that the food budget should be multiplied by four instead of three to estimate poverty. Polls conducted of American consumers reveal they believe the Poverty Guidelines for a family of four is set about $3,000 too low.[43]

It is also very indicative how inappropriate the Poverty Guidelines are when you consider that many other agencies of the U.S. Government reject the scale and use other government guidelines. For example, until 1985, the Bureau of Labor Statistics (BLS) calculated its own measure of poverty. The scale was designed to estimate a budget of minimum adequacy. Living below that level was considered to be subminimal existence. The BLS guideline was substantially higher than the Poverty Guidelines.[44] Even though the BLS no longer produces these figures, the Department of Labor (DOL) updates the figures annually since they are used to measure eligibility for certain job training programs.[45]

Significantly, many federal and state need-based assistance programs do not use the Poverty Guidelines.[46] The Department of Housing and Urban Development (HUD) links eligibility with the median income, not the Poverty Guidelines. For example, HUD classifies families earning between 50-80% of the median income as "Lower Income Families." Those earning less than 50% of the median income are "Very Low-Income Families." The HUD guidelines for low-income levels are higher than those of the Poverty Guidelines. The Legal Service Corporation (LSC) determined that people whose incomes do not exceed 125% of the Poverty Guidelines are poor enough to receive free legal services. In certain circumstances, this may extend up to 150% of the Poverty Guidelines. For tax determination, the Earned Income Tax Credits (EICs) are granted to families far

above the Poverty Guidelines. EIC are characterized as a welfare payment made through the tax system to low-income families. Congress, in developing the EIC program, believed that families with incomes well above the Poverty Guidelines were entitled to the tax break to help lift them out of "poverty."[47] The Department of Education defines low-income as borrowers with incomes not exceeding 125% of the Poverty Guidelines. Such a designation qualifies them for extended repayment periods on direct education loans.[48] Finally, Aid to Families with Dependent Children (AFDC), does not set an income eligibility criteria at all, but rather leaves it up to each individual state to establish.

Even sociologists, who strive to define social yardsticks, do not agree on the correct measure of poverty. There are three major schools of sociological thought viewing poverty — absolute definitions, relativistic definitions, and sociocultural definitions. Moreover, within these schools are subgroups of thought. Overall, there is no consensus as to how to define "poverty" and when it is used. Poverty is a social construct molded by the nature for how it will be used.

Linking the Federal Poverty Guidelines to undue hardship is, and has been, arbitrary. Neither Congress, the Bankruptcy Code, nor the Department of Education regulations require student debtors, who are subjected to an undue hardship analysis, to be evaluated against the Poverty Guidelines. The Poverty Guidelines is not an accurate measure of poverty and bear "no relationship at all to bankruptcy law or the fresh start policy."[49] Debtors need to challenge the use of the Federal Poverty Guidelines during their undue hardship analysis.

D. Discrediting the Value of the Education

Initially, when courts evaluated undue hardship cases, they questioned whether or not the debtor benefited financially from the education the loan helped to finance (otherwise known as "educational value" of the loan). This was formalized in the third prong (*policy* test) of the Johnson Test. Under the policy test, if a debtor did not benefit from the education, e.g., obtain employment in the field of his or her degree or certificate, then the student loan debt was open to being discharged.

This position was rejected by the Brunner court. The court believed that since student loans were made without consideration of credit worthiness to the student, there was an expectation of payment from future income as a financial quid pro quo; additionally students accepted the responsibility to repay the loans regardless of the benefit they received from their education.[50] The court further stated that it was improper to consider educational benefit because it placed the government in the role of insurer of educational value.[51] Since the Brunner test has become the primary test in bankruptcy courts throughout the United States, this position prevails.

We believe the Brunner court was wrong. The relevance of educational value was expressly noted by the 1978 Congressional Bankruptcy Commission. The Commission recommended making student loans nondischargeable because they believed obtaining an education leads people to earn greater income.[52] The converse of this statement is true. If borrowers do not earn greater income from employment related to their educational degree or certificate, then the loans used to obtain this education should be dischargeable. Contrary to the Brunner court, it would seem that attention to educational value is mandated in undue hardship cases.

Although the Brunner court was concerned about the government becoming insurer of educational value, this is unfounded. The insurance analogy is not appropriate. True schooling insurance would provide income supplement to graduates who are unable to use their education to enhance their financial status. Simply allowing for the discharge of student loans is not income supplementation. Instead, allowing for the discharge of student loans, if the debtor is unable to obtain appropriate employment, is better seen as a form of credit insurance, i.e., insurance to reduce the impact of financial failure. Viewed this way, a student loan discharge based on lack of educational value is consistent with the fresh start policy and the role of bankruptcy to the economy and society. Debtors should insist that bankruptcy courts include

review of the educational value of their loans during the undue hardship analysis.

Summary concerning definition of "undue hardship:"

- The Department of Education and courts have misinterpreted the undue hardship clause of §523(a)(8) to mean "certainty of hopelessness." This is not what Congress intended and violates the fresh start policy (see previous section analyzing *fresh start*). The wide interpretation of the phrase indicates the law is inequitably applied and should be sent back to Congress for clarification.
- Courts have engaged in judicial lawmaking as evidenced by:
  o Granting partial discharges and modifying repayment plans—neither of which are authorized by law.
  o Wide variance in undue hardship tests; wide variance in court decisions
  o Inclusion of the Federal Poverty Guidelines for which there is no Congressional authorization to do so.
  o Discrediting the Value of the Education ignores the recommendations of the Bankruptcy Commission

The undue hardship clause of §523(a)(8) is extremely vague. The courts need to reject §523(a)(8) for its vagueness and send it back to Congress for clarification. Until that time, student loans should be handled by the bankruptcy courts as common unsecured loans and discharged accordingly.

Challenges to Income Contingent Repayment (ICR) Plan

The Income Contingent Repayment (ICR) Plan is the most flexible repayment plan offered by the Department of Education for Direct Loans. A complicated formula is used to calculate how much a debtor should be able to afford to make toward loan repayments (*see* Appendix A). If a debtor experiences hard times and his or her income drops, payments drop accordingly— sometimes to zero. Each year the repayment schedule is recalculated to reflect the financial condition of the debtor. The plan lasts for 25 years and any outstanding debt remaining at the end of the plan is discharged. <u>However, debtors are liable for the income taxes on the amount discharged</u>.

It is often stated by Department of Education attorneys that ICR makes it impossible for debtors to discharge their student loans in bankruptcy. They contend that anyone can make "zero dollar" payments, thus negating the undue hardship exception of §523(a)(8). In many cases this is true. But for some debtors the ICR is inappropriate. As a debtor who might suffer undue hardship caused by participating in an ICR, he or she has the right to contest such a judgment. We discuss two approaches to the problem. Perhaps you can think of other approaches.

<u>For All Debtors:</u> The ICR is calculated using the Federal Poverty Guidelines. Earlier in this chapter, it was discussed at length why using the Poverty Guidelines is *arbitrary* and why the Poverty Guidelines violate the *fresh start* policy of the Bankruptcy Code. *All debtors filing an adversary proceeding could make these two arguments in court.*

<u>For Debtors on Restricted or Fixed Income:</u> Imagine being over 65-years of age and living on Social Security, or disabled and living off some form of government benefit (SDI, Worker Compensation, and others), or on a fixed income and your ICR finishes; the remaining debt on your student loan is discharged. You are now hit with an income tax bill for an amount equal to the discharged debt. Could you manage? Many people living on fixed incomes are often living near the poverty level and have very little, if any, discretionary income. A huge tax liability would be devastating; it is a liability that cannot be discharged through bankruptcy. Debtors over 50 years of age or living on government benefits have successfully argued that the ICR poses an undue hardship and cannot be imposed in their cases.

2005 Changes to Bankruptcy Code

In April 2005, Congress passed a major revision to the Bankruptcy Code. Primarily, debtors now must pass a <u>means test</u> to determine if they qualify for a Chapter 7 bankruptcy or are forced into Chapter 13 reorganization. Also, persons filing for bankruptcy must take an approved Credit Counseling Course within 6 months of filing. During the process, an approved Financial Management Course must be taken and completed.

The Bankruptcy Institute of American estimates approximately 5% of those currently filing a Chapter 7 bankruptcy will not qualify and, instead, be redirected into a Chapter 13 bankruptcy. Thus, the changes in bankruptcy law may affect relatively few of those who commonly use Chapter 7 bankruptcy.

Chapter 13 Bankruptcies

For those debtors forced into a Chapter 13 bankruptcy by the new means test, the process of discharging student loans has become legally confused. What has happened is that some debtors have listed their student loans in their Chapter 13 plan without filing an adversary proceeding and judges have approved their plan. Creditors (including educational loan agencies) have been duly informed, the plan executed, and judges have discharged the student loans once the plan was completed. The educational creditors have come back to say that the discharges were improper because there was no adversary proceeding. At issue is whether or not bankruptcy judges in Chapter 13 bankruptcies can alter the terms of student loans, including their discharge, without an adversary proceeding decision. The case, *Espinosa v. United Student Aid Funds* (Ninth Circuit Court of Appeals No. 06-16421), is working its way to the U.S. Supreme Court.

What does this mean for debtors? Until the final ruling comes through, it is best if debtors file an adversary proceeding in conjunction with a Chapter 13 plan. If the US Supreme Court rules that judges have this power, then the adversary proceeding will be unnecessary in Chapter 13 filings unless the educational creditor objects to the plan. (In the *Espinosa* case, Student Aid Funds did not complain about being listed in the Chapter 13 plan until years after the debt was discharged—even though they received legal notice of the plan.) We advocate that judges should have the right to include student loans in Chapter 13 plans without the need of an adversary proceeding.

Student loan payments may be reduced during the five years of Chapter 13 court oversight. However the entire loan balance comes due, PLUS, the interest accrued during the time at the end of the process. If this happens to you, your only recourse is to negotiate with your student loan agency for a new repayment plan. Debtors faced with this situation may want to argue any of the challenges given previously to have the court rule 11 U.S.C.A. §523(a)(8) invalid. Then the debt can be discharged similarly as any other unsecured debt.

Summary

- Chapter 11, Section 523(a)(8) is bad law
- Chapter 11, Section 523(a)(8) passage was unnecessary
  - Only 1/2 to 3/4 of 1% of all matured education loans discharged in bankruptcy in the 1970s.
  - High loan default rate is not related to the ability to bankrupt student loans.
  - Better debt collection techniques by the Department of Education drove down the default rate, not the enforcement of Section 523(a)(8) in bankruptcy court.
- Chapter 11, Section 523(a)(8) violates the Equal Protection Clause
  - Different debtors treated differently.
  - Single debtors without medical conditions are treated most stringently by the court.
  - Debtors with dependents and medical condition fair the best in court.
- Chapter 11, Section 523(a)(8) has disproportionate impact on debtors who are poor and/or member of a minority
  - Mostly poor default on student loans.
  - Mostly minorities default on student loans.
  - Mostly those attending proprietary schools default on student loans.
  - Section 523(a)(8) was targeted at the upwardly mobile professional who wanted to skip repaying their student loans. In actuality, mostly the poor and minorities have been subjected to section 523(a)(8).
- Chapter 11, Section 523(a)(8) violates bankruptcy's *fresh start* policy

- Goal of fresh start policy is to help honest debtors restore financial health through bankruptcy.
  - Fresh start policy takes precedence over section 523(a)(8).
  - Fresh start is evaluated within the parameters of the middle class standard of living.
- Congress failed to define *undue hardship* in §523(a)(8)
  - Most courts have interpreted this harshly to mean *certainty of hopelessness*.
  - Should be evaluated at the middle class standard of living.
- Courts have engaged in judicial lawmaking
  - Granting partial discharges and modifying repayment plans—neither of which courts are authorized to do by law.
  - Wide variance in undue hardship tests; wide variance in court decisions.
  - Inclusion of the Federal Poverty Guidelines for which there is no Congressional authorization to do so.
  - Discrediting the Value of the Education ignores the recommendations of the Bankruptcy Commission.
- Income Contingent Repayment (ICR) Plan
  - Most flexible repayment plan offered by the Department of Education.
  - Debt remaining after 25 years is discharged.
  - Debtor is liable for the income taxes due on the discharged amount.
  - ICR violates the fresh start policy of the Bankruptcy Code.
  - ICR violates the undue hardship exception for debtors on restricted or fixed income.
- 2005 Changes to the Bankruptcy Code
  - Established means test to qualify for Chapter 7.
  - Can be forced into Chapter 13 reorganization if debtor fails means test.
  - Chapter 13 reduces loan payments over 5 years, the balance plus interest becomes due.
  - Only recourse is to renegotiate loan with the agency that granted the student loan.
  - May need to file adversary proceeding during Chapter 13 plan.
  - OK to contest Chapter 11, Section 523(a)(8) as invalid.

[1] H.R. Rep. No. 95-595, at 133 (1978), reprinted in 1978 U.S.C.C.A.N. 5963, 6094.

[2] A&P 123 Cong. Rec. H11690, H11705 (Oct. 27, 1977) (statement of Rep. Volkmer).

[3] See H.R. Rep. No. 95-595, at 133 (1977), reprinted in 1978 U.S.C.C.A.N 5963, 6094.

[4] See also A&P 124 Cong. Rec. 1794 (daily ed. Feb. 1, 1978) (statement of Rep. Dodd) ("The GAO report also recites the number of bankruptcies or the increase in the student loan bankruptcies in comparison to the overall increase in bankruptcies across the country and shows that they have been relatively stable, and I am quoting relatively stable.").

[5] *National Bankruptcy Review Commission Report*. (Oct. 20, 1997). Pub. L. No. 103-394, at 179.

[6] A&P 124 Cong. Rec. 1796 (daily ed. Feb. 1, 1978); see also supra notes 44-45.

[7] Fossey, Richard. (1997). The certainty of hopelessness: Are courts to harsh toward bankrupt student loan debtors? *J. L. & Educ., (26)*, 29.

[8] See Fossey, Richard (1997). The certainty of hopelessness: Are courts too harsh toward bankrupt student loan debtors? *Journal of Law and Education, (26)*, 29, 30 (supra note 251).

[9] National Center for Education Statistics. (May 1993). *Financing Undergraduate Education, (1990)*, at 27.

[10] U.S. Gen. Acct. office Defaulted Student Loans: Preliminary Analysis of Student Loan Borrowers and Defaulters. (June 1998). GAO HRD 88-1128. [Herein noted as 1988 GAO Report.]

[11] 1988 GAO REPORT, Supra Note 43

[12] Volkwein, James F. & Cabrera, Alberto F.\ (1998). Factors associated with student loan default in borrowing against America's future. Richard Fossey & Mark Bateman (Eds.), *Student loans, higher education and public policy*.

[13] 1988 GAO REPORT, Supra Note 43.

[14] Winerip, Martin, et al. (Feb. 4, 1994). Overhauling school grants: Much debate but little gain. *N.Y. Times*.

[15] Correll v. Union Nat'l Bank of Pittsburgh (*In re Correll*), 105 B.R. 302, 304-07 (Bankr. W.D. Pa. 1989) at 304.

[16] Jackson, Thomas H. (1985). The fresh start policy in bankruptcy law. *Harvard Law Rev., (98)*, 1393, 1420.

[17] King, Lawrence & Cook, Michael. (1996). *Creditors' rights, debtors' protection, and bankruptcy* (3rd Edition). New York, NY: Matthew Bender and Col., Inc.

[18] See Howard, Margaret. (1987). A Theory of Discharge in Consumer Bankruptcy, *Ohio St. L.J., (48)*, 1047, 1085-87 supra note 23, at 1085 ("The availability of a debtor's earning capacity as an asset free from the reach of creditors is what gives the debtor a new start.").

[19] Other priority claims include: rental security deposits, contributions to employee benefit plans, and claims for alimony and support. See id. s 507(a)(4), (a)(6) & (a)(7).

[20] Fox v. Pennsylvania Higher Educ. Assistance Agency (*In re Fox*), 163 B.R. 975, 978 (Bankr. M.D. Pa. 1993).

[21] See, e.g., Baker v. University of Tenn. at Chattanooga (*In re Baker*), 10 B.R. 870, 872 (Bankr. E.D. Tenn. 1981) (stating that Congress did not intend make student loans generally nondischargeable to those who fell on hard times); Clay v. Westmar College (*In re Clay*), 12 B.R. 251, 255 (Bankr. N.D. Iowa 1981) (stating that the fresh start policy would be defeated if continuing liability on a loan would impose an undue hardship on debtor). The court in Lohman v. Connecticut Student Loan Foundation (*In re Lohman*), 79 B.R. 576 (Bankr. D. Vt. 1987) actually stated that undue hardship requires courts to consider the "premise for discharge." Id. at 580.

[22] Comm'n Report, supra note 40, pt. II, at 141.

[23] One dictionary defines "Poverty" as, "1. the condition or quality of being poor; indigence; need 2. deficiency in necessary properties or desirable qualities, or in a specific quality, etc.; inadequacy ... 3. smallness in amount; scarcity; paucity." Webster's New World Dictionary of the American Language 1116 (David B. Guralnik ed., 2d ed. 1970).

[24] Salvin, Robert F. (1996). Student loans, bankruptcy, and the fresh start policy: Must debtors be impoverished to discharge educational loans? Tul. L. Rev. (71), Supra note 178.

[25] See Healey v. Massachusetts Higher Educ. (*In re Healey*), 161 B.R. 389, 392 (E.D. Mich. 1993); Law v. Educational Resources Inst., Inc. (*In re Law*), 159 B.R. 287, 291 (Bankr. D.S.D. 1993); Bakkum v. Great Lakes Higher Educ. Corp. (*In re Bakkum*), 139 B.R. 680, 682 (Bankr. N.D. Ohio 1992); Evans v. Higher Educ. Assistance Found. (*In re Evans*), 131 B.R. 372, 374-75 (Bankr. S.D. Ohio 1991); Johnson v. USA Funds, Inc. (*In re Johnson*), 121 B.R. 91, 93 (Bankr. N.D. Okla. 1990); Burton v. Pennsylvania Higher Educ. Assistance Agency (*In re Burton*), 117 B.R. 167, 169 (Bankr. W.D. Pa. 1990); D'Ettore v. Devry Inst. of Tech. (*In re D'Ettore*), 106 B.R. 715, 718 (Bankr. M.D. Fla. 1989); Coleman v. Higher Educ. Assistance Found. (*In re Coleman*), 98 B.R. 443, 447 (Bankr. S.D. Ind. 1989); Bey v. Dollar Sav. Bank (*In re Bey*), 95 B.R. 376, 377 (Bankr. W.D. Pa. 1989); Conner v. Illinois State Scholarship Comm'n (*In re Conner*), 89 B.R. 744, 747 (Bankr. N.D. Ill. 1988); United States v. Brown (*In re Brown*), 18 B.R. 219, 222 (Bankr. D. Kan. 1982); Briscoe v. Bank of N.Y. (*In re Briscoe*), 16 B.R. 128, 130-31 (Bankr. S.D.N.Y. 1981); see also Smith v. Pittsburgh Nat'l Bank (*In re Smith*), Adv. No. 87-0399, 1988 WL 59209, at *3 (Bankr. W.D. Pa. June 7, 1988) ("[A]ll those

petitioning for relief under the bankruptcy laws are presumed to be suffering severe financial difficulties.").

[26] See Law, 159 B.R. at 291; Evans, 131 B.R. at 374-75; Johnson, 121 B.R. at 93; Burton, 117 B.R. at 169; D'Ettore, 106 B.R. at 718; Coleman, 98 B.R. at 448; Bey, 95 B.R. at 377; Pendergrast v. Student Loan Servicing Ctr. (*In re Pendergrast*), 90 B.R. 92, 94 (Bankr. M.D. Pa. 1988) ("[L]iving on a tight budget is a common rather than an undue hardship."); Childs v. Higher Educ. Assistance Found. (*In re Childs*), 89 B.R. 819, 820 (Bankr. D. Neb. 1988); Courtney v. Gainer Bank (*In re Courtney*), 79 B.R. 1004, 1010-11 (Bankr. N.D. Ind. 1987); North Dakota State Bd. of Higher Educ. v. Frech (*In re Frech*), 62 B.R. 235, 243 (Bankr. D. Minn. 1986); Brunner v. New York State Higher Educ. Servs. Corp. (*In re Brunner*), 46 B.R. 752, 755 (Bankr. S.D.N.Y. 1985), aff'd, 831 F.2d 395 (2d Cir. 1987); Panteli v. New York State Higher Educ. Servs. Corp., 41 B.R. 856, 858 (Bankr. S.D.N.Y. 1984) (requiring a certainty of hopelessness to discharge student loan); Shoberg v. Minnesota Higher Educ. Coordinating Council, 41 B.R. 684, 687 (Bankr. D. Minn. 1984) (stating that student loans are discharged only under exceptional circumstances); Brown, 18 B.R. at 222; Briscoe, 16 B.R. 130-31; Virginia Educ. Loan Auth. v. Archie (*In re Archie*), 7 B.R. 715, 718 (Bankr. E.D. Va. 1980).

[27] See Healey, 161 B.R. at 393; Law, 159 B.R. at 291; Evans, 131 B.R. at 374-75; D'Ettore, 106 B.R. at 718; Coleman, 98 B.R. at 448; Courtney, 79 B.R. at 1010-11; Frech, 62 B.R. at 243; Brunner, 46 B.R. at 753; see also Love v. United States, (*In re Love*), 33 B.R. 753, 755 (Bankr. E.D. Va. 1983) (stating that undue hardship is more than the "unpleasantness" associated with the repayment of an educational debt).

[28] Financial Collection Agencies v. Norman (*In re Norman*), 25 B.R. 545, 549 (Bankr. S.D. Cal. 1982) (quoting Fischer v. State Univ. (*In re Fischer*), 23 B.R. 432, 433 (Bankr. W.D. Ky. 1982)).

[29] *In re Roberson*, 999 F.2d 1132, 1136 (7th Cir. 1993); Barrows v. Illinois Student Assistance Comm'n (*In re Barrows*), 182 B.R. 640, 648 (Bankr. D.N.H. 1994); Healey, 161 B.R. at 392-93; Ford v. Tennessee Student Assistance Corp. (*In re Ford*), 151 B.R. 135, 138-39 (Bankr. M.D. Tenn. 1993); Kraft v. New York State Higher Educ. Servs. Corp. (*In re Kraft*), 161 B.R. 82, 84 (Bankr. W.D.N.Y. 1993); Phillips v. Great Lakes Higher Educ. Corp. (*In re Phillips*), 161 B.R. 945, 947-48 (Bankr. N.D. Ohio 1993); Reyes v. Oklahoma State Regents For Higher Educ. (*In re Reyes*), 154 B.R. 320, 322-23 (Bankr. E.D. Okla. 1993); Woodcock v. Chemical Bank (*In re Woodcock*), 149 B.R. 957, 961-63 (Bankr. D. Colo. 1993), aff'd, 45 F.3d 363 (10th Cir. 1995); Cadle Co. v. Webb (*In re Webb*), 132 B.R. 199, 201-02 (Bankr. M.D. Fla. 1991);

Garneau v. New York State Higher Educ. Servs. Corp. (*In re Garneau*), 122 B.R. 178, 180 (Bankr. W.D.N.Y. 1990); D'Ettore, 106 B.R. at 718; Coleman, 98 B.R. at 454; Taylor v. Tennessee Student Assistance Corp. (*In re Taylor*), 95 B.R. 550, 552 (Bankr. E.D. Tenn. 1989); Gearhart v. Clearfield Bank & Trust Co. (*In re Gearhart*), 94 B.R. 392, 393 (Bankr. W.D. Pa. 1989); Strauss v. United States Dep't of Educ. (*In re Strauss*), 91 B.R. 872, 874 (Bankr. E.D. Mo. 1988); Childs, 89 B.R. at 820-21; Courtney, 79 B.R. at 1010-11; Craig v. Pennsylvania Higher Educ. Assistance Agency (*In re Craig*), 64 B.R. 854, 857 (Bankr. W.D. Pa. 1986); Brunner, 46 B.R. at 754- 55; Holzer v. Wachovia Servs., Inc. (*In re Holzer*), 33 B.R. 627, 631 (Bankr. S.D.N.Y. 1983); Lezer v. New York State Higher Educ. Servs. Corp. (*In re Lezer*), 21 B.R. 783, 787-88 (Bankr. N.D.N.Y. 1982); Brown, 18 B.R. at 222; Briscoe, 16 B.R. at 129-30; Rappaport v. Orange Sav. Bank (*In re Rappaport*), 16 B.R. 615, 616-17 (Bankr. D.N.J. 1981); Virginia Educ. Loan Auth. v. Archie (*In re Archie*), 7 B.R. 715, 717-18 (Bankr. E.D. Va. 1980); New York State Higher Educ. Servs. Corp. v. Kohn (*In re Kohn*), 5 Bankr. Ct. Dec. (CRR) 419, 424 (Bankr. S.D.N.Y. 1979); see also Myers v. Pennsylvania Higher Educ. Assistance Agency (*In re Myers*), 150 B.R. 139, 142 (Bankr. W.D. Pa. 1993); Harris v. Pennsylvania Higher Educ. Assistance Agency (*In re Harris*), 103 B.R. 79, 82 (Bankr. W.D.N.Y. 1989); Medeiros v. Florida Dep't of Educ. (*In re Medeiros*), 86 B.R. 284, 286 (Bankr. M.D. Fla. 1988) ("To prove undue hardship, the Debtor must show that his financial resources will allow him to live only at a poverty level standard for the foreseeable future ...."); Preisser v. University of Maine (*In re Preisser*), 33 B.R. 63, 65 (Bankr. D. Me. 1983) ("[D]ebtor must demonstrate that it would be impossible 'in the foreseeable future' for him to generate enough income to pay off the loan and maintain himself and his dependents above the poverty level.")

[30] Correll v. Union Nat'l Bank of Pittsburgh (*In re Correll*), 105 B.R. 302, 304-07 (Bankr. W.D. Pa. 1989); Dyer, 40 B.R. at 874

[31] *See* Johnson, 5 Bankr. Ct. Dec. (CRR) at 544.

[32] *See* Pashman, Scott. (2001). Note, Discharge of student loan debt under 11 U.S.C.A. § 523(A)(8): Reassessing "undue hardship" after the elimination of the seven-year exception *N.Y.L. Sch. L. Rev.*, (44). 605, 617-18, at 618.

[33] 11 U.S.C.A. § 105(a) (2000).

[34] United States v. Sutton, 786 F.2d 1305, 1307 (5th Cir. 1986).

[35] Skaggs v. Great Lakes Higher Educ. Corp. (*In re Skaggs*), 196 B.R. 865, 867 (Bankr. W.D. Okla. 1996).

[36] Chapter 13 proceedings must be voluntary. See 11 U.S.C.A. s 303(a) (stating that involuntary cases may be filed only under Chapters 7 and 11); id. s 706(c) (indicating

that a case may be converted to Chapter 13 only on request of debtor); see also Gross, supra note 229, at 119- 20 (observing that the purpose of Chapter 13 is to give debtors the voluntary choice of repaying creditors).

[37] *In re Heckathorn*, 199 B.R. at 194.

[38] Johnson v. USA Funds, Inc. (*In re Johnson*), 121 B.R. 91, 93 (Bankr. N.D. Okla. 1990).

[39] See Bryant, 72 B.R. at 915.

[40] Even the federal government admits the official poverty level is subjective. See Bureau of the Census, U.S. Department of Commerce, Series P-60, No. 178, Workers With Low Earnings: 1964-1990, at B-3 (1992) (hereinafter Census II) ("The choice of a threshold for determining whether annual earnings are low or not low is necessarily subjective.") Cf. Teresa A. Sullivan et al., Forklore and Facts: A Preliminary Repot from the Consumer Bankruptcy Project, 60 Am. Bankr. L.J. 293, 294, 312, 314 (1986) ("[A]ny inference from the data will still require a normative view about when repayment appears so onerous that the debtor 'can't pay'.")

[41] See Census II, supra note 241, at 9 ("[T]he USDA food budget that underlies the SSA index is at best a measure of temporary/emergency food needs and thus not appropriate as a long-run market basked.")

[42] Winnick, Andrew J. (1989). *Toward two societies: The changing distributions of income and wealth in the U.S. since 1960* (p. 10-11). New York: Praeger.

[43] See Ross, Sonya. (December 8, 1994). Americans think welfare benefits are higher than they are. *Phila. Inquirer*, at A30; Rainwater, Lee. (1974). What money buys. *Tul. L. Rev.. (31)*, supra note 233, at 132-33.

[44] Winnick, Andrew J. (1989). *Toward two societies: The changing distributions of income and wealth in the U.S. since 1960* (p. 24-25). New York: Praeger.

[45] *See* Notice of Determination of Lower Living Standard Income Level, 59 Fed. Reg. 19241-46 (1994).

[9] Salvin, Robert F. (1996). Student loans, bankruptcy, and the fresh start policy: Must debtors be impoverished to discharge educational loans? Tul. L. Rev. (71), 139, at 10.

[47] McGinley, Laurie. (March 31, 1993). Outline is given for expansion of a tax credit (supra note 298). *Wall St. Journal*.

[48] See 34 C.F.R. s 674.33(c)(2).

[49] Salvin, Robert F. (1996). Student loans, bankruptcy, and the fresh start policy: Must debtors be impoverished to discharge educational loans? Tul. L. Rev. (71), 139 at 11.

[50] See Brunner, 46 B.R. at 756

[51] See Brunner, 46 B.R. at 755 n.3 & 756.

[52] The 1978 Bankruptcy Commission described the reasons for limiting the dischargeability of student loans in the following terms: A separate clause to provide for a limited nondischargeability of educational loan debts is desirable for two kinds of reasons. First, a loan or other credit extended to finance higher education that enables a person to earn substantially greater income over his working life should not as a matter of policy be dischargeable before he has demonstrated that for any reason he is unable to earn sufficient income to maintain himself and his dependents and to repay the educational debt. Second, such a policy cannot be appropriately carried out under any other nondischargeability provision. Comm'n Report, supra note 40, pt. II, at 140 (emphasis added).

Whew!

Take a deep breath.

You can do it.

It takes planning and determination.

CHAPTER 8

Preparing for the
Adversary Proceeding

This chapter helps you gather all the data and documents you will need to prove your claim that having to repay your federally guaranteed student loan(s) will cause you an "undue hardship" and, therefore, should be discharged.

It does not matter if you are filing an adversary proceeding as part of a Chapter 7, Chapter 11, Chapter 12 or Chapter 13 bankruptcy, or attempting to have your loans discharged through Compromise or Write-Off (*see* Chapter 2), the preparation is similar. This chapter discusses only the adversary proceeding. See Chapter 10 for details for preparing a Compromise or Write-Off.

Some courts have developed forms to gather the data needed to establish undue hardship. For example, see Appendix B to view a sample of the Interrogatories used by the United States Bankruptcy Court for the Western District of Kentucky. Most courts use the Brunner Test to determine undue hardship, whereas a few courts use the other tests detailed in Chapter 4. Regardless of which test is used by the court or forms used to gather information, the categories of information are very much the same as described in Chapter 5.

Many of the steps below refer to forms or worksheets located in Appendix C, D, and E. **The Chapter 7 bankruptcy forms in Appendix C are for the Central District of California. They are there for illustrative purposes only. You will need to locate the corresponding forms used in your bankruptcy court.**

Items that are bulleted and bolded are the data or documents you need to collect or create.

If you are filing an *adversary proceeding*, read this chapter. If you are attempting to discharge your student loans through a *Compromise* or *Write-Off*, see Chapters 10 and 11.

The Adversary Proceeding

An adversary proceeding is filed in conjunction with a bankruptcy filing. The steps below assume you have already filed, or are planning to file, a bankruptcy. You will need copies of some of the forms used in your bankruptcy filing.

PRE-INFO—
Undue Hardship Test and Student Loan History

Before you file the bankruptcy, it is important for you to be up-to-date about all your student loans. Thus, you need to contact each lender and get a copy of your student loans and their payment histories. It is most important to know payment, forbearance, and deferment dates.

> **Step 1 • Obtain** a printout from your lenders of the history of your student loans. It is important to know the payment amounts, forbearances and deferment dates for each loan. **Transfer** this information on the Student Loan History worksheet found in Appendix D.

Comments about what constitutes a "student loan"— One of the major questions asked of the author of this book is whether or not particular student loans are federally guaranteed or not. This is an important question because loans made for schooling that are not federally guaranteed can be included in a bankruptcy without having to file an adversary proceeding. In reality, virtually all loans made for schooling are federally guaranteed. Further, the Bankruptcy Abuse Prevention and Consumer Protection Act of 2005 amended the US Bankruptcy Code to include "qualified education loans" within the scope of the exception for discharging student loans. Private loans that are not "school certified" generally do not meet the definition of qualified education loans. "School certified" means the school complies with restrictions imposed by 26 USC 221(d)(l) which enforces limits on the amount of debt and other qualifications. Why would a school give private loans that are not "qualified education loans?" Easy, the school can lend more money than they otherwise would be permitted on a school-certified loan. Thus, if you received private loans you need to determine if the school is "certified" as described above. [*See* Kantrowitz, Mark (August 19, 2007). *Limitations on Exception to Discharge of Private Student Loans*, FinAid.org.]

> **Step 2 • Ask** the court which hardship test they use **and/or obtain** Interrogatories Form. Ask for a sample from the court. Often they are available on-line for download. You will use this information later to tailor the data to meet the needs of the hardship test.

Chapter 5 detailed the kinds of information you must provide in order to achieve the claim of undue hardship. These were identified as *Characteristics*:

- **Characteristic A**—Current Living Condition and the Impact of Repaying Loan on "Minimal Living" Standard
- **Characteristic B**—Prospects for Repaying the Loans
- **Characteristic C**—Good Faith and Loan Repayment

Each *Characteristic* will be discussed below in detail along with the sequential steps used to produce the appropriate documents. The problem of the *Income Contingent Repayment (ICR) Plan* also is addressed.

CHARACTERISTIC A—
Current Living Condition and the Impact of Repaying Loan on "Minimal Living" Standard

First, you need to establish your current financial and living conditions. When you filed a bankruptcy, you gave information concerning your family, and you and your spouse's income, net pay, and total monthly income. Forms for a Chapter 7 bankruptcy will be used to illustrate the following steps.

> **Step 3 •** From your Chapter 7 bankruptcy filing; **make a copy** of your *Form B6I—Schedule I-Current Income of Individual Debtor* (this is a California Central District form, use your state's equivalent Chapter 7 bankruptcy form). If you have business income/expenses, make a copy of that form also (sample in Appendix C). A sample is included in the Appendix C if you need a blank form. If you have multiple employers, you may need to make additional copies of Form B6I.

The time span from when you first file your bankruptcy and then enter into mediation or trial for the adversary proceeding may be 6 months or longer. As such, your income and living conditions may have changed since the bankruptcy filing and needs to be updated.

> **Step 4 • Update** your income and living conditions by **making a copy** of the worksheet *Current Income Status* (in Appendix D), **fill in** old information using your Form B6I, and **write** in any new changes.

—WARNING—
A Word of Caution about Income Statements

The income you list on Form B6I of your Chapter 7 bankruptcy should match the income you claim during the adversary proceeding— which should match the income you claim with the IRS. *If these are not similar, the court will view you with suspicion.*

As you will learn later, part of the strategy of proving undue hardship or negotiating a Compromise or Write-off is for you to present yourself as a hopeless and helpless debtor who is representing him or herself. As such, it is **best not to let the defendant or court know that you are using this book**. Instead of handing them the *Current Income Status* worksheet, we suggest that you write, in your own words and on a blank piece of paper, the changes in your financial and living status. The *Current Income Status* worksheet will help guide you in your writing in that process.

Step 5 • **On** a <u>blank piece of paper</u>, **write** your name, adversary case number, and date. Title the page "Current Income and Family Status" (or similar words). Below this, write a few short paragraphs telling how your income or family has changed, if at all, since filing your Chapter 7 bankruptcy. *See* a sample in Appendix D— <u>Current Income and Family Status</u>.

It is recommended that you write all these documents on a computer and save the files. Later, you will be asked to blend all the documents together into one master document. If you write them on a computer, all you will have to do is cut and paste the sections, thereby eliminating the need to retype everything.

Now we evaluate your expenditures.

Step 6 • From your Chapter 7 bankruptcy filing; **make a copy** of your *Form B6J—Schedule J- Current Expenditures of Individual Debtor* (again, this is a California Central District form, use your equivalent Chapter 7 bankruptcy form). A sample is included in the Appendix C if you need a blank form.

As with the income statement being updated as necessary, you need to update your expenses if they have changed between the time of filing the bankruptcy, to the time of the adversary proceeding mediation or trial.

Step 7 • **Update** your expense conditions by **making a copy** of the worksheet *Current Expenditure Status* (in Appendix D), **fill in** old

information (column 1) using your Form B6J, and **write in** any new changes (column 2).

Also, you need to demonstrate that your expenses are comparable to a similarily situated debtor. This is achieved by showing: (a) that your income is within range of the Federal Poverty Guidelines for a family your size, and (b) your expenses are similar to other families of your size and circumstances.

Step 8 • **Go to** the website of the United States Department of Health and Human Services (http://aspe.hhs.gov/poverty/poverty.shtml) and **download a copy** of the current Federal Poverty Guidelines(a copy of this homepage and document are in Appendix B). If you do not have access to the web, your local library should have a copy of this government publication. Be sure it is the current year. **Write** your information on the *Current Expenditure Status* worksheet.

Step 9 • Go **to the website** of the IRS to gather data on Collection Financial Standards (www.irs.gov/individuals/article/0,,id=96543,00.h tml). The IRS has established standards used to determine the ability of taxpayers to make delinquent payments. Use the data found here to **fill-in** the National Norms (column 3) on the *Current Expenditure Status* worksheet.

Step 10 • For those cases where there are significant differences between your expenditures and the national norms, **write** an explanation for each on the *Current Expenditure Status* worksheet (column 4).

—WARNING—
A Word of Caution about Expense Statements

The expenses you list on Form B6J of your Chapter 7 bankruptcy should match the expense you claim during the adversary proceeding— which should match the expenses you claim with the IRS. *If these are not similar, the court will view you with suspicion.*

You need to explain that you have minimized your living expenses and are not living extravagantly, and that there is no extra income available to pay on your student loans.

Step 11 • On a <u>blank piece of paper</u>, write your name, adversary case number, and date. Title the page "Current Expenditures and Minimalized Living" (or similar words). Below this, write a few short paragraphs telling how your expenditures have changed (if it has changed since filing your bankruptcy), how you live frugally, and that it would be impossible to make payments on your student loans. *See* a sample and instructions in Appendix D— <u>Current Expenditure and Minimalized Living</u>.

CHARACTERISTIC B—
<u>Prospects for Repaying the Loans</u>

In so many cases, debtors make a strong showing for their situation only to have the court reject the claim and tell the debtor to get a part-time, minimum-wage job and use that money to make loan payments. Regardless of how laughable or tragic this may seem, it happens all the time. Thus, the debtor needs to <u>account for his or her time working or providing dependent care, or both</u>. Debtors need to clearly point out to the court that asking the debtor to take on any more work would push him or her over a standard workweek, and that would be an undue hardship.

Step 12 • Make a copy of the worksheet *Work Time Accounting Table* (Appendix D) and complete it as instructed. **Write** on a blank piece of paper you name, date and adversary number and entitle it *Work Time Accounting* (or similar words). In your own words (using the *Work Time Accounting Table*), explain why all your available time is committed making it impossible for you to take on another job. *See* a sample document in the Samples section of Appendix D under *Work Time Accounting Statement*.

The debtor needs to address in detail any <u>personal limitations</u> that may impact the ability to obtain appropriate employment. This includes personal medical limitations, support of dependents (and their medical conditions, if applicable), and lack of useable job skills. These need to be described in detail, with supporting documents (like medical records), etc.

Step 13 • On a blank piece of paper, **write** your name, date and adversary number and entitle it *Personal Limitations* (or similar words). Here you explain why medical problems for you and/or your dependents, the lack of usable job skills, and/or the existence of a large number of dependents impacts your future ability to work at a job that will provide sufficient income to service your student loan debt. *See* a sample document in the Samples section of Appendix D under *Personal Limitations Statement*. **In general, you must show there are "unique" or "exceptional" circumstances that impact future employment and earnings.**

The final step to this Characteristic is to discuss the impact of <u>external factors</u> on your future employment. Courts have been hesitant to include these factors since it would require them to accept the fact that not all employment doors are open to all workers, i.e., the American dream is not really attainable by all.

External factors that affect future employment opportunities include:
- U.S. Economy
- Discrimination based on age, race, ethnicity, gender, sexual orientation, and others.
- Reverse Discrimination
- Past Terminations
- Whistleblower
- And others

Chapter 5 explained in greater detail about these issues. In many cases, academic papers on these topics are included in Appendix F.

Step 14 • On a blank piece of paper, **write** your name, date and adversary number and entitle it *External Factors* (or similar words). In general, it is suggested that you first develop your argument through academic research of the societal problem that impacts future employment, and then make it specific with examples from <u>your</u> own life story. You need to tell the court about the factors that impact your ability to secure employment. It is important to emphasize how this impacts your future earnings. No sample is provided in the Appendix because each case is very specific to the debtor and no generalization is possible.

The process described above explains for the court the reasons why you can't take on any more work and why your future employment is not going to improve. As such, you will not be able to service your student loans and request they be discharged as an undue hardship.

CHARACTERISTIC C—
Good Faith and Loan Repayment

Debtors are required to demonstrate "good faith" attempts to repay student loans. There is an expectation that any time the debtor's net income exceeded the Federal Poverty Guidelines, payments were made on the student loans. During times of financial difficulty, debtors must show that they worked with the lender to resolve the issue instead of letting loans fall into arrears. When contemplating filing a bankruptcy, keep in mind that student loans should not exceed about 50% of the debtor's total debt load, otherwise the court will be suspicious that the primary purpose of the bankruptcy is to discharge the student loans. Additionally, at least 5 or more years should have passed since obtaining the last student loan before filing an adversary proceeding, otherwise the courts have a presumption of fraud which the debtor must overcome.

Step 15 • Make copies of your IRS Income Tax filings for each year since receiving your last student loan. **Fill out** the worksheet *Income and Student Loan Payment* (Appendix D). Instructions are on the worksheet form. This form tracks your income for the years since obtaining your most recent student loans and the status of student loan repayments.

You now have everything needed to write a history of your employment, attempts to find work, family income, and servicing your student loans. The purpose of the narrative is to show that you have been

diligent in trying to make income sufficient to repay your student loans.

Step 16 • On a blank piece of paper, **write** your name, date and adversary number, and entitle it *Good Faith and Loan Repayment* (or similar words). Here, you write a history of your employment, family income, and student loan repayment. Be sure to indicate when your family income dropped below the Federal Poverty Guidelines, that you received deferments or forbearances whenever you were unable to make payments, and more. You want to show you have been diligent in servicing your student loans, and that there is no fraud in seeking their discharge. Review the sample provided in Appendix D entitled *Good Faith and Loan Repayment Statement*.

INCOME CONTINGENT REPAYMENT (ICR) PLAN

Finally, the last problem that must be addressed is the *Income Contingent Repayment (ICR) Plan*. As described at length in Chapter 7, the ICR allows debtors to make loan payments when they can, and sometimes pay nothing at all if his or her income drops below a particular level. The plan lasts for 25 years and any outstanding student loan debt remaining at the end of the plan is discharged. However, and this is a big however, debtors are liable for the income taxes on the discharged amount.

It is often stated by Department of Education attorneys that ICR makes it impossible for debtors to discharge their student loans in bankruptcy or otherwise. They contend that anyone can make "zero dollar" payments, thus negating the undue hardship exception of §523(a)(8).

In many cases, this is true. But, we argue in Chapter 7, for some debtors, the ICR is inappropriate. Perhaps you are one of the debtors who would benefit from arguing that the ICR causes you an undue hardship.

Step 17 • On a blank piece of paper, **write** your name, date and adversary number, and entitle it *Income Contingent Repayment* (or similar words).

Tell why, in your case, the ICR is not appropriate and causes an undue hardship. See *Income Contingent Repayment* statement in Appendix D for a sample.

Review

If you have completed all 17 steps listed above, you have all the necessary documents and arguments to file an adversary proceeding. There will be no surprises and you will have all the facts and documents needed to defend your position.

To review; you have completed the following forms and worksheets:

Step 1 — Contacted your student loan lenders and obtained a complete history of their payment and status. Completed the Student Loan History worksheet (Appendix D).

Step 2 — Contacted your local bankruptcy court and determined which undue hardship test will be used in your jurisdiction and/or obtained a copy of interrogatories, if used.

Step 3 — Made a copy of your bankruptcy Schedule I—Current Income of Individual Debtor (Appendix C)(or similar form used in your bankruptcy court) and business income/expense (if needed).

Step 4 — Completed the Current Income Status worksheet (Appendix D).

Step 5 — Wrote a **Current Income and Family Status*** statement on a blank piece of paper (Appendix D).

Step 6 — Made a copy of your bankruptcy Schedule J—Current Expenditures of Individual Debtor (Appendix C)(or similar form used in your bankruptcy court).

Step 7 — Completed most of the Current Expenditure Status worksheet (Appendix D).

Step 8 — Downloaded a copy of the U.S. Department of Health and Human Services Federal Poverty Guidelines and completed more of the Current Expenditure Status worksheet.

Step 9 — Went to IRS website, obtained Collection Financial Standards, and used the data to fill in the Current Expenditure Status worksheet.

Step 10 — Compared your family expenditures against the national norms and completed the Current Expenditure Status worksheet.

Step 11 — Wrote a **Current Expenditures and Minimalized Living***. (Appendix D) statement on a blank piece of paper

Step 12 — Completed the Work Time Accounting Table worksheet (Appendix D). Wrote a **Work Time Accounting Statement*** (Appendix D) on a blank piece of paper.

Step 13 — Wrote a **Personal Limitations*** (Appendix D) statement on a blank piece of paper.

Step 14 — Wrote an **External Factors*** (Appendix D) statement on a blank piece of paper.

Step 15 — Made copies of your IRS Income Tax forms. Completed the Income and Student Loan Payment worksheet.

Step 16 — Wrote a **Good Faith and Loan Repayment*** (Appendix D) statement on a blank piece of paper.

Step 17 — Wrote an **Income Contingent Repayment*** (Appendix D) statement on a blank piece of paper.

(Each underlined item is either a worksheet from the Appendix, letter you wrote, or document you downloaded. **Each bolded and asterisked items are documents you wrote on a blank piece of paper that will be used in the adversary proceeding**. We suggest that you do not submit or show the attorneys for the Department of Education any of the worksheets you used. You do not want to tip them off that you are using this book.)

The next chapter will give step-by-step guidance on how to file an adversary proceeding and strategies for forcibly making the case to have your student loans discharged. If you are not filing an adversary proceeding but trying to negotiate a discharge of your debt through Compromise or Write-off, see Chapter 10.

CHAPTER 9
Step-By-Step Procedures for The Adversary Proceeding

This chapter presents the steps required to file and argue an adversary proceeding as part of a bankruptcy. The steps here are based on the personal experience of the author and are not legal advice.

The previous chapter helped you to bring together all the documents and data needed to present your case. Hopefully, you have read the rest of this book to familiarize yourself with the legal concepts, language and court cases that are used to prove cases of "undue hardship." Remember, the strength of the case will ultimately rest on your shoulders and the better prepared you are the greater the chance of prevailing and having your student loans discharged or severely reduced.

A check off box is placed in front of each step. Once you have completed a step, check-off the box so as to keep track where you are in the process.

The Adversary Proceeding

Chapter 11, Section 523(a)(8) of the 1998 U.S.C.A. Bankruptcy Reform Act declares that government backed student loans are not dischargeable unless there is evidence showing that repaying the loans would cause an "undue hardship." To prove this point, the debtor must file a formal complaint with the bankruptcy court. This is legally termed an "adversary proceeding."

An adversary proceeding is the bankruptcy court's execution of a civil complaint. It is governed by Federal Rules of Bankruptcy Procedure (FRBP) Rule 7001 and is used to determine the dischargeability of a debt, as well as other purposes. Since student loans

backed by the government are considered not dischargeable, *an adversary proceeding asks the court to determine if they are dischargeable*.

An adversary proceeding is just like any other formal court action and consists of the following steps:

- Filing the Complaint with Proof of Service
- Status Hearing
- Mediation
- Pre-Trial Hearing
- Trial

Some of these steps may be combined or skipped at the discretion of the court. For example, the court where the person who won a discharge of $225,000 of student loans did not hold a status hearing or send the parties to mediation but rather used interrogatories to gather the information for the judge to make a determination. Still, being prepared for each of these steps helps prepare you for any variation in process since the same basic questions will be asked.

Before Filing the Complaint

Before filing the adversary complaint, you must clarify some of the legal details for your specific bankruptcy court. Then, you will prepare your documents for filing.

Bankruptcy Filing

Remember to list ALL outstanding student loans in your bankruptcy (one of the cases listed in Chapter 6 illustrates how courts become confused by debtors who fail to list all student loans and conclude there is something wrong with, or being hidden, by the debtor). Chapter 7 forms will be used here to illustrate the process. Student loans are listed on Form B6F *Schedule F - Creditors Holding Unsecured Nonpriority Claims*. A sample and blank form are provided in the Appendix C.

Court Details

Although federal law dictates bankruptcy law, each district court, and in fact some judges, have very specific rules related to how to file the case, the layout of the documents, court procedures, costs, and more. Further, you need the specific forms for the court. Most bankruptcy courts make all these documents available on-line for free download.

Local Bankruptcy Rules and Forms

❑ **Step 1:**
Contact or go on-line to your bankruptcy district court and obtain a copy of:
(1) *Local Bankruptcy Rules*
(2) *Adversary Proceeding Sheet (Cover)*
(3) *Summons*
(4) *Proof of Service*
(5) *Joint Status Report*

The samples given in this book are for the Central District of California. The *Local Bankruptcy Rules* gives many details, such as the size of the paper, blue back, hole spacing, number of lines maximum per document, and much more. Review these, and if necessary, modify the samples in this book to comply with your local rules.

Time Frame for Filing and Federal Addresses

In general, you need to file the adversary proceeding within 60 days of the meeting of the creditors for Chapter 7, 11, and 12 cases. [Bankruptcy Rules 4007 (c)]

For Chapter 13 cases the time for notifying the creditors is 30 days. [Bankruptcy Rules 4007 (d)] As discussed in Chapter 7, it is unclear when, or if, a debtor files and adversary proceeding as part of a Chapter 13 bankruptcy. Please check our website— www.BankruptYourStudentLoans.com— for update on this issue.

❑ **Step 2:**
Although the *Local Bankruptcy Rules* should list the time frame for filing an adversary proceeding, it may be difficult to locate. Thus, we suggest you contact your local United States Attorney. This is the office that will be defending the United States Department of Education against your adversary proceeding. In this initial phone call, you want to find out:

(a) Ask for the time frame for filing the adversary proceeding

Write the time frame here: _____

(b) Ask for the correct mailing address for the defendant (the Department of Education)

Write the name and address here:

_____

_____

_____

_____

(c) Ask for the proper person and address for hand delivery of the complaint.

Write the name and address here:

_____

_____

_____

_____

Do not be alarmed that they will keep a record of when you call them. They may be very "helpful," so much so they may try to engage you in a lengthy conversation and try to convince you not to file the adversary proceeding. They may lie to you saying that you cannot bankrupt the loans. They will probably tell you that the Income Contingent Repayment (ICR) Plan guarantees that you will lose the case. If you have come this far in the book, you have already developed your arguments to satisfy this condition. It is probably best that you do not engage them in lengthy discussion. Just find out the three items listed above in Step 2.

If you have missed the time for filing the adversary proceeding, you may still be able to file. Some courts have allowed filings years later, whereas other courts insist upon the stated time frame. It costs you nothing to file, so you might as well try. Another approach is to re-open your bankruptcy for the purpose of filing an adversary proceeding. See Chapter 1 for details on reopening a bankruptcy.

Fees and Verify Bankruptcy Addresses

<u>There should be no fee for filing an adversary proceeding if it is filed within the stipulated time frame and by the debtor.</u> However, in some bankruptcy districts, the fee may be as high as $150.

❏ **Step 3**:
Contact your <u>bankruptcy district court</u>:

(a) Ask what the fee is for filing a Complaint to Determine Dischargeability. You may need to remind them that you are filing within the time frame specified for an adversary proceeding as part of a bankruptcy and that you are the debtor. In fact, the instructions given on the back of the *Adversary Proceeding Sheet (Cover)* states, "The fee is not required if the plaintiff is the United States government or the debtor." Thus, there should be no fee in your case. (In the author's experience, the clerks at the California Central Distinct Court thought there was a fee. A supervisor had to be called over, who then verified that the fee was zero.)

Write the fee here: _____

(b) Ask for the mailing address of the trustee in your Chapter 7 case. You should already know this from your Chapter 7 bankruptcy filing. But ask anyway just to verify.

Write the address here:

_____

_____

_____

_____

(c) Ask for the mailing address of the U.S. trustee, i.e., the U.S. trustee who oversees all bankruptcies in your district.

Write the address here:

_____

_____

_____

_____

(d) Ask the time frame for filing an adversary proceeding.

Write the time frame here: _____

Review

In preparation for filing a complaint, you have:
1. Listed all your student loans in your Chapter 7 bankruptcy.
2. Obtained a copy of rules and forms you will need to file—(1) *Local Bankruptcy Rules*, (2) *Adversary Proceeding Sheet* (Cover), (3) *Summons*, (4) *Proof of Service*, and (5) *Joint Status Report*.
3. Used your *Local Bankruptcy Rules* to adjust forms, and more, to conform to the rules.

4. Contacted the local United States Attorney and verified: (a) the time frame for filing an adversary proceeding, (b) the mailing address for the defendant, and (c) the address for hand delivery (serving) of the complaint.

5. Contacted the bankruptcy district court and verified: (a) the filing fee, (b) address of your Chapter 7 trustee, (c) address of the U.S. trustee, and (d) the time frame for filing an adversary proceeding.

You may have noticed that we have had you ask similar questions of the United States Attorney and the bankruptcy district court. Their responses should be the same. If there are differences between the two, you need to contact both and resolve the differences. This way you avoid having your case delayed or thrown out for simple mistakes such as serving the wrong people or missing deadlines.

Let's summarize the final data you will need for the filing. Fill out the table (*Adversary Proceeding Data Summary*) with the data you clarified in Steps 1-3. You will use this table to complete your adversary proceeding.

ADVERSARY PROCEEDING DATA SUMMARY

Write the time frame for filing an adversary proceeding (e.g., within 60 days of meeting with the creditors):
_____

Write the filing fee (if any) here: _____

Names and addresses of people and agencies you need to serve:
- Civil process clerk at the office of the United States attorney for the district in which the action is brought (local U.S. Attorney used to defend the case). This is who you hand deliver the complaint and summons. Everyone else you mail a copy.
  Write the Name and Address here:_____

  _____

  _____

- Office of the U.S. Trustee in you bankruptcy district.
  Write the Name and Address here:_____

  _____

  _____

- The Attorney General in Washington, D.C.
  Write the Name and Address here:_____

  _____

  _____

- Particular agency named in or affected by the lawsuit (in another words, the agency you are suing—most likely the Dept. of Education).
  Write the Name and Address here:_____

  _____

  _____

- Your Chapter 7 bankruptcy trustee.
  Write the Name and Address here:_____

  _____

  _____

  _____

Filing and Serving the Complaint

In this section we will first have you prepare your documents for filing, and then show you how to file them with the court and serve them to the defendants.

There are 2 separate document packages that need to be prepared— the Complaint package and the Proof of Service package.

Appendix E contains instructions, samples, and blanks of these forms in these packets. Remember, the forms in the Appendix are for the U.S. Bankruptcy Court for the Central District of California. You should have obtained blanks of these forms in Step 1 (above) for your specific bankruptcy court district.

Preparing the Complaint Package

The Adversary Complaint package is made up of 3 documents and a backing:
- A. *Summons*
- B. *Adversary Proceeding Sheet* (otherwise known as the *Cover* form)
- C. *Adversary Complaint*
- D. Blue Back

❑ **Step 4:**
> Obtain a few sheets of legal (pleading) paper. A blank is provided in Appendix E if you want to make photocopies.
>
> Obtain a few sheets of blue back. See Appendix E for details on how to prepare the backing and how court documents are assembled.

❑ **Step 5:**
> Prepare the *Summons*. See Appendix E for instructions, samples and blank form. Sometimes the *Summons* form can only be obtained at the clerk's window. In this case, we suggest that you complete the form in this book and take it with you as a sample.

❑ **Step 6:**
> Prepare the *Adversary Proceeding Sheet (Cover)*. See Appendix E for instructions, samples and blank form.

❑ **Step 7:**
> Prepare the *Adversary Complaint*. See Appendix E for instructions and sample form.

❑ **Step 8:**
> Make 8 copies each of the *Adversary Proceeding Sheet (Cover)* and Adversary *Complaint*. These spare copies will be used to serve all parties during the Proof of Service step.
>
> Assemble one Adversary Complaint package as follows (top to bottom) using one of each document:
> - A. *Adversary Proceeding Sheet (Cover)*
> - B. *Adversary Complaint*
>
> The documents are stapled to the Blue Back with just one staple in the left corner.
>
> Assemble the 7 remaining copies into similar sets.
>
> The *Summons* is not stapled into this package since the clerk has to handle it separately to assign a court date. Place the *Summons* loosely on top of the Complaint package.

Preparing the Proof of Service

The *Summons* and Adversary Complaint package must be served upon the defendant and other parties. You, the plaintiff, are not allowed to serve these documents. Instead, most states allow you to use a friend or other non-relative for this purpose. Some states restrict "service of process" (serving the documents) to law enforcement officers (sheriff, marshal or constable) or a licensed private process server. Some states allow all the documents to be served by mail, whereas most states require the defendant to be served personally and all others served by mail. Check with the Local Rules, or directly with the bankruptcy court to clarify who can serve the documents and how they are served.

The example in this section assumes you will have a friend personally serve the defendant and mail copies to all others.

The Proof of Service package is made up of 3 documents and a backing:

    A. *Proof of Service Cover*
    B. *Proof of Service*
    C. *Mail Matrix*
    D. Blue Back

❑ **Step 9:**

Prepare the *Proof of Service Cover*, *Proof of Service* with *Mail Matrix*. The names and addresses used on the *Proof of Service* and *Mail Matrix* comes from the summary of Step 3 (above). The person who will be performing the "service of process" for you completes and signs the *Proof of Service*. See Appendix E for instructions, samples and blank forms.

Filing the Complaint and Serving/Filing the Proof of Service

You are now ready to file your complaint and serve the documents.

❑ **Step 10:**

Take your Adversary Complaint package to the bankruptcy court. Bring along your checkbook in case there are any fees. Be sure you are filing before the deadline.

When you get to the clerk, hand him or her your *Summons*. If you did not fill one out in advance, ask for a blank *Summons* form.

If you are handed a blank *Summons* form, get out of line and fill it out on the spot. You may use a pen (it does not have to be typed).

Get back in line with the completed *Summons* and give it to the clerk along with the Adversary Complaint package (the one you have bound in a Blue Back) plus one more copy. The clerk will stamp everything. The court will keep the original complaint (the one that is Blue Back) plus the one copy. If needed, you will pay fees at this time.

Then give the clerk the other copies of the *Adversary Proceeding Sheet (Cover)* and

Adversary Complaint to stamp (i.e., be "conformed"). These will be handed back to you.

❑ **Step 11:**

You will now receive a date for the "status conference" hearing.

Some bankruptcy clerk offices will issue the status conference date at the same time you file the *Adversary Complaint*. If so, usually they make a copy of the *Summons* and write the court date and address information on it, or they may give you a separate piece of paper with this information (known as the *Order*). In either case, you need to leave with a copy of the *Summons* (and *Order* if given) that contains the status conference date and details.

Some bankruptcy clerk offices will mail the *Summons/Order* to you.

Make 9 copies of the final *Summons* and any *Order* giving the details of the "status conference."

❑ **Step 12:**

Finally, the documents must be served.

Most courts require the *Adversary Complaint* and *Summons* with any *Order* to be served within 10 days of the filing. Check with your bankruptcy court or local rules to be sure.

❑ Preparing the Envelopes

Obtain a quantity of 9" x 12" (or larger) envelopes equal to the number of addresses on the Mail Matrix plus one. (In the sample given in Appendix E, there are 4 names/addresses on the Mail Matrix. Thus, 5 envelopes would be needed).

In each envelope, place a copy of:
    A. *Adversary Proceeding Sheet (Cover)*
    B. *Adversary Complaint*
    C. *Summons/Order*

Serving the Documents

The defendant listed on the *Proof of Service* must be hand-delivered a set of documents. Take one of the envelopes prepared above and have your friend (or who ever agreed to deliver the *Summons* and who signed the *Proof of Service*) go to the address and deliver the envelope. Usually a secretary will accept the envelope, not the person listed. Ask the name of the person receiving the envelope and write it on the *Proof of Service* next to the address.

Make copies of this *Proof of Service* (the one that has written on it the name of the person who accepted it) and *Mail Matrix* equal to the number names/address on the *Mail Matrix* plus 3 more. (In the sample in Appendix E, this would be 4 plus 3 for a total of 7).

Mailing the Documents

Take the remaining envelopes and prepare each one for mailing by writing a name/address from the *Mail Matrix*. Place a copy of the notated Proof *of Service* with *Mail Matrix* inside along with the other documents. Use sufficient postage and mail the envelopes.

Filing the Documents

Now you are ready to file with the court your *Proof of Service*.

Assemble one *Proof of Service* package as follows (top to bottom) using one of each document:
  A. *Proof of Service Cover*
  B. *Proof of Service* (the one that contains your notation of who accepted it)
  C. *Mail Matrix*
  D. *Adversary Proceeding Sheet (Cover)* (conformed copy)
  E. *Adversary Complaint* (conformed copy)
  F. *Summons/Order*

The documents are stapled to the Blue Back with just one staple in the left corner.

Assemble the 2 remaining copies into similar sets (without the Blue Back).

Return to the bankruptcy court clerk. Hand him or her the Proof of Service package (with Blue Back) plus one copy. They will stamp these and accept them. Hand them the one last copy to have them stamp; it will be handed back to you as your conformed copy.

Congratulations! You have finished filing your adversary complaint. Each court is different and the procedure outlined above could be different. You need to learn to adapt to the situation. Sometimes clerks tell you something different than what you know or ask a question you are not sure how to answer. Often, courts have a help desk to clarify these steps. They cannot offer legal advice, but they can guide you in which documents are needed and how they are filed.

The important thing to remember is the process. You are asking the court to appoint a date to hear your complaint. Obviously, you must let the defendant and related people know that you are taking these legal actions and where and when the court action will take place. The court needs to know that you have properly notified all interested parties with enough time to respond.

It must be emphasized that you are now entering into a formal legal process that is much different than the simple bankruptcy procedures. It is highly recommended that you get a copy of Bergman and Berman-Barrett, *Represent Yourself in Court* (NOLO Press) or similar type of book. Although this book will discuss ways to avoid pit falls of a typical lawsuit, you should be prepared for anything.

Status Hearing

Typically, the defendant (probably the Department of Education) has 60-days in which to file a response to your complaint. Of course, they will deny your complaint.

You may, if you wish, respond to the defendant's response. See the Bergman and Berman-Barrett book for details on filing a response. It is probably better not to respond at this point and let the negotiations occur during mediation.

The *Summons* and *Order* you received were for a Status Hearing. The court does not make a decision at a Status Hearing and it is not a trial. It simply is a step where the court wants to know if the two parties are talking and trying to resolve the problem.

❑ **Step 13:**

Approximately 2 weeks before the Status Hearing a report must be filed with the court. The court wants to know if the two parties have come to some kind of agreement, and if not, do they want to enter into mediation. Typically the defendant's attorney (local U.S. Attorney) will offer to prepare a *Joint Status Report*. They will fill out their part, send you a copy, you fill out your part and mail it back. They will file it with the court. The form asks if you want to go into mediation. You want to check off "yes." It is mediation where you will win your case. A sample and blank form of a *Joint Status Report* is provided in Appendix E. Be sure to file your own status report if a joint one is not filed by the defendant.

❑ **Step 14:**

Attend your Status Hearing. This is probably the first time you'll meet the U.S. attorney who is representing the defendant (U.S. Department of Education). Be calm. The judge will ask you to come forward and identify yourself. He or she will ask if you agree to mediation. By responding, "yes," the judge will direct the case to mediation.

Mediation

You will receive notice in the mail about the mediation. Sometimes you are given the opportunity to select the mediator. Most often you do not know who the mediators are. Probably it is best to just go with whomever the court assigns, particularly if the mediation site is nearby.

MEDIATION AND NEGOTIATION ARE WHERE YOU WIN YOUR CASE!

<u>You really don't want to go to trial</u>. Review the cases presented in Chapter 6 and you will notice how the courts usually rule against the debtor. There is an unreasonable bias against debtors that the courts reinforce.

The Department of Education also does not want to go to trial. It costs them a lot of money to defend against adversary proceedings. Before the trial, they will have to put you through a deposition and other steps that all cost money. Further, they want to avoid having a court make an adverse decision against them that may affect their future ability to defend against similar adversary proceedings.

Strategies

Going into mediation and negotiating with the attorney's for the Department of Education requires some strategy. In general, they believe the Income Contingent Repayment (ICR) Plan precludes anyone from discharging his or her student loans regardless of meeting the "undue hardship" court requirement. They will be aggressive and intimidating. They may, in fact, lie to you. Thus, you need to prepare for the negotiations.

There are three levels of strategy to mediation the author found effective. They are identified as:

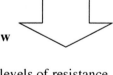

* **Playing the Game**

* **Resisting Their Arguments**

* **Attacking the Agency and Law**

The strategies represent increasing levels of resistance to the psychological and legal intimidation they will use on you.

Playing the Game

Section 523(a)(8) of the bankruptcy laws require you to show that it would cause an undue hardship to you and your dependants if you were required to repay your student loans. Twenty years of litigation on this issue has resulted in the courts developing a number of tests. Most courts use the Brunner test as discussed in Chapters 4 and 5. In Chapter 8, we had you verify with your court which test they use.

In Chapter 5, we developed a set of guidelines needed to prove undue hardship. In Chapter 8, we had you complete a number of worksheets that helped you develop and compose written responses to prove these guidelines.

Your first step is to comply with proving the "undue hardship" test used by your court. We call this "playing the game" because the court expects you to make this proof, whereas the Department of Education believes that the Income Contingent Repayment (ICR) Plan negates any "undue hardship" test.

- First— you need to show that your current family income does not allow you to make repayments on your student loans. To that end you composed in Chapter 8 the letter *Current Income and Family Status*.

- Second— you need to show that your family expenditures are minimized and equal to other similarly situated families. To that end you composed in Chapter 8 the letter *Current Expenditures and Minimalized Living*.

- Third— you need to show that there are personal limitations and external factors that impact your ability to find better paying work. To that end you composed in Chapter 8 the letters *Personal Limitations* and *External Factors*.

- Fourth— you need to show that you have been diligent in making student loan payments when you were financially able, and received deferments or forbearances whenever you were unable to make payments. To that end you composed in Chapter 8 the letter *Good Faith and Loan Repayment*.

We want to blend these 5 documents into one letter and deliver it to the defendant a few weeks before the

Mediation. By doing so, you are showing the court that you are trying to work with the defendant by honestly presenting your case. Hopefully, you wrote all these documents on a computer so you only have to cut and paste the sections into one master document. If you did not, or could not, use a computer; you will have to retype all the letters.

❑ **Step 15:**
A few weeks before your Mediation, write one letter that contains all 5 documents—
Current Income and Family Status
Current Expenditures and Minimalized Living
Personal Limitations
External Factors
Good Faith and Loan Repayment
Address the letter to the attorney representing the defendant. On the first lines of the letter state that, "repaying my student loans represents an undue hardship because . . . " (now copy each of your letters, one-by-one, in the order above). Mail the letter to the attorney. Be sure to keep a copy of the master letter for yourself (or if on a computer, save the file). A few days after you mail the letter, call the attorney to see that he or she received it.

A word about grammar and wording: If you have a high college degree such as Ph.D. or Master's, take time to use proper wording and grammar. If you have a technical degree, no degree or limited education, or are mentally disabled, do not worry that your letter is not perfect; they expect you to make mistakes. If your letter is too good, they may suspect you had professional help.

You should not expect to hear from the attorney for the defendant before the Mediation. The attorney should forward the letter to the defendant.

A word about the attorney for the defendant: Usually, this person is not a direct employee of the Department of Education. Instead, he or she is an attorney for the U.S. Attorney's office and is retained to negotiate for the Department. Ultimately, a decision to accept an out-of-court settlement comes from the Department itself, not from the attorney. The attorney is just a conduit to the Department although the attorney will fully represent the Department if your case goes all the way to trial.

You should feel proud that you have taken the effort to present your position. Many, if not most, people filing an adversary proceeding do not make their position clear. They leave it up to the attorney for the defendant and court to pull this information out of the debtor. As such, they control how they present your information; and you can be sure it is not in your best interest. By clearly stating your position, you have taken control of the process.

It is now time for the mediation.

Before going to the Mediation, we want you to be prepared for a number of contingencies:

- Although the attorney probably will be very pleasant at the beginning of the Mediation, he or she may try to unnerve you soon into the Mediation by pointing out "problems" in your master letter. These may or may not be true. You may answer the best you can, but it would be better to write down the supposed problem for you to work on after the Mediation.

- If your "undue hardship" arguments are strong, the attorney will most likely ignore your master letter and attack other "problems." Write these down for you to research after the Mediation.

- Regardless if the discussion begins with reference to your letter or not, eventually the attorney is going to claim that you should agree to an Income Contingent Repayment (ICR) Plan. You must have a strong answer for this. You prepared a letter in Chapter 8 to address this issue. Thus, a day before going to the Mediation, review your letter *Income Contingent Repayment*. Don't bring this with you, just know the contents so you can recite the reasons ICR is inappropriate for you.

- Similarly the attorney is going to claim that you can work more to make more income that

can be used toward student loan payments. In Chapter 8, you prepared a letter to address this issue. The day before the Mediation, review your letter *Work Time Accounting Statement*. Don't bring this letter with you, but know the contents so you can recite why you are not able to take on more work.

- The attorney will most likely tell a story about some other debtor he or she is currently negotiating who is in much worse financial stress than you and that the Department of Education is not accepting his or her claim of "undue hardship." This is meant to unnerve you and make you feel that the process is hopeless. Don't give up.

- Give some thought to a "fair" settlement for your particular situation. Maybe your situation is so dire that complete discharge of the loans is necessary. However, maybe you could pay a portion of the loans. In the banking industry, bad debts are often settled at 10 cents on the dollar. Ask yourself if you could pay 10% of your loan. The Department of Education will not accept payments less than $50 a month because of bookkeeping expenses. For example, let's say you owe $60,000; maybe you could pay $50 a month for 10 years. That works out to a total of $6,000 repayment saving you $54,000. If you owe a smaller amount, maybe you could pay $50 a month for 5 years, or whatever. Try not to have the loan last more than 10 years. Also, consider the issue of furlough. Obviously, you would like the ability to have a number of furloughs available just in case something terrible goes wrong and you do not have money for a short time. The problem about including furloughs in your settlement is that then your repayment program begins to look too much like the ICR plan. Congress set the terms for the ICR and the Department of Education does not have the authority to amend them. We suggest that if you seek a reduced loan settlement, ask for furloughs knowing that you are using them as bargaining chips. Be sure to have any discharged loan amount passed through your bankruptcy (see the *Stipulation* sample in Appendix E). This means you *will not owe any income tax on the discharged amount*.

❑ **Step 16:**

The day before the Mediation, review the letters you wrote in Chapter 8 —
Income Contingent Repayment
Work Time Accounting Statement
Be prepared to cite the reasons listed in these letters.

❑ **Step 17:**

Attend your Mediation. Be early. Be rested. Take a copy of your master letter with you to make notes on. Remember, they already have this letter. *Do not take any other letters or worksheets*. Take a pen and pencil and writing paper.

The first thing that is going to happen at the Mediation is that they are going to have you sign a non-disclosure form. It means that you cannot call the mediator or attorney to court to testify that various statements or promises were made.

The purpose of the mediator is to help both sides discuss the issues and hopefully find a mutually agreed resolution. <u>The mediator is not to take anyone's side</u>. About three-fourths the way into the time allotted for the mediation, the mediator most likely will try to get you and the attorney to come to some settlement. Here is where you "hold tuff," keeping in mind what you consider a "fair" settlement (as discussed above).

Negotiate strongly. Here is a hierarchy of possible proposals from the greatest discharge to least. Be aware of where your lowest "fair" settlement is:

• The entire loan is discharged through the bankruptcy.

• A monthly payment of $50 for so many years with 5 furloughs. The remaining portion of the loan to be discharged through the bankruptcy.

• A monthly payment of $50 for so many years with no furloughs. The remaining portion of the loan to be discharged through the bankruptcy.

• A modified Income Contingent Repayment (ICR) Plan for so many years. The remaining portion of the loan to be discharged through the bankruptcy. (We've included this idea because, in reality, the Department of Education could conceivably obtain the most money through such a program but they are not allowed to offer such a plan because Congress specified 25-year terms and no opportunity to discharge the remaining portion through a bankruptcy. However, bringing up this idea makes you look fair and not greedy.)

Perhaps you can think of other settlement plans. Remember that whatever amount is discharged, be sure it is discharged through the bankruptcy, so as to avoid owing income taxes on the amount discharged.

If you are seeking a portion settlement (like $50 a month for so many years), they will write into the settlement that you have the right to prepay the loan. This means that if you have a lump sum available to pay on the loan, you could negotiate paying only this sum immediately, and the rest is discharged through the bankruptcy.

If you and the attorney come to an impasse, the mediator will move you into separate rooms. Typically, the mediator will meet with you first to clarify what you are trying to offer. Then, the mediator will go to the attorney to see if he or she will accept the terms. The mediator may go back and forth a few times to each of you. Eventually, the mediator will bring the two of you back together where, hopefully, you have made clear your offer. The attorney may not agree with you, but has an obligation to take your offer to the Department of Education for their approval. Remember, the attorney cannot make a binding offer. That has to come from the Department of Education.

One more thing about Mediation: most likely, the attorney representing the Department of Education will speak down to you and treat you with contempt. He or she may even laugh at you by making snide remarks about your "feeble attempt" to have the loans discharged. Don't get mad. Stay focused. Realize it is a psychological tactic to make you feel inadequate and give up. Listen to what the attorney has to say, however. In his or her arrogance, he or she may give leads to how to succeed later in the negotiation process. Remember, the attorney does not make the final decision about a negotiated settlement, the Department of Education does.

Congratulations, you have gotten through the Mediation.

A few weeks may go by before the attorney gets back to you with the Department of Education's response. Hopefully, they will have accepted your offer. If so, the attorney will write up a stipulation detailing the settlement. Appendix E contains a sample stipulation. A stipulation is a document that tells the court what you and the defendant have agreed to. This is presented to the judge who almost always approves the stipulation whereupon it is recorded making it legally binding. A trial or judgment is no longer needed.

Let's take some time to review the *Stipulation (Sample)* in Appendix E. It is important for you to know the elements of the stipulation so that you can be assured the discharged portion of your student loans is discharged through the bankruptcy. Otherwise, you will owe income tax on the discharged amount.

On page 2 of *Stipulation (Sample)*, Item 1 gives the repayment terms— so much per month for so many years, when due each month, when the plan begins, and how payment is made (check, electronic transfer, etc.). Page 3, Item 2 is the most important item. It states that the "remaining amount of the Debt will be considered by Education as discharged through Plaintiff's bankruptcy." This eliminates income taxes on the discharged amount. Think about it. **The stipulation means you were successful at bankrupting your student loans**; maybe not the entire debt, but some of it. Take pride in the fact that you succeeded at something most lawyers claim is impossible; and you did it yourself. Item 3 allows you to prepay the debt. Item 4 spells out the consequences of not making the payments specified in Item 1. The other items are important legal clarifications. If you and the Department of Education enter into a stipulation, be sure it is similar to this sample.

If the Department of Education rejects your offer, we go to the next step of the process— "Resisting Their Arguments." When the attorney calls you to inform you of the rejection, he or she should give you some idea why it was rejected. Also, during the Mediation, you should have been aware of concerns expressed by the attorney.

You still have time before going to trial to try and seek a settlement.

Resisting Their Arguments

❑ **Step 18:**
   Write another letter to the Department of Education. In this letter you need to address any issues that came up in the Mediation. Further, cut and paste from the Chapter 8 letters— *Income Contingent Repayment* and *Work Time Accounting Statement*. You need to be clear why the ICR is not appropriate for you and why you cannot take on any more work. The ICR is the major sword used by the Department of Education to convince the court that you cannot meet the

provisions of the undue hardship tests. Reiterate your points in the letter and restate your offer; emphasis that it is fair. Mail the letter to the attorney.

If the Department of Education accepts your offer, a stipulation will be written and the case will be over (see discussion above on stipulation).

But, if the Department of Education rejects your offer, the author found it effective to make a very aggressive attack on the Department of Education and the bankruptcy law. Most people who read the cases presented in Chapter 6 shake their heads in disbelief over the injustice perpetrated on so many honest poor debtors. Basically, 11 U.S.C.A. §523(a)(8) is bad law that has been distorted through aggressive enforcement by the Department of Education.

The author took a 3-fold strategy:

> **First**—request lots and lots of documents from the Department of Education to prove the concerns discussed in Chapter 7.

> **Second**–let the Department of Education know that you expect to bring up during the trial many of the concerns discussed in Chapter 7. In general, the Department does not want a court ruling on many of these issues as they may loose— resulting in 11 U.S.C.A. §523(a)(8) being overturned.

> **Third**—be such an annoyance that they will be encouraged to settle in your favor before the trial.

Attacking the Agency and Law

❏ **Step 19:**
Immediately write a new letter to the Department of Education. At the top of the letter, express your dissatisfaction with their rejection of your fair offer. Then continue writing the letter similar to that presented in *Request for Documents from Department of Education (Sample)* found in Appendix E. Mail the letter to the attorney.

Hopefully, the attorney will call to say that the Department of Education has accepted your offer, a stipulation will be written, most if not all of your debt discharged, and the case closed.

If they do not accept your offer, you have no choice but to continue to the trial.

Pretrial Hearing and Trial

It is impossible to write in any detail about what could happen between now and the pre-trial hearing or at the trial. So much depends on the state the court is located, the court itself, and the particular judge. Writing generalized instructions is impossible.

The defendant may subpoena you to take your deposition. Or you may be given interrogatories to fill out. Don't panic. They will be asking for information that you have already prepared in Chapter 8. If you are being depositioned, request a copy of the questions they intend to ask before you go. They legally must provide you these questions if you ask.

The Department of Education probably will not provide you with the documents you requested in your previous letter. You can demand this information through what is termed discovery. Be sure to let the court know that the Department failed to provide you with the information you requested. You want the court to see how difficult and uncooperative the Department of Education is toward resolving this issue.

If your case has not been settled and you have gotten this far, we really recommend you obtain the Berman & Berman-Barrett book *Represent Yourself in Court* (NOLO) or similar type book. Or, you may want to bring in an attorney.

In Appendix B— *Precedent Setting Cases*, there is a summary of an article that reviewed hundreds of adversary proceedings related to student loans and categorized them. This article has hot links to each court case when viewed through Westlaw. As such, it allows you to conduct a quick search of adversary proceedings that addresses your issues. From this research you can develop your legal arguments in the form courts want them presented, i.e., a particular court ruled a particular way in a similar situation. This is known as finding "precedent" for your case. If your case has reached the Pretrial Hearing stage, you most likely will want to conduct a legal search of comparable court cases.

In many states, the next step will be the *Pretrial Hearing*. By law, this hearing is to occur as close to the trial time as reasonable under the circumstances. Here, you, the defendant, and judge develop a plan for the trial. The judge will want you and the defendant's attorney to agree to the legal issues to be decided, documents to be submitted, and more. Once this has been resolved, the judge will issue a *Pretrial Order*. In many ways, this is the most important document for the trial. It supplants the original pleading and establishes the legal theories that will be presented during the trial. Thus, it is important that you have included in the Pretrial Order any of the arguments you want brought to the court's attention, including the "undue hardship" tests, but also the advocacy issues described in Chapter 7 if you want to pursue them.

In some bankruptcy courts, the judge will provide you with guidelines for preparing for the trial since you are representing yourself.

❏ **Step 20:**
Read, understand, and respond to any document sent to you by the defendant's attorney or the court. Do so in a timely manner.

Attend the *Pretrial Hearing*. You may want to try to negotiate one more time with the defense attorney before going to trial. Remember, it has been shown time and again that leaving it up to judges to decide the merits of an "undue hardship" case usually goes poorly for the debtor.

Prepare a Statement. Often times court can be so emotionally daunting for those who are not attorneys that you may want to prepare and read a statement to the court. The court should allow you to read your statement. We suggest that it not exceed 3-4 pages and emphasize your financial hardship explaining why it will not improve in the future. Make it larger type size and double-spaced. This will make it easier to read under stress.

Attend the *Trial*.

*

The author of this book would like to hear the results of your adversary proceeding or Compromise or Write-Off. Although the author cannot provide legal advice, he would like to hear how your case developed and was resolved. Also, any comments, corrections, or insight concerning the content of this book would be appreciated. Contact information is given in "About the Author."

CHAPTER 10
Preparing Your Case for
Compromise or _Write-Off_

This chapter helps you prepare documents for arguing for a _Compromise_ or _Write-Off_ directly to the Department of Education. This section helps you pull together all the documents and data necessary to prove repaying your student loans would cause an "undue hardship."

We suggest you complete the Chapter 7 bankruptcy forms located in Appendix C. These forms— Schedule I, Schedule J, and Business Income and Expense— form the basis of your financial arguments and are familiar to the Department of Education.

PRE-INFO—
Student Loan History

Before you even attempt to have your student loans discharged through _Compromise_ or _Write-Off_, it is important for you to be up-to-date about all your student loans. Thus, you need to contact each lender and get a copy of your student loans and their payment histories. It is most important to know payment, forbearance, and deferment dates.

> **Step 1 • Obtain** a printout from your lenders of the history of your student loans. It is important to know the payment amounts, forbearances and deferment dates for each loan. **Transfer** this information on the Student Loan History worksheet found in Appendix D.

Chapter 5 detailed the kinds of information you must provide in order to achieve the claim of undue hardship.

These were identified as _Characteristics_:

- **Characteristic A**—Current Living Condition and the Impact of Repaying Loan on "Minimal Living" Standard
- **Characteristic B**—Prospects for Repaying the Loans
- **Characteristic C**—Good Faith and Loan Repayment

Each _Characteristic_ will be discussed below in detail along with the sequential steps used to produce the appropriate documents. The problem of the _Income Contingent Repayment (ICR) Plan_ also is addressed.

CHARACTERISTIC A—
Current Living Condition and the Impact of Repaying Loan on "Minimal Living" Standard

First, you need to establish your current financial and living conditions.

> **Step 2 • Make a copy and complete** _Schedule I-Current Income of Individual Debtor._). If you have business income/expenses, make a copy of that form also. Samples and blank forms are included in Appendix C. If you have multiple employers, you may need to make additional copies of Form B6I.

As you will learn later, part of the strategy of proving undue hardship or negotiating a Compromise or Write-Off is for you to present yourself as a hopeless and helpless debtor who is representing him or herself. As such, it is **best not** to let the Department of Education know that **you are using this book**. Instead of handing them *Schedule I*, we suggest that you write, in your own words and on a blank piece of paper, your financial and living status.

> **Step 3** • On a <u>blank piece of paper</u>; **write** your name and date. Title the page "Current Income and Family Status" (or similar words). Below this, in your own words, write a few short paragraphs telling how your family and income. Use *Schedule I* as a basis for discussion. *See* a sample in Appendix D— <u>Current Income and Family Status</u>.

It is recommended that you write all these documents on a computer and save the files. Later, you will be asked to blend all the documents together into one master document. If you write them on a computer, all you will have to do is cut and paste the sections, thereby eliminating the need to retype everything.

Now we evaluate your expenditures.

—WARNING—
<u>A Word of Caution about Income and Expense Statements</u>

The income you list during the *Compromise* or *Write-Off* should match the income you claim with the IRS. If these are not similar, you will be viewed with suspicion.

The expenses you list during the *Compromise* or *Write-Off* should match the expenses you claim with the IRS. If these are not similar, you will be viewed with suspicion.

Step 4 • **Make a copy and complete** *Schedule J-Current Expenditures of Individual Debtor*. This form is found in Appendix C under Chapter 7 Bankruptcy Forms.

Step 5 • **Transfer** your expense data from *Schedule J-Current Expenditures of Individual Debtor* to column 2 of the *Current Expenditure Status* worksheet.

You need to demonstrate that your expenses are comparable to a similarily situated debtor. This is achieved by showing: (a) that your income is within range of the Federal Poverty Guidelines for a family your size, and (b) your expenses are similar to other families of your size and circumstances.

> **Step 6** • **Go to** the website of the United States Department of Health and Human Services (http://aspe.hhs.gov/poverty/poverty.shtml) and **download a copy** of the current Federal Poverty Guidelines(a copy of this homepage and document are in Appendix B). If you do not have access to the web, your local library should have a copy of this government publication. Be sure it the current year. **Write** your information on the *Current Expenditure Status* worksheet.

> **Step 7** • **Go to the website** of the IRS to gather data on Collection Financial Standards (www.irs.gov/individuals/article/0,,id=96543,00.html). The IRS has established standards used to determine the ability of taxpayers to make delinquent payments. Use the data found here to **fill-in** the National Norms (column 3) on the *Current Expenditure Status* worksheet.

> **Step 8** • For those cases where there are significant differences between your expenditures and the national norms, **write** an explanation for each on the *Current Expenditure Status* worksheet (column 4).

You need to explain that you have minimized your living expenses and are not living extravagantly, and that there is no extra income available to pay on your student loans.

Step 9 • On a blank piece of paper; write your name and date. Title the page "Current Expenditures and Minimalized Living" (or similar words). Below this, write a few short paragraphs telling how you live frugally and that it would be impossible to make payments on your student loans. *See* a sample and instructions in Appendix D— Current Expenditure and Minimalized Living.

CHARACTERISTIC B—
Prospects for Repaying the Loans

In so many cases, debtors make a strong showing for their situation, only to have the Department of Education reject the claim and tell the debtor to get a part-time minimum-wage job and use that money to make loan payments. Regardless of how laughable or tragic this may seem, it happens all the time. Thus, the debtor needs to account for his or her time working or providing dependent care, or both. Debtors need to clearly point out to the court that asking the debtor to take on any more work would push him or her over a standard workweek, and that would be an undue hardship.

Step 10 • **Make a copy** of the worksheet *Work Time Accounting Table* (Appendix D) and complete it as instructed. **Write** on a blank piece of paper you name and date and entitle it *Work Time Accounting* (or similar words). In your own words (using the *Work Time Accounting Table*), explain why all your available time is committed making it impossible for you to take on another job. *See* a sample document in the Samples section of Appendix D under *Work Time Accounting Statement*.

The debtor needs to address in detail any personal limitations that may impact the ability to obtain appropriate employment. This includes personal medical limitations, support of dependents (and their medical conditions, if applicable), and lack of useable job skills. These need to be described in detail, with supporting documents (like medical records), etc.

Step 11 • On a blank piece of paper, **write** your name and date and entitle it *Personal Limitations* (or similar words). Here you explain why medical problems for you and/or your dependents, the lack of usable job skills, and/or the existence of a large number of dependents impact your future ability to work at a job that will provide sufficient income to service your student loan debt. *See* a sample document in the Samples section of Appendix D under *Personal Limitations Statement*. **In general, you must show there are "unique" or "exceptional" circumstances that impact future employment and earnings.**

The final step to this Characteristic is to discuss the impact of external factors on your future employment. Courts and the Department of Education have been hesitant to include these factors since it would require them to accept the fact that not all employment doors are open to all workers, i.e., the American dream is not really attainable by all.

External factors that affect future employment opportunities include:
- U.S. Economy
- Discrimination based on age, race, ethnicity, gender, sexual orientation, and others.
- Reverse Discrimination
- Past Terminations
- Whistleblower
- And others

Chapter 5 explained in greater detail about these issues. In many cases, academic papers on these topics are included in Appendix F.

Step 12 • On a blank piece of paper, **write** your name and date and entitle it *External Factors* (or similar words). In general, it is suggested that you first develop your argument with academic research of the societal problem that impacts future employment, and then make it specific with examples from your own life story. You need to tell the Department of Education about the factors that impact your ability to secure employment. It is important to emphasize how this impacts your future earnings. No sample is provided in the Appendix because each case is very specific to the debtor and no generalization is possible.

The process described above documents for the Department of Education the reasons why you can't take on any more work and why your future employment is not going to improve. As such, you will not be able to service your student loans and request they be discharged as an undue hardship.

CHARACTERISTIC C—
Good Faith and Loan Repayment

Debtors are required to demonstrate "good faith" attempts to repay student loans. There is an expectation that any time the debtor's net income exceeded the Federal Poverty Guidelines, payments were made on the student loans. Whenever there were times of financial difficulty, debtors must show that they worked with the lender to resolve the issue instead of letting loans fall into arrears. Additionally, at least 5 or more years should have passed since obtaining the last student loan, otherwise there is a presumption of fraud, which the debtor must overcome.

> **Step 13 • Make copies** of your IRS Income Tax filings for each year since receiving your last student loan. **Fill out** the worksheet *Income and Student Loan Payment* (Appendix D). Instructions are on the worksheet form. This form tracks your income for the years since obtaining your most recent student loans and the status of student loans repayment.

You now have everything needed to write a history of your employment, attempts to find work, family income, and servicing your student loans. The purpose of the narrative is to show that you have been diligent in trying to make income sufficient to service your student loans.

> **Step 14 •** On a blank piece of paper, **write** your name and date and entitle it *Good Faith and Loan Repayment* (or similar words). Here, you

write a history of your employment, family income, and student loan repayment. Be sure to indicate when your family income dropped below the Federal Poverty Guideline, that you received deferments or forbearances whenever you were unable to make payments, and more. You want to show you have been diligent in servicing your student loans and that there is no fraud in seeking their discharge. Review the sample provided in Appendix D entitled *Good Faith and Loan Repayment Statement*.

INCOME CONTINGENT REPAYMENT (ICR) PLAN

Finally, the last problem that must be addressed is the *Income Contingent Repayment (ICR) Plan*. As described at length in Chapter 7, the ICR allows debtors to make loan payments when they can, and sometimes pay nothing at all if his or her income drops below a particular level. The plan lasts for 25 years and any outstanding student loan debt remaining at the end of the plan is discharged. However, and this is a big however, debtors are liable for the income taxes on the discharged amount.

It is often stated by Department of Education attorneys that ICR makes it impossible for debtors to discharge their student loans in bankruptcy or otherwise. They contend that anyone can make "zero dollar" payments, thus negating the undue hardship exception of §523(a)(8).

In many cases, this is true. But, as argued in Chapter 7, for some debtors, the ICR is inappropriate. Perhaps you are one of the debtors who would benefit from arguing that the ICR causes you an undue hardship.

> **Step 15 •** On a blank piece of paper, **write** your name and date and write the title *Income Contingent Repayment* (or similar words). Tell why, in your case, the ICR is not appropriate and causes an undue hardship. See *Income Contingent Repayment* statement in Appendix D for a sample.

Review

If you have completed all 15 steps listed above, you are ready to file a *Compromise* or *Write-Off*. There will be no surprises and you will have all the facts and documents needed to defend your position.

To review, you have taken these actions and completed the following forms and worksheets:

Step 1 — Contacted your student loan lenders and obtained a complete history of their payment and status. Completed the Student Loan History worksheet (Appendix D).

Step 2 — Made a copy of and completed Schedule I—Current Income of Individual Debtor (Appendix C) and business income/expense (if needed).

Step 3 — Wrote a **Current Income and Family Status*** (Appendix D) statement on a blank piece of paper.

Step 4 — Made a copy and completed Schedule J—Current Expenditures of Individual Debtor (Appendix C).

Step 5 — Completed most of the Current Expenditure Status worksheet (Appendix D).

Step 6 — Downloaded a copy of the U.S. Department of Health and Human Services Federal Poverty Guidelines and completed more of the Current Expenditure Status worksheet.

Step 7 — Went to IRS website, obtained Collection Financial Standards and used the data to fill in the Current Expenditure Status worksheet.

Step 8 — Compared your family expenditures against the national norms and completed the Current Expenditure Status worksheet.

Step 9 — Wrote a **Current Expenditures and Minimalized Living*** statement (Appendix D) on a blank piece of paper.

Step 10 — Completed the Work Time Accounting Table worksheet (Appendix D). Wrote a **Work Time Accounting Statement***

(Appendix D) on a blank piece of paper.

Step 11 — Wrote a **Personal Limitations*** statement (Appendix D) on a blank piece of paper.

Step 12 — Wrote an **External Factors*** statement (Appendix D) on a blank piece of paper.

Step 13 — Made copies of your IRS Income Tax forms. Completed the Income and Student Loan Payment worksheet (Appendix D).

Step 14 — Wrote a **Good Faith and Loan Repayment*** statement (Appendix D) on a blank piece of paper.

Step 15 — Wrote an **Income Contingent Repayment*** statement (Appendix D) on a blank piece of paper.

(Each underlined item is either a worksheet from the Appendix, letter you wrote, or document you downloaded. **Each bolded and asterisked items are documents you wrote on a blank piece of paper that will be used in the** *Compromise* **or** *Write-Off.* We suggest that you do not submit or show the attorneys for the Department of Education any of the worksheets you used. You do not want to tip them off that you are using this book.)

The next chapter will give step-by-step guidance on how to negotiate directly with the Department of Education through use of a *Compromise* or *Write-Off* to have your student loans discharged.

CHAPTER 11

Step-By-Step Negotiations for
Compromise or _Write-Off_

This section discusses negotiation strategies to improve your chances at having all, or part, of your student loans discharged.

Chapter 2 discussed the conditions under which the Department of Education may Compromise or Write-Off student loans. The details are summarized here.

Compromise

Under the **Compromise** plan, the Department is allowed to accept less than the total amount due to fully satisfy the conditions of the loan (and end a default status). This policy was specified in a regulation the Director of the U.S. Department of Education, Policy Development Division approved on 12/23/93. (_See_ Appendix B for letter authorizing _Standardized Compromise and Write-Off Procedures_.)

The collections supervisor at a guarantee agency may reduce ("compromise") your loan under the following conditions:

- If you agree to pay the full amount of the loan—principal and interests owed on defaulted loans—then all collection costs, including the standard 25% collection fee may be waived.

- If you agree to pay the remaining principal and interest owed on a defaulted loan, then up to 30% of the principal and interest may be waived.

- If you are in dire financial straits and it looks like you won't be able to service your loans in the future, the agency's director has the authority to waive even more than 30% of the principal and interest of your defaulted loans.

- If you agree to pay off the entire principal of your defaulted loans within 30 days of negotiating the compromise (and paid with a certified check), then all interests charges may be waived.

The agency determines if the Compromise represents the best interest of the _government_. Obviously, this is very subjective and open to the judgment of the agency director. If you can show that you have very limited income and that it will not change in the future, they may accept your request since the alternative is to sue, which is a fairly expensive process for the government.

As a strategy, Compromise works best for old loans where most of the principal has been paid and has been in default for a while. If you can afford to pay the remaining principal in one lump sum, they are most likely to cancel the interest and collection fees.

Write-Off

An even more radical idea is to ask the guarantee agency of the Department of Education to **Write-Off** your loans. This works only if you are in dire financial straits, do not believe you will ever be able to repay your loans, and you don't qualify for other forms of discharge or Compromise. The three conditions most likely to be written-off include:

- The balance on your principal is $100 or less.

- The total balance of your loans does not exceed $1000.

- The balance of your loans is for interest, court fees, collection costs, and costs other than the principal, regardless the total loan amount.

If you can convince the Department of Education that your situation is financially hopeless, it can write-off much larger loans and end collection efforts.

Contacting the Agency

❑ **Step 1:**
Review the conditions for <u>Compromise</u> and <u>Write-Off</u> described above and determine which plan best meets your situation. Write that information here:

I will be seeking a: ❑ Compromise ❑ Write-Off

I will be asking to have \$_____ discharged.

This amount represents:

Principal: \$ _____

Interest: \$ _____

Court Fees: \$ _____

Collection Costs: \$ _____

Other: \$ _____

The loans are currently in default: ❑ Yes ❑ No

Other Conditions: _____

_____

_____

(Note: you should have the specifics about your loans since you were asked to gather that information in the last chapter.)

Now you need to know who to contact at the Department of Education and learn if any forms or guidelines have been developed concerning Compromise or Write-Off.

❑ **Step 2:**
Contact the Department of Education and find out who has the authority to approve a Compromise or Write-Off (we will refer to this person as a Supervisor). Contact the Supervisor and explain

that you have severe financial problems that will make it impossible to repay your student loans. Ask how to file for a Compromise or Write-Off. *We advise you not to talk too long with this person; just find out if they have developed some procedures or forms for these kinds of discharges.* The Supervisor will probably ask if you have spoken with a counselor at the Department of Education about changing your repayment plan, furloughs, the Income Contingent Repayment (ICR) Plan and more. Be courteous, but be firm explaining that none of these options work for you and that you really need to apply for a Compromised or Write-Off.

They may have developed some guidelines for filing such claims. If they have forms or guidelines, ask to have them mailed to you.

Write the Supervisor's contact information here:
Name: _____

Title: _____

Agency: _____

Department: _____

Mailing Address: _____

_____

_____

_____

Telephone: _____

Fax: _____

E-mail: _____

Are there forms or guidelines? ❑ Yes ❑ No

If they are sending you some guidelines, wait and see what they state. More than likely, there are no guidelines or forms. Regardless, if they are sending you forms and/or guidelines, the basic problem you have is to convince the Department of Education that your financial situation is hopeless and that it would cost them more to sue you than what they would recover. This is similar to proving "undue hardship" under the bankruptcy laws and we will proceed as such.

Section 523(a)(8) of the bankruptcy laws require you to show that it would cause an undue hardship to you and your dependants if you were required to repay your student loans. Twenty years of litigation on this issue has resulted in the courts developing a number of tests. Most courts use the Brunner test as discussed in Chapters 4 and 5.

In Chapter 5, a set of guidelines was developed and used to prove undue hardship. In the last chapter, you completed a number of worksheets that helped you develop and compose written responses to prove these guidelines. They are:

- First— you need to show that your current family income does not allow you to make repayments on your student loans. To that end, you composed the letter *Current Income and Family Status*.

- Second— you need to show that your family expenditures are minimized and equal to other similarly situated families. To that end you, composed the letter *Current Expenditures and Minimalized Living*.

- Third— you need to show that there are personal limitations and external factors that impact your ability to find better paying work. To that end, you composed the letters *Personal Limitations* and *External Factors*.

- Fourth— you need to show that you have been diligent in making student loan payments when you were financially able, and received deferments or forbearances whenever you were unable to make payments. To that end, you composed the letter *Good Faith and Loan Repayment*.

We want to blend these 5 documents into one letter and deliver it to the Supervisor. Hopefully, you wrote

all these documents on a computer so you only have to cut and paste the sections into one master document. If you did not, or could not, use a computer; you will have to retype all the letters.

Writing the Agency

❑ **Step 3:**
Write one letter containing all 5 documents—
Current Income and Family Status
Current Expenditures and Minimalized Living
Personal Limitations
External Factors
Good Faith and Loan Repayment
Address the letter to the Supervisor. On the first lines of the letter state that, "repaying my student loans represents an undue hardship because . . . " (now copy each of your letters, one-by-one, in the order above). <u>At the end of the letter, state that you want your entire student loan debt to be discharged.</u> Mail the letter to the Supervisor. Be sure to keep a copy of the master letter for yourself (or if on a computer, save the file). A few days after you mail the letter, call the Supervisor to see that he or she received it.

A word about grammar and wording: If you have a graduate college degree such as Ph.D. or Master's, take time to use proper wording and grammar. If you have a technical degree, no degree or limited education, a high school diploma, or are mentally disabled, do not worry if your letter is not perfect. They expect you to make mistakes. If your letter is too good, they may suspect you had professional help.

Notice that we have purposely left out discussion about the Income Contingent Repayment (ICR) Plan, or your time commitment. The strategy is to see if what you have submitted is sufficient. If not, then you have more to send. This gives a little backup to the negotiation process.

Expect it to take a few weeks for the Supervisor to get back to you. Hopefully, they accept your arguments and discharge your entire loan. *If they discharge your loans, you will be responsible for the income tax on that amount.* Only through a bankruptcy can the discharge be tax-free.

The supervisor most likely will tell a story of some other debtor he or she is currently negotiating who is in much worse financial stress than you and that the Department of Education is not accepting his or her claim of "undue hardship." *This is meant to unnerve you and make you feel that the process is hopeless.* Your situation is unique. Don't give up.

They most likely will not accept your request the first time asked.

Stronger Negotiations

❑ **Step 4:**

If your request is rejected, ask for specific details as to why it was rejected. Now compose a letter back to the Supervisor that addresses the specific reasons for the rejection <u>and</u> include the arguments you developed in the *Income Contingent Repayment* and *Work Time Accounting Statement*. You need to be clear why the ICR is not appropriate for you and why you cannot take on any more work. The ICR is the major sword used by the Department of Education to convince the court that you cannot meet the provisions of the undue hardship tests.

Again, they may or may not accept your arguments and discharge your entire loan. You still have one more negotiation attempt.

<u>Give some thought to a "fair" settlement for your particular situation</u>. Maybe your situation is so dire that complete discharge of the loans is the only solution. However, maybe you could pay a portion of the loans. In the banking industry, bad debts are often settled at 10 cents on the dollar. Ask yourself if you could pay 10% of your loan. The Department of Education will not accept payments less than $50 a month because of bookkeeping expenses. For example, let's say you owe $60,000; maybe you could pay $50 a month for 10 years. That works out to a total of $6,000 repayment saving you $54,000. If you owe a smaller amount, maybe you could pay $50 a month for 5 years, or whatever. Try not to have the loan last more than 10 years. Also, consider the issue of furlough. Obviously, you would like the ability to have a number of furloughs available just in case

something terrible goes wrong and you do not have money for a short time. The problem about including furloughs in your negotiated repayment plan is that your repayment program then begins to look too much like the ICR plan. Congress set the terms for the ICR and the Department of Education does <u>not</u> have the authority to amend them. We suggest that if you seek a reduced loan settlement, ask for furloughs, knowing that you are using them as bargaining chips.

Negotiate strongly. Here is a <u>discharge hierarchy</u> of possible proposals from the greatest discharge to least. Be aware of where your lowest "fair" settlement is:

DISCHARGE HIERARCHY

- The entire loan is discharged.

- Only a portion of the loan is paid right now and the rest is discharged.

- A monthly payment of $50 for so many years with 5 furloughs.

- A monthly payment of $50 for so many years with no furloughs.

- A modified Income Contingent Repayment (ICR) Plan for so many years; the remaining portion of the loan to be discharged. (We've included this idea because, in reality, the Department of Education could conceivably obtain the most money through such a program but they are not allowed to offer such a plan because Congress specified 25-year terms and no opportunity to discharge the remaining portion through a bankruptcy. However, bringing this idea up makes you look fair and not greedy.)

Perhaps you can think of other settlement plans.

If you are seeking to negotiate a new repayment plan (like $50 a month for so many years) it should include wording that you have the right to prepay the loan. This means that if you have a lump sum available to pay on the loan, you could negotiate paying only this sum immediately and the rest is discharged.

Proposing a Settlement

❑ **Step 5:**

If your request is rejected, again ask for the reasons it was rejected. <u>If you seem to be at an impasse, now is the time to consider proposing a new repayment plan or settlement plan for some percentage of your loan (as described above) instead of the entire amount.</u> Compose a letter back to the Supervisor where you propose a "fair" repayment or settlement plan. Mail it to the Supervisor.

<u>If the Department of Education rejects your offer after all these efforts, it may be necessary to file for bankruptcy, in which you also file an adversary proceeding.</u> See Chapter 8 and 9 for details for this process. Decide if it is worth it to you to go through the challenge of a bankruptcy while attempting to have your student loans discharged.

We wish you the best.

Just Who Does the Negotiations at DOE?

Since the release of the first edition of this book, many people have asked how realistic is the Compromise or Write-Off strategy. There are many debtors who only have large student loan burdens that are causing hardship. They don't want to file a bankruptcy since the rest of their financial situation is livable. So, let's look at who it is that you will be negotiating with at the Department of Education.

Yes, the DOE is a large bureaucratic institution, but there are real people that you must negotiate with. How are these people rated on job performance? Will forgiving your loan look bad on their job performance? Like with a bank or other financial institution, there are loan managers who handle a caseload of loans. Because few workers stay on the exact same job for more than a few short years, loan managers are not evaluated on how much money they bring in but on how many loans are classified as "current," "late," "troubled," or in "default." The goal of any loan manager is to have all loans "current." In the case of student loans that means payments are up to date or the loans are in forbearance or deferment. Obviously DOE employees don't care how much money is actually coming in, just that the loans are current. Thus, you can see their motivation for severe hardship cases to shift the debtor to the Income Contingency Repayment or similar plan. It doesn't matter that they may not get any money for 25 years, but that the loan is technically "current." Although DOE claims a default rate of a few percentage points, other research indicates as much as two-thirds of all education loan will ultimately default. This is something DOE and Congress does not want to confront.

From this perspective, when negotiating with DOE think about how you can make your loan "current" or that you bring up issues so threatening to their house of cards that they would be hesitant to go to court. For example, the author of this book settled for paying $50 a month for ten years for a total of $6,000 while discharging $54,000 through the bankruptcy. Since the monthly payments are on time, the loan is considered "current" which makes the loan officer look good.

If your situation is dire but you are not in the position to file a bankruptcy at this time, maybe the ICR is an acceptable option. This can always be change due to future circumstances. Perhaps your financial situation deteriorates, then file for bankruptcy. If you become disabled, then file for a disability discharge. Of course, if you live to a ripe old age, the loans should be able to be discharged with a disability discharge. The worst thing to do is become delinquent with the loans since, if you need to file for bankruptcy, this will make you look bad and negatively impact your success with the adversary proceeding.

*

The author of this book would like to hear the results of your adversary proceeding or Compromise or Write-Off. <u>Although the author cannot provide legal advice</u>, he would like to hear how your case developed and was resolved. Also, any comments, corrections, or insight concerning the content of this book would be appreciated. Contact information is given in "About the Author."

APPENDIX

APPENDIX A — Department of Education Repayment Plans and Discharge Optons

APPENDIX B — Laws and Legal Guidelines

APPENDIX C — Chapter 7 Bankruptcy Forms

APPENDIX D — Worksheets

APPENDIX E — Forms

APPENDIX F — Academic Articles

APPENDIX G — Resources

APPENDIX A

Department of Education Repayment Plans and Discharge Options

Postponing Repayments

This discussion is found at:
www.ed.gov/offices/OSFAP/DirectLoan/avoid.html

Repayment of student loans may be delayed by obtaining either a *deferment* or *forbearance*, or the use of loan *consolidation*.

Deferment

[U.S. Department of Education webpage located at:
www.studentaid.ed.gov/students/publications/repaying_loans/2003_2004/english/repayment-options-deferment.htm]

Deferment is a postponement of repayment under various, specific circumstances:
- For Federal Perkins Loans, subsidized FFEL Stafford Loans, and subsidized Direct Stafford Loans, you don't have to pay principal or interest during deferment.
- For unsubsidized FFEL Stafford Loans, unsubsidized Direct Stafford Loans, FFEL PLUS Loans, and Direct PLUS Loans, you can postpone paying principal, but you (or your parents, for PLUS Loans) are responsible for the interest. You can pay the interest during the deferment period, or the loan holder can capitalize the interest when the deferment ends. Remember that capitalization will increase the loan balance.

The deferments listed apply to all Federal Perkins Loan borrowers and to Direct Loan borrowers and FFEL borrowers who received their first loan on or after July 1, 1993. Other deferments might also be available if you have an outstanding balance on a federal student loan made before July 1, 1993. For more information, FFEL Stafford Loan borrowers should contact their lenders or agencies. Direct Stafford Loan borrowers can contact the Direct Loan Servicing Center at:

The Direct Loan Servicing Center
Borrower Services: 1-800-848-0979 or 1-315-738-6634 Fax: 1-800-848-0984 TTY: 1-800-848-0983 http://www.dl.ed.gov

Schools must automatically defer your Federal Perkins Loans during the time you perform any service that qualifies you for loan cancellation (see service cancellations).

TABLE—LOAN DEFERMENT SUMMARY

Deferment Condition	Direct Loans [1,2]	FFELs [1,3]	Perkins Loans
At least half time study at a postsecondary school	YES	YES	YES
Study in an approved graduate fellowship program or in an approved rehabilitation training program for the disabled	YES	YES	YES
Unable to find full-time employment	Up to 3 years	Up to 3 years	Up to 3 years
Economic hardship	Up to 3 years [4]	Up to 3 years [4]	Up to 3 years [4]
Engages in service listed under discharge/cancellation conditions	NO	NO	YES [5]

- For PLUS Loans and unsubsidized student loans, only principal is deferred. Interest continues to accrue.
- Direct Loan borrowers who have outstanding balances on FFEL Loans disbursed prior to July 1993, might be eligible for additional deferments, provided the outstanding balance on the FFEL existed when the borrower received his or her first Direct Loan.
- Applies to loans first disbursed on or after July 1, 1993, to borrowers who have no outstanding FFELs or Federal Supplemental Loans for Students (Federal SLS Program) on the date they signed their promissory note. (Note that the Federal SLS Program was repealed beginning with the 1994-1995 award year.)
- Many Peace Corps volunteers will qualify for a deferment based on economic hardship.
- More information on teaching service deferments can be found on the Internet at http://www.studentaid.ed.gov. At the site, Click on "Repaying," then click on "Cancellation and Deferment Options for Teachers."

In most cases, you aren't just granted a deferment automatically; you must formally request one through the procedures your loan holder has established. Often, you need to complete a deferment form. You'll need to provide documentation showing how you qualify for the deferment you're applying for. Make sure all your paperwork is in order and make sure the loan holder receives it.

Here's one of the most important things to remember: You must continue to make payments on the loan until you've been notified the deferment has been approved. Sometimes borrowers apply for deferment and don't hear anything back and assume things are fine. Or, as soon as they send a deferment form and their paperwork, they think they can immediately stop payment. Even if the paperwork is received without any problem, it takes a while to process. So, don't skip the next payment when it's due. First, check with the loan holder. If your deferment has not been processed, make your payment! You might go into default otherwise. <u>You can't get any deferment on a defaulted loan.</u>

Forbearance

[This discussion is available at the U.S. Department of Education webpage: www.studentaid.ed.gov/students/publications/repaying_loans/2003_2004/english/repayment-options-forbearance.htm]

If you find you can't meet your repayment schedule but you're not eligible for a deferment, you might be granted forbearance for a limited and specified period. During forbearance, your payments are temporarily postponed or reduced. Unlike deferment, whether your loans are subsidized or unsubsidized, you'll be charged interest during forbearance. If you don't pay the interest as it accrues, it will be capitalized.

As is true with deferment, you aren't just granted forbearance automatically; you must formally request one from your loan holder. You might have to provide documentation to support your request. You might be granted forbearance if you are:
- unable to pay due to poor health or other unforeseen personal problems.
- serving in a medical or dental internship or residency serving in a position under the National Community Service Trust Act of 1993 (forbearance can be granted for this reason for a Direct or FFEL Stafford Loan, but not for a PLUS Loan).
- obligated to make payments on certain federal student loans that are equal to or greater than 20 percent of your monthly gross income.

This is not a complete list of conditions that might qualify you for forbearance. For more information, contact your loan holder.

Unlike deferment, which you're entitled to receive, the loan holder does <u>not</u> have to grant forbearance except in certain mandatory circumstances (check with your loan holder for details). In most cases, however, lenders are willing to work with you if you show you're willing, but temporarily unable, to repay your debt.

Consolidation

Consolidation allows you to simplify the repayment process by combining several types of federal education loans into one loan, so you make just one payment a month. Also, that monthly payment might be lower than what you're currently paying. It also restarts the clock for all deferments and forbearances— thus postponing when you must begin repaying your student loans.

[This discussion is located at U.S. Department of Education webpage: www.studentaid.ed.gov/students/publications/repaying_loans/2003_2004/english/repayment-options-consolidation.htm]

You can get a Direct Consolidation Loan, available from ED, or a Federal (FFEL) Consolidation Loan from participating FFEL lenders. Under both programs, the loan holder pays off the existing loans and makes one Consolidation Loan to replace them. If you have subsidized and unsubsidized loans, they'll be grouped accordingly when you consolidate so you won't lose your interest subsidy on the subsidized loans.

There are three categories of Direct Consolidation Loans: Direct Subsidized Consolidation Loans, Direct Unsubsidized Consolidation Loans, and Direct PLUS Consolidation Loans. If you have loans from more than one category, they can be combined into one Direct Consolidation Loan, and make only one monthly payment.

Under the FFEL Program, you can receive a Subsidized and/or an Unsubsidized FFEL Consolidation Loan, depending on the types of loans you're consolidating. (FFEL PLUS Consolidation Loans are included under the Unsubsidized FFEL Consolidation Loan category.)

You can also consolidate Federal Perkins Loans and other federal education loans. To get a complete list of the kinds of federal student loans that can be consolidated:
- contact the Direct Loan Origination Center's Consolidation Department if you're applying for a Direct Consolidation Loan. You can reach them by calling 1-800-557-7392. TTY users can call 1-800-557-7395. Or visit http://www.loanconsolidation.ed.gov
- contact a participating FFEL lender if you're applying for a FFEL Consolidation Loan.

Under FFEL consolidation, if the same holder holds all the loans you want to consolidate, you must obtain your consolidation loan from that holder.

To get a Direct Consolidation Loan, you must consolidate at least one Direct Loan or FFEL. If you have a FFEL, you must first contact a FFEL lender that makes FFEL Consolidation Loans to ask about obtaining a FFEL Consolidation Loan. If you can't get such a loan, or you can't get one with income-sensitive repayment terms acceptable to you and you're eligible for the Direct Loan Income Contingent Repayment Plan, your best bet is to apply for a Direct Consolidation Loan.

Even if you're in default, you might be eligible for a Consolidation Loan if certain conditions are met. Talk to your loan holder(s).

What is the Interest Rate on a Consolidation Loan?

As of February 1, 1999, both FFEL and Direct Consolidation Loans had the same interest rate, which is a fixed rate set according to a formula established by law. The rate is the weighted average rate of the current rates charged on the loans being consolidated, rounded up to the nearest one-eighth of a percent. The rate you'll pay won't be more than one-eighth of a percent more than the effective rate on your individual loans. The rate is fixed for the life of the Consolidation Loan.

Before February 1, 1999, Consolidation Loans had variable interest rates. For information on interest rates on these loans, contact the Direct Loan Origination Center's Consolidation Department by calling 1-800-557- 7392, if you have a Direct Consolidation Loan, or check with your lender if you have a FFEL Consolidation Loan. If you have a Stafford Loan made on or after July 1, 1995, you can reduce your consolidation rate by up to half a percentage point or more if you are able to consolidate before the end of the grace period.

What is the Repayment Period for Consolidation Loans?

The repayment period for consolidation loans ranges from 10 to 30 years, depending on the amount of your debt and the repayment option you choose.

What are my Repayment Options?

All the FFEL Stafford Loan repayment plans (see FFEL Plans) are available to FFEL Consolidation Loan borrowers. For Direct Consolidation Loan borrowers, the Direct Loan repayment plans generally are available. An exception is that Direct PLUS Consolidation Loans, which are not eligible to be repaid under the Income Contingent Repayment Plan, or might not be eligible for some discharge/cancellation benefits.

Deciding for Consolidation

Although consolidation can simplify loan repayment and might lower your monthly payment, you should carefully consider whether it is best to consolidate all your loans. For example, you might lose some discharge (cancellation) benefits if you include a Federal Perkins Loan either of the loan consolidation choices. Consolidating only your FFELs or only your Direct Loans would not jeopardize options on your Federal Perkins Loan(s). Also, you wouldn't want to lose any borrower benefits offered under your existing nonconsolidated loans, such as interest rate discounts or principal rebates, which can significantly reduce the cost of repaying your loans.

You can have a longer period of time to repay your consolidation loan than for the individual student loans you're currently repaying, but this means you'll also pay more interest over time. In fact, consolidation can double total interest expense. If you don't need monthly payment relief, you should compare the cost of repaying your unconsolidated loans against the cost of repaying a consolidation loan. To help you figure the costs, contact your lender or loan servicer.

Once made, consolidation loans can't be unmade because the loans that were consolidated have been paid off and no longer exist. So, take the time to study your consolidation options before you apply. For more details on loan consolidation, contact your loan holder or servicer.

Repayment Plans

This discussion is found at:
www.ed.gov/offices/OSFAP/DirectLoan/pubs/repabook/rep2.html

When repaying Federal Direct Stafford/Ford Loans (Direct Subsidized Loans) and Federal Direct Unsubsidized Stafford /Ford Loans (Direct Unsubsidized Loans), student borrowers may choose from four repayment plans:

- Standard Repayment Plan
- Extended Repayment Plan
- Graduated Repayment Plan
- Income Contingent Repayment (ICR) Plan

Parent borrowers may repay their Federal Direct PLUS Loans (Direct PLUS Loans) through the Standard, Extended, and Graduated Repayment Plans. The Income Contingent Repayment Plan is not available to Direct PLUS Loan borrowers.

The repayment plan you choose will cover all of your Direct Loans. An exception is made for parent borrowers who are repaying Direct PLUS Loans received for their children and student loans they received for themselves. In this circumstance, a borrower may use two repayment plans -- one for all of their parent loans and one for all of their student loans. Shortly before your loan repayment period begins, the Servicing Center will send you information about the various repayment plans including the amount you would pay under each plan. You are to select one. If you do not select a plan, your loans will automatically be placed in the Standard Repayment Plan. Generally, your monthly payment will be adjusted to account for changes in the annual interest rate. Your selection of a repayment plan does not affect your interest rate. Note that the length of your repayment period does not include periods of deferment for forbearance (postponements of repayments).

Standard Repayment Plan

With the Standard Plan, the payment is a fixed amount each month until your loans are paid in full. Monthly payments will be at least $50, and you'll have up to 10 years to repay your loans. The Standard Plan is good for you if you can handle higher monthly payments because you'll repay the loans more quickly. The monthly payment under the Standard Plan may be higher than it would be under the other plans because your loans will be repaid in the shortest time. For the same reason--the 10-year limit on repayment--you may pay the least interest.

Example A: Let's say you owe $15,000 in Direct Subsidized Loans when your repayment period begins, and your loans will be repaid at an 8.25 percent interest rate. Under the Standard Plan, you'll pay approximately $184 a month for 10 years totaling about $22,078 ($15,000 in principal and $7,078 in interest).

EXAMPLE A, STANDARD REPAYMENT OPTION DIRECT SUBSIDIZED LOANS		
This example shows Direct Subsidized Loans repaid at 8.25 percent interest under the Standard Repayment Plan for 10 years (120 payments).		
Loan Amount	Beginning Monthly Payment	Total Amount Repaid
$15,000	$184	$22,078*
*$15,000 in principal and $7,078 in interest		

Example B: You borrowed $15,000 in Direct Unsubsidized Loans to attend school ($2,000 your first year, $3,000 your second year, and $5,000 in each of your third and fourth years), and you chose to repay your loans under the Standard Repayment Plan. Because you chose not to pay the interest on your loans as it accumulated, the interest was capitalized when your repayment period began. At an interest rate of 8.25 percent, the amount of capitalized interest added to the original balance was $2,641, making the total principle balance of your loans $17,641. Your monthly payments will be calculated using this amount. At 8.25 percent interest, the monthly payments will be about $216 a month under the

Standard Plan. You will repay a total of approximately $25,964 ($17,641 in original principal and capitalized interest and $8,323 in additional interest).

EXAMPLE B, STANDARD REPAYMENT OPTION DIRECT UNSUBSIDIZED LOANS					
This example shows Direct Unsubsidized Loans (with capitalized interest) repaid at 8.25 percent under the Standard Repayment Plan.					
Loan Amount	Capitalized Interest	Principal to Be repaid	Monthly Payments	Number of Payments	Total Repayment
$15,000	$2,641	$17,641	$216	120	$25,964**
*Interest was capitalized once, when the borrower entered repayment					
**$17,641 in principal and capitalized interest and $8,323 in additional interest					

Extended Repayment Plan

Under the Extended Plan, minimum monthly payments are at least $50, but you can take from 12 to 30 years to repay the loans. The length of the repayment period will depend on the total amount owed when the loans go into repayment (see table below). This is a good plan if you will need to make smaller monthly payments. Because the repayment period will generally be at least 12 years, your monthly payments will be less than with the Standard Plan. However, you may pay more in interest because you're taking longer to repay the loans. Remember, the longer your loans are in repayment, the more interest you will pay.

Example C: With $15,000 in Direct Subsidized Loans, an 8.25 percent interest rate, and a repayment period of 15 years, payments are about $146 a month. By the end of the 15 years, you will have paid a total of about $26,196 ($15,000 in principal and $11,193 in interest).

EXAMPLE C, EXTENDED REPAYMENT PLAN DIRECT SUBSIDIZED LOANS		
This example shows Direct Subsidized Loans at 8.25 percent interest under the Extended Repayment Plan for 15 years (180 payments).		
Loan Amount	Beginning Monthly Payment	Total Amount Repaid
$15,000	$146	$26,196*
*$15,000 in principal and $11,193 in interest		

Graduated Repayment Plan

With this plan, payments start out low, and then increase about every two years. The length of the repayment period will depend on the total amount owed when the loans go into repayment (see the table below). If you expect your income to increase steadily over time, this plan may be right for you. Your initial monthly payments will be equal to either the interest that accumulates on your loans, or half of the payment you would make each month using the Standard Plan, whichever is greater. However, the monthly payments will never increase to more than 1.5 times what you would pay with the Standard Plan.

TABLE—GRADUATED/EXTENDED REPAYMENT SCHEDULE

Amount of Debt	Repayment Period May Not Exceed
Less than $10,000	12 Years
$10,000-$19,999	15 Years
$20,000-$39,999	20 Years
$40,000-$59,999	25 Years
$60,000 or more	30 Years

Example D: Let's say that you owe $15,000 in Direct Subsidized Loans when your loans enter repayment and that the interest rate on your loans is 8.25 percent. Under the Graduated Plan, the repayment period may be as long as 15 years, with beginning payments of about $103 each month. By the last year of your repayment period is reached, your monthly payments will have increased to about $244. In this example, you will repay a total of about $28,762 ($15,000 in principal and $13,762 in interest).

EXAMPLE D, GRADUATED REPAYMENT PLAN DIRECT UNSUBSIDIZED LOANS			
This example shows Direct Unsubsidized Loans repaid at 8.25 percent interest under the Graduated Repayment Plan for 15 years (180 payments).			
Loan Amount	Beginning Monthly Payment	Ending Monthly Payment	Total Amount Repaid
$15,000	$103	$244	$28,762*
*$15,000 in principal and $13,762 in interest			

Income Contingent Repayment (ICR) Plan

This plan gives you the flexibility to meet your Direct Loan obligations without causing undue financial hardship. Each year, your monthly payments will be calculated on the basis of your Adjusted Gross Income (AGI), family size, and the total amount of your direct loans. To participate in the ICR plan, you must sign a form that permits the Internal Revenue Service to provide information about your income to the U.S. Department of Education. This information will be used to recalculate your monthly payment, adjusted annually based on the updated information.

If your payments are not large enough to cover the interest that has accumulated on your loans, the unpaid interest will be capitalized once each year. However, capitalization will not exceed 10 percent of the original amount initially owed when you entered repayment. Interest will continue to accumulate but will no longer be capitalized. The maximum repayment period is 25 years. If you make payments under the Standard Plan or the 12-year extended plan and then switch to the ICR plan, those periods are counted toward your 25-year repayment period. Time spent in other plans or in deferment or forbearance does not count toward the maximum 25 years. If you haven't fully repaid your loans after 25 years under this plan, the unpaid portion will be discharged. You will, however, have to pay income taxes on the amount that is discharged.

The ICR Formula

You will pay an amount based on the adjusted gross income (AGI) reported on your federal income tax returns, or, if you submit alternative documentation of income, you will pay an amount based on that current income. If you are married, the amount paid will be based on your income and your spouse's income. Under the ICR plan, you will pay the lesser of:
- the amount you would pay if you repaid your loan in 12 years multiplied by an income percentage factor that varies with your annual income.
- 20 percent of your discretionary income, which is your AGI minus the poverty level for your family size, divided by 12.

Calculating your monthly payment under the ICR plan involves the following series of steps.

Step 1: Determine monthly payments based on what you would pay over 12 years using equal monthly installments. To do this, multiply the principal balance by the constant multiplier for the interest rate on your loan. See Chart D below in *Constant Multiplier and Other Charts* section. If the exact interest rate is not listed, choose the next highest rate for estimation purposes.

Step 2: Multiply the result by the income percentage factor that corresponds to your income. If you are married, choose the factor that corresponds to your and your spouse's combined income. See Chart E below in *Constant Multiplier and Other Charts* section for Income Percentage Factors. If your income is not listed, choose the income percentage factor that corresponds to the next highest income for estimation purposes, or interpolate to determine the correct income percentage factor. (See this worksheet to follow the steps necessary to interpolate.)

Step 3: Next, calculate your discretionary income by subtracting the poverty level for your family size from your adjusted gross income. (See the Poverty Guidelines chart below). Then use the following equation to figure your monthly payment as a portion of your discretionary income: Monthly discretionary income payment = (Discretionary income x .20) / 12.

Step 4: Compare the results of steps 2 and 3. Your payment will be the lesser of these results.

Example E: You are a single borrower with a family size of one, and your prior year AGI was $15,000. You owe $15,000 in Direct Subsidized Loans when your repayment period begins, and the interest rate on your loans is 8.25 percent. Your beginning payment would be about $104 a month. This amount is less than 20 percent of your monthly discretionary income (which would be $116). In this example, you would repay your loans in about 25 years, and you would repay a total of $35,096 ($8,991 in principal and $26,105 in interest). Note that in this example, you would not repay the total principle amount. After 25 years, the remaining balance on the loan would be discharged.

EXAMPLE E, ICR DIRECT UNSUBSIDIZED LOANS				
This example shows Direct Unsubsidized Loans (with capitalized interest) repaid at 8.25 percent under the Income Contingent Repayment (ICR) Plan.				
Loan Amount	Adjusted Gross Income	Beginning Monthly Payment	Number of Years in Repayment	Total Repayment
$15,000	$15,000	$104*	25	$35,096**

*Calculated as follows:

- Step 1: Multiply the principal balance by the constant multiplier for 8.25% interest (.0109621). (For constant multipliers, see Chart D) 0.0109621 x 15,000 = 164.4315
- Step 2: Multiply the result by the income percentage factor that corresponds to the borrower's income. (For income percentage factors, see Chart E). 63.85% (0.8887) x 164.4315 = $104
- Step 3: Determine 20 percent of discretionary income. (See the poverty guidelines) *** [$15,000 - $8,050] x 0.20 / 12 = $116
- Step 4: Payment is the amount determined in step 2 because it is less than 20 percent of discretionary income.

**$8,991 in principal and $26,105 in interest   ***Poverty guideline for a family size of one

Example F: You are a borrower with a family size of one, and your prior year AGI was $30,000. You owe $15,000 in direct subsidized loans when your repayment period begins, and the interest rate on your loans is 8.25 percent. Your beginning monthly payment would be $146. This amount is less than 20 percent of your monthly discretionary income (which would be $366). In this example, you would repay your loans in about 14 years and would repay a total of about $25,034 ($15,000 in principal and $10,034 in interest).

EXAMPLE F, ICR DIRECT SUBSIDIZED LOANS				
This example shows a borrower with a family size of one and a $30,000 AGI repaying $15,000 in direct subsidized loans at 8.25 percent interest under the **ICR Plan**.				
Loan Amount	Adjusted Gross Income	Beginning Monthly Payment	Number of Years in Repayment	Total Repayment
$15,000	$30,000	$146*	14	$25,034**

*Calculated as follows:

- Step 1: Multiply the principal balance by the constant multiplier for 8.25% interest (.0109621). (For constant multipliers, see Chart D below). 0.0109621 x 15,000 = 164.4315
- Step 2: Multiply the result by the income percentage factor that corresponds to the borrower's income. (For income percentage factors, see Chart E below). 88.77% (0.9089) x 164.4315 = $146
- Step 3: Determine 20 percent of discretionary income. (See the Poverty Guidelines below)*** [$30,000 - $8,050] x 0.20 / 12 = $366
- Step 4: Payment is the amount determined in step 2 because it is less than 20 percent of discretionary income.

**$15,000 in principal and $10,034 in interest   ***Poverty guideline for a family size of one

Constant Multiplier and Other Charts

This discussion is found at:
www.ed.gov/offices/OSFAP/DirectLoan/pubs/repabook/rep8.html

The *constant multiplier* is a factor that allows you to estimate your monthly payment under each direct loan repayment plan. Because the constant multiplier is calculated on the basis of an annual interest rate, it will change as the interest rate on your loan changes.

Instructions for using the constant multiplier charts:

1. Determine the current interest rate on your direct loan. (If your loan has a lower interest rate during in-school, grace, and deferment periods than during repayment, *make sure you are using the rate that applies during periods in which you are required to make payments*.) If you do not know the interest rate, you can obtain this information by calling your servicing center.
2. Select the repayment plan for which you want to calculate your estimated monthly payment.
3. On the chart for that repayment plan (beginning below), find your interest rate. If your exact interest rate is not listed, choose the next highest rate. (For example, if the current rate were 7.62 percent, you would select 7.75 percent.) You'll find your constant multiplier in the cell below your interest rate.
4. If you are calculating an estimated monthly payment for the extended repayment plan, first find the repayment period on your loan. Then in the chart below you will find your constant multiplier in the cell where the interest rate column and repayment period row cross.

CHART A: STANDARD REPAYMENT PLAN, CONSTANT MULTIPLIER
This chart is accessed at: www.ed.gov/offices/OSFAP/DirectLoan/pubs/repabook/rep8.html

Interest Rate	7.00%	7.25%	7.46%	7.50%	7.75%	8.00%
Constant Multiplier	.0116108	.0117401	.0118493	.0118702	.0120011	.0121328
Interest Rate	8.25%	8.38%	8.50%	8.75%	9.00%	
Constant Multiplier	.0122653	.0123345	.0123986	.0125327	.0126676	

CHART B: EXTENDED REPAYMENT PLAN, CONSTANT MULTIPLIER
This chart is accessed at: www.ed.gov/offices/OSFAP/DirectLoan/pubs/repabook/rep8.html

Length of Repayment Period (in years)	Interest Rate					
	7.0%	7.25%	7.46%	7.50%	7.75%	8.00%
12	.0102838	.0104176	.0105306	.0105523	.0106879	.0108245
15	.0089883	.0091286	.0092474	.0092701	.0094128	.0095565
20	.0077530	.0079038	.0080315	.0080559	.0082095	.0083644
25	.0070678	.0072281	.0073639	.0073899	.0075533	.0077182
30	.0066530	.0068218	.0069348	.0069921	.0071641	.0073376
	8.25%	8.38%	8.50%	8.75%	9.00%	
12	.0109621	.0110340	.0111006	.0112400	.0113803	
15	.0097014	.0097772	.0098474	.0099945	.0101427	
20	.0085207	.0086024	.0086782	.0088371	.0089973	
25	.0078845	.0079716	.0080523	0082214	.0083920	
30	.0075127	.0076043	.0076891	.0078670	.0080462	

CHART C: GRADUATED REPAYMENT PLAN, CONSTANT MULTIPLIER						
This chart is accessed at: www.ed.gov/offices/OSFAP/DirectLoan/pubs/repabook/rep8.html						
Interest Rate	7.00%	7.25%	7.46%	7.50%	7.75%	8.00%
Constant Multiplier	.005833	.006042	.006217	.006250	.006458	.006667
Interest Rate	8.25%	8.38%	8.50%	8.75%	9.00%	
Constant Multiplier	.006875	.006983	.007083	.007292	.007500	

CHART D: INCOME CONTINGENT REPAYMENT PLAN, CONSTANT MULTIPLIER						
This chart is accessed at: www.ed.gov/offices/OSFAP/DirectLoan/pubs/repabook/rep8.html						
Interest Rate	7.00%	7.25%	7.46%	7.5%	7.75%	8.00%
Constant Multiplier	.0102838	.0104176	.0105306	.0105523	.0106879	.0108245
Interest Rate	8.25%	8.38%	8.50%	8.75%	9.00%	
Constant Multiplier	.0109621	.0110340	.0111006	.0112400	.0113803	

Charts E and F are used in calculating your payment amount under the Income Contingent Repayment Plan.

CHART E: INCOME PERCENTAGE FACTORS (BASED ON ANNUAL INCOME)			
This chart is accessed at: www.ed.gov/offices/OSFAP/DirectLoan/pubs/repabook/charte.html			
SINGLE		MARRIED AND HEAD OF HOUSEHOLD	
Income	% Factor	Income	% Factor
7,669	55.00%	7,669	50.52%
8,050	55.37%	10,850	54.94%
10,552	57.79%	12,101	56.68%
13,578	60.57%	14,422	59.56%
15,000	63.17%	15,000	60.63%
16,673	66.23%	18,853	67.79%
19,629	71.89%	20,000	69.68%
20,000	72.73%	23,356	75.22%
23,356	80.33%	29,337	87.61%
25,000	82.65%	30,000	88.71%
29,337	88.77%	36,793	100.00%
30,000	89.77%	40,000	100.00%
36,793	100.00%	44,251	100.00%
40,000	100.00%	50,000	104.83%
44,251	100.00%	55,438	109.40%
50,000	107.59%	60,000	113.22%
53,185	111.80%	70,000	121.59%
60,000	117.15%	74,080	125.00%
68,101	123.50%	80,000	128.54%
70,000	124.69%	90,000	134.52%
80,000	130.93%	100,180	140.60%
90,000	137.17%	120,000	145.27%
96,452	141.20%	140,106	150.00%
100,000	143.41%	150,000	155.57%
110,592	150.00%	200,000	183.71%
150,000	172.81%	228,943	200.00%
196,984	200.00%		

Poverty Guidelines

This chart is accessed at: www.ed.gov/offices/OSFAP/DirectLoan/pubs/repabook/chartf.html

To use the Poverty Guidelines chart:
- First— determine your family size, which is the number of the people whom you support. Include your children if they get more than half their support from you. Include other people only if they live with you, get more than half their support from you, and will continue to get that support from you. Support includes money, gifts, loans, housing, food, clothes, car, medical and dental care, payment of college costs, and so on.
- Second— find the column that represents your place of residence. Read down to your family size. This is the poverty guideline for you.

CHART—POVERTY GUIDELINES, DEPARTMENT OF EDUCATION 2004

Family size	All States and the District of Columbia (except Alaska, Hawaii)	Alaska	Hawaii
1	$8,050	$10,070	$9,260
2	10,850	13,570	12,480
3	13,650	17,070	15,700
4	16,450	20,570	18,920
5	19,250	24,070	22,140
6	22,050	27,570	25,360
7	24,850	31,070	28,580
8	27,650	34,570	31,800
For each person above 8 add:	2,800	3,500	3,220

[U.S. Department of Education webpage located at:
www.studentaid.ed.gov/students/publications/repaying_loans/2003_2004/english/loan-discharge-cancellation.htm]

In some cases, federal student loans can be discharged (canceled). A discharge releases you from all obligations to repay the loan. Lists of cancellation provisions for FFEL/Direct Loans and Federal Perkins Loans are given on this page and the next.

Your loan can't be merely discharged because you didn't complete the program of study at the school (unless you couldn't complete the program for a valid reason—see introduction), you didn't like the school or the program of study, or you didn't get a job after completing the program of study.

For more information about discharge, contact the Direct Loan Servicing Center by calling 1-800-848-0979 if you have a Direct Loan. If you have a FFEL, contact the lender or agency that holds your loan. If you have a Federal Perkins Loan, contact the school that made you the loan.

Direct Loan and FFEL Discharge

TABLE—DIRECT LOAN AND FFEL DISCHARGE/CANCELLATION SUMMARY		
Cancellation Conditions	**Amount Forgiven**	**Notes**
Borrower's total and permanent disability[1] or death	100%	For a PLUS Loan, includes death but not disability of the student for whom the parents borrowed.
Full-time teacher for five consecutive years in a designated elementary or secondary school serving students from low-income families	Up to $5,000 of the aggregate loan amount that is outstanding after completion of the fifth year of teaching. A borrower might qualify for loan forgiveness under the Direct Consolidation and the FFEL Consolidation Loan programs. If so, only the portion of the consolidation loan used to repay Direct Stafford Loans or FFEL Stafford Loans qualifies.	For Direct and FFEL Stafford Loans received on or after October 1, 1998, by a borrower with no outstanding loan balance as of that date. At least one of the five consecutive years of teaching must occur after the 1997-98 academic year. (To find out whether your school is considered a low-income school, visit http://www.studentaid.ed.gov. Click on "Repaying," then click on "Cancellation and Deferment Options for Teachers." Or, call 1-800-4-FED-AID.)
Bankruptcy (in rare cases)	100%	Cancellation is possible only if the bankruptcy court rules that repayment would cause undue hardship.
Closed school (before student could complete program of study) or false loan certification	100%	For loans received on or after January 1, 1986.
School does not make required return of loan funds to the lender	Up to the amount that the school was required to return.	For loans received on or after January 1, 1986.

1. Beginning July 1, 2002, a borrower who is determined to be totally and permanently disabled will have his or her loan placed in a conditional discharge period for three years from the date the borrower became totally and permanently disabled. During this conditional period, the borrower doesn't have to pay principal or interest. If the borrower continues

to meet the total-and-permanent disability requirements during, and at the end of, the three-year conditional period, the borrower's obligation to repay the loan is canceled. If the borrower doesn't continue to meet the cancellation requirements, the borrower must resume payment. Total and permanent disability is defined as the inability to work and earn money because of an injury or illness that is expected to continue indefinitely, or to result in death. More information on this discharge can be found in the promissory note and by contacting the loan holder.

Perkins Discharge

Table—Perkins Discharge/Cancellation Summary [1]		
Cancellation Conditions	**Amount Forgiven**	**Notes**
Borrower's total and permanent disability2 or death	100%	Service qualifies for deferment also.
Full-time teacher in a designated elementary or secondary school serving students from low-income families	Up to 100%	Service qualifies for deferment also.
Full-time special education teacher (includes teaching children with disabilities in a public or other nonprofit elementary or secondary school)	Up to 100%	Service qualifies for deferment also.
Full-time qualified professional provider of early intervention services for the disabled	Up to 100%	Service qualifies for deferment also.
Full-time teacher of math, science, foreign languages, bilingual education, or other fields designated as teacher shortage areas	Up to 100%	Service qualifies for deferment also.
Full-time employee of a public or nonprofit child- or family-services agency providing services to high-risk children and their families from low-income communities	Up to 100%	Service qualifies for deferment also.
Full-time nurse or medical technician	Up to 100%	Service qualifies for deferment also.
Full-time law enforcement or corrections officer	Up to 100%	Service qualifies for deferment also.
Full-time staff member in the education component of a Head Start Program	Up to 100%	Service qualifies for deferment also.
Vista or Peace Corps volunteer	Up to 70%	Service qualifies for deferment also.
Service in the U.S. Armed Forces	Up to 50% in areas of hostilities or imminent danger.	Service qualifies for deferment also.
Bankruptcy (in rare cases)	Up to 100%	Cancellation is possible only if the bankruptcy court rules that repayment would cause undue hardship.
Closed school (before student could complete program of study	100%	For loans received on or after January 1, 1986.

Notes:
1. As of October 7, 1998, all Perkins Loan borrowers are eligible for all cancellation benefits regardless of when the loan was made or the terms of the borrower's promissory note. However, this benefit is not retroactive to services performed before that date.
2. Beginning July 1, 2002, a borrower who is determined to be totally and permanently disabled will have his or her loan placed in a conditional discharge period for three years from the date the borrower became totally and permanently disabled. During this conditional period, the borrower doesn't have to pay principal or interest. If the borrower continues

to meet the total-and-permanent disability requirements during, and at the end of, the three-year conditional period, the borrower's obligation to repay the loan is canceled. If the borrower doesn't continue to meet the cancellation requirements, the borrower must resume payment. Total and permanent disability is defined as the inability to work and earn money because of an injury or illness that is expected to continue indefinitely, or to result in death. For more information on qualifying for this discharge, review your promissory note and contact your loan holder.

More information on teaching service cancellation/deferment options can be found at www.studentaid.ed.gov. At the site, click on "Repaying," then on "Cancellation and Deferment Options for Teachers."

Other Discharge Options

- Your state might offer programs that cancel or reduce part of your loan for certain types of service you perform (such as teaching or nursing). Contact your state agency for postsecondary education to see what programs are available in your state. For the address and telephone number of your state agency, call the Federal Student Aid Information Center at 1-800-4-FED-AID (1-800-433-3243). You can also find this information at http://www.studentaid.ed.gov. At the site, click on the "Funding" tab, and then go to "State Aid."

- You should also contact professional, religious, or civic organizations to see if any benefits would be available to you.

- Although not a loan cancellation, some branches of the military offer loan repayment programs as an incentive for service. Check with your local recruiting office for more information.

- Another type of repayment assistance (again, not a discharge) is available through the Nursing Education Loan Repayment Program (NELRP) to registered nurses in exchange for service in eligible facilities located in areas experiencing a shortage of nurses. All NELRP participants must enter into a contract agreeing to provide full-time employment in an approved eligible health facility (EHF) for 2 or 3 years. In return, the NELRP will pay 60 percent of the participant's total qualifying loan balance for 2 years or 85 percent of the participant's total qualifying loan balance for 3 years. For more information, call NELRP, toll-free, at 1-866-813-3753 or visit http://www.bhpr.hrsa.gov/nursing/loanrepay.htm

- The AmeriCorps Program allows participants to earn education awards— including money to repay student loans—in return for national service. For more information, contact the Corporation for National Service, which administers the AmeriCorps Program:

Corporation for National and Community Service
1201 New York Avenue NW
Washington, DC 20525
1-800-94-ACORPS (1-800-942-2677)
202-606-5000
TTY: 1-800-833-3722
Web site: http://www.americorps.org
E-mail: Questions@americorps.org

Loan Default

[U.S. Department of Education webpage located at:
www.studentaid.ed.gov/students/publications/repaying_loans/2003_2004/english/default.htm]

What is default?

For a Federal Perkins Loan, default occurs if you don't make an installment payment when due or don't comply with the promissory note's other terms. Default for a FFEL or Direct Loan occurs if you become 270 days delinquent if you're making monthly payments, or 330 days delinquent if you pay less often than monthly. Explore all the options you can—the last thing you want to do is default.

What happens if I default?

The consequences of default are severe:
The entire loan balance (principal and interest) can be immediately due and payable.

- You'll lose your deferment options.
- You won't be eligible for additional federal student aid.
- Your account might be turned over to a collection agency. If so, you'll have to pay additional interest charges, late fees, collection costs, and possibly court costs and attorney fees. These costs really add up, and it will take you even longer to pay off your student loan.
- As mentioned earlier, your account will be reported to national credit bureaus and your credit rating can be damaged. You might find it very difficult to receive other types of credit, such as credit cards, car loans, or mortgages. Because many landlords do credit checks, it might be hard to rent an apartment. Some employers check to see if you're responsible by looking at your credit rating, so bad credit could even affect getting a job. On top of this, your default will remain on your credit report for up to seven years.
- Your federal income tax refunds (and in some states, your state income tax refunds) might be withheld and applied toward your loan repayment. This happens frequently to defaulters, and it can really hurt if you were counting on that refund.
- Your employer, at the request of the loan holder, may withhold (garnish) part of your wages.
- You might be unable to obtain a professional license in some states.

Do these sound serious? They are, so don't let any of them happen to you! Make sure to contact your lender as soon as you think you might have trouble making payments. Don't ignore any calls or letters from your lender or servicer, either. Putting things off is never the answer because these loans won't go away; talk to your lender and discuss all the options for making payment easier that you've seen in this booklet. Get the details from your lender/servicer on how you can benefit from these options. Don't default!

APPENDIX B
Laws and Legal Guidelines

Precedent Setting Cases

Andrew M. Campbell, J.D., conducted a major review of bankruptcy cases and categorized the findings. In preparing your defense, we encourage you to: (1) look at the Index below and see if your situation matches any one of these listed, (2) if yes, use Westlaw to locate this article, (3) while on-line, click on the link after each category and you will be taken to the related cases. By doing this, you can conduct your own research toward preparing your brief. Visit your local law library or public library with Westlaw access and work with the librarian to seek out the cases related to your situation.

- - - - - - - -

American Law Reports (ALR)
Annotation. 144 A.L.R. Fed. 1

BANKRUPTCY DISCHARGE OF STUDENT LOAN ON GROUND OF UNDUE HARDSHIP UNDER § 523(A)(8)(B) OF BANKRUPTCY CODE OF 1978 (11 U.S.C.A. § 523(A)(8)(B)) DISCHARGE OF STUDENT LOANS

By Andrew M. Campbell, J.D.

This annotation collects and analyzes the federal cases applying §523(a)(8)(B) of the Bankruptcy Code and a predecessor provision. This Index lists some of the circumstances evaluated by bankruptcy cases related to student loan discharges.

INDEX

Abdominal pain
Absence from work Academic probation
Accounting
Acting and theater
Additional hours of work as possible source of income
Adjustment or deferral of payments
Advancement, prospect of
Age as affecting ability to pay
Agoraphobia
Agricultural consumer finance, associate's degree in
Airline, computer programmer for
Air traffic control
Alcohol problems and alcoholism
Allergies, debtor
Allergies, dependent child
Ambulatory schizophrenic
Amount paid on loan prior to filing bankruptcy petition
Anesthesiologist, inability to become
Anorexia
Antibiotic purchases, necessity of
Antibiotics, dependent children allergic to
Anxiety disorders
Apartment, new
Appendix, ruptured
Applied science, associate's degree in

Area in which employment sought
Area where there was shortage of doctors, medical
　　student's agreement to serve in
Army private, spouse as
Arrearages in child support
Arthritis, debtor
Arthritis, spouse
Artificial leg
Art institute, master's degree from
Asbestosis
Assets, which could be liquidated to pay off student loan
Assistant manager of shoe store, spouse as
Assistant professor
Associate's degree
Asthma, debtor
Asthma, dependent child
Attention deficit hyperactivity disorder, dependent
　　children with
Attorneys' fees
Autism, dependent child with
Automobile, repossession of
Automobile accident
Automobile assembly plant, spot welder at
Automobile body repair
Automobile debt, payment of
Automobile loan, reaffirmation of
Automobile loan taken out after bankruptcy

Automobile mechanics, course in
Automobile parts store
Automobiles owned or purchased
Availability of loans to future students
Aviation
Bachelor's degree
Back problems
Bad or good faith
Bakery, employment in
Bankrupt school, prepaid tuition
Banks, employment in
Bar exam, law school graduate failing
Bartenders
Beauty college
Benefit from education financed
Biology, bachelor's degree in
Bipolar disorder or manic-depression
Bladder problems
Blind, partially
Block and brick masonry course
Blood disorder
Boat, ownership of
Bookkeeper, inability to find job as
Borderline psychotic
Bottling plant, employment at
Bowel disorder
Boyfriend, girlfriend, or fiancée, cohabitation with or
    receiving assistance from
Brain tumor, dependent child with
Bronchitis
Budget analyst
Burden of proof
Bus driver
Business degree
Cable television expense
Caring for mother
Carpal tunnel syndrome
Cashiers
Cat, health insurance for
Census taker
Certified public accountant
Cervical cancer
Chapter 13
Charitable expenditures
Checking account in excess of amount of student loan
Chemical engineering degree
Chemical mixer at chemical plant
Chemistry degree, daughter having
Child-care costs
Child leaving home at future time, effect on expenses
Children, having as showing bad faith
Children's higher education, saving for
Child support income

Child support obligations
Chimney sweep
Chiropractic degree
Choice of hardship
Choral music teacher, spouse as
Chosen field, employment outside
Chosen specialty, abandonment of medical education
Christmas club savings account
Chronic fatigue syndrome
Chronic glomerulonephritis
Church contributions
Church member donating down payment for car
Church school, sending child to
Cigarettes, expenditures for
Civil service examination, high score on
Classified paste artist for newspaper
Clerical jobs
Clerk, employment as
Clerk, spouse employed as
Client services representative at securities firm
Closing of school
Clothes, making own
Clothing plant worker
Cocaine addiction, disbarment of lawyer for
Colitis
Collection remedies, lender left to
College degrees, debtors with
Common and ordinarily accepted meaning of words used
    in statutes
Common sense approach
Communications, master's degree in
Community college
Community college, counselor at
Commuting
Computer data entry, certificate in
Computer salesperson
Computers and computer programming
Concentrate, inability to
Congenital nerve damage
Congressional policy, violation of
Consolidation loans
Construction, work in
Continuing education
Continuing hardship
Conviction of crime
Correctional probation officer
Cost-of-living increases
Counselor, financial
Counselor at community college
Court-assigned cases, law school graduate working on
CPA
Creative writing
Credit card debts

Credit risks
Credit union
Criminal justice, degree in
Custodians
Cystic fibrosis, dependent child with
Cystoceles, recurring
Daughter, payment of debt owed to
Day-care costs
Death of dependent child, freeing debtor to obtain
    employment
Debt consolidation loan
Declaration of nondischargeability, consequences of
Deferral of loan repayments
Degenerative arthritis
Degenerative disc disease
Dental expenses
Dental hygiene, associate's degree in
Dentists and dental school
Dependents, debtors with
Depression and bi-polar disorder
Developmentally disabled dependent child
Developmentally disabled persons, caring for
Diabetes, debtor
Diabetes, dependent child
Dietary supervisor
Disability benefits
Disbarment of lawyer
Discount stores, buying clothing at
Dismissal from medical school
Distributor, work at home as
Divorce settlement, failure to use to repay loan
Dog track winnings, failure to use to repay loans
Dominant purpose of bankruptcy filing
Downsizing, loss of job because of
Drafting program
Drama
Drinking problems and alcoholism
Drivers and trucking jobs
Dropping out of school
Drug abuse or addiction
Drugs or medications, expense of
Drunk driving convictions
Duodenal ulcer
Dyslexia
Ear and mouth surgery
Ear infections, dependent children having
Early intervention specialist at mental health center
Economic prospects
Economic value of education financed
Edema
Education, degree in
Efforts to secure employment
Eighth grade education

Electronic repair technician
Elementary education, degree in
Elementary school teacher
Emotional problems or illnesses, generally
Emphysema
Employment, efforts to secure
Endometriosis
English, degree in
English, inability to speak
Epilepsy, adult non-dependent child
Epilepsy, debtor
Epstein-Barr syndrome
Equity, bankruptcy courts as courts of
Equity in home
Equity in house debtor did not live in
Expenses, attempt to minimize, generally
Eye, growth on
Eye or vision problems
Factory work
Failing of bar exam by law school graduate
Failing of licensing examination by medical school
    graduate
Failing out of school
Failure to enforce support obligation of former spouse
Failure to make loan payments or negotiate deferral
Farm equipment manufacturer, layoff from job at
Fast food restaurants, eating at
Fast food restaurants, work at
Fatigue
Feet and legs, problems with
Fiancée, boyfriend, or girlfriend, cohabitation with or
    assistance from
Fibrocystic breast disease
Field engineer, spouse of debtor as
Financial counselor
Fine arts degree
Firewood, gathering on beach to heat home
Flight school
Flunking out of school
Flutist
Flying lessons
Food stamps
Foreseeable and voluntarily assumed hardships
Former spouse, payment of educational loans which
    benefited
Former spouse, support or other payments by
Friends, living with or assistance from
Friends, payment of debts owed to
Gall bladder tumors
Gambling, failure to use money won to repay loans
Gambling losses
Garage sales, buying clothing at
Garnishing of wages

Gas station attendant
GED or high school equivalency diploma
GI bill
Girlfriend, boyfriend, or fiancée, cohabitation with or
    assistance from
Girlfriend, combining of financial affairs with
Girlfriend and her children as dependents
Glomerulonephritis, chronic
Good faith, generally
Good Will stores, purchase of clothes for dependent
    child at
Gout
Graduation of dependent children from high school or
    college, impact on debtor's expenses
Graphic arts
Group home coordinator, director, or shift worker
Growth on eye
Hair stylist
Hand, injury or limitation on use of
Headaches
Health club as unnecessary expense
Health insurance, lack of
Health insurance for cat
Health of debtors and dependents
Hearing loss
Heart attacks
Heart conditions
Heating and air conditioning work
Hemorrhoids
High blood pressure or hypertension
Higher income debtors
High school equivalency diploma
High school graduates
History, bachelor's degree in
History teacher, high school
Hodgkin's disease as reason for dropping out of college
Home, work at
Home caring for children
Home economics, bachelor's degree in
Home insurance, amount budgeted for
Homicide conviction
Honors, graduation with
Horseback lessons and riding camp
Hospital caseworker
Hostess/waitress
Housecleaner
House trailer or mobile home, living in
House trailer or mobile home which could be liquidated
Human resources administration, bachelor's degree in
Hyperactive dependent child
Hypertension or high blood pressure
Income tax refund
Inconvenience, mere

Industrial technology, Bachelor of Science degree in
Inheritance as source of funds
Insurance
Insurance industry, work in
Interest on loan, accrual of as interfering with fresh start
Internal Revenue Service, payment of debts owed to
Internal Revenue Service, work for
Introduction to annotation
Iritis
IRS, payment of debts owed to
IRS, work for
Janitors
Jewelry purchases
Judgment against former spouse
Junior college
Keypunch operator training
Kidney problems
Kidney stones
Laborer
Lab technician
Laundry, no money budgeted for
Law clerk
Law school and law school graduates
Layoffs
Leaving of home by child, effect on expenses
Legal assistant
Legs and feet, problems with
Librarian
Library page, work as
Licenses, professional, revocation of
Licenses to sell insurance and real estate
Lift, ability to
Literacy, teaching
Lower income debtors
Lumbar strain
Lupus
Machine operator
Main purpose of bankruptcy filing
Management accounting, master's degree in
Manager, restaurant
Manic-depression and bipolar disorder
Masonry, block and brick masonry course
Master's degree
Maximize income, attempt to, generally
MBA
Mechanical test, generally
Medicaid benefits
Medical and dental assistants
Medical problems and expenses
Medical schools and students
Medical technician course
Meniere's disease
Mental health, associate's degree in

Mental health center, early intervention specialist at
Mental illness, generally
Mentally retarded dependent child
Mentally retarded persons, caring for
Migraine headaches
Military providing benefits to adult daughter with
    epilepsy
Minimal standard of living, generally
Minimize expenses, attempt to, generally
Minimum wage
Minister
Misconduct, denial of discharge for
Mobile home or house trailer, living in
Mobile home, which could be liquidated
Mortgage on parent's home taken out to finance
    education, debtor paying
Motorcycle, failure to sell
Motor vehicle, repossession of
Motor vehicle accident
Motor vehicle assembly plant, spot welder at
Motor vehicle body repair
Motor vehicle debt, payment of
Motor vehicle loan, reaffirmation of
Motor vehicle loan taken out after bankruptcy
Motor vehicle mechanics, course in
Motor vehicle parts store
Motor vehicles owned or purchased
Mouth and ear surgery
Multiple sclerosis
Music therapist
Neck injury
Neck spasms
Negotiate deferral, failure to
Nerve damage
Nervous condition or disorder
New position, starting
Newspaper, classified paste artist for
Ninth grade education
Number of dependents, large
Nursery, work at
Nurse's aide
Nurses and nursing
Nursing home, work at
Nutritionist
Obsessive-compulsive disorder
Obstructing justice, conviction of
Occupational therapy assistant
Odd jobs
Older children in family, use of for child care
Only debt, student loan as
Operations manager for railroad
Osteoporosis
Other favored creditor, payment of debt owed to

Outside chosen field, employment
Overdose of prescription drug
Overqualified, debtor denied employment as
Overtime, availability of
Overweight, inability to obtain employment because of
    being
Own business
Pain
Painting, experience in
Panic attacks
Paralegal
Paralegal, spouse employed as
Paranoid reaction, manic depressive condition with
Parents, assistance from or living with
Parents, debtor supporting or caring for
Parents also obligated, reaffirmation of debt
    consolidation loan
Parent's home, debtor paying mortgage taken out to
    finance education
Parochial school teacher
Part-time work
Paste artist for newspaper
Payment of other debts
Payments, failure to make
Payments made until filing for bankruptcy
People skills, lack of
Percentage of student loan to total indebtedness
Persistence of hardship, likelihood of
Pharmaceutical salesman
Pharmacist
Photography business
Physical education
Physicians
Physician's assistant
Piloting and air traffic control, associate's degrees in
Pizza deliveryman
Plant closings
Podiatrist
Police officers
Policy test
Poor educational choices
Postal Service, employment with
Posttraumatic stress disorder
Poverty line
Practice pointers
Pregnancy
Preliminary matters
Private schools for children
Private school teacher
Process server
Promotions and advancement, prospect of
Psoriasis
Psychiatric aide

Psychiatric disorders, generally
Psychology, bachelor's degree in
Psychotherapy, undergoing to keep up on latest
    techniques
Public administration
Public assistance, danger of forcing family onto
Public assistance and welfare
Public health, master's degree in
Public housing
Purpose of bankruptcy filing, dominant
Quadruple bypass procedure
Railroad employees
Ratio of student loan to total indebtedness
Reaffirmation of debts
Real estate business
Receptionist
Records clerk
Recreation expense
Reduction or deferral of payments
Refusal of early or partial payments by lender
Rehabilitation program
Related annotations
Relative or other favored creditor, payment of debt owed
    to
Relatives, choosing to assist
Relatives and friends, assistance from
Relatives or friends, living with
Reliability of income
Religious beliefs, free exercise of
Religious or theological studies
Relocate, unwillingness to
Renegotiation or restructuring of loan
Rent, unpaid, record of evictions and judgments for
Rent-free housing at Air Force base
Rent payments, debtor delinquent in
Repossession of automobile
Reservationist for ski resort
Residency program, dropping out of
Respiratory problems, dependent children with
Respiratory technician degree
Respiratory therapist
Restaurant jobs
Restaurants, eating at
Restitution of amounts stolen from clients
Restructuring of loan
Retirement account, payments into
Retirement benefits, absence of
Rosacea
Router
Sailor, spouse as
Sales
Sallie Mae, application for assistance through

Salvation Army stores, purchase of clothes for dependent
    child at
Satellite dish salesman
Schizophrenia
School bus driver
Scoliosis
Scope of annotation
Seamstress
Search for employment
Second job
Secretaries and secretarial training
Security guard
Self-employment
Seniority, likelihood of pay increase
Senior recorder, employment as
Shipbuilding industry
Shirt presser
Shoe salesperson
Shortage of doctors, medical student's agreement as to
    where to serve
Shoulder, partial permanent disability
Sit, ability to
Site of job, expenses incurred by living at
Skin rash
Ski resort, reservationist for
Sleep difficulties
Social Security benefits
Social work, Bachelor of Arts degree with major in
Social work, master's degree in
Social workers
Sociology, master's degree in
Specialty, abandonment of medical education
Speech therapy
Spendthrift philosophy of debtor
Spina bifida
Spot welder at automobile assembly plant
Spouse, former, payment of educational loans which
    benefited
Spouse, former, support or other payments by
Spouse's income
Stability of employment
Stability of family, threat to
Stand, ability to
State employee
State unemployment agency, registration with
Steelworker
Stock clerk
Store, employment in
Store clerk, spouse employed as
Stress related problems
Substitute teaching
Suicide attempt
Summary

Support or other payments by ex-spouse
Surgery
Tax debts, payment of
Tax refunds
Tax work by attorney
Teacher's aide
Teachers and instructors
Technical or trade school
Telephone consultations with psychiatrist
Telephone expenditures
Tenth grade education
Tests for determining undue hardship
Theater and acting
Theological or religious studies
Thrift stores, buying clothing at
Thyroid condition
Time having passed since graduation
Time passing between time student loan became due and
    filing of bankruptcy petition
Tire business
Tobacco, expenditures for
Toll collector, debtor's spouse as
Totality of circumstances test
Trade or technical school
Trailer or mobile home, living in
Trailer or mobile home which could be liquidated
Travel or tourism industry
Truck drivers and trucking
Trust fund to pay dependent child's expenses
Tuberculosis, debtor having positive test for
Two loans, paying one
Two residences, maintaining
Ulcers
Uncertainty in financial situation, periodic layoffs as
    contributing to
Underachiever
Underemployment or underutilization of education
Unearned income as source of funds
Unemployed debtor
Unemployed ex-spouse
Unemployed spouse
Unemployment compensation
University, employment by
Unrealistic employment goals
Unrealistic expectations
Unremunerative occupation, selection of curriculum
    leading to
Unskilled work
Unstable employment
Urban studies
Urinary tract problems
Usefulness of education financed
Uterus, prolapsed

Vacation days, cashing in
Value of education financed
VCR, debtor not owning
Veterans disability claims, pursuing
Veterinarian
Vietnam war service, disabilities resulting from
Violation of congressional policy
Vision problems
Vocational rehabilitation
Vocational technical education, undergraduate degree in
Voluntary choice of hardship
Wafer fabrication room of technical company,
    employment in
Waitress
Warehouse, laborer in
Water meter reader
Welding school
Welfare agency of state, employment by
Welfare and public assistance
Wheelchair, use of
Woman's shelter, employment at
Word processing
Workers compensation award
Work placement specialist
Writers and writing

31 U.S.C.A. §3716 — Administrative Offset of Federal Benefits

(a) After trying to collect a claim from a person under section 3711(a) of this title, the head of an executive, judicial, or legislative agency may collect the claim by administrative offset. The head of the agency may collect by administrative offset only after giving the debtor -

(1) written notice of the type and amount of the claim, the intention of the head of the agency to collect the claim by administrative offset, and an explanation of the rights of the debtor under this section;

(2) an opportunity to inspect and copy the records of the agency related to the claim;

(3) an opportunity for a review within the agency of the decision of the agency related to the claim; and

(4) an opportunity to make a written agreement with the head of the agency to repay the amount of the claim.

(b) Before collecting a claim by administrative offset, the head of an executive, judicial, or legislative agency must either -

(1) adopt, without change, regulations on collecting by administrative offset promulgated by the Department of Justice, the General Accounting Office, or the Department of the Treasury; or

(2) prescribe regulations on collecting by administrative offset consistent with the regulations referred to in paragraph (1).

(c) (1) (A) Except as otherwise provided in this subsection, a disbursing official of the Department of the Treasury, the Department of Defense, the United States Postal Service, or any other government corporation, or any disbursing official of the United States designated by the Secretary of the Treasury, shall offset at least annually the amount of a payment which a payment certifying agency has certified to the disbursing official for disbursement, by an amount equal to the amount of a claim which a creditor agency has certified to the Secretary of the Treasury pursuant to this subsection.

(B) An agency that designates disbursing officials pursuant to section 3321(c) of this title is not required to certify claims arising out of its operations to the Secretary of the Treasury before such agency's disbursing officials offset such claims.

(C) Payments certified by the Department of Education under a program administered by the Secretary of Education under title IV of the Higher Education Act of 1965 shall not be subject to administrative offset under this subsection.

(2) Neither the disbursing official nor the payment certifying agency shall be liable -

(A) for the amount of the administrative offset on the basis that the underlying obligation, represented by the payment before the administrative offset was taken, was not satisfied; or

(B) for failure to provide timely notice under paragraph (8).

(3) (A) (i) Notwithstanding any other provision of law (including sections 207 and 1631(d)(1) of the Social Security Act (42 U.S.C. 407 and 1383(d)(1)), section 413 (b) of Public Law 91-173 (30 U.S.C. 923(b)), and section 14 of the Act of August 29, 1935 (45 U.S.C. 231m)), except as provided in clause (ii), all payments due to an individual under -

(I) the Social Security Act,

(II) part B of the Black Lung Benefits Act, or

(III) any law administered by the Railroad Retirement Board (other than payments that such Board determines to be tier 2 benefits), shall be subject to offset under this section.

(ii) An amount of $9,000 which a debtor may receive under Federal benefit programs cited under clause (i) within a 12-month period shall be exempt from offset under this subsection. In applying the $9,000 exemption, the disbursing official shall -

(I) reduce the $9,000 exemption amount for the 12-month period by the amount of all Federal benefit payments made during such 12-month period which are not subject to offset under this subsection; and

(II) apply a prorated amount of the exemption to each periodic benefit payment to be made to the debtor during the applicable 12-month period. For purposes of the preceding sentence, the amount of a periodic benefit payment shall be the amount after any reduction or deduction required under the laws authorizing the program under which such payment is authorized to be made (including any reduction or deduction to recover any overpayment under such program).

(B) The Secretary of the Treasury shall exempt from administrative offset under this subsection payments under means-tested programs when requested by the head of the respective agency. The Secretary may exempt other payments from administrative offset under this subsection upon the written request of the head of a payment certifying agency. A written request for exemption of other payments must provide justification for the exemption under standards prescribed by the Secretary. Such standards shall give due consideration to whether administrative offset would tend to interfere substantially with or defeat the purposes of the payment certifying agency's program. The Secretary shall report to the Congress annually on exemptions granted under this section.

(C) The provisions of sections 205 (b)(1) and 1631(c) (1) of the Social Security Act shall not apply to any administrative offset executed pursuant to this section against benefits authorized by either title II or title XVI of the Social Security Act, respectively.

(4) The Secretary of the Treasury may charge a fee sufficient to cover the full cost of implementing this subsection. The fee may be collected either by the retention of a portion of amounts collected pursuant to this subsection, or by billing the agency referring or transferring a claim for those amounts. Fees charged to the agencies shall be based on actual administrative offsets completed. Amounts received by the United States as fees under this subsection shall be deposited into the account of the Department of the Treasury under section 3711 (g) (7) of this title, and shall be collected and accounted for in accordance with the provisions of that section.

(5) The Secretary of the Treasury in consultation with the Commissioner of Social Security and the Director of the Office of Management and Budget, may prescribe such rules, regulations, and procedures as the Secretary of the Treasury considers necessary to carry out this subsection. The Secretary shall consult with the heads of affected agencies in the development of such rules, regulations, and procedures.

(6) Any Federal agency that is owed by a person a past due, legally enforceable nontax debt that is over 180 days delinquent, including nontax debt administered by a third party acting as an agent for the Federal Government, shall notify the Secretary of the Treasury of all such nontax debts for purposes of administrative offset under this subsection.

(7) (A) The disbursing official conducting an administrative offset with respect to a payment to a payee shall notify the payee in writing of -

> (i) the occurrence of the administrative offset to satisfy a past due legally enforceable debt, including a description of the type and amount of the payment otherwise payable to the payee against which the offset was executed;
>
> (ii) the identity of the creditor agency requesting the offset; and
>
> (iii) a contact point within the creditor agency that will handle concerns regarding the offset.

(B) If the payment to be offset is a periodic benefit payment, the disbursing official shall take reasonable steps, as determined by the Secretary of the Treasury, to provide the notice to the payee not later than the date on which the payee is otherwise scheduled to receive the payment, or as soon as practical thereafter, but no later than the date of the administrative offset. Notwithstanding the preceding sentence, the failure of the debtor to receive such notice shall not impair the legality of such administrative offset.

(8) A levy pursuant to the Internal Revenue Code of 1986 shall take precedence over requests for administrative offset pursuant to other laws.

(d) Nothing in this section is intended to prohibit the use of any other administrative offset authority existing under statute or common law.

(e) This section does not apply -

(1) to a claim under this subchapter that has been outstanding for more than 10 years; [NO LONGER TRUE SINCE U.S. SUPREME COURT DECISION IN DECEMBER 2005, *LOCKHART V. U.S., 04-881*] or

(2) when a statute explicitly prohibits using administrative offset or setoff to collect the claim or type of claim involved.

(f) The Secretary may waive the requirements of sections 552a(o) and (p) of title 5 for administrative offset or claims collection upon written certification by the head of a State or an executive, judicial, or legislative agency seeking to collect the claim that the requirements of subsection (a) of this section have been met.

(g) The Data Integrity Board of the Department of the Treasury established under 552a(u) of Title 5 shall review and include in reports under paragraph (3)(D) of that section a description of any matching activities conducted under this section. If the Secretary has granted a waiver under subsection (f) of this section, no other Data Integrity Board is required to take any action under section 552a (u) of title 5.

(h) (1) The Secretary may, in the discretion of the Secretary, apply subsection (a) with respect to any past-due, legally-enforceable debt owed to a State if -

(A) the appropriate State disbursing official requests that an offset be performed; and

    (B) a reciprocal agreement with the State is in effect which contains, at a minimum -

        (i) requirements substantially equivalent to subsection (b) of this section; and

        (ii) any other requirements which the Secretary considers appropriate to facilitate the offset and prevent duplicative efforts.

(2) This subsection does not apply to -

    (A) the collection of a debt or claim on which the administrative costs associated with the collection of the debt or claim exceed the amount of the debt or claim;

    (B) any collection of any other type, class, or amount of claim, as the Secretary considers necessary to protect the interest of the United States; or

    (C) the disbursement of any class or type of payment exempted by the Secretary of the Treasury at the request of a Federal agency.

(3) In applying this section with respect to any debt owed to a State, subsection (c)(3)(A) shall not apply. Source (Added Pub. L. 97-452, Sec. 1(16)(A), Jan. 12, 1983, 96 Stat. 2471; amended Pub. L. 104-134, title III, Sec. 31001(c)(1), (d)(2), (e), (f), Apr. 26, 1996, 110 Stat. 1321-359, 1321-362.)

Standardized Compromise and Write-Off Procedures

Bob — copy out to SAM

UNITED STATES DEPARTMENT OF EDUCATION

WASHINGTON, D.C. 20202-_____

(SAM)

JAN 21 1994

JAN 2 6 1994

NOTICE TO ALL GUARANTY AGENCIES

Dear Agency Director:

The enclosed compromise and write-off procedures have been approved for use by all guaranty agencies. These procedures supersede all existing compromise and write-off procedures previously approved by the U.S. Department of Education, and must be used for any compromise or write-off authorized on or after March 1, 1994.

In developing these procedures, the National Council of Higher Education Loan Programs (NCHELP) and the Department worked with a variety of program participants, including lenders, servicers, and student advocate groups. Our goal was to develop *standardized* procedures that could be used by all guaranty agencies.

Two of the major objectives in developing standardized compromise and write-off procedures were to protect the federal taxpayer's interests and ensure equitable treatment of borrowers throughout the country. In keeping with those objectives, we will not permit an agency to alter these procedures unless the proposed change is a truly minor one that is justified because of a unique administrative requirement of the agency. Any proposed change must be submitted for the Department's review and approval.

Sincerely yours,

Robert W. Evans

Robert W. Evans
Director, Division of Policy Development
and Member, Direct Student Loan Task Force

Enclosure

cc: DOUG
MER
SS

STANDARDIZED COMPROMISE AND WRITE-OFF PROCEDURES

The following guidelines are established to allow a guaranty agency to compromise amounts owing on a defaulted reinsured student loan and to write-off accounts where the loan(s) is determined to be uncollectible and the agency seeks to discontinue its semi-annual reviews as required under the due diligence requirements. Write off in this context does not relate to "writing the loan off the books" but only relates to the cessation of collection activity. In all cases, the reasons for the agency's decision and actions will be documented in the borrower's file.

COMPROMISE AUTHORITY

Compromise refers to a negotiated agreement between the debtor and the guaranty agency to accept a payment of a lesser portion of the total debt as full liquidation of the entire indebtedness. A guaranty agency will be permitted in certain cases to accept a compromise amount from a debtor as full satisfaction of the debt to all parties, including the U.S. Department of Education. The authority to accept a compromise as full satisfaction of the debt is intended to maximize collections on defaulted loans. The guaranty agency may compromise a loan at any time after it pays a default claim on that loan.

A guaranty agency will be permitted to compromise under the following circumstances and in the following amounts:

1. An agency can compromise an amount up to an amount equal to all collection costs in order to obtain payment in full of all principal and interest owing on a defaulted loan(s). The agency shall consider the litigative risk of seeking a judgment on a reinsured loan, the likelihood and timing of the collection of the loan, and the borrower's current and expected financial condition.

2. An agency can compromise an amount up to 30% of all principal and interest owing in order to obtain a payment in full of the reinsured portion of a loan(s). The agency shall consider the litigative risk of seeking a judgment on a reinsured loan, the likelihood and timing of the collection of the loan, and the borrower's current and expected financial condition.

3. An agency can compromise in situations that do not meet the criteria in #1 and #2 above, provided the agency can demonstrate and document the reasons for doing so and the compromise is approved by the agency director. Compromises approved by the agency director allow the guaranty agency to waive the Secretary's right to collect the remaining balance due.

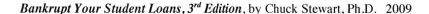

Approval authority for the write-off of a loan(s) will be individualized within each agency. However, the following minimum guidelines will apply:

1.   Balances up to $5,000 can be approved by the supervisor responsible for collection of the loan(s).

2.   Balances up to $20,000 can be approved by the next level of management within the guaranty agency if the documents authorizing a write-off contain the signatures of each agency official participating or concurring in the write-off decision.

3.   Balances exceeding $20,000 can be approved by the division/agency director if the documents authorizing a write-off contain the signatures of each agency official participating or concurring in the write-off decision.

In each case, upon approval of the write-off, the account will be scheduled for permanent assignment to the U.S. Department of Education under the provisions in 34 CFR 682.409, et seq. (except those previously noted.)

A debtor who benefits from a write-off must reaffirm the amount written off if he or she later wants to receive an FFEL Program loan.

Interrogatories— Kentucky

This document is for illustration only. Your own Circuit Court will provide its own Interrogatories if needed.

UNITED STATES BANKRUPTCY COURT
FOR THE WESTERN DISTRICT OF KENTUCKY

IN RE:

CASE #

Debtor

Plaintiff

vs.   ADV. #

KENTUCKY HIGHER EDUCATION
ASSISTANCE AUTHORITY
Defendant(s)

*   *   *   *   *   *

INTERROGATORIES

Pursuant to Rule 33 of the Federal Rules of Bankruptcy Procedure and the Rules of the United States District Court for the Western District of Kentucky, Defendant serves the following written interrogatories upon Plaintiff, XXXXXXXX   XXXXX, which shall be answered separately and fully in writing under oath and served upon Defendant within thirty (30) days from service hereof.

Pursuant to FRCP Rule 26(e), XXXXXX-XXXXX, is under a duty to seasonably supplement his/her responses with respect to any question directly addressed to the identity and location of persons having knowledge of discoverable matters, and to amend a prior response if he/she obtains information upon the basis of which he/she knows that the response was incorrect when made, or the response is no longer true.

The answers of XXXXXX-XXXXX to the interrogatories should include all information which is in his/her possession or control, or within the possession or control of his/her attorneys, investigators, agents, employees or other representatives of XXXXXX-XXXXX.

> Melissa F. Justice
> Attorney for Defendant
> KHEAA
> 1050 U.S. 127 South
> Frankfort, Kentucky 40601
> (502) 696-7309

Interrogatory No. 1: State your full name, address, telephone number, date of birth, date of marriage(s), date of divorce(s).
    ANSWER:

Interrogatory No. 2: State whether you and/or your spouse/and or any family member who resides with you and/or any person dependent on you for support are employed, the names and addresses of all employers, dates of employment with each employer, position held with each employer, respective duties of each position

held, and the amount of income received from employment for each of the years from December 1, 1997, through the present (including salary, commission, tips, bonuses, profit sharing, and overtime pay).
ANSWER:

Interrogatory No. 3: For each person referred to in Interrogatory No. 2, state the present amount of take home income (income after deductions) received each pay period; whether this income is received monthly, twice per month, bi-weekly (every 2 weeks), weekly, or otherwise; and state the amounts and respective types of deductions taken from each paycheck each pay period.
ANSWER:

Interrogatory No. 4: State in detail all facts and information you have to support your allegation that your debt to Defendant will impose an undue hardship on you and your dependents.
ANSWER:

Interrogatory No. 5: State your current monthly budget of expenses and your monthly budget of expenses for the last three years, for you, your spouse, and your dependents, including rent, utilities, telephone, gasoline, food, clothes, insurance and any other expenses. If you rent your place of residence, please state the name, business address and telephone number of your landlord.
ANSWER:

Interrogatory No. 6: Do you have any roommates and/or any family members (either immediate or non-immediate) who reside with you? If so, state the amount of money each roommate and/or family member contributes toward each expense listed in your answer for Interrogatory No. 5.
ANSWER:

Interrogatory No. 7: State the respective dates, names and locations of schools attended, major areas of study, and degrees and/or certificates obtained as a result of all postsecondary education and/or training you, your spouse, and any other person dependent on you for support have received, including participation in college (other than Sullivan College), vocational schools, correspondence courses, and technical or union training programs.
ANSWER:

Interrogatory No. 8: State the dates, locations, and results of any and all efforts by you to locate employment or better paying employment since December 1, 1997, including the name and address of each potential employer with whom you have actually applied for work.
ANSWER:

Interrogatory No. 9: State what specific action you have taken to attempt to maximize your income and minimize your expenses in order to make some payment towards your student loan.
ANSWER:

Interrogatory No. 10: Do you and/or your spouse, and/or your dependents presently suffer any permanent injury, persistent infirmity, chronic illness or disability? If so, state the person afflicted, the nature of the condition and:
(a) Whether you and/or your dependents undergo any recurring examination, treatment, counseling, or nursing care for this condition.
(b) The names, addresses, and phone numbers of all treating physicians, other persons, or entities which provide care and/or services for this condition.
(c) The particular way in which the injury or disability incapacitates the person afflicted.
(d) Whether any physician, or other medical personnel, has since December 1, 1997, assigned a disability rating for it, and, if so, the name of such physician and the percentage of the disability rating.
(e) The amount of recurring expenses (including doctors, hospitalization, rehabilitation, prescriptions, nursing care, etc.) not reimbursed through health insurance, disability income, or government assistance.
ANSWER:

Interrogatory No. 11: State the name, address and telephone number of each person whom you intend to call as a witness at the trial of this action, and provide a summary of the testimony of each witness.
ANSWER:

Interrogatory No. 12: If you own your place of residence, state whether you own it jointly or in common with any other person or persons, the nature and extent of their interest in the property, the approximate date(s) whereupon the person or persons acquired the interest in the property, whether the interest of the person or persons was acquired by gift, bequest, or purchase?
ANSWER:

Interrogatory No. 13: Do you have any boarders, tenants, and/or subtenants at your place of residence? If so, give their name(s), the amount of rent payable to you, when and how often rent is to be paid to you, and whether it is paid in cash, by check, or otherwise.
ANSWER:

Interrogatory No. 14: Do you own or hold any interest in any real estate other than your place of residence? If so, identify the property, state the nature and extent of your interest in the property, state whether you obtained the interest and how much money or property was given in exchange for the interest.
ANSWER:

Interrogatory No. 15: Are you a proprietor, part-owner, stockholder, officer, and/or director of any business organization(s)? If so, state the name and location of such organization(s) and your relationship to the organization(s).
ANSWER:

Interrogatory No. 16: Do you have, in your own name or jointly with any other person or organization, a bank, credit union, and/or savings and loan account, either commercial or personal, either savings, checking or otherwise, any shares of stock, bonds, mutual fund shares, certificates of deposit, money market certificates, bills, notes, or other instruments representing money or other property owned by or payable to you? If so, state where and the balance of the account(s).
ANSWER:

Interrogatory No. 17: Do you and/or your spouse and/or any other person dependent on you for support own or use or have you and/or your spouse and/or any other person dependent on you for support owned and used, within the last 6 months, any credit cards. If so, state the company or companies which issued the cards and state the balance owed for any credit card owned.
ANSWER:

Interrogatory No. 18: Does any person or organization owe you money or other property and/or do you anticipate that any person or organization will or may owe you money or other property as the result of a loan, contract, judgment, insurance settlement, accident settlement, conditional transfer, bequest or devise, as payment for services rendered, or otherwise? If so, give full details as to the debtor's identity and location, the amount and type of debt, the date upon which payment or conveyance of property is due, and any encumbrances on such money or other property.
ANSWER:

Interrogatory No. 19: State the amount of income which you and/or your spouse and/or any other person dependent on you for support and/or any family member who resides with you receives from any of the following sources and state whether this income is received weekly, bi-weekly (every two weeks), twice per month, once per month, or otherwise:

(a)   Disability or severance pay:

(b)   Unemployment compensation:

(c)   Workman's compensation:

(d)   Social Security:

(e)   Veteran's benefits:

(f)   Aid to Families with Dependent Children:

(g)   Food stamps:

(h)   Alimony:

(i)   Child support:

(j)   Interest and/or dividends:

(k)   Inheritance or trust income:

(l)   Income received from parents, in-laws, or other relatives:

(m)   Farm income (including subsidy payments):

(n)   Federal income tax refund for the most recent previous four years:

(o)   State income tax refund for the most recent previous four years:

ANSWER:

Interrogatory No. 20: State the names and respective dates of birth, social security numbers, and relationships to you, of all persons dependent on you for support (including your spouse, children, other relatives, etc.).
ANSWER:

Interrogatory No. 21: State the respective names, addresses and phone numbers of all other persons who have a legal obligation to provide support to any of the dependents identified in Interrogatory No. 21 and identify the dependent(s) to whom such legal obligation relates. If you are owed child support based on a legal obligation, describe what efforts you have made to enforce such obligation.
ANSWER:

Interrogatory No. 22: If you are currently unemployed, state the information requested as follows:
(a)   When and in which position you were last employed?
(b)   Were you laid off or did your voluntarily leave your last job?
ANSWER:

Interrogatory No. 23: State the information requested as follows:
(a)   The number of years and type of occupations, trades, or professions in which you have work experience:

(b)   Have you sought employment in fields other than those in which you have work experience or educational training?

(c)   Have you registered for work with private or governmental employment agencies or services?

(d)   Have you sought retraining through any educational institution or governmental program for occupations in which employment opportunities are available in your community?

ANSWER:

Interrogatory No. 24: Other than the student loans which are the subject of this action, identify the creditor, outstanding balance, and the nature of all debts that you have reaffirmed or that are exempt from discharge so that such debts will not be discharged in this bankruptcy (include student loans which are the subject of other actions not joined with this case).
ANSWER:

Interrogatory No. 25: State the reason and date you ceased enrollment at Sullivan University, and what program(s) of study did you major in while you were enrolled?
ANSWER:

****

The signatory hereof certifies under oath that the foregoing responses to interrogatories are true, complete, and accurate to the best of my knowledge.

_____
DATE   PLAINTIFF(S)

Subscribed and Sworn to before me by XXXXXX-XXXXX on this ___ day of _____, 2000.

_____
NOTARY PUBLIC   MY COMMISSION EXPIRES

****

CERTIFICATE OF SERVICE

The undersigned hereby certifies that a true copy of the foregoing Interrogatories were mailed to Plaintiff's Attorney, Nick Thompson, 12404 Aquarius Road, Louisville, Kentucky 40243-1508, on this day by regular mail.

_____
Date   Melissa F. Justice
                                             Attorney for Defendant
                                             Kentucky Higher Education Assistance Authority
                                             1050 U.S. 127 South
                                             Frankfort, Kentucky 40601
                                             (502) 696-7309

UNITED STATES BANKRUPTCY COURT
FOR THE WESTERN DISTRICT OF KENTUCKY

IN RE:

CASE #

Plaintiff/Debtor

vs.

**REQUEST FOR PRODUCTION
OF DOCUMENTS**

ADV. #

KENTUCKY HIGHER EDUCATION
ASSISTANCE AUTHORITY
Defendant(s)

****

Pursuant to Rule 7034 of the Rules of Bankruptcy Procedure and Rule 34 of the Federal Rules of Civil Procedure, Defendant, Kentucky Higher Education Assistance Authority, requests Plaintiff to respond within 30 days to the following requests:

1.   That Plaintiff submit to the Defendant or produce and permit Defendant to inspect and to copy each of the following documents:

(a) Copies of Plaintiff's state and federal tax returns (form 1040 or its equivalent and attached schedules) and W-2 forms for the three most recent tax years and those of each family member residing in the household.

(b) Copies of all of Plaintiff's cancelled checks for the six most recent preceding months and those of each family member residing in the household.

(c) Current pay stubs for the six most recent preceding months (showing total year-to-date earnings, including wages, commissions, tips and deductions) for each family member (including Plaintiff) residing in the household.

(d) Copies of all of Plaintiff's credit card statements for the six most recent preceding months, and those of each family member residing in the household.

(e) Copies of Medical Records of each family member (including Plaintiff) with an illness or disability which Plaintiff may allege as contributing to an undue hardship in repayment of this debt.

(f) A current rent or mortgage receipt.

(g) A current utilities bill for water, gas and electricity usage.

(h) A current phone bill.

(i) Current receipts for childcare and tuition.

(j) Payment receipts for the six most recent preceding months which show amounts paid or received for child support.

(k) A copy of Plaintiff's(s) bankruptcy petition and schedules.

(l) Copies of Plaintiff's college and/or vocational school transcripts.

(1) Copies of any and all correspondence which relate to requests by the Plaintiff(s) for employment, requests for job interviews, rejection letters, or any other correspondence to or from the Plaintiff(s) relating to job searches by the Plaintiff(s).

(2) Said documents are to be produced at the office of Kentucky Higher Education Assistance Authority, 1050 U.S. 127 South, Suite 102, Frankfort, Kentucky 40601 between 8 a.m. and 4 p.m.

(3) In lieu of said production at the place previously designated, Plaintiff may, at its discretion, mail copies of said documents to the undersigned at Kentucky Higher Education Assistance Authority, 1050 U.S. 127 South, Suite 102, Frankfort, Kentucky 40601; provided that Plaintiff understands that use of this alternative procedure constitutes an admission that each of the documents so mailed is an authentic and genuine copy of the original document.

Diana L. Barber
Attorney for Defendant
KHEAA
1050 U.S. 127 South
Frankfort, Kentucky 40601
(502) 696-7298

CERTIFICATE OF SERVICE

I hereby certify that the foregoing Request for Production of Documents was served upon Plaintiff by mailing a true and accurate copy of same to Plaintiff's attorney: Nick C. Thompson, 12404 Aquarius, Louisville, Kentucky 40243, this the _____ day of January, 1999.

_____
Diana L. Barber

IRS Collection Financial Standards

The IRS has established standards used to determine the ability of taxpayers to make delinquent payments. The main webpage links to other pages that give standards for food, clothing, housing, utilities, transportation, and other expenses. You will use these numbers to show your family expenses are comparable to other similarly situated families. Visit the website — www.irs.gov/individuals/article/0,,id=96543,00.html— for updated information.

 Internal Revenue Service IRS.gov

DEPARTMENT OF THE TREASURY

Collection Financial Standards

General

Collection Financial Standards are used to help determine a taxpayer's ability to pay a delinquent tax liability.

Allowances for food, clothing and other items, known as the National Standards, apply nationwide except for Alaska and Hawaii, which have their own tables. Taxpayers are allowed the total National Standards amount for their family size and income level, without questioning amounts actually spent.

Maximum allowances for housing and utilities and transportation, known as the Local Standards, vary by location. Unlike the National Standards, the taxpayer is allowed the amount actually spent or the standard, whichever is less.

Food, Clothing and Other Items

National Standards for reasonable amounts have been established for five necessary expenses: food, housekeeping supplies, apparel and services, personal care products and services, and miscellaneous.

All standards except miscellaneous are derived from the Bureau of Labor Statistics (BLS) Consumer Expenditure Survey (CES). The miscellaneous standard has been established by the IRS.

Alaska and Hawaii

Due to their unique geographic circumstances and higher cost of living, separate standards for food, clothing and other items have been established for Alaska and Hawaii .

Housing and Utilities

The housing and utilities standards are derived from Census and BLS data, and are provided by state down to the county level.

Transportation

The transportation standards consist of nationwide figures for monthly loan or lease payments referred to as ownership costs, and additional amounts for monthly operating costs broken down by Census Region and Metropolitan Statistical Area (MSA). Public transportation is included under operating costs. A conversion chart has been provided with the standards which shows which IRS districts fall under each Census Region, as well as the counties included in each MSA. The ownership cost portion of the transportation standard, although it applies nationwide, is still considered part of the Local Standards.

The ownership costs provide maximum allowances for the lease or purchase of up to two automobiles if allowed as a necessary expense. The operating costs are derived from BLS data.

If a taxpayer has a car payment, the allowable ownership cost added to the allowable operating cost equals the allowable transportation expense. If a taxpayer has no car payment, or no car, only the operating costs portion of the transportation standard is used to come up with the allowable transportation expense.

The link on the IRS Collection Financial Standards main webpage will take you to the standards for Allowable Living Expenses. You need to visit the website to gather current data. www.irs.gov/businesses/small/article/0,,id=104627,00.html

National Standards for Allowable Living Expenses

Collection Financial Standards for Food, Clothing and Other Items. Due to their unique geographic circumstances and higher cost of living, separate standards have been established for Alaska and Hawaii .

One Person National Standards
Based on Gross Monthly Income

Item	less than $833	$833 to $1,249	$1,250 to $1,666	$1,667 to $2,499	$2,500 to $3,333	$3,334 to $4,166	$4,167 to $5,833	$5,834 and over
Food	197	215	231	258	300	339	369	543
Housekeeping supplies	19	20	25	26	29	36	37	51
Apparel & services	60	61	70	75	100	124	134	207
Personal care products & services	19	24	26	27	40	42	43	44
Miscellaneous	108	108	108	108	108	108	108	108
Total	$403	$428	$460	$494	$577	$649	$691	$953

Two Persons National Standards
Based on Gross Monthly Income

Item	less than $833	$833 to $1,249	$1,250 to $1,666	$1,667 to $2,499	$2,500 to $3,333	$3,334 to $4,166	$4,167 to $5,833	$5,834 and over
Food	336	337	338	424	439	487	559	691
Housekeeping supplies	36	37	38	48	52	53	107	108
Apparel & services	81	88	91	95	125	132	164	276
Personal care products & services	33	34	35	43	44	51	56	71
Miscellaneous	134	134	134	134	134	134	134	134
Total	$620	$630	$636	$744	$794	$857	$1,020	$1,280

Three Persons National Standards
Based on Gross Monthly Income

Item	less than $833	$833 to $1,249	$1,250 to $1,666	$1,667 to $2,499	$2,500 to $3,333	$3,334 to $4,166	$4,167 to $5,833	$5,834 and over
Food	467	468	469	470	490	546	622	778
Housekeeping supplies	41	42	43	49	53	55	108	109
Apparel & services	132	144	157	158	159	188	204	303
Personal care products & services	34	36	37	44	45	52	61	79
Miscellaneous	161	161	161	161	161	161	161	161
Total	$835	$851	$867	$882	$908	$1,002	$1,156	$1,430

Four Persons National Standards
Based on Gross Monthly Income

Item	less than $833	$833 to $1,249	$1,250 to $1,666	$1,667 to $2,499	$2,500 to $3,333	$3,334 to $4,166	$4,167 to $5,833	$5,834 and over
Food	468	525	526	527	528	640	722	868
Housekeeping supplies	42	43	44	50	54	61	109	110
Apparel & services	146	169	170	171	174	189	217	317
Personal care products & services	37	42	43	45	46	53	62	81
Miscellaneous	188	188	188	188	188	188	188	188
Total	$881	$967	$971	$981	$990	$1,131	$1,298	$1,564

More than Four Persons National Standards
Based on Gross Monthly Income

Item	less than $833	$833 to $1,249	$1,250 to $1,666	$1,667 to $2,499	$2,500 to $3,333	$3,334 to $4,166	$4,167 to $5,833	$5,834 and over
For each additional person, add to four person total allowance:	$134	$145	$155	$166	$177	$188	$199	$209

effective January 1, 2005

The link on the IRS Collection Financial Standards main webpage will take you to the standards for Housing and Utilities Allowable Living Expenses. These are specific for each state. Click on your state and see the standard. The California Standard is given below. Visit the website to gather current data for your state.
www.irs.gov/businesses/small/article/0,,id=104696,00.html

Local Standards: Housing and Utilities

Disclaimer: IRS Collection Financial Standards are intended for use in calculating repayment of delinquent taxes. These Standards are effective on March 1, 2009 for purposes of federal tax administration only. Expense information for use in bankruptcy calculations can be found on the website for the U.S. Trustee Program.

Please choose a state or territory.

Alabama	Montana
Alaska	Nebraska
American Samoa	Nevada
Arizona	New Hampshire
Arkansas	New Jersey
California	New Mexico
Colorado	New York
Connecticut	North Carolina
Delaware	North Dakota
District of Columbia	Northern Mariana Islands
Florida	Ohio
Georgia	Oklahoma
Guam	Oregon
Hawaii	Pennsylvania
Idaho	Puerto Rico
Illinois	Rhode Island
Indiana	South Carolina
Iowa	South Dakota
Kansas	Tennessee
Kentucky	Texas
Louisiana	Utah
Maine	Vermont
Maryland	Virgin Islands
Massachusetts	Virginia
Michigan	Washington
Minnesota	West Virginia
Mississippi	Wisconsin
Missouri	Wyoming

The link on the IRS Collection Financial Standards—Housing and Utilities Allowable Living Expenses are specific for each state. The California Standard is given below as an example. Visit the website to gather current data for your state. www.irs.gov/businesses/small/article/0,,id=104701,00.html

California - Housing and Utilities Allowable Living Expenses

Collection Financial Standards
Financial Analysis - Local Standards: Housing and Utilities (effective 1/1/2005)

Maximum Monthly Allowance

County	Family of 2 or less	Family of 3	Family of 4 or more
Alameda County	1,745	2,053	2,361
Alpine County	1,254	1,475	1,696
Amador County	1,175	1,382	1,590
Butte County	1,045	1,229	1,413
Calaveras County	1,167	1,372	1,578
Colusa County	968	1,139	1,309
Contra Costa County	1,718	2,021	2,324
Del Norte County	1,012	1,191	1,370
El Dorado County	1,463	1,721	1,979
Fresno County	1,087	1,279	1,471
Glenn County	887	1,044	1,201
Humboldt County	1,024	1,204	1,385
Imperial County	1,067	1,256	1,444
Inyo County	1,135	1,336	1,536
Kern County	1,029	1,211	1,393
Kings County	1,023	1,203	1,384
Lake County	1,018	1,198	1,377
Lassen County	1,007	1,184	1,362
Los Angeles County	1,563	1,839	2,114
Madera County	1,036	1,219	1,402
Marin County	2,318	2,727	3,136
Mariposa County	1,047	1,232	1,417
Mendocino County	1,164	1,369	1,574
Merced County	1,058	1,244	1,431
Modoc County	729	858	987
Mono County	1,480	1,741	2,002
Monterey County	1,526	1,795	2,065

Napa County	1,555	1,830	2,104
Nevada County	1,353	1,592	1,830
Orange County	1,748	2,057	2,366
Placer County	1,536	1,807	2,077
Plumas County	1,044	1,228	1,412
Riverside County	1,317	1,549	1,781
Sacramento County	1,254	1,475	1,696
San Benito County	1,757	2,067	2,377
San Bernardino County	1,253	1,474	1,695
San Diego County	1,633	1,922	2,210
San Francisco County	1,883	2,216	2,548
San Joaquin County	1,265	1,488	1,711
San Luis Obispo County	1,412	1,661	1,910
San Mateo County	2,124	2,499	2,874
Santa Barbara County	1,529	1,799	2,069
Santa Clara County	2,048	2,410	2,771
Santa Cruz County	1,813	2,133	2,453
Shasta County	1,066	1,254	1,443
Sierra County	945	1,112	1,279
Siskiyou County	865	1,017	1,170
Solano County	1,473	1,733	1,993
Sonoma County	1,575	1,853	2,131
Stanislaus County	1,149	1,351	1,554
Sutter County	1,091	1,283	1,476
Tehama County	922	1,085	1,248
Trinity County	901	1,060	1,219
Tulare County	989	1,163	1,338
Tuolumne County	1,126	1,325	1,523
Ventura County	1,704	2,005	2,306
Yolo County	1,375	1,617	1,860
Yuba County	917	1,079	1,240

The link on the IRS Collection Financial Standards main webpage will take you to the standards for Transportation. Visit the website to gather current data for your state. www.irs.gov/businesses/small/article/0,,id=104623,00.html

Allowable Living Expenses for Transportation

Collection Financial Standards
Financial Analysis - Local Standards: Transportation *

Ownership Costs		
National	**First Car**	**Second Car**
	$475	$338

Operating Costs & Public Transportation Costs			
Region	**No Car**	**One Car**	**Two Cars**
Northeast Region	$230	$298	$393
New York	$302	$384	$479
Philadelphia	$236	$298	$392
Boston	$259	$284	$380
Pittsburgh	$161	$286	$380
Midwest Region	$194	$251	$345
Chicago	$257	$329	$422
Detroit	$312	$376	$469
Milwaukee	$212	$247	$341
Minneapolis-St. Paul	$276	$303	$397
Cleveland	$198	$293	$387
Cincinnati	$222	$272	$365
St. Louis	$203	$287	$383
Kansas City	$246	$291	$384
South Region	$197	$242	$336
Washington, D.C.	$289	$313	$407
Baltimore	$225	$240	$334
Atlanta	$283	$258	$351
Miami	$284	$344	$439
Tampa	$255	$265	$359
Dallas-Ft. Worth	$309	$332	$425
Houston	$281	$367	$462
West Region	$246	$305	$399
Los Angeles	$275	$353	$448
San Francisco	$317	$373	$466
San Diego	$311	$318	$415
Portland	$189	$246	$339
Seattle	$258	$335	$427
Honolulu	$295	$314	$409
Anchorage	$312	$336	$431

Phoenix	$273	$326	$420
Denver	$302	$351	$442

* Does not include personal property taxes. (effective January 1, 2005)

For Use with Allowable Transportation Expenses Table

The Operating Costs and Public Transportation Costs sections of the Transportation Standards are provided by Census Region and Metropolitan Statistical Area (MSA). The following table lists the states that comprise each Census Region. Once the taxpayer's Census Region has been ascertained, to determine if an MSA standard is applicable, use the definitions below to see if the taxpayer lives within an MSA (MSAs are defined by county and city, where applicable). If the taxpayer does not reside in an MSA, use the regional standard.

Northeast Census Region

Maine, New Hampshire, Vermont, Massachusetts, Rhode Island, Connecticut, Pennsylvania, New York, New Jersey

MSA		COUNTIES
New York	in NY:	Bronx, Dutchess, Kings, Nassau, New York, Orange, Putnam, Queens, Richmond, Rockland, Suffolk, Westchester
	in NJ:	Bergen, Essex, Hudson, Hunterdon, Mercer, Middlesex, Monmouth, Morris, Ocean, Passaic, Somerset, Sussex, Union, Warren
	in CT:	Fairfield, Litchfield, Middlesex, New Haven
	in PA:	Pike
Philadelphia	in PA:	Bucks, Chester, Delaware, Montgomery, Philadelphia
	in NJ:	Atlantic, Burlington, Camden, Cape May, Cumberland, Gloucester, Salem
	in DE:	New Castle
	in MD:	Cecil
Boston	in MA:	Bristol, Essex, Hampden, Middlesex, Norfolk, Plymouth, Suffolk, Worcester
	in NH:	Hillsborough, Merrimack, Rockingham, Strafford
	in CT:	Windham
	in ME:	York
Pittsburgh	in PA:	Allegheny, Beaver, Butler, Fayette, Washington, Westmoreland

Midwest Census Region

North Dakota, South Dakota, Nebraska, Kansas, Missouri, Illinois, Indiana, Ohio, Michigan, Wisconsin, Minnesota, Iowa

MSA		COUNTIES (unless otherwise specified)
Chicago	in IL:	Cook, DeKalb, DuPage, Grundy, Kane, Kankakee, Kendall, Lake, McHenry, Will
	in IN:	Lake, Porter
	in WI:	Kenosha
Detroit	in MI:	Genesee, Lapeer, Lenawee, Livingston, Macomb, Monroe, Oakland, St. Clair, Washtenaw, Wayne
Milwaukee	in WI:	Milwaukee, Ozaukee, Racine, Washington, Waukesha
Minneapolis-St. Paul	in MN:	Anoka, Carver, Chisago, Dakota, Hennepin, Isanti, Ramsey, Scott, Sherburne, Washington, Wright
	in WI:	Pierce, St. Croix
Cleveland	in OH:	Ashtabula, Cuyahoga, Geauga, Lake, Lorain, Medina, Portage, Summit
Cincinnati	in OH:	Brown, Butler, Clermont, Hamilton, Warren
	in KY:	Boone, Campbell, Gallatin, Grant, Kenton, Pendleton
	in IN:	Dearborn, Ohio
St. Louis	in MO:	Crawford, Franklin, Jefferson, Lincoln, St. Charles, St. Louis, Warren, St. Louis city
	in IL:	Clinton, Jersey, Madison, Monroe, St.Clair
Kansas City	in MO:	Cass, Clay, Clinton, Jackson, Lafayette, Platte, Ray
	in KS:	Johnson, Leavenworth, Miami, Wyandotte

South Census Region

Texas, Oklahoma, Arkansas, Louisiana, Mississippi, Tennessee, Kentucky, West Virginia, Virginia, Maryland, District of Columbia, Delaware, North Carolina, South Carolina, Georgia, Florida, Alabama

MSA		COUNTIES (unless otherwise specified)
Washington, D.C.	*in* DC:	District of Columbia
	in MD:	Calvert, Charles, Frederick, Montgomery, Prince George's, Washington
	in VA:	Arlington, Clarke, Culpepper, Fairfax, Fauquier, King George, Loudoun, Prince William, Spotsylvania, Stafford, Warren, Alexandria city, Fairfax city, Falls Church city, Fredericksburg city, Manassas city, Manassas Park city
	in WV:	Berkeley, Jefferson
Baltimore	*in* MD:	Anne Arundel, Baltimore, Carroll, Harford, Howard, Queen Anne's, Baltimore city
Atlanta	*in* GA:	Barrow, Bartow, Carroll, Cherokee, Clayton, Cobb, Coweta, DeKalb, Douglas, Fayette, Forsyth, Fulton, Gwinnett, Henry, Newton, Paulding, Pickens, Rockdale, Spalding, Walton
Miami	*in* FL:	Broward, Miami-Dade
Tampa	*in* FL:	Hernando, Hillsborough, Pasco, Pinellas
Dallas-Ft. Worth	*in* TX:	Collin, Dallas, Denton, Ellis, Henderson, Hood, Hunt, Johnson, Kaufman, Parker, Rockwall, Tarrant
Houston	*in* TX:	Brazoria, Chambers, Fort Bend, Galveston, Harris, Liberty, Montgomery, Waller

West Census Region:

New Mexico, Arizona, Colorado, Wyoming, Montana, Nevada, Utah, Washington, Oregon, Idaho, California, Alaska, Hawaii

MSA		COUNTIES (unless otherwise specified)
Los Angeles	*in* CA:	Los Angeles, Orange, Riverside, San Bernadino, Ventura
San Francisco	*in* CA:	Alameda, Contra Costa, Marin, Napa, San Francisco, San Mateo, Santa Clara, Santa Cruz, Solano, Sonoma
San Diego	*in* CA:	San Diego
Portland	*in* OR:	Clackamas, Columbia, Marion, Multnomah, Polk, Washington, Yamhill
	in WA:	Clark
Seattle	*in* WA:	Island, King, Kitsap, Pierce, Snohomish, Thurston
Honolulu	*in* HI:	Honolulu
Anchorage	*in* AK:	Anchorage borough
Phoenix	*in* AZ:	Maricopa, Pinal
Denver	*in* CO:	Adams, Arapahoe, Boulder, Denver, Douglas, Jefferson, Weld

The United States Department of Health and Human Services publishes the Federal Poverty Guideline. Current versions can be found at their website at: http://aspe.hhs.gov/poverty/poverty.shtml

---

Poverty Guidelines, Research, and Measurement   05/23/2005 02:21 PM

Skip Navigation

● **HHS Home**
● **Questions?**
● **Contact Us**
● **Site Map**

[   ] **Search**

United States, Department of
Health & Human Services

Poverty Guidelines, Research, and Measurement

Poverty Guidelines
- **2005 HHS Poverty Guidelines** 🔳
- **Prior HHS Poverty Guidelines and** *Federal Register* **References**
- **Frequently Asked Questions** (FAQs) on the Poverty Guidelines and Poverty 🔳
- **Information Contacts and References** on the Poverty Guidelines/Thresholds/Lines and Their History

---

Research

The following organizations have received support from ASPE to conduct and report on research related to poverty:

- **The Institute for Research on Poverty** at the University of Wisconsin
- **The Joint Center for Poverty Research** of Northwestern University and the University of Chicago
- **The National Poverty Center** at the University of Michigan
- **The Kentucky Center for Poverty Research** at the University of Kentucky
- **The RUPRI Rural Poverty Research Center** at the University of Missouri

The **Census Bureau** is the federal agency that prepares statistics on the number of people in poverty in the United States.

Poverty Measurement: Papers, Articles, and a Report

Papers and Articles on:

- **How Mollie Orshansky Developed the Poverty Thresholds**
- **Unofficial Poverty Lines in the U.S. Before 1965**

The 1995 Report of the National Research Council's Panel on Poverty and Family Assistance

Papers by David Betson on Poverty Measurement Issues

- Looking for information on the **number of people in poverty** in the U.S. or a state or county? Visit the Census Bureau's **Poverty Web site** or its **Question and Answer Center**.

Last Revised: March 18, 2005

http://aspe.hhs.gov/poverty/poverty.shtml   Page 1 of 2

Skip Navigation
● **HHS Home**
● **Questions?**
● **Contact Us**
● **Site Map**

Search

THE 2005 HHS POVERTY GUIDELINES

One Version of the [U.S.] Federal Poverty Measure

[*Federal Register* Notice with 2005 Guidelines - Full Text]
[Prior Poverty Guidelines and *Federal Register* References Since 1982]
[Frequently Asked Questions (FAQs)]
[Information Contacts/References - Poverty Guidelines/Thresholds/Lines and Their History]
[Computations for the 2005 Poverty Guidelines]

There are two slightly different versions of the federal poverty measure:

- The poverty thresholds, and
- The poverty guidelines.

The **poverty thresholds** are the original version of the federal poverty measure. They are updated each year by the **Census Bureau** (although they were originally developed by Mollie Orshansky of the Social Security Administration). The thresholds are used mainly for **statistical** purposes — for instance, preparing estimates of the number of Americans in poverty each year. (In other words, all official poverty population figures are calculated using the poverty thresholds, not the guidelines.) Poverty thresholds since 1980 and weighted average poverty thresholds since 1959 are available on the Census Bureau's Web site. For an example of how the Census Bureau applies the thresholds to a family's income to determine its poverty status, see "How the Census Bureau Measures Poverty" on the Census Bureau's web site.

The **poverty guidelines** are the other version of the federal poverty measure. They are issued each year in the *Federal Register* by the **Department of Health and Human Services** (HHS). The guidelines are a simplification of the poverty thresholds for use for **administrative** purposes — for instance, determining financial eligibility for certain federal programs. (The full text of the *Federal Register* notice with the 2005 poverty guidelines is available here.)

The poverty guidelines are sometimes loosely referred to as the "federal poverty level" (FPL), but that phrase is ambiguous and should be avoided, especially in situations (e.g., legislative or administrative) where precision is important.

Key differences between poverty thresholds and poverty guidelines are outlined in a table under Frequently Asked Questions (FAQs). See also the discussion of this topic on the Institute for Research on Poverty's web site.

2005 HHS Poverty Guidelines

Persons in Family Unit	48 Contiguous States and D.C.	Alaska	Hawaii
1	$ 9,570	$11,950	$11,010
2	12,830	16,030	14,760
3	16,090	20,110	18,510
4	19,350	24,190	22,260
5	22,610	28,270	26,010
6	25,870	32,350	29,760
7	29,130	36,430	33,510
8	32,390	40,510	37,260
For each additional person, add	3,260	4,080	3,750

SOURCE: *Federal Register*, Vol. 70, No. 33, February 18, 2005, pp. 8373-8375.

The separate poverty guidelines for Alaska and Hawaii reflect Office of Economic Opportunity administrative practice beginning in the 1966-1970 period. Note that the poverty thresholds — the original version of the poverty measure — have never had separate figures for Alaska and Hawaii. The poverty guidelines are not defined for Puerto Rico, the U.S. Virgin Islands, American Samoa, Guam, the Republic of the Marshall Islands, the Federated States of Micronesia, the Commonwealth of the Northern Mariana Islands, and Palau. In cases in which a Federal program using the poverty guidelines serves any of those jurisdictions, the Federal office which administers the program is responsible for deciding whether to use the contiguous-states-and-D.C. guidelines for those jurisdictions or to follow some other procedure.

The poverty guidelines apply to both aged and non-aged units. The guidelines have never had an aged/non-aged distinction; only the Census Bureau (statistical) poverty thresholds have separate figures for aged and non-aged one-person and two-person units.

Programs using the guidelines (or percentage multiples of the guidelines — for instance, 125 percent or 185 percent of the guidelines) in determining eligibility include Head Start, the Food Stamp Program, the National School Lunch Program, the Low-Income Home Energy Assistance Program, and the Children's Health Insurance Program. Note that in general, cash public assistance programs (Temporary Assistance for Needy Families and Supplemental Security Income) do NOT use the poverty guidelines in determining eligibility. The Earned Income Tax Credit program also does NOT use the poverty guidelines to determine eligibility. For a more detailed list of programs that do and don't use the guidelines, see the Frequently Asked Questions (FAQs).

The poverty guidelines (unlike the poverty thresholds) are designated by the year in which they are issued. For instance, the guidelines issued in February 2005 are designated the 2005 poverty guidelines. However, the 2005 HHS poverty guidelines only reflect price changes through calendar year 2004; accordingly, they are approximately equal to the Census Bureau poverty thresholds for calendar year 2004. (The 2004 thresholds are expected to be issued in final form in August 2005; a preliminary version of the 2004 thresholds is now available from the Census Bureau.)

The computations for the 2005 poverty guidelines are available.

The poverty guidelines may be formally referenced as "the poverty guidelines updated periodically in

Skip Navigation
● **HHS Home**
● **Questions?**
● **Contact Us**
● **Site Map**

Search

Prior HHS Poverty Guidelines
and *Federal Register* References

Poverty guidelines since 1982 for the 48 contiguous states and the District of Columbia can be calculated by addition using the figures shown below. (This simple calculation procedure gives correct guideline figures for each year, but it is not identical to the procedure by which the poverty guidelines are calculated from the poverty thresholds each year; see an <u>example calculation</u>.) Before 1982, the poverty guidelines were issued by the Office of Economic Opportunity/Community Services Administration.

HHS Poverty Guidelines

Year	First Person	Each Additional Person	(Four-Person Family)	Page with Complete Details
2005	$9,570	$3,260	($19,350)	**2005 Guidelines**
2004	9,310	3,180	(18,850)	**2004 Guidelines**
2003	8,980	3,140	(18,400)	**2003 Guidelines**
2002	8,860	3,080	(18,100)	**2002 Guidelines**
2001	8,590	3,020	(17,650)	**2001 Guidelines**
2000[1/]	8,350	2,900	(17,050)	**2000 Guidelines**
1999[1/]	8,240	2,820	(16,700)	**1999 Guidelines**
1998	8,050	2,800	(16,450)	**1998 Guidelines**
1997	7,890	2,720	(16,050)	**1997 Guidelines**
1996	7,740	2,620	(15,600)	**1996 Guidelines**
1995	7,470	2,560	(15,150)	
1994	7,360	2,480	(14,800)	
1993	6,970	2,460	(14,350)	
1992	6,810	2,380	(13,950)	
1991	6,620	2,260	(13,400)	
1990[2/]	6,280	2,140	(12,700)	

1989 2/	5,980	2,040	(12,100)	
1988	5,770	1,960	(11,650)	
1987	5,500	1,900	(11,200)	
1986	5,360	1,880	(11,000)	
1985	5,250	1,800	(10,650)	
1984	4,980	1,740	(10,200)	
1983	4,860	1,680	(9,900)	
1982 3/	4,680	1,540	(9,300)	

1. Note that 1999 and 2000 poverty guidelines figures should **NOT** be used in connection with determining poverty population figures from 2000 Decennial Census data. Poverty population figures are calculated using the Census Bureau poverty thresholds, not the poverty guidelines.
2. Note that 1989 and 1990 poverty guidelines figures should **NOT** be used in connection with determining poverty population figures from 1990 Decennial Census data. Poverty population figures are calculated using the Census Bureau poverty thresholds, not the poverty guidelines.
3. Figures for nonfarm families only.

For a table showing the poverty guidelines for all family sizes back to 1965, see Table 3.E8 in the most recent *Annual Statistical Supplement* of the *Social Security Bulletin*. This table is also available on the Social Security Administration's Web site at http://www.ssa.gov/policy/docs/statcomps/supplement/2003/3e.html.

Poverty guidelines for the years shown above can be found in the *Federal Register* as follows:

2005 — Vol. 70, No. 33, February 18, 2005, pp. 8373-8375
2004 — Vol. 69, No. 30, February 13, 2004, pp. 7336-7338
2003 — Vol. 68, No. 26, February 7, 2003, pp. 6456-6458
2002 — Vol. 67, No. 31, February 14, 2002, pp. 6931-6933
2001 — Vol. 66, No. 33, February 16, 2001, pp. 10695-10697

2000 — Vol. 65, No. 31, February 15, 2000, pp. 7555-7557
1999 — Vol. 64, No. 52, March 18, 1999, pp. 13428-13430
1998 — Vol. 63, No. 36, February 24, 1998, pp. 9235-9238
1997 — Vol. 62, No. 46, March 10, 1997, pp. 10856-10859
1996 — Vol. 61, No. 43, March 4, 1996, pp. 8286-8288

1995 — Vol. 60, No. 27, February 9, 1995, pp. 7772-7774
1994 — Vol. 59, No. 28, February 10, 1994, pp. 6277-6278
1993 — Vol. 58, No. 28, February 12, 1993, pp. 8287-8289
1992 — Vol. 57, No. 31, February 14, 1992, pp. 5455-5457
1991 — Vol. 56, No. 34, February 20, 1991, pp. 6589-6861

1990 — Vol. 55, No. 33, February 16, 1990, pp. 5664-5666
1989 — Vol. 54, No. 31, February 16, 1989, pp. 7097-7098

TITLE 11. BANKRUPTCY UNITED STATES CODE

Chapter 5. Creditors, the Debtor and the Estate

Subchapter II. Debtor's Duties and Benefits

11 USC § 523. Exceptions to discharge

(a) A discharge under section 727, 1141, 1228(a), 1228(b), or 1328(b) of this title does not discharge an individual debtor from any debt--

  (1) for a tax or a customs duty--

    (A) of the kind and for the periods specified in section 507(a)(3) or 507(a)(8) of this title, whether or not a claim for such tax was filed or allowed;

    (B) with respect to which a return, or equivalent report or notice, if required--

      (i) was not filed or given; or

      (ii) was filed or given after the date on which such return, report, or notice was last due, under applicable law or under any extension, and after two years before the date of the filing of the petition; or

    (C) with respect to which the debtor made a fraudulent return or willfully attempted in any manner to evade or defeat such tax;

  (2) for money, property, services, or an extension, renewal, or refinancing of credit, to the extent obtained by--

    (A) false pretenses, a false representation, or actual fraud, other than a statement respecting the debtor's or an insider's financial condition;

    (B) use of a statement in writing--

      (i) that is materially false;

      (ii) respecting the debtor's or an insider's financial condition;

      (iii) on which the creditor to whom the debtor is liable for such money, property, services, or credit reasonably relied; and

      (iv) that the debtor caused to be made or published with intent to deceive; or

    (C)

      (i) for purposes of subparagraph (A)--

        (I) consumer debts owed to a single creditor and aggregating more than $500 [$550] for luxury goods or services incurred by an individual debtor on or within 90 days before the order for relief under this title are presumed to be nondischargeable; and

        (II) cash advances aggregating more than $750 [$825] that are extensions of consumer credit under an open end credit plan obtained by an individual debtor on or within 70 days before the order for relief under this title, are presumed to be nondischargeable; and

[Dollar amounts in subsections 523(a)(2)(C)(i) and (ii) are adjusted on April 1 every 3 years by section 104. Adjusted amounts effective 4-1-07 are in brackets.]

(ii) for purposes of this subparagraph--

(I) the terms "consumer", "credit", and "open end credit plan" have the same meanings as in section 103 of the Truth in Lending Act; and

(II) the term "luxury goods or services" does not include goods or services reasonably necessary for the support or maintenance of the debtor or a dependent of the debtor.

(3) neither listed nor scheduled under section 521(1) of this title, with the name, if known to the debtor, of the creditor to whom such debt is owed, in time to permit--

(A) if such debt is not of a kind specified in paragraph (2), (4), or (6) of this subsection, timely filing of a proof of claim, unless such creditor had notice or actual knowledge of the case in time for such timely filing; or

(B) if such debt is of a kind specified in paragraph (2), (4), or (6) of this subsection, timely filing of a proof of claim and timely request for a determination of dischargeability of such debt under one of such paragraphs, unless such creditor had notice or actual knowledge of the case in time for such timely filing and request;

(4) for fraud or defalcation while acting in a fiduciary capacity, embezzlement, or larceny;

(5) for a domestic support obligation;

(6) for willful and malicious injury by the debtor to another entity or to the property of another entity;

(7) to the extent such debt is for a fine, penalty, or forfeiture payable to and for the benefit of a governmental unit, and is not compensation for actual pecuniary loss, other than a tax penalty--

(A) relating to a tax of a kind not specified in paragraph (1) of this subsection; or

(B) imposed with respect to a transaction or event that occurred before three years before the date of the filing of the petition;

(8) unless excepting such debt from discharge under this paragraph would impose an undue hardship on the debtor and the debtor's dependents, for--

(A)

(i) an educational benefit overpayment or loan made, insured, or guaranteed by a governmental unit, or made under any program funded in whole or in part by a governmental unit or nonprofit institution; or

(ii) an obligation to repay funds received as an educational benefit, scholarship, or stipend; or

(B) any other educational loan that is a qualified education loan, as defined in section 221(d)(1) of the Internal Revenue Code of 1986, incurred by a debtor who is an individual;

(9) for death or personal injury caused by the debtor's operation of a motor vehicle, vessel, or aircraft if such operation was unlawful because the debtor was intoxicated from using alcohol, a drug, or another substance;

(10) that was or could have been listed or scheduled by the debtor in a prior case concerning the debtor under this title or under the Bankruptcy Act in which the debtor waived discharge, or was denied a discharge under section 727(a)(2), (3), (4), (5), (6), or (7) of this title, or under section 14c(1), (2), (3), (4), (6), or (7) of such Act;

(11) provided in any final judgment, unreviewable order, or consent order or decree entered in any court of the United States or of any State, issued by a Federal depository institutions regulatory agency, or contained in any settlement agreement entered into by the debtor, arising from any act of fraud or defalcation while acting in a fiduciary capacity committed with respect to any depository institution or insured credit union;

(12) for malicious or reckless failure to fulfill any commitment by the debtor to a Federal depository institutions regulatory agency to maintain the capital of an insured depository institution, except that this paragraph shall not extend any such commitment which would otherwise be terminated due to any act of such agency;

(13) for any payment of an order of restitution issued under title 18, United States Code;

(14) incurred to pay a tax to the United States that would be nondischargeable pursuant to paragraph (1);

(14A) incurred to pay a tax to a governmental unit, other than the United States, that would be nondischargeable under paragraph (1);

(14B) incurred to pay fines or penalties imposed under Federal election law;

(15) to a spouse, former spouse, or child of the debtor and not of the kind described in paragraph (5) that is incurred by the debtor in the course of a divorce or separation or in connection with a separation agreement, divorce decree or other order of a court of record, or a determination made in accordance with State or territorial law by a governmental unit;

(16) for a fee or assessment that becomes due and payable after the order for relief to a membership association with respect to the debtor's interest in a unit that has condominium ownership , in a share of a cooperative corporation, or a lot in a homeowners association, for as long as the debtor or the trustee has a legal, equitable, or possessory ownership interest in such unit, such corporation, or such lot, but nothing in this paragraph shall except from discharge the debt of a debtor for a membership association fee or assessment for a period arising before entry of the order for relief in a pending or subsequent bankruptcy case;

(17) for a fee imposed on a prisoner by any court for the filing of a case, motion, complaint, or appeal, or for other costs and expenses assessed with respect to such filing, regardless of an assertion of poverty by the debtor under subsection (b) or (f)(2) of section 1915 of title 28 (or a similar non-Federal law), or the debtor's status as a prisoner, as defined in section 1915(h) of title 28 (or a similar non-Federal law);

(18) owed to a pension, profit-sharing, stock bonus, or other plan established under section 401, 403, 408, 408A, 414, 457, or 501(c) of the Internal Revenue Code of 1986, under--

(A) a loan permitted under section 408(b)(1) of the Employee Retirement Income Security Act of 1974, or subject to section 72(p) of the Internal Revenue Code of 1986; or

(B) a loan from a thrift savings plan permitted under subchapter III of chapter 84 of title 5, that satisfies the requirements of section 8433(g) of such title;

but nothing in this paragraph may be construed to provide that any loan made under a governmental plan under section 414(d), or a contract or account under section 403(b), of the Internal Revenue Code of 1986 constitutes a claim or a debt under this title; or

(19) that--

(A) is for--

(i) the violation of any of the Federal securities laws (as that term is defined in section 3(a)(47) of the Securities Exchange Act of 1934), any of the State securities laws, or any regulation or order issued under such Federal or State securities laws; or

(ii) common law fraud, deceit, or manipulation in connection with the purchase or sale of any security; and

(B) results, before, on, or after the date on which the petition was filed, from--

(i) any judgment, order, consent order, or decree entered in any Federal or State judicial or administrative proceeding;

(ii) any settlement agreement entered into by the debtor; or

(iii) any court or administrative order for any damages, fine, penalty, citation, restitutionary payment, disgorgement payment, attorney fee, cost, or other payment owed by the debtor.

For purposes of this subsection, the term "return" means a return that satisfies the requirements of applicable nonbankruptcy law (including applicable filing requirements). Such term includes a return prepared pursuant to section 6020(a) of the Internal Revenue Code of 1986, or similar State or local law, or a written stipulation to a judgment or a final order entered by a nonbankruptcy tribunal, but does not include a return made pursuant to section 6020(b) of the Internal Revenue Code of 1986, or a similar State or local law.

(b) Notwithstanding subsection (a) of this section, a debt that was excepted from discharge under subsection (a)(1), (a)(3), or (a)(8) of this section, under section 17a(1), 17a(3), or 17a(5) of the Bankruptcy Act, under section 439A of the Higher Education Act of 1965, or under section 733(g) of the Public Health Service Act in a prior case concerning the debtor under this title, or under the Bankruptcy Act, is dischargeable in a case under this title unless, by the terms of subsection (a) of this section, such debt is not dischargeable in the case under this title.

(c)

    (1) Except as provided in subsection (a)(3)(B) of this section, the debtor shall be discharged from a debt of a kind specified in paragraph (2), (4), or (6) of subsection (a) of this section, unless, on request of the creditor to whom such debt is owed, and after notice and a hearing, the court determines such debt to be excepted from discharge under paragraph (2), (4), or (6) , as the case may be, of subsection (a) of this section.

    (2) Paragraph (1) shall not apply in the case of a Federal depository institutions regulatory agency seeking, in its capacity as conservator, receiver, or liquidating agent for an insured depository institution, to recover a debt described in subsection (a)(2), (a)(4), (a)(6), or (a)(11) owed to such institution by an institution-affiliated party unless the receiver, conservator, or liquidating agent was appointed in time to reasonably comply, or for a Federal depository institutions regulatory agency acting in its corporate capacity as a successor to such receiver, conservator, or liquidating agent to reasonably comply, with subsection (a)(3)(B) as a creditor of such institution-affiliated party with respect to such debt.

(d) If a creditor requests a determination of dischargeability of a consumer debt under subsection (a)(2) of this section, and such debt is discharged, the court shall grant judgment in favor of the debtor for the costs of, and a reasonable attorney's fee for, the proceeding if the court finds that the position of the creditor was not substantially justified, except that the court shall not award such costs and fees if special circumstances would make the award unjust.

(e) Any institution-affiliated party of an insured depository institution shall be considered to be acting in a fiduciary capacity with respect to the purposes of subsection (a)(4) or (11).

Chapter 7 Bankruptcy Forms (California Central District)

Schedule I-Current Income of Individual Debtor (Form B6I)

Form B6I - (Rev. 12/03)		2003 USBC, Central District of California
In re _____ Debtor.	Case No.: _____ (If known)	

SCHEDULE I - CURRENT INCOME OF INDIVIDUAL DEBTOR(S)

The column labeled "Spouse" must be completed in all cases filed by joint debtors and by a married debtor in a chapter 12 or 13 case whether or not a joint petition is filed, unless the spouses are separated and a joint petition is not filed.

Debtor's Marital Status:	DEPENDENTS OF DEBTOR AND SPOUSE	
	RELATIONSHIP	AGE

Employment:	DEBTOR	SPOUSE
Occupation		
Name of Employer		
How Long Employed		
Address of Employer		

Income: (Estimate of average monthly income)	DEBTOR	SPOUSE
Current monthly gross wages, salary, and commissions (prorate if not paid monthly)	$_____	$_____
Estimated monthly overtime	$_____	$_____
SUBTOTAL	$_____	$_____
LESS PAYROLL DEDUCTIONS		
a. Payroll taxes and Social Security	$_____	$_____
b. Insurance	$_____	$_____
c. Union dues	$_____	$_____
d. Other (specify) _____	$_____	$_____
SUBTOTAL OF PAYROLL DEDUCTIONS	$_____	$_____
TOTAL NET MONTHLY TAKE HOME PAY	$_____	$_____
Regular income from operation of business or profession or farm (attach detailed statement)	$_____	$_____
Income from real property	$_____	$_____
Interest and dividends	$_____	$_____
Alimony, maintenance or support payments payable to the debtor for the debtor's use or that of dependents listed above.	$_____	$_____
Social security or other government assistance (Specify) _____	$_____	$_____
Pension or retirement income	$_____	$_____
Other monthly income	$_____	$_____
(Specify) _____	$_____	$_____
_____	$_____	$_____
TOTAL MONTHLY INCOME	$_____	$_____
TOTAL COMBINED MONTHLY INCOME $_____	(Report also on Summary of Schedules)	

Describe any increase or decrease of more than 10% in any of the above categories anticipated to occur within the year following the filing of this document:

Schedule J-Current Expenditures of Individual Debtor (Form B6J)

Form B6J - (Rev. 12/03)   2003 USBC, Central District of California

In re	Case No.:
Debtor.	(If known)

SCHEDULE J - CURRENT EXPENDITURES OF INDIVIDUAL DEBTOR(S)

Complete this schedule by estimating the average monthly expenses of the debtor and the debtor's family. Prorate any payments made bi-weekly, quarterly, semi-annually, or annually to show monthly rate.

☐ Check this box if a joint petition is filed and debtor's spouse maintains a separate household. Complete a separate schedule of expenditures labeled "Spouse."

Rent or home mortgage payment (include lot rented for mobile home) $_____

Are real estate taxes included?   Yes _____   No _____
Is property insurance included?   Yes _____   No _____

Utilities: Electricity and heating fuel $_____
                Water and sewer $_____
                Telephone $_____
                Other _____ $_____
Home Maintenance (Repairs and Upkeep) $_____
Food $_____
Clothing $_____
Laundry and dry cleaning $_____
Medical and dental expenses $_____
Transportation (not including car payments) $_____
Recreation, clubs and entertainment, newspapers, magazines, etc. $_____
Charitable contributions   _____ $_____
Insurance (not deducted from wages or included in home mortgage payments):
     Homeowner's or renter's $_____
     Life $_____
     Health $_____
     Auto $_____
     Other _____ $_____
Taxes (not deducted from wages or included in home mortgage payments)
(specify) _____ $_____
Installment payments (In chapter 12 and 13 cases, do not list payments to be included in the plan)
     Auto $_____
     Other _____ $_____
     Other _____ $_____
Alimony, maintenance, and support paid to others $_____
Payments for support of additional dependents not living at your home $_____
Regular expenses from operation of business, profession, or farm (attach detailed statement) $_____
Other _____ $_____

TOTAL MONTHLY EXPENSES (Report also on Summary of Schedules) $_____

[FOR CHAPTER 12 AND 13 DEBTORS ONLY]
Provide the information requested below, including whether plan payments are to be made bi-weekly, monthly, annually, or at some other regular interval.

A. Total projected monthly income $_____
B. Total projected monthly expenses $_____
C. Excess income (A minus B) $_____
D. Total amount to be paid into plan each _____
                                   (interval)

UNITED STATES BANKRUPTCY COURT
Central District of California

In re: :   Case No. _____

Chapter   7

BUSINESS INCOME AND EXPENSES

FINANCIAL REVIEW OF THE DEBTOR'S BUSINESS (NOTE: ONLY INCLUDE information directly related to the business operation.)

PART A - GROSS BUSINESS INCOME FOR PREVIOUS 12 MONTHS:

    1. Gross Income For 12 Months Prior to Filing: $ _____

PART B - ESTIMATED AVERAGE FUTURE GROSS MONTHLY INCOME:

    2. Gross Monthly Income: $ _____

PART C - ESTIMATED FUTURE MONTHLY EXPENSES:

    3. Net Employee Payroll (Other Than Debtor) $ _____
    4. Payroll Taxes   _____
    5. Unemployment Taxes   _____
    6. Worker's Compensation   _____
    7. Other Taxes   _____
    8. Inventory Purchases (Including raw materials)   _____
    9. Purchase of Feed/Fertilizer/Seed/Spray   _____
    10. Rent (Other than debtor's principal residence)   _____
    11. Utilities   _____
    12. Office Expenses and Supplies   _____
    13. Repairs and Maintenance   _____
    14. Vehicle Expenses   _____
    15. Travel and Entertainment   _____
    16. Equipment Rental and Leases   _____
    17. Legal/Accounting/Other Professional Fees   _____
    18. Insurance   _____
    19. Employee Benefits (e.g., pension, medical, etc.)   _____
    20. Payments to Be Made Directly By Debtor to Secured Creditors For

        Pre-Petition Business Debts (Specify):

        None   _____

    21. Other (Specify):

        None   _____

    22. Total Monthly Expenses (Add items 3 - 21) $ _____

PART D - ESTIMATED AVERAGE NET MONTHLY INCOME:

    23. AVERAGE NET MONTHLY INCOME (Subtract Item 22 from Item 2) $ _____

Form B6F (Official Form 6F) - (Rev. 12/03)   2003 USBC, Central District of California

In re **Name**		Case No.:	
	Debtor.		(If known)

SCHEDULE F - CREDITORS HOLDING UNSECURED NONPRIORITY CLAIMS

State the name, mailing address, including zip code, and last four digits of the account number, if any, of all entities holding unsecured claims without priority against the debtor or the property of the debtor, as of the date of filing of the petition. Do not include claims listed in Schedules D and E. If all creditors will not fit on this page, use the continuation sheet provided.

If any entity other than a spouse in a joint case may be jointly liable on a claim, place an "X" in the column labeled "Codebtor," include the entity on the appropriate schedule of creditors, and complete Schedule H - Codebtors. If a joint petition is filed, state whether husband, wife, both of them, or the marital community may be liable on each claim by placing an "H," "W," "J," or "C" in the column labeled "Husband, Wife, Joint, or Community."

If the claim is contingent, place an "X" in the column labeled "Contingent." If the claim is unliquidated, place an "X" in the column labeled "Unliquidated." If the claim is disputed, place an "X" in the column labeled "Disputed." (You may need to place an "X" in more than one of these three columns.)

Report total of all claims listed on this schedule in the box labeled "Total" on the last sheet of the completed schedule. Report this total also on the Summary of Schedules.

☐ Check this box if debtor has no creditors holding unsecured nonpriority claims to report on this Schedule F.

CREDITOR'S NAME AND MAILING ADDRESS INCLUDING ZIP CODE	CODEBTOR	HUSBAND, WIFE, JOINT, OR COMMUNITY	DATE CLAIM WAS INCURRED, AND CONSIDERATION FOR CLAIM, IF CLAIM IS SUBJECT TO SETOFF, SO STATE	CONTINGENT	UNLIQUIDATED	DISPUTED	AMOUNT OF CLAIM
Last four digits of ACCOUNT NO. 8233 U. S. Dept. of Education Direct Loan Servicing System PO Box 4609 Utica, NY 13504-4609			Student Loan December 2003				$50,000.00
Last four digits of ACCOUNT NO.							
Last four digits of ACCOUNT NO.							
Last four digits of ACCOUNT NO.							
				Subtotal ➤			$
_____ Continuation Sheets attached				Total ➤			$
				(Report total also on Summary of Schedules)			

In re		Case No.:
	Debtor.	(If known)

SCHEDULE F - CREDITORS HOLDING UNSECURED NONPRIORITY CLAIMS

State the name, mailing address, including zip code, and last four digits of the account number, if any, of all entities holding unsecured claims without priority against the debtor or the property of the debtor, as of the date of filing of the petition. Do not include claims listed in Schedules D and E. If all creditors will not fit on this page, use the continuation sheet provided.

If any entity other than a spouse in a joint case may be jointly liable on a claim, place an "X" in the column labeled "Codebtor," include the entity on the appropriate schedule of creditors, and complete Schedule H - Codebtors. If a joint petition is filed, state whether husband, wife, both of them, or the marital community may be liable on each claim by placing an "H," "W," "J," or "C" in the column labeled "Husband, Wife, Joint, or Community."

If the claim is contingent, place an "X" in the column labeled "Contingent." If the claim is unliquidated, place an "X" in the column labeled "Unliquidated." If the claim is disputed, place an "X" in the column labeled "Disputed." (You may need to place an "X" in more than one of these three columns.)

Report total of all claims listed on this schedule in the box labeled "Total" on the last sheet of the completed schedule. Report this total also on the Summary of Schedules.

☐ Check this box if debtor has no creditors holding unsecured nonpriority claims to report on this Schedule F.

CREDITOR'S NAME AND MAILING ADDRESS INCLUDING ZIP CODE	CODEBTOR	HUSBAND, WIFE, JOINT, OR COMMUNITY	DATE CLAIM WAS INCURRED, AND CONSIDERATION FOR CLAIM, IF CLAIM IS SUBJECT TO SETOFF, SO STATE	CONTINGENT	UNLIQUIDATED	DISPUTED	AMOUNT OF CLAIM
Last four digits of ACCOUNT NO.							
Last four digits of ACCOUNT NO.							
Last four digits of ACCOUNT NO.							
Last four digits of ACCOUNT NO.							

_____ Continuation Sheets attached

Subtotal ► $

Total ► $

(Report total also on Summary of Schedules)

Motion to Reopen Bankruptcy Sample

SAMPLE

UNITED STATES BANKRUPTCY COURT
SOUTHERN DISTRICT OF OHIO
EASTERN DIVISION

IN RE:

Chuck Stewart,	) Case No.: 06-1234
	) Chapter 7
SSN: 123-45-6789	) Judge: Judy Smith
	)
Debtor(s).	)

<u>MOTION TO REOPEN BANKRUPTCY CASE</u>

Chuck Stewart HEREBY MOVES THIS Court for an order reopening the above-referenced bankruptcy case pursuant to 11 U.S.C. § 350(b) and Bankruptcy Rule 5010 in order to file an Adversary Proceeding to determine dischargability of student loan(s) debt pursuant to 11 U.S.C. §532(a)(8). Movant had filed original bankruptcy under the mistaken belief that it was impossible to bankrupt student loans. Only now has Movant learned of the possibility for filing an Adversary Proceeding and would like to take that action.

1. The Debtor(s) filed a voluntary bankruptcy petition under Chapter 7 on May, 16, 2005.

2. The Debtor received a discharge on August 15, 2003.

3. The bankruptcy case was closed on August 15, 2003.

4. The movant seeks to file an Adversary Proceeding to determine dischargability of student loan(s) debt pursuant to 11 U.S.C. §532(a)(8).

WHEREFORE, movant respectfully requests that the Court enter on order reopening this bankruptcy case.

Dated: June 20, 2009   _____

                                          Chuck Stewart

Motion to Reopen Bankruptcy Case - 1

UNITED STATES BANKRUPTCY COURT
(Title of District)

IN RE:

_____,) Case No.: [**Case number**]
)
                  Debtor(s).) Chapter
)
)
_____   )

MOTION TO REOPEN BANKRUPTCY CASE

_____ HEREBY MOVES THIS Court for an order reopening the above-referenced bankruptcy case pursuant to 11 U.S.C. § 350(b) and Bankruptcy Rule 5010 in order to file an Adversary Proceeding to determine dischargability of student loan(s) debt pursuant to 11 U.S.C. §532(a)(8). Movant had filed original bankruptcy under the mistaken belief that it was impossible to bankrupt student loans. Only now has Movant learned of the possibility for filing an Adversary Proceeding and would like to take that action.

    1. The Debtor(s) filed a voluntary bankruptcy petition under Chapter _ on

        _____.

    2. The Debtor received a discharge on _____.

    3. The bankruptcy case was closed on _____.

    4. The movant seeks to file an Adversary Proceeding to determine

        dischargability of student loan(s) debt pursuant to 11 U.S.C. §532(a)(8).

WHEREFORE, movant respectfully requests that the Court enter on order reopening this bankruptcy case.

Dated: _____   _____

                                        [Movant]

UNITED STATES BANKRUPTCY COURT
SOUTHERN DISTRICT OF FLORIDA
www.flsb.uscourts.gov

In re:
                               Case No.
                               Chapter 7

_____ Debtor _____ /

ORDER REOPENING CASE TO ADD OMITTED CREDITOR(S)

THIS CAUSE having come before the court upon debtor's Motion to Reopen Case pursuant to 11 U.S.C. §350, Bankruptcy Rule 5010, and Local Rule 5010-1(B) and the court having considered the motion and having determined that good cause has been shown, and being otherwise fully advised in the premises, it is

ORDERED:

1.   This case is reopened. No filing fee is required to be paid to the clerk unless the debtor fails to comply with paragraph 3 of this order and the case is closed pursuant to paragraph 4. No trustee shall be appointed.

2.   Within 15 days from the entry of this order, the debtor shall amend the schedules (and pay applicable amendment fee) to add the name(s) and address(es) of the creditor(s) previously omitted from the original schedules. A supplemental matrix of creditors as required by the "Clerk's Instructions for Preparing, Submitting and Obtaining Service Matrices" must accompany the amended schedules.

3.   The debtor (or the debtor's attorney) is directed to furnish a complete and correct copy of this order to all affected parties, including the added creditor and a copy of the clerk's notice of meeting of creditors must also be served on the creditor as required under Local Rule 1009-1(D). A certificate of service must be filed as required under Local Rule 2002-1(F).

4.   Within 15 days from the entry of this order, the debtor shall file an adversary proceeding(s) to determine whether the debt(s), subject to such amendment(s), is/are or is/are not dischargeable under 11 U.S.C. §523(a).

5.   Upon the filing of the adversary case(s) by the debtor, or upon the debtor's failure to comply with this order, the case will be reclosed by the clerk's office.

###

Submitted by:

Copies to:
Debtor (or Debtor's Attorney)

SAMPLE

UNITED STATES BANKRUPTCY COURT
SOUTHERN DISTRICT OF OHIO
EASTERN DIVISION

IN RE:

    Chuck Stewart   ) Case No.: 07-12345
) Chapter7
      SSN: 123-45-6789   ) Judge: Judy Smith
)
)
      Debtor.   )

AMENDMENT TO SCHEUDLE F

CREDITOR HOLDING UNSECURED CLAIMS

The Debtor Amends Schedule F to add the following creditor, as described below:

Creditor	Description	Amount
U.S. Dept. of Education	Student Loan	$50,000.00
Direct Loan Servicing System	Date of debt: 2003	
PO Box 4609		
Utica, NY 13504-4609		

Dated: June 20, 2009   _____

                                     Plaintiff (*sign your name*)

Amend Schedule F - 1

UNITED STATES BANKRUPTCY COURT
(Title of District)

IN RE:

_____,) Case No.: [**Case number**]
) Chapter
                    Debtor(s).   ) Judge:
)
)
_____   )

AMENDMENT TO SCHEUDLE F

CREDITOR HOLDING UNSECURED CLAIMS

The Debtor Amends Schedule F to add the following creditor, as described below:

Creditor   Description   Amount

Dated: _____   _____
                                                 Plaintiff (*signature*)

Amend Schedule F - 1

Student Loan History

It is important to know the status of your student loans. The table below helps to organize that information. If you do not have current information, contact your lender for a complete printout of your loans.

Use additional copies of this table as needed.

	Loan 1	Loan 2	Loan 3	Loan 4	Loan 5	Loan 6
Name of Loan						
Guarantor						
Amount						
Date of Issuance						
Payment Status						
Amount Repaid to date						
Payment dates						

Current Income Status

This worksheet is used to establish your current income at the time of the adversary proceeding mediation or trial. Use *Chapter 7 Bankruptcy (Form B6I)— Schedule I-Current Income of Individual Debtor(s)* for data. Use additional sheets as necessary.

Debtor's Martial Status:	DEPENDENTS OF DEBTOR AND SPOUSE		
	RELATIONSHIP		AGE
Employment:	**DEBTOR**		**SPOUSE**
Occupation			
Name of Employer			
How Long Employed			
Address of Employer			

	Col. 1	Col. 2	Col. 3	Col. 4
Instruction: In columns 1 & 2, write the numbers listed with your Chapter 7 bankruptcy form B6I. The 3rd & 4th columns are the numbers updated at the time the adversary proceeding mediation or trial.	At time of Chapter 7 filing	At time of Chapter 7 filing	Current Status (date)	Current Status (date)
Income: (Estimate of average monthly income)	Debtor	Spouse	Debtor	Spouse
Current monthly gross wages, salary, and commissions (prorate if not paid monthly)				
Estimated monthly overtime				
SUBTOTAL				
LESS PAYROLL DEDUCATIONS				
a. Payroll taxes and Social Security				
b. Insurance				
c. Union dues				
d. Other (specify)				
SUBTOTAL OF PAYROLL DEDUCTIONS				
TOTAL NET MONTHLY TAKE HOME PAY				
Regular income form operation of business or profession or farm (attach detailed statement)				
Income from real property				
Interest and dividends				
Alimony, maintenance or support payments payable to the debtor for the debtor's use of that of dependents listed above.				
Social security or other government assistance (Specify) _____				
Pension or retirement income				
Other monthly income (Specify) _____				
(Specify) _____				
TOTAL MONTHLY INCOME				
TOTAL COMBINED MONTHLY INCOME				

Current Expenditure Status

This 2-page worksheet is used to establish your current expenses at the time of the adversary proceeding mediation or trail and to compare these expenses to national norms.

INSTRUCTIONS:

FIRST: Go to the United States Department of Health and Human Services (http://aspe.hhs.gov/poverty/poverty.shtml) and **download a copy** of the current Federal Poverty Guideline. This is also available at your local library. The table gives the Poverty level as related to family size. Look up your family size and fill in below:

    _____ : Size of your Family Unit
    _____ : Total Yearly Income (see your Current Financial Status worksheet)
    _____ : Yearly Income as specified by the Federal Poverty Guideline

Comment: If your Yearly Income is very different than what is established by the Federal Poverty Guideline, you need to explain the discrepancy. Most courts, rightly or wrongly, use the Federal Poverty Guidelines as a baseline for determining "undue hardship" when considering discharging federally guaranteed student loans. Very few courts have understood that undue hardship is to be evaluated at the middle class level and reject the Federal Poverty Guidelines analysis. Thus, if your family income is more than 1 ½ time greater than that established by the Federal Poverty Guideline, be prepared to advocate the use of a more moderate middle-class analysis. See Chapter 7 for this discussion.

SECOND: Complete the Current Expenditure Status table on the next page.

Column 1— Use the data from your *Chapter 7 Bankruptcy (Form B6J)— Schedule J-Current Expenditures of Individual Debtor(s)* to fill in column 1.

Column 2 — If there have been any changes to your expenditures listed in column 1, make the changes in column 2.

Column 3 — These are national norms developed by the IRS. Go to the IRS website for Collection Financial Standards (www.irg.gov/individuals/article/0,,id=96543,00.html. Follow the links to the various standards. The boxes in column 3 represent values pulled from the IRS Collection Financial Standards. In most cases they represent a summation of a number of expenditures. Below is indicated which Collection Financial Standards are placed in the table and the expenditures they correspond. Samples of the Collection Financial Standards are in the Appendix.

    Box 1—Food, Clothing and Other Items (www.irs.gov/businesses/small/article/0,,id=104627,00.html) is the same as the sum of Food, Clothing, and Laundry and dry cleaning.

    Box 2—Housing and Utilities (www.irs.gov/businesses/small/article/0,,id=104701,00.html) is the same as the sum of Rent, Electricity and Heating Fuel, Water and Sewer, and Telephone.

    Box 3—Transportation (ownership) (www.irs.gov/businesses/small/article/0,,id=104623,00.html) is the same as Installment payments—Auto.

    Box 4—Transportation (operating costs and public transportation costs) (www.irs.gov/businesses/small/article/0,,id=104623,00.html) is the same as Transportation (not including car payments) and Insurance—auto.

Column 4 — If your expenditures are significantly higher or lower than the national norm, then you need to write an explanation. For example, your housing costs are higher than the national norm because you live in a high rent area. A good explanation is that you live closer to work and thus save on transportation costs. Or, this places you closer to a grandparent who provided free daily childcare for your young children. Maybe your automobile expenses are higher due to higher insurance rates for those living in the city, or maybe they are very old cars requiring much repair.

Current Expenditure Status	Col. 1	Col. 2	Col. 3	Col. 4
See Instructions for how to use this chart.	At time of Chapter 7 filing	Current Status (date)	National Norms	Comment
Rent or home mortgage payment (include lot rented for mobile home)			Box 2	
Are real estate taxes included? Yes ___ No ____				
Is property insurance included? Yes ___ No ___				
Utilities: Electricity and heating fuel				
Water and sewer				
Telephone				
Other _____				
Home Maintenance (Repairs and Upkeep)				
Food			Box 1	
Clothing				
Laundry and dry cleaning				
Medical and dental expenses				
Transportation (not including car payments)			Box 4	
Recreation, clubs and entertainment, newspapers, magazines, etc.				
Charitable contributions				
Insurance (not deducted from wages or included in home mortgage payments):				
Homeowner's or renter's				
Life				
Health				
Auto			Box 4	
Other _____				
Taxes (not deducted from wages or included in home mortgage payments) (specify)_____				
Installment payments (in chapter 12 and 13 cases, do not list payments to be included in the plan)				
Auto			Box 3	
Other _____				
Other _____				
Alimony, maintenance, and support paid to others				
Payments for support of additional dependents not living at your home				
Regular expenses from operation of business, profession, or farm (attach detailed statement)				
Other _____				
TOTAL MONTHLY EXPENSES				

Work Time Accounting Table

Goal: You want to show that your time working (jobs for which you receive money or expect to) and taking care of dependents exceeds approximately 60 hours a week—so that the court can't come back to you and insist that you get another job. If you are medically restricted to work fewer hours per week, make a detailed notation in the job description. Still, the goal is to show that your time is fully committed.

Make sure the work hours listed here match your income statement on your Chapter 7 bankruptcy—Schedule I. See the next worksheet: Financial Status to collaborate the numbers here. Create this table on your own paper.

Current Work Time Load	Hours Per Week
Job #1: Title and Company: Duties:	
Job #2: Title and Company: Duties:	
Job #3: Title and Company: Duties:	
Job #4: Title and Company: Duties:	
Dependents: (give names, ages, any medical condition)	
Dependents: (give names, ages, any medical condition)	
Total	

Income and Student Loan Payment

The purpose of this worksheet is to present your income tax reports for all years since obtaining your most recent student loan, determine if the income exceeded the Federal Poverty Guidelines, and if you made payments on your student loans.

Instructions:

1. Make a copy of the top page of your income tax filings <u>for every year from current, back to the year you last received a student loan</u>. The chart below shows you which lines of the Form 1040, 1040A and 1040 EZ apply. Fill in the <u>Income (Gross)</u>, <u>Total Income</u>, and <u>Taxable Income</u> in the marked columns in the large chart on the next page for each year.

Where to Find Tax Information by Form and Line Number

	Income (Gross)	Total Income	Taxable Income
Line Number Form 1040	7	22	36
Line Number Form 1040A	7	15	21
Line Number Form 1040 EZ	1	4	6

2. Go to the website of the United States Department of Health and Human Services (http://aspe.hhs.gov/poverty/poverty.shtml) and download a copy of the Federal Poverty Guidelines (a copy of this homepage and document are in Appendix B) for all years since receiving your last student loan until now. If you do not have access to the web, your local library should have a copy of this government publication. Locate your size family in the Guidelines and write the income number in the column marked <u>Federal Poverty Guideline</u>. Indicate your family size.

3. Now compare your Total Income with the Federal Poverty Guideline. If your <u>Total Income</u> is greater than the <u>Federal Poverty Guidelines</u> for your size family, write the word "yes" in the column marked <u>Are You Above Poverty Level?</u>

4. Previously, you prepared the worksheet *Student Loan History*. From that worksheet, you should be able to tell which years you made payments on your student loans. In the chart below, indicate which years you made payments on your student loans by writing the dollar amount in the column marked <u>Student loan payments?</u> If your student loans were in forbearance or deferment, write the words "forbearance" or "deferment" as necessary in the <u>Student loan payments?</u> column.

5. If there are years in which you failed to make student loan payments or they were not in deferment or forbearance, AND your income was above the poverty level, you need to write some explanation.

Income Tax Report by Year (SAMPLE)

Year	Income (Gross)	Total Income	Taxable Income	Federal Poverty Guideline Family Size= 3	Are You Above Poverty Level?	Student loan payments?
(year you received your last student loan) 2000	15,000	14,000	13,500	14,150	no	deferment
2001	14,000	13,900	13,200	14,630	no	deferment
2002	15,000	14,500	14,500	15,020	no	deferment
2003	17,000	16,000	14,200	15,260	yes	no
2004	23,000	21,000	20,400	15,670	yes	$1,200
2005	17,500	17,000	16,500	16,090	yes	forbearance

Comments: <u>In 2003, my family had large medical bills that made paying student loans impossible. In 2004, I got a new job that allowed me to make student loan payments. Unfortunately, I lost that job and got a new one at lower pay in 2005 and had to delay paying my student loans.</u>

Income Tax Report by Year

Year	Income (Gross)	Total Income	Taxable Income	Federal Poverty Guideline Family Size=	Are You Above Poverty Level?	Student loan payments?
(year you received your last student loan)						

Comments: _____

_____

_____

_____

_____

_____

_____

_____

Current Income and Family Status

On a blank piece of paper, write a similar letter using data from the *Current Financial Status* worksheet. **Use your own words**.

Name   SAMPLE
Date
Adversary Number [*omit if filing a Compromise or Write-Off*]

(*Put the rest of this document in your own words. If you are not filing an adversary proceeding, remove all references to Chapter 7 bankruptcy and its forms.*)

Current Income and Family Status
(use some other combination of terms for this title)

Since filing my Chapter 7 bankruptcy in (date), there have been changes in my income and family. My current income is $(amount).

The income I reported on Form B6I—Schedule I-Current Income of Individual Debtor(s)(give the name of the form used in your court), needs to be (increased or decreased) by ($ amount). This is due to (list reasons such as getting or loosing a job, divorce or getting married, increase or reduction in federal benefits or alimony or child support, unemployment, etc.)

My family consists of:

Yourself. (Write about yourself giving your age and medical condition. If you have medical conditions that limit your ability to work, give details about the medical conditions, how long you have had them, how it limits your ability to work, the prognosis, and include the name and contact information for your medical doctors.)

Spouse and Dependents. (Give their names, ages, how they are related, and whether or not they are working. If they have medical conditions, tell how they are disabled, how long they have been disabled, the prognosis, and detail how you support them. Be sure to tell if you have to limit work to care for a medically ill spouse or dependent. List the contact information for the medical doctors involved.)

(Medical note: If you or your spouse or dependents have medical conditions, obtain a letter from your physician that summarizes the problem and states the long-term prognosis.)

Current Expenditures and Minimalized Living

On a blank piece of paper, write a letter similar as shown below using data from the *Current Expenditure Status* and the *Current Income Status* worksheets. Use your own words. This letter has 3 parts: (1) an update of your expense reported in your chapter 7 bankruptcy, (2) to demonstrate that all your expenses are reasonable and are kept to a minimum, and (3) it would be impossible to pay on your student loans without creating an undue hardship. Remember, you want to show that you live without extravagance, that all expenditures are necessary and minimal, and that your income just meets your expenses— thereby leaving no excess income available to pay toward student loan debt. In fact, you want to show that if you had to make student loan payments, then your family would drop to a sub-standard level of living. **Use your own words**.

Name   SAMPLE
Date
Adversary Number [*omit if filing a Compromise or Write-Off*]

(*Put the rest of this document in your own words. If you are not filing an adversary proceeding, remove all references to Chapter 7 bankruptcy and its forms.*)

Current Expenditures and Minimalized Living
(use some other combination of terms for this title)

Since filing my Chapter 7 bankruptcy in (date), there have been changes in my family expenses. The expenses I reported on Form B6J—Schedule J-Current Expenditure of Individual Debtor(s) (give the name of the form used in your court), needs to be (increased or decreased) by ($ amount). This is due to (list reasons such as divorce or getting married, moving, more medical problems, auto repair problems, birth or death of spouse or dependent, house repair, etc.)

My family lives at the Federal Poverty Level. (Write about how difficult it is to live so poorly). (Note: if you live well above the Federal Poverty Level, do not mention it here. You will address this later.)

My family expenses are kept to a minimum with no extras. (Write some more about how you save money buying used clothes at thrift stores, buying food in bulk at discount warehouse stores, that you almost never eat out or take in a movie or sporting event or other entertainment, and more. Be sure to mention if you do not have health insurance, bank savings, or any retirement funds. If medical expenses are a major problem, be sure to mention them.)

My family expenses just match (or exceed) my family income. If I were required to pay on my student loans, then my family would be pushed into a sub-minimal living standard and this would be an undue hardship.

Work Time Accounting Statement

On a blank piece of paper, write a letter similar to the one shown below using data from the *Work time Account Table* worksheets. Explain in your own words why all your time is committed and it would be impossible for you to take on another job. **Use your own words**.

Name   SAMPLE
Date
Adversary Number [*omit if filing a Compromise or Write-Off*]

(Put the rest of this document in your own words.)

Work Time Accounting
(use some other combination of terms for this title)

I currently work (quantity) hours a week as a (title) with (company name). With travel time included, (quantity) hours a week are devoted to paid employment. (If you have more than one paying job, expand this paragraph to list each one.)

I also work part-time for (company name) performing (sales, grant writing, etc.—something where you are only paid if you make a sale). This takes (quantity) hours per week and I am only paid if I make the (sale, grant, promotion, etc.).

At home, I take care of (list dependents) for (quantity) hours per week. (If they have medical needs, list the problems).

Combining my time on the job and caring for my dependents, I am committed (quantity—should be more than a 40-hour week) each week. It would be impossible for me to take on any more work or responsibility.

Personal Limitations Statement

The purpose of this letter is to detail any <u>personal limitations</u> that may impact your ability to work and, therefore, service your student loan debt. This includes personal medical limitations, support of dependents (and their medical conditions, if applicable), and lack of useable job skills. These need to be described in detail and with supporting documents (like medical records). Your letter will probably be longer than one page.

Here are the guidelines for composing your letter:

• Medical Limitations

If you have medical problems that contributed to your bankruptcy, discuss the following:

1. How your medical condition contributed to your bankruptcy. Here you need to give a complete history of your medical condition and subsequent loss of work and income.

2. That your medical condition will continue into the future, most likely become worse, and that it will be impossible to make payments on the student loans. It helps to find a physician who will write you a letter claiming that you are disabled, or partially disabled, and that is will persist for many years to come.

• Dependents

Courts are aware that dependents cause time constraints for debtors who otherwise could use the time for employment. Thus, the greater the number of dependents and the time involved in their care directly impact the debtor's ability to repay student loans.

1. <u>Children</u>: Courts make the assumption that children will leave home at 18-years of age. Thus, courts will calculate when the youngest child is expected to leave home and try to determine if the debtor would then be capable of resuming payments on his or her student loans. Extenuating circumstances would be if the child is disabled and will continue to reside with the parent.

2. <u>Spouse, Civil Union, or Domestic Partner</u>: Courts are sensitive to the situation where debtors provide financial and emotional support for medically ill spouses (whether by marriage, Civil Union, or Domestic Partnership). Unlike with children, there is no assumption the spouse will leave the home. You are encouraged to combine the care of a medically ill spouse with other factors that will impact your future ability to make income.

3. <u>Elderly or Medically Ill Parents or Siblings</u>: There have been a number of cases where courts have shown themselves insensitive to debtors who take care of elderly or medically ill parents or siblings. The courts question why the debtor is taking care of these people. It may seem obvious to the debtor, but it is not to the court. Debtors need to make a strong case as to why it is they, and not their siblings, parents, or government taking care of these people. If this is your situation, you may want to discuss your moral or religious convictions that have influenced you to be the caretaker of these people. Too often courts take the position that the debtor should not take on this responsibility and, instead, focus on paying back student loans.

• Lack of Useable Job Skills

A good number of debtors filing bankruptcy have student loans from training programs they either did not complete, or the program was of such dubious value that the debtor gained no improved job skills. Courts have been sensitive to debtors who lack useable job skills. They are aware that without proper job skills, it is very difficult for debtors to obtain high-paying employment and, subsequently, be able to make student loan payments. In this situation, you are encouraged to forcibly show the court how your low job skills are preventing you from getting a good job. Of course, the court may respond by asking why you don't educate yourself further and get a better job. The best answer is to show working <u>and</u> taking care of dependents is taking all your time making it impossible to obtain more education.

<u>**Use your own words**</u>.

Name   SAMPLE
Date
Adversary Number [*omit if filing a Compromise or Write-Off*]

(*Put the rest of this document in your own words.*)

Personal Limitations
(create your own title)

I have a number of personal issues that limit my future ability to work and earn sufficient income to service my student loan debt.

(Talk about yours and your dependent's medical conditions and how they will persist into the future.)

(Write about your dependents and how their care interferes with you obtaining higher income.)

(Explain how your low work skills are impacting your ability to work.)

These conditions affect my future ability to make sufficient income to service my student loans. There is no indication that I will ever earn enough to repay my student loans.

[Your letter should be much longer and in greater detail.]

Good Faith and Loan Repayment Statement

Instructions:

On a blank piece of paper, write a letter similar to the one shown on the next page. You will be blending the data you created on the worksheets *Income and Student Loan Payment* and *Student Loan History* with your own work and life history. The goal of the narrative is to show:

1. That you worked. If you were out of work or your income was too low, you sought work or had a legitimate medical disability.
2. Whenever your family income exceeded the Federal Poverty Guideline, you made payments on your student loans. If you could not make payments due to medical or other problems, you obtained deferments or forbearances on the loans.
3. If your family income dropped below the Federal Poverty Guideline, you obtained deferments or forbearances on the loans.
4. Ultimately, you want to show that it will be impossible to service your student loan debt.

In many cases, debtors will be deposition by the Department of Education attorneys regarding your work and family history. This can be nerve racking. By writing this history in advance, you will be clear about details. You can take your time and accurately compile information without being under pressure. In fact, if you give this history to the other side before mediation, the deposition may be waived.

In your work and life history, include any and all topics below that apply):

Employments/ Job Firings   Marriages/ Divorces
Dependents   Discriminations
Schooling and Career Choices   Medical Conditions
Changes in living conditions   And more to show your struggles

Tell your story in your own words.

Name   SAMPLE

Date

Adversary Number [*omit if filing a Compromise or Write-Off*]

(Put the rest of this document in your own words. If you are not filing an adversary proceeding, remove all references to Chapter 7 bankruptcy and its forms.)

Good Faith and Loan Repayment
(use some other combination of terms for this title)

My student loan debt of $(amount) represent about (quantity)% of my total debt that is being discharged through Chapter 7 bankruptcy. The last time I received a student loan was (how many) years ago.

I obtained my (degree or certificate) in (year) and is the last year I received a student loan. I immediately looked for higher paying work. I applied for more than 200 jobs but did not get any new job (be sure you can verify the efforts to find work). I contacted my lender who granted a deferment.

The next two years, I applied for hundreds more jobs but without success. I did get an additional part-time job that increased the family's income to just above the poverty level. However, my spouse experienced severe medical problems (specify in detail) that consumed all spare cash. Later that year, I lost my job and my student loans became due because of failure to make payment. Luckily, in early 2004, I got a well-paying job that increased our family income to almost $5,000 above the Federal Poverty Level. That year I paid $1,200 toward my student loans.

2005 was a rough year. I lost my job but found another a few months later paying just above the Federal Poverty Level. My spouse is ill again and we have no savings. I contacted my student loan lender and received a forbearance.

I have been diligent in trying to service my student loans and there is no fraud in seeking their discharge.

(Your letter may be much longer and in greater detail than this sample.)

Income Contingent Repayment

On a blank piece of paper, write a statement similar to the one shown below. Use your own words. You are stating why the ICR is not an appropriate repayment plan in your situation.

Use your own words.

Name   SAMPLE
Date
Adversary Number [*omit if filing a Compromise or Write-Off*]

(Put the rest of this document in your own words)

Income Contingent Repayment
(use some other combination of terms for this title)

The Income Contingent Repayment plan is not an appropriate repayment plan for my student loans. I am (over 50 years old, or living on federal benefits) and the tax liability after 25 years would prove an undue hardship. It will be impossible for me, because I will be living on a fixed and limited income to pay the income taxes on the discharged loans. As such, the ICR represents an undue hardship and cannot be implemented in my case.

(Your letter may be much longer and in greater detail than this sample.)

APPENDIX E
Forms for Adversary Proceeding

This section of the Appendix contains all the legal forms needed to file an Adversary Proceeding. The forms are presented three ways—

- First, the forms are given with detailed **INSTRUCTION(S)** regarding their completion.

- Second, the forms are completed using fictitious names and data so you can see a finished **SAMPLE** form.

- Third, **BLANK** form are provide for you to fill in with your specific information.

This section of the Appendix gives detailed instructions for completing several of the forms needed for filing an adversary proceeding.

Blue Back

Many courts require all papers filed with the clerk to be assembled in what is termed a "blue back." How it is constructed is shown on the next page.

Adversary Proceeding Sheet (Cover)

The bankruptcy court where the adversary complaint is filed requires a cover sheet to be placed on top of the complaint. The federal form F 7004-1 has two pages. Both pages need to be completed along with a mailing matrix.

Adversary Proceeding Complaint

There are many variations for writing an adversary complaint. Here is shown a basic version that can be altered according to the needs of the court and whether or not you want to advocate for the abolition of §523(a)(8).

Summons

The court issues a summons for the first court hearing (otherwise known as a status hearing). The instructions here are for the federal form F 7004-1 page 1. Check with the clerk for one for your district.

Proof of Service

After serving the complaint and summons, the court needs documentation that the service was done appropriately; Federal form F 7004-1 page 2 fulfills that need.

Mail Matrix

Attached to the Proof of Service is the Mail Matrix.

Proof of Service Cover

To file the proof of service, a cover may be required by the court. A sample is given here.

Blue Back

All original petitions and pleadings must be "backed" to aid in easy identification of documents in case files. "Backing" is paper that resembles construction paper. The Court requires blue backs in the standard size of 9" wide by 11 ¾" in length with a ¾" top flap. You may obtain backing from any stationery store. The court does not sell nor is it obligated to provide blue backs. Staple the backing to the petition or pleading in the following manner:

- Mount original petition or pleading on backing, face side up and flush with the top, centered.
- Staple complete ORIGINAL petition or pleading on the left corner only.
- Hole-punch original petition or pleading by placing two standard size holes, centered 2 ¾" apart. A standard home/office stapler usually has adjustments to allow this spacing.
- Type a short title of petition or pleading on the lower right-hand corner of the backing. You may type this on a small label and place the label in the lower right-hand corner.

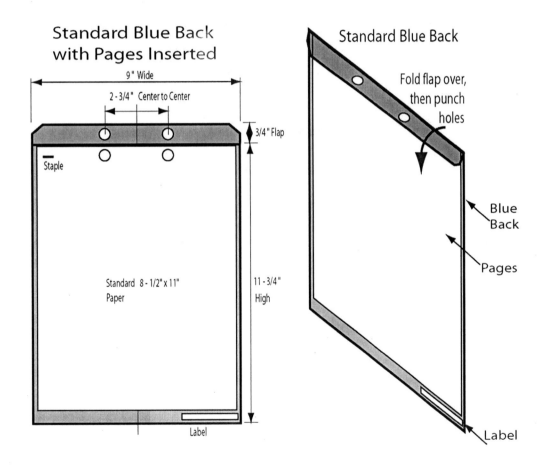

Adversary Proceeding Sheet (Cover)

The following page shows where you fill in the form. A finished sample is given in the next section of the Appendix. A blank form is given in the Appendix.

It is suggested that you type your response. However, the person who successfully had $225,000 in student loans discharged through bankruptcy hand printed his information in the forms. Obviously, you don't need to type these forms.

Instructions:

BOX MARKED AS—	ACTION
PLAINTIFFS	type your first and last name, address, city, state, and zip code
DEFENDANTS	type the name of the defendant along with their address. Most likely the defendant is the United States Department of Education Direct Loan Servicing. Verify this by contacting the Department of Education.
ATTORNEYS (under Plaintiffs)	type — *None*
ATTORNEYS (under Defendants)	type — *In Pro Per*
PARTY	place check mark in second box — *2 U.S. Defendant*
CAUSE OF ACTION	type — *Plaintiff seeks dischargeability of debt pursuant to 11 U.S.C.A. §532(a)(8).*
NATURE OF SUIT	place check mark in box next to — *426 To determine the dischargeability of a debt 11 U.S.C.A. §523.*
ORIGIN OF PROCEEDING	place check mark in box next to— 1. *Original Proceeding.*
NEAREST THOUSAND	type approximate amount of debt.
NAME OF DEBTOR	type your first and last name
BANKRUPTCY CASE NUMBER	type your bankruptcy case number
DISTRICT IN WHICH CASE IS PENDING	type the name of your district court
DIVISIONAL OFFICE	type the division the bankruptcy court is located
FILING FEE	You need to check with the court to determine the fee. In general, the fee for a debtor filing his or her own adversary proceeding (In Pro Per) is zero. If so, place a check in the box next to *Fee Not Required*.
DATE	type the date the adversary proceeding is filed.
SIGNATURE OF ATTORNEY (OR PLAINTIFF)	sign your name.

B. 104 (Rev. 8/99)	**ADVERSARY PROCEEDING SHEET** (Instructions on Reverse)	ADVERSARY PROCEEDING NUMBER (For Court Use Only)

PLAINTIFFS	**(Your Name)**	DEFENDANTS	**(Most likely this address:**
Address	**(Your street, city, state, zip)**	Address	**United States Department of Education Direct Loan Servicing PO Box 4609 Utica, NY 13504-4609)**

ATTORNEYS (Firm Name, Address, and Telephone Number) **None**	ATTORNEYS (if known) **In Pro Per**

PARTY (Check one box only) ☐ 1. U.S. PLAINTIFF ☑ 2. U.S. DEFENDANT ☐ 3. U.S. NOT A PARTY

CAUSE OF ACTION (Write a brief statement of cause of action, including all U.S. statutes involved)

Plaintiff seeks dischargeability of debt pursuant to 11 U.S.C. §532(a)(8).

NATURE OF SUIT
(Check the one most appropriate box only)

☐ 454 To recover money or property	☐ 455 To revoke an order of confirmation of a Chapter 11 or Chapter 13 Plan	☐ 456 To obtain a declaratory judgment relating to any of the foregoing causes of action
☐ 435 To determine validity, priority, or extent of a lien or other interest in property	☑ 426 To determine the dischargeability of a debt 11 U.S.C. § 523	☐ 459 To determine a claim or cause of action removed to a bankruptcy court
☐ 458 To obtain approval for the sale of both the interest of the estate and of a co-owner in property	☐ 434 To obtain an injunction or other equitable relief	☐ 498 Other (specify)
☐ 424 To object or to revoke a discharge 11 U.S.C. § 727	☐ 457 To subordinate any allowed claim or interest except where such subordination is provided in a Plan	

ORIGIN OF PROCEEDING (Check one box only)	☑ 1 Original Proceeding	☐ 2 Removed Proceeding	☐ 4 Reinstated or Reopened	☐ 5 Transferred from Another Bankruptcy Court	☐ CHECK IF THIS IS A CLASS ACTION UNDER F.R.C.P. 23

DEMAND	NEAREST THOUSAND **‡(your debt amount)**	OTHER RELIEF SOUGHT	☐ JURY DEMAND

BANKRUPTCY CASE IN WHICH THIS ADVERSARY PROCEEDING ARISES

NAME OF DEBTOR **(your name)**	BANKRUPTCY CASE NUMBER **(your case number)**

DISTRICT IN WHICH CASE IS PENDING **(your bankruptcy court district)**	DIVISIONAL OFFICE **(your divisional office)**	NAME OF JUDGE

RELATED ADVERSARY PROCEEDING (IF ANY)

PLAINTIFF	DEFENDANT	ADVERSARY PROCEEDING NUMBER
DISTRICT	DIVISIONAL OFFICE	NAME OF JUDGE

FILING FEE (Check one box only)	☐ FEE ATTACHED	☑ FEE NOT REQUIRED	☐ FEE IS DEFERRED

DATE **(date of filing)**	PRINT NAME	SIGNATURE OF ATTORNEY (OR PLAINTIFF)

ADVERSARY PROCEEDING COVER SHEET (Reverse Side)

This cover sheet must be completed by the plaintiff's attorney (or by the plaintiff if the plaintiff is not represented by an attorney) and submitted to the Clerk of the Court upon the filing of a complaint initiating an adversary proceeding.

The cover sheet and the information contained on it **do not** replace or supplement the filing and service of pleadings or other papers as required by law, the Bankruptcy Rules, or the local rules of court. This form is required for the use of the Clerk of the Court to initiate the docket sheet and to prepare necessary indices and statistical records. A separate cover sheet must be submitted to the Clerk of the Court for each complaint filed. The form is largely self-explanatory.

Parties. The names of the parties to the adversary proceeding *exactly* as they appear on the complaint. Give the names and addresses of the attorneys if known. Following the heading "Party," check the appropriate box indicating whether the United States is a party named in the complaint.

Cause of Action. Give a brief description of the cause of action including all federal statutes involved. For example, "Complaint seeking damages for failure to disclose information, Consumer Credit Protection Act, 15 U.S.C. § 1601 et seq.," or "Complaint by trustee to avoid a transfer of property by the debtor, 11 U.S.C. § 544."

Nature of Suit. Place an "X" in the appropriate box. Only one box should be checked. If the cause fits more than one category of suit, select the most definitive.

Origin of Proceedings. Check the appropriate box to indicate the origin of the case:

1. Original Proceeding.
2. Removed from a State or District Court.
4. Reinstated or Reopened.
5. Transferred from Another Bankruptcy Court.

Demand. On the next line, state the dollar amount demanded in the complaint in thousands of dollars. For $1,000, enter "1," for $10,000, enter "10," for $100,000, enter "100," if $1,000,000, enter "1000." If $10,000,000 or more, enter "9999." If the amount is less than $1,000, enter "0001." If no monetary demand is made, enter "XXXX." If the plaintiff is seeking non-monetary relief, state the relief sought, such as injunction or foreclosure of a mortgage.

Bankruptcy Case In Which This Adversary Proceeding Arises. Enter the name of the debtor and the docket number of the bankruptcy case from which the proceeding now being filed arose. Beneath, enter the district and divisional office where the case was filed and the name of the presiding judge.

Related Adversary Proceedings. State the names of the parties and six-digit adversary proceeding number from any adversary proceeding concerning the same two parties or the same property currently pending in any bankruptcy court. On the next line, enter the district where the related case is pending and the name of the presiding judge.

Filing Fee. Check one box. The fee must be paid upon filing unless the plaintiff meets one of the following exceptions. The fee is not required if the plaintiff is the United States government or the debtor. If the plaintiff is the trustee or a debtor in possession and there are no liquid funds in the estate, the filing fee may be deferred until there are funds in the estate. (In the event no funds are ever recovered for the estate, there will be no fee.) There is no fee for adding a party after the adversary proceeding has been commenced.

Signature. This cover sheet must be signed by the attorney of record in the box on the right of the last line of the form. If the plaintiff is represented by a law firm, a member of the firm must sign. If the plaintiff is *pro se*, that is, not represented by an attorney, the plaintiff must sign.

The name of the signatory must be printed in the box to the left of the signature. The date of the signing must be indicated in the box on the far left of the last line.

Adversary Proceeding Complaint

The following pages show where you fill in the form. A finished sample is given in the next section of the Appendix.

The sample given here is for a <u>basic adversary complaint</u>. There are two variations of this form that are discussed below. Some courts may require you to give details in the initial complaint as to why you cannot repay the loan. In general, if you are going to be pushed into mediation, you can use the simpler basic form given below. During mediation and subsequent deposition, all the particular information about your dire condition will come out. So, before filling out this form, find out if you will be going to mediation. More than 90% of the bankruptcy courts will require you to go to mediation. Of course, you can always request mediation. If you need to include in the adversary complaint greater information about why you cannot repay your loans, look at the <u>Alternate Ending1</u> shown later in this Appendix.

The second condition that will alter this form is if you are going to advocate changing or rescinding the bankruptcy law 11 U.S.C.A. §523(a) (8). This is discussed at length in the book. If you want to include challenges to the law, there are additional items to include in the adversary complaint. These are detailed below as <u>Alternate Ending 2</u>.

Instructions:

It is suggested that you type your response. However, the person who successfully had $225,000 in student loans discharged through bankruptcy whited-out the appropriate sections of the form and hand printed his information. Obviously, you don't need to type these forms.

Use this instructional form and sample to show you how to type the complaint. Use legal paper as instructed by the court. Blank legal paper is provided in this book. Make copies of the blank paper. However, remember that every time you make a photocopy, it shrinks by 2% and typing on such paper may be difficult to line up in your typewriter. It is strongly suggested that you buy legal numbered paper at a stationery store.

If you look at the bottom of the form, you will see that a short title of the document is printed to the left of the page number and your name, address, and phone number is printed to the right of the page number. You do not need to include this kind of information in the footer. It is a convenience for the court. However, you must have the page number <u>centered in the footer</u>. Notice that the footer is below the last numbered line.

Copy the next page onto numbered legal paper. Items that are italicized are items that you need to fill in. The following table guides you in filling in the italicized items:

Line Number	Action
Page 1	
1.	type your first and last name, and that of your spouse if you are filing jointly.
2.	type your address.
2.5	type your city, state, zip.
3.	type your phone number.
4.	type — *In Pro Per*.
8.	type the name of the district bankruptcy court.

9.	type the name of the bankruptcy court division.
11.	type your first and last name.
12.	type your bankruptcy case number.
16.	type the name of the defendant. Most likely this is the *United States Department of Education*. This may include a guarantee agency and any other collection agency.
16.	type the date the complaint was filed.

At this point, you may want to make a few copies of the page so far. This "header" paper may be necessary for future filings (like filing the *Proof of Service* described later) and it will save you time and potential mistakes to use these copies. Now take one of your copies and continue copying and filling in from line 20 on down.

24.	type your first and last name.
26.	type your first and last name.
27.	type the date you filed your chapter 7 bankruptcy.
27.	type the name of your chapter 7 trustee.
Page 2	
2.	if you have dependents, include the line.
5.	type the name of the defendant.
6.	type the names of the educational institutions from which the loans were used. Indicated if a degree was attained.
10.	type the name of the defendant.
11.	type the address of the defendant.
21.	type the approximate amount of the debt.

Once your complete copying down to and including line 24, you will need to decide if you are going to use one of the alternate endings (changes to item 8). If you are filing the basic complaint, continue on. If you are using one of the alternate forms, see details below.

27.	type your pronoun.
Page 3	
1.	type your pronoun.
4.	type your pronoun.
8.	type the date.
12.	sign your name.
13.	type your first and last name.

Alternate Endings

Alternate Ending 1— If you are required to include details about why you cannot repay the debt, item 8 (line 25 page 2) of the basic adversary complaint needs to be expanded.

Follow all the steps above for pages 1 and 2, stopping at line 25 page 2.
Instead of items 8 and 9, we are expanding item 8 into 3 more items and renumbering item 9 as item 11. Copy the following onto your complaint. Italicized items need your input. Replace items 8 and 9 with the following:

8. Based on the Debtor(s) current income and expenses, the Debtor(s) cannot maintain a minimal standard of living and at the same time repay (*his/her*) student loan(s). (*Now give details about your current income, the sources of your income, your employment, education, work skills, potential for work, personal and family health, and support obligations.*)

9. The Debtor(s)' current financial status most likely will continue for a significant portion of the repayment period of the loan. (*Now give details about the conditions that are preventing you from*

getting more income. Examples would be poor health, care of dependents and more. You have developed your arguments in Chapter 8.)

10. The Debtor(s) has made a good-faith effort to repay on (*his/her*) student loans. (*Give details about your student loan payment history and other attempts to repay or reschedule the loans.*)

11. The Debtor has filed for bankruptcy for reasons other than just to discharge (*his/her*) student loans.

Now finish the complaint and copy page 3 line 5 to 13, filing in the date, your name, and signing the document.

<u>Alternate Ending 2</u> — If you want to include challenges to the bankruptcy law, you must list challenges in the Adversary Complaint. Chapter 7 discussed a wide-range of deficiencies in the law that are open to legal challenges. We really advise you seek the help of an attorney to word your challenges correctly. Another approach is to seek the help of law students who need a special project for school and may take on the opportunity to help you in your challenge of the law.

Challenging the law may result in it being overturned. That would be a big help to so many other honest debtors. Challenging the law is also about the only avenue open to middle-class debtors who otherwise would not qualify for an "undue hardship" discharge.

1	(*your name*)
2	(*address*)
3	(*city, state, zip*)
	(*telephone*)
4	In Pro Per
5	
6	
7	UNITED STATED BANKRUPTCY COURT
8	(*name of district*)
9	(*name of division*)
10	

11	(your name)	) CHAPTER 7 BANKRUPTCY CASE
12		) (*bankruptcy case number*)
13	PLAINTIFF,	)
		)
14	vs.	) ADV. NO.
15		)
16	(*name of defendant-- most likely*	) COMPLAINT FILED: (*date*)
17	*UNITED STATES DEPARTMENT*	) DEPT:
	OF EDUCATION),	) JUDGE:
18		)
19	DEFENDANT	)
20	———————————————————	)

21   COMPLAINT TO DETERMINE DISCHARGEABILITY OF DEBT

22   PURSUANT TO 11 U.S.C. §523(a)(8)

23

24   (*your name*), Debtor and Plaintiff in the above captioned adversary

25 proceeding, represents as follows:

26   1.   (*your name*) filed a voluntary petition for relief under Chapter 7 of the

27 United States Bankruptcy Code on (*date*). (*name*) is the duly appointed Chapter 7

28

PLAINTIFF'S COMPLAINT TO DETERMINE
DISCHARGEABILITY OF DEBT

- 1 -

YOUR NAME
ADDRESS
CITY, STATE, ZIP
TELEPHONE

1   trustee. This complaint seeks to determine the dischargeability of a student loan as

2   it presents an undue hardship for the Debtor (*and his/her dependents*).

3   2.   One of the unsecured debts owing by the Debtor and listed on

4   Schedule F—Creditors Holding Unsecured Nonpriority Claims— is a student loan

5   owing to (*most likely United States Department of Education*).

6   3.   This loan was incurred to pay expenses at (*list colleges where debt*

7   *was assumed and indicate if degree was obtained*).

8

9   JURISDICTION

10   4.   Defendant (*most likely United States Department of Education*)

11   maintains its (*address – most likely Direct Loan Servicing Center in Utica, New*

12   *York*) (*verify this address*).

13   5.   Jurisdiction exists under 28 U.S.C. §1334. Venue is proper under 28

14   U.S.C. §1409(a). The District Court has generally referred these matters to the

15   Bankruptcy Court for hearing pursuant to 28 U.S.C. §157(a). This is a core

16   proceeding within the meaning of 28 U.S.C. §157(b)(2)(I). This adversary

17   complaint is brought pursuant to 11 U.S.C. §523(a)(8).

18

19   <u>FIRST CAUSE OF ACTION [11 U.S.C. §523(a)(8)]</u>

20   6.   Plaintiff is indebted to the Defendant in the approximate sum of

21    $(*amount*) for education loans made by Defendant to Plaintiff.

22   7.   Requiring Plaintiff to repay these debts will impose undue hardship on

23   the Debtor and the Debtor's dependents as contemplated under 11 U.S.C.

24   §523(a)(8).

25   8.   Based upon Plaintiff's current income and expenses, Plaintiff cannot

26   maintain a minimum standard of living if forced to repay the loan. Plaintiff

27   believes that (*his/her*) economic state of affairs is likely to persist for a significant

28

PLAINTIFF'S COMPLAINT TO DETERMINE
DISCHARGEABILITY OF DEBT

- 2 -

YOUR NAME
ADDRESS
CITY, STATE, ZIP
TELEPHONE

1 portion of the repayment period and (*he/she*) has made good faith efforts to repay

2 the loans.

3   9.   The Debtor has filed for bankruptcy for reasons other than just to

4 discharge (*his/her*) student loan.

5   WHEREFORE, the Debtor asks this court to enter an Order declaring the

6 student loan debt to be dischargeable.

7

8 Date: (*date*).

9

10

11

12

13

                                    _____

Plaintiff (*your name*)

14

15

16

17

18

19

20

21

22

23

24

25

26

27

28

PLAINTIFF'S COMPLAINT TO DETERMINE
DISCHARGEABILITY OF DEBT

                - 3 -

YOUR NAME
ADDRESS
CITY, STATE, ZIP
TELEPHONE

Summons

You may or may not need to fill out this form before filing the adversary complaint with the bankruptcy clerk. Usually, you ask for the form from the clerks, they give you a blank one, you fill in the information, then get back in line to complete filing the adversary complaint. They fill out the rest and give you a conformed copy (stamped). Regardless, seeing the form here will prepare you for when you are given one. We suggest that you complete this form and take it with you even if you don't use it.

The form here is for the Central District of California. It will help in preparing your own form. Use the correct form specified for your bankruptcy court.

Instructions for *Summons and Notice of Status Conference — Page 1*:

BOX MARKED AS—	ACTION
ATTORNEY OR PARTY	type your first and last name, address, city, state, and zip code
ATTORNEY OR PLAINTIFF	type — *In Pro Per*
DEBTOR	type your first and last name
PLAINTIFF(S), VS. DEFENDANT(S)	type your first and last name alongside Plaintiff(s). type name of Defendant— most likely the *United States Dept. of Education Direct Loan Servicing*.
CHAPTER	type — 7
CASE NUMBER	type your bankruptcy case number

The clerk will assign:

- Adversary Case Number
- Status Conference:
    - Date and time of Hearing
    - Court Address indicating Courtroom and Floor

Attorney or Party Name, Address, Telephone & FAX Numbers, and California State Bar Number	FOR COURT USE ONLY
(name) **(address)** **(city, state, zip)** *Attorney for Plaintiff* **In Pro Per**	

UNITED STATES BANKRUPTCY COURT
CENTRAL DISTRICT OF CALIFORNIA

In re: **(your name)** Debtor.	CHAPTER ___7___ CASE NUMBER **(bankruptcy number)** ADVERSARY NUMBER **(adversary number)**
(your name) Plaintiff(s), vs. **(most likely United States Dept. of Education Direct Loan Servicing)** Defendant(s).	*(The Boxes and Blank Lines below are for the Court's Use Only) (Do Not Fill Them In)* **SUMMONS AND NOTICE OF STATUS CONFERENCE**

TO THE DEFENDANT: A Complaint has been filed by the Plaintiff against you. If you wish to defend yourself, you must file with the Court a written pleading, in duplicate, in response to the Complaint. You must also send a copy of your written response to the party shown in the upper left-hand corner of this page. Unless you have filed in duplicate and served a responsive pleading by _____, the Court may enter a judgment by default against you for the relief demanded in the Complaint.

A Status Conference on the proceeding commenced by the Complaint has been set for:

Hearing Date:	**Time:**	**Courtroom:**	**Floor:**

❑   **255 East Temple Street, Los Angeles**   ❑   **411 West Fourth Street, Santa Ana**

❑   **21041 Burbank Boulevard, Woodland Hills**   ❑   **1415 State Street, Santa Barbara**

❑   **3420 Twelfth Street, Riverside**

PLEASE TAKE NOTICE that if the trial of the proceeding is anticipated to take less than two (2) hours, the parties may stipulate to conduct the trial of the case on the date specified, instead of holding a Status Conference. Such a stipulation must be lodged with the Court at least two (2) Court days before the date set forth above and is subject to Court approval. The Court may continue the trial to another date if necessary to accommodate the anticipated length of the trial.

Date of Issuance: _____

Clerk of the Bankruptcy Court

By: _____
Deputy Clerk

This form is mandatory. It has been approved for use by the United States Bankruptcy Court for the Central District of California.

Revised December 1998 (COA-SA)

F 7004-1

Proof of Service with Mail Matrix and Cover

Once the complaint has been filed and the court summons issued, the papers must be served on all parties and the court given proof that they were served. Here is an illustrative sample Proof of Service with Mail Matrix and Cover used in the California Central District. Check with your court for their forms. It is the person who performs the service that fills out these forms, not the debtor.

Before filling out this form, contact the Department of Education and the bankruptcy court to verify the names and addresses for service:

- Office of the U.S. Trustee in you bankruptcy district.
- Civil process clerk at the office of the United States attorney for the district in which the action is brought (local U.S. Attorney used to defend the case).
- The Attorney General in Washington, D.C.
- Particular agency named in or affected by the lawsuit (most likely the Dept. of Education).
- Your Chapter 7 bankruptcy trustee.

Samples of these forms are given later in the Appendix.

Instructions for *Summons and Notice of Status Conference – Page 2*:

BOX OR LINE	ACTION
IN RE	type your first and last name (name of debtor)
CHAPTER	type — *7*
CASE NUMBER	type your bankruptcy case number
Under the box marked CHAPTER	type — *Adversary Number* (with your number)
STATE OF CALIF., COUNTY OF	type your county
1.	type your county
In space below item 1	type the business address of the person who is serving the notice.
2. (first line)	Check off box and type — *See Attached Service List*
2. (last line)	type name of city notice mailed from
3.	Check off box and type name of local U.S. Attorney.
4.	type name and address of local U.S. Attorney
4. (box)	Check off box indicating *Names and Address continued on attached page* (otherwise known as a Mail Matrix).
DATED	type date
TYPE NAME	Type the name of the person making the hand delivery and mailing the notices.
SIGNATURE	The person making the deliveries of these notices signs the form.

Instructions for *Mail Matrix* attachment:
See the Mail Matrix form. It is self-explanatory.

Instructions for *Proof of Service* cover: After the Summons and Complaint are hand-delivered and mailed to all parties, the Proof of Service is filed with the court.

When you prepared your Adversary Complaint, we asked that you make a few extra copies of the first page after completing the "header" but before writing the title or body. This provided you with "header" paper for future filings. Here is where we will use one of these copies. Simply type in the title *PROOF OF SERVICE OF SUMMONS AND COMPLAINT* on line 19.

For your reference, an instructional header is given two pages from here and given the title "Proof of Service of Summons and Complaint."

If you need to create a new header paper for this cover, here are the steps:

<u>On lined legal paper type the following</u>—

Line Number	Action
Page 1	
1.	type your first and last name, and that of your spouse if you are filing jointly.
2.	type your address.
2.5	type your city, state, zip.
3.	type your phone number.
4.	type — *In Pro Per*.
8.	type the name of the district bankruptcy court.
9.	type the name of the bankruptcy court division.
11.	type your first and last name.
12.	type your bankruptcy case number.
13.	type your adversary case number.
16.	type the name of the defendant. Most likely this is the *United States Department of Education*. This may include a guarantee agency and any other collection agency.
16.	type the date the complaint was filed.
17.	type the name of the presiding judge.
19.	type — *PROOF OF SERVICE OF SUMMONS AND COMPLAINT*.

In re

(your first and last name)

Debtor.

CHAPTER _7___
(bankruptcy case number)
CASE NUMBER

Adversary Number (your number)

PROOF OF SERVICE

STATE OF CALIFORNIA, COUNTY OF ___(county)_____

1. I am employed in the County of ___(county)_____, State of California. I am over the age of 18 and not a party to the within action. My business address is as follows:

> (address
> city, state, zip)

2. ☑ **Regular Mail Service:** On___See Attached Service List_____, I served the foregoing Summons and Notice of Status Conference (and any instructions attached thereto), together with the Complaint filed in this proceeding, on the Defendant(s) at the following address(es) by placing a true and correct copy thereof in a sealed envelope with postage thereon fully prepaid in the United States Mail at ___(city mailed from)___, California, addressed as set forth below.

3. ☑ **Personal Service:** On (name of local US Attorney) personal service of the foregoing Summons and Notice of Status Conference (and any instructions attached thereto), together with the Complaint filed in this proceeding, was made on the Defendant(s) at the address(es) set forth below.

4. Defendant(s) and address(es) upon which service was made:

> (name and address of local U.S. Attorney
> in the bankruptcy court district)

☑ Names and Addresses continued on attached page

I declare under penalty of perjury under the laws of the United States of America that the foregoing is true and correct.

Dated: (date)

(first and last name)

_____   _____
Type Name   *Signature*

This form is mandatory. It has been approved for use by the United States Bankruptcy Court for the Central District of California.

Revised December 1998 (COA-SA)

F 7004-1

(This is the *Mail Matrix* that is attached to the Proof of Service form.)

In re: (*debtor's name*)
Case Number (*debtor's bankruptcy case number*)

Regular Mail Service

Name and address (*office of the U.S. Trustee in you bankruptcy district*)

Name and address (*the Attorney General in Washington, D.C.*)

Name and address (*particular agency named in or affected by the lawsuit*, most likely the Dept. of Education)

Name and address (*debtor's Chapter 7 bankruptcy trustee*)

(This is the *Cover* used when filing the Proof of Service with the court.)

```
 1 │ (your name)
   │ (address)
 2 │ (city, state, zip)
 3 │ (telephone)
   │ In Pro Per
 4 │
 5 │
 6 │
 7 │              UNITED STATED BANKRUPTCY COURT
 8 │                    (name of district)
 9 │                    (name of division)
10 │
11 │  (your name)                    )  CHAPTER 7 BANKRUPTCY CASE
12 │                                 )  (bankruptcy case number)
13 │  PLAINTIFF,                     )
   │                                 )
14 │  vs.                            )  ADV. NO.
15 │                                 )
16 │  (name of defendant-- most likely )  COMPLAINT FILED:   (date)
17 │  UNITED STATES DEPARTMENT       )  DEPT:
   │  OF EDUCATION),                 )  JUDGE:
18 │                                 )
19 │  DEFENDANT                      )
20 │  _____ )
21 │         PROOF OF SERVICE OF SUMMONS AND COMPLAINT
22 │
23 │
24 │
25 │
26 │
27 │
28 │
   │  PROOF OF SERVICE                              (NAME)
   │                        - 1 -                  (ADDRESS)
   │                                           (CITY, STATE, ZIP)
   │                                              (TELEPHONE)
```

Forms—Samples

This section contains samples of the following documents:

Adversary Proceeding Sheet (Cover)

Adversary Proceeding Complaint

Summons

Proof of Service

Mailing Matrix

Proof of Service Cover

Joint Status Report

Request for Documents from Department of Education

Stipulation

Adversary Proceeding Sheet (Cover) (Sample)

B. 104 (Rev. 8/99)	**ADVERSARY PROCEEDING SHEET** (Instructions on Reverse)	ADVERSARY PROCEEDING NUMBER (For Court Use Only)

PLAINTIFFS	Bob Smith	DEFENDANTS	United States Department of Education Direct Loan Servicing
Address	3722 Anystreet #1 Los Angeles, CA 90034	Address	PO Box 4609 Utica, NY 13504-4609

ATTORNEYS (Firm Name, Address, and Telephone Number)	ATTORNEYS (if known)
None	In Pro Per

PARTY (Check one box only) ☐ 1 U.S. PLAINTIFF ☑ 2 U.S. DEFENDANT ☐ 3 U.S. NOT A PARTY

CAUSE OF ACTION (Write a brief statement of cause of action, including all U.S. statutes involved)

Plaintiff seeks dischargeability of debt pursuant to 11 U.S.C. §532(a)(8).

NATURE OF SUIT
(Check the one most appropriate box only)

☐ 454 To recover money or property

☐ 455 To revoke an order of confirmation of a Chapter 11 or Chapter 13 Plan

☐ 456 To obtain a declaratory judgment relating to any of **the foregoing causes of action**

☐ 435 To determine validity, priority, or extent of a lien or other interest in property

☑ 426 To determine the dischargeability of a debt 11 U.S.C. § 523

☐ 459 To determine a claim or cause of action removed to a bankruptcy court

☐ 458 To obtain approval for the sale of both the interest of the estate and of a co-owner in property

☐ 434 To obtain an injunction or other equitable relief

☐ 498 Other (specify)

☐ 424 To object or to revoke a discharge 11 U.S.C. § 727

☐ 457 To subordinate any allowed claim or interest except where such subordination is provided in a Plan

ORIGIN OF PROCEEDING (Check one box only) ☑ 1 Original Proceeding ☐ 2 Removed Proceeding ☐ 4 Reinstated or Reopened ☐ 5 Transferred from Another Bankruptcy Court ☐ CHECK IF THIS IS A CLASS ACTION UNDER F.R.C.P. 23

DEMAND	NEAREST THOUSAND $ 55,000.00	OTHER RELIEF SOUGHT	☐ JURY DEMAND

BANKRUPTCY CASE IN WHICH THIS ADVERSARY PROCEEDING ARISES

NAME OF DEBTOR	Bob Smith	BANKRUPTCY CASE NUMBER	LA 04-19681-ER

DISTRICT IN WHICH CASE IS PENDING **Central District of California**	DIVISIONAL OFFICE **Los Angeles**	NAME OF JUDGE

RELATED ADVERSARY PROCEEDING (IF ANY)

PLAINTIFF	DEFENDANT	ADVERSARY PROCEEDING NUMBER
DISTRICT	DIVISIONAL OFFICE	NAME OF JUDGE

FILING FEE (Check one box only) ☐ FEE ATTACHED ☑ FEE NOT REQUIRED ☐ FEE IS DEFERRED

DATE 8-2-2004	PRINT NAME	SIGNATURE OF ATTORNEY (OR PLAINTIFF) *Bob Smith*

Adversary Proceeding Complaint (Sample)

```
 1   Bob Smith
 2   3722 Anystreet #1
     Los Angeles, CA  90034
 3   555-000-0000
 4   In Pro Per

 5

 6

 7                   UNITED STATED BANKRUPTCY COURT

 8                   CENTRAL DISTRICT OF CALIFORNIA

 9                      (LOS ANGELES DIVISION)

10

11   BOB SMITH                    ) CHAPTER 7 BANKRUPTCY CASE
12                                ) NO. LA 04-19681-ER
13   PLAINTIFF,                   )
                                  )
14   vs.                          ) ADV. NO.
15                                )
16   UNITED STATES DEPARTMENT     ) COMPLAINT FILED:    8/2/2004
     OF EDUCATION,                ) DEPT:
17                                ) JUDGE:
18   DEFENDANT                    )
19   _____ )

20
          COMPLAINT TO DETERMINE DISCHARGEABILITY OF DEBT
21               PURSUANT TO 11 U.S.C. §523(a)(8)
22

23        Bob Smith, Debtor and Plaintiff in the above captioned adversary

24   proceeding, represents as follows:

25        1.    Bob Smith filed a voluntary petition for relief under Chapter 7 of the

26   United States Bankruptcy Code on April 28, 2004.  Jane Doe        is the duly

27   appointed Chapter 7 trustee.  This complaint seeks to determine the

28
```

PLAINTIFF'S COMPLAINT TO DETERMINE
DISCHARGEABILITY OF DEBT

- 1 -

BOB SMITH
3722 ANYSTREET #1
LOS ANGELES, CA 90034
555-000-0000

1   dischargeability of a student loan as it presents an undue hardship for the Debtor

2   and his dependents.

3   2.   One of the unsecured debts owing by the Debtor and listed on

4   Schedule F—Creditors Holding Unsecured Nonpriority Claims— is a student loan

5   owing to United States Department of Education.

6   3.   This loan was incurred to pay expenses at California State University,

7   Chico for a Secondary Teaching Credential, and University of Southern California

8   for a Ph.D. in Education (both were attained).

9

10   JURISDICTION

11   4.   Defendant United States Department of Education maintains its Direct

12 Loan Servicing Center in Utica, New York.

13   5.   Jurisdiction exists under 28 U.S.C. §1334. Venue is proper under 28

14 U.S.C. §1409(a). The District Court has generally referred these matters to the

15 Bankruptcy Court for hearing pursuant to 28 U.S.C. §157(a). This is a core

16 proceeding within the meaning of 28 U.S.C. §157(b)(2)(I). This adversary

17 complaint is brought pursuant to 11 U.S.C. §523(a)(8).

18

19   FIRST CAUSE OF ACTION [11 U.S.C. §523(a)(8)]

20   6.   Plaintiff is indebted to the Defendant in the approximate sum of

21 $55,000 for education loans made by Defendant to Plaintiff.

22   7.   Requiring Plaintiff to repay these debts will impose undue hardship on

23 the Debtor and the Debtor's dependents as contemplated under 11 U.S.C.

24 §523(a)(8).

25   8.   Based upon Plaintiff's current income and expenses, Plaintiff cannot

26 maintain a minimum standard of living if forced to repay the loan. Plaintiff

27 believes that his economic state of affairs is likely to persist for a significant

28

PLAINTIFF'S COMPLAINT TO DETERMINE
DISCHARGEABILITY OF DEBT
                                    - 2 -

BOB SMITH
3722 ANYSTREET #1
LOS ANGELES, CA 90034
555-000-0000

1   portion of the repayment period and he has made good faith efforts to repay the

2   loans.

3   9.   The Debtor has filed for bankruptcy for reasons other than just to

4   discharge his student loan.

5   WHEREFORE, the Debtor asks this court to enter an Order declaring the

6   student loan debt to be dischargeable.

7

8   Date: August 2, 2004.

9

10

11

12   *Bob Smith*

13   Plaintiff   BOB SMITH

14

15

16

17

18

19

20

21

22

23

24

25

26

27

28

PLAINTIFF'S COMPLAINT TO DETERMINE
DISCHARGEABILITY OF DEBT

- 3 -

BOB SMITH
3722 ANYSTREET #1
LOS ANGELES, CA 90034
555-000-0000

Summons (Sample)

<table>
<tr><td colspan="2">Attorney or Party Name, Address, Telephone & FAX Numbers, and California State Bar Number

Bob Smith
1111 Anystreet #1
Los Angeles, CA 90034</td><td>FOR COURT USE ONLY</td></tr>
<tr><td colspan="2">Attorney for Plaintiff   In Pro Per</td><td></td></tr>
</table>

UNITED STATES BANKRUPTCY COURT
CENTRAL DISTRICT OF CALIFORNIA

In re: Bob Smith _Debtor._	CHAPTER ___7___ CASE NUMBER LA 04-19681-ER ADVERSARY NUMBER AD04-02232
Bob Smith _Plaintiff(s),_ United States Dept. of Education Direct Loan Servicing _Defendant(s)._	_(The Boxes and Blank Lines below are for the Court's Use Only) (Do Not Fill Them In)_ **SUMMONS AND NOTICE OF STATUS CONFERENCE**

TO THE DEFENDANT: A Complaint has been filed by the Plaintiff against you. If you wish to defend yourself, you must file with the Court a written pleading, in duplicate, in response to the Complaint. You must also send a copy of your written response to the party shown in the upper left-hand corner of this page. Unless you have filed in duplicate and served a responsive pleading by _____, the Court may enter a judgment by default against you for the relief demanded in the Complaint.

A Status Conference on the proceeding commenced by the Complaint has been set for:

Hearing Date:	**Time:**	**Courtroom:**	**Floor:**

- ☐ 255 East Temple Street, Los Angeles
- ☐ 21041 Burbank Boulevard, Woodland Hills
- ☐ 3420 Twelfth Street, Riverside
- ☐ 411 West Fourth Street, Santa Ana
- ☐ 1415 State Street, Santa Barbara

PLEASE TAKE NOTICE that if the trial of the proceeding is anticipated to take less than two (2) hours, the parties may stipulate to conduct the trial of the case on the date specified, instead of holding a Status Conference. Such a stipulation must be lodged with the Court at least two (2) Court days before the date set forth above and is subject to Court approval. The Court may continue the trial to another date if necessary to accommodate the anticipated length of the trial.

Date of Issuance: _____

Clerk of the Bankruptcy Court

By: _____
Deputy Clerk

This form is mandatory. It has been approved for use by the United States Bankruptcy Court for the Central District of California.

Revised December 1998 (COA-SA)   **F 7004-1**

Proof of Service (Sample)

F 7004-1

In re		CHAPTER 7	LA 03-19681-ER
	Bob Smith		
	Debtor.	CASE NUMBER	

Adversary Number AB 04-022320ER

PROOF OF SERVICE

STATE OF CALIFORNIA, COUNTY OF ___Los Angeles___

1. I am employed in the County of ___Los Angeles___, State of California. I am over the age of 18 and not a party to the within action. My business address is as follows:

   2222 Anystreet #2
   Los Angeles, CA 90034

2. ☑ **Regular Mail Service:** On___See Attached Service List___, I served the foregoing Summons and Notice of Status Conference (and any instructions attached thereto), together with the Complaint filed in this proceeding, on the Defendant(s) at the following address(es) by placing a true and correct copy thereof in a sealed envelope with postage thereon fully prepaid in the United States Mail at ___Los Angeles___, California, addressed as set forth below.

3. ☑ **Personal Service:** On___Debra Hoffer___, personal service of the foregoing Summons and Notice of Status Conference (and any instructions attached thereto), together with the Complaint filed in this proceeding, was made on the Defendant(s) at the address(es) set forth below.

4. Defendant(s) and address(es) upon which service was made:

   Debra Hoffer
   1200 U.S. Courthouse
   312 N. Spring Street
   Los Angeles, Ca 90012
   For Defendant-Creditor
   U.S. Dept. of Education

   ☑ Names and Addresses continued on attached page

I declare under penalty of perjury under the laws of the United States of America that the foregoing is true and correct.

Dated: 9/21/04

Michael Hughes
_____   _____ *Michael Hughes* _____
Type Name   **Signature**

This form is mandatory. It has been approved for use by the United States Bankruptcy Court for the Central District of California.

Revised December 1998 (COA-SA)

F 7004-1

Mail Matrix (Sample)

In re: Bob Smith
Case Number LA 04-19681-ER

Regular Mail Service

U. S. Dept. of Education
Direct Loan Servicing System
PO Box 4609
Utica, NY 13504-4609

Office of U.S. Trustee
725 S. Figueroa
26th Floor
Los Angeles, CA 90017

Attorney General
U.S. Dept. of Justice
10th Constitution Ave. NW
Washington, D.C. 20530

Jane Doe
Trustee
Law Offices of Jane Doe
221 N. Figueroa St. Suite 1200
Los Angeles, CA 90012

Proof of Service Cover (Sample)

```
 1   Bob Smith
 2   1111 Anystreet #1
     Los Angeles, CA  90034
 3   555-000-0000
 4   In Pro Per

 5

 6

 7                    UNITED STATED BANKRUPTCY COURT

 8                    CENTRAL DISTRICT OF CALIFORNIA

 9                         (LOS ANGELES DIVISION)

10

11   BOB SMITH                  )  CHAPTER 7 BANKRUPTCY CASE
12                              )  NO. LA 04-19681-ER
     PLAINTIFF,                 )
13                              )
14   vs.                        )  ADV. NO.  AB 04-02232ER
15                              )
16   UNITED STATES DEPARTMENT   )  COMPLAINT FILED:   8/2/2004
     OF EDUCATION,              )  DEPT:
17                                 JUDGE:              T M.
18   DEFENDANT
19   _____   )

20             PROOF OF SERVICE OF SUMMONS AND COMPLAINT
21

22

23

24

25

26

27

28
```

PROOF OF SERVICE
                                    - 1 -

Joint Status Report (Sample)

<table>
<tr>
<td colspan="2">Attorney or Party Name, Address, Telephone & FAX Numbers and California State Bar Number

Don Sing
U.S. Attorney Office
312 N. Spring St., Room 512
Los Angeles, CA 90012
213-555-5555

Attorney for **U.S. Department of Education**</td>
<td>FOR COURT USE ONLY</td>
</tr>
<tr>
<td colspan="2" align="center">UNITED STATES BANKRUPTCY COURT
CENTRAL DISTRICT OF CALIFORNIA</td>
<td></td>
</tr>
<tr>
<td colspan="2">In re:

Bob Smith

Debtor.</td>
<td></td>
</tr>
<tr>
<td>**Bob Smith**</td>
<td>Plaintiff(s).</td>
<td>CHAPTER ___7___

CASE NUMBER **LA 04-19681-ER**</td>
</tr>
<tr>
<td rowspan="2" align="center">vs.</td>
<td rowspan="2"></td>
<td>ADVERSARY NUMBER **04-02232-ER**</td>
</tr>
<tr>
<td>DATE: **12/16/04**</td>
</tr>
<tr>
<td>**United States Department of Education**</td>
<td>Defendant(s).</td>
<td>TIME: **10:00 a.m.**
PLACE: **Crtrm 1568**</td>
</tr>
</table>

JOINT STATUS REPORT
LOCAL BANKRUPTCY RULE 7016-1(a)(2)

TO THE HONORABLE UNITED STATES BANKRUPTCY JUDGE:

The parties submit the following JOINT STATUS REPORT in accordance with Local Bankruptcy Rule 7016-1(a)(2):

A. **PLEADINGS/SERVICE:**

1. Have all parties been served? ☑ Yes ☐ No

2. Have all parties filed and served answers to the complaint/ counter-complaints/etc.? ☑ Yes ☐ No

3. Have all motions addressed to the pleadings been resolved? ☑ Yes ☐ No

4. Have counsel met and conferred in compliance with Local Bankruptcy Rule 7026-1? ☑ Yes ☐ No

5. If your answer to any of the four preceding questions is anything other than an unqualified "YES," then please explain below (or on attached page):

(Continued on next page)

Rev 1/01   This form is optional. It has been approved for use by the United States Bankruptcy Court for the Central District of California.   **F 7016-1.1**

In re		CHAPTER ___7___
Bob Smith	Debtor.	CASE NUMBER LA 04-19681-ER

B.   READINESS FOR TRIAL:

1.   When will you be ready for trial in this case?

Plaintiff	Defendant
January 2005	April 2005

2.   If your answer to the above is more than four (4) months after the summons issued in this case, give reasons for further delay.

Plaintiff	Defendant
	Defendant belies a mediation conference may lead to settlement.

3.   When do you expect to complete your discovery efforts?

Plaintiff	Defendant
January 2005	March 2005

4.   What additional discovery do you require to prepare for trial?

Plaintiff	Defendant
None	Depositions, Requests for Admission, Interrogatories, Document Production

C.   TRIAL TIME:

1.   What is your estimate of the time required to present your side of the case at trial (including rebuttal stage if applicable)?

Plaintiff	Defendant
Two hours	One or two hours

2.   How many witnesses do you intend to call at trial (including opposing parties)?

Plaintiff	Defendant
None	One or two

3.   How many exhibits do you anticipate using at trial?

Plaintiff	Defendant
Twenty to fifty.	Ten to twenty.

(Continued on next page)

Rev 1/01   This form is optional. It has been approved for use by the United States Bankruptcy Court for the Central District of California.   **F 7016-1.1**

Bankrupt Your Student Loans, 3ʳᵈ Edition, by Chuck Stewart, Ph.D. 2009   **APPENDIX E**   Page 218

F 7016-1.1

In re	Bob Smith	CHAPTER 7
	Debtor.	CASE NUMBER LA 04-19681-ER

D.   PRE-TRIAL CONFERENCE:

A pre-trial conference is usually conducted between a week to a month before trial, at which time a pre-trial order will be signed by the court. [See Local Rule 7016-1.] If you believe that a pre-trial conference is not necessary or appropriate in this case, please so note below, stating your reasons:

Plaintiff	Defendant
Pre-trial conference ✔ (is)/ ___ (is not) requested. Reasons: _____	Pre-trial conference ✔ (is)/ ___ (is not) requested. Reasons: _____

Plaintiff	Defendant
Pre-trial conference should be set <u>after</u>:	Pre-trial conference should be set <u>after</u>:
(date) 02/04/05	(date) 03/07/05

E.   SETTLEMENT:

1.   What is the status of settlement efforts?

2.   Has this dispute been formally mediated?   ☐   Yes   ✔   No
     If so, when?

3.   Do you want this matter sent to mediation at this time?

Plaintiff	Defendant
✔ Yes ☐ No	✔ Yes ☐ No

(Continued on next page)

Rev 1/01   This form is optional. It has been approved for use by the United States Bankruptcy Court for the Central District of California.

F 7016-1.1

In re	Bob Smith		CHAPTER ___7___
		Debtor.	CASE NUMBER LA 04-19681-ER

F.   ADDITIONAL COMMENTS/RECOMMENDATIONS RE TRIAL: *(Use additional page if necessary.)*

Respectfully submitted,

Dated: _____11/30/04_____   Dated: _____

_____   United States Attorney's Office

Firm Name   _____

                                         Firm Name

By: _____   By: _____

Name: _____Bob Smith_____   Name: _____Don Sing_____

                                                  U.S. Department of Education

Attorney for: _____   Attorney for: _____

Request for Documents from Department of Education (Sample)

This is a sample letter to be sent to the Department of Education requesting documents. The strategy is three – fold: first— to obtain information to prove your claim; second– to bring up issues the Department of Education does not want to be decided in court, and; third— to be an annoyance that will encourage them to settle in your favor before the trial.

In general, this letter is asking for information from the Department of Education to clarify and prove many of the issues brought forward in Chapter 7—Advocacy. 11 U.S.C.A. §523(a)(8) is bad law and should be overturned. Reread Chapter 7 to help you with your writing.

Remember, if you choose to write a letter like this, you **must** put it in your own words. Do not copy it as is.

Dear Department of Education,

This letter asks for data from the Department of Education for use in my own adversary proceeding.

A. I strongly believe the aggressive drive by the Department of Education to lower the student loan default rate has led to a terrible misreading of the law.

I've read many, many adversarial court cases and see a pattern of aggressive attempts to squeeze money out of destitute debtors. I've read many academic papers on the issue of student loan defaults and find virtually all writers in agreement that the current enforcement system is biased against debtors. This seems to stem from directives by Congress and the Department of Education to lower the default rates at all costs. What we see is the restructuring of loans in ways that make no economic sense just to say that a loan in not in "default." For example, placing a 65-year-old debtor living at the poverty level on SSI with $50,000 in student loans on an Income Contingent Repayment plan makes no sense. Technically, the loan will not be in default, but, realistically, the person will NEVER be able to pay back the loan, much less keep up with the interest payments. The Department of Education will spend thousands of dollars over 25 years just maintaining the loan on the books and working with collection agencies. This is a loss to taxpayers and violates the reason to reduce default rates—that is to recover more money. Commercial banks understand that it is better to get 10 cents on the dollar than incur years of additional expense when collection is near impossible.

I need more information to prove this point. **I request** copies of any internal directives, memorandums, position papers, strategy papers, and more since 1995 from the Department of Education about their efforts to lower default rates. For example, are there settlement goals employees are required to meet each month? Are employees trained to guide debtors who are in trouble to the ICR? I need Department level documents that can answer these questions.

B. I believe the Department of Education has consistently violated debtor rights during the adversary proceeding litigation.

Many attorneys told me that it is impossible to bankrupt my student loans. I conducted my own research and found that it was possible to bankrupt student loans but only through an adversary proceeding. When I contacted the Department of Education, I was never told about bankruptcy, or compromise, or write-off as possible ways to have my student loans discharged. There seems to be a concerted effort by the Department of Education to deny honest debtors relief through bankruptcy, compromise or write-off.

There is also much evidence that the Department of Education fails to follow the Debt Reduction Act and pursues debtors whose debt cannot be recovered.

I need more information to prove this point. **I request** copies of documents spanning the past 5 years that provide the following information:

- Number of student loan defaults.
- Number of Chapter 7 filings in which student loans are listed
- Number of people filing an "adversarial proceeding" seeking discharge of student loans.
- How the adversarial proceedings were resolved, e.g.
- Number found in favor of the debtor
- How many settled before trial and their results
- How many go to trial and the final results
- Reports from the Department of Education on discharges of loans and adversarial proceedings.
- Reports, papers, analysis, recommendations, and guidance made by the legal department of the Department of Education detailing legal strategies surrounding the discharge of student loans through the adversarial proceeding process.
- Reports on how many debtors have debts that more than 10-years old, are living on government benefits, and the Department of Education is actively pursuing.

C. I believe the Department of Education has incorrectly employed used of the Federal Poverty Guidelines as a measure of "undue hardship."

Someplace in the history of defending against adversary proceedings, the Department of Education suggested to the court to measure "undue hardship" against the Federal Poverty Guidelines. I've never read any rationale as to why this happened and why the courts accepted the arguments. There seems to be no legislative guidance in this area. There are many other measure that could have been used, but the Federal Poverty Guidelines are the most restrictive measure of poverty. I believe this happened because the Department of Education was too aggressive in its defense against bankruptcy.

I need more information to prove this point. **I request** copies of internal documents created by the Department of Education where it was decided to employ the strategy of using the Federal Poverty Guidelines as the measure of "undue hardship."

D. I believe the Department of Education discriminates against certain protected classes in its defense against student loan bankruptcies. I am in one of these classes.

A number of reports have pointed out that not all classes of debtors fair as well in their adversary proceeding. Those that fail most in securing a discharge of their student loans are racial minorities, single people, the well-educated, those living above the poverty level, and other classes.

I need more information to prove this point. **I request** copies of any studies, reports, memos, E-mails, or analysis that show the Department of Education is aware of its discriminatory practices, whether or not policies and programs have been established to assure the fair treatment of all debtors, and the results of these policies and programs.

E. I believe the Department of Education defense against the adversary proceeding has been too severe, so much so, that they violate debtor's "fresh start" policy of the United States Bankruptcy laws.

The Bankruptcy Code reveals that the fresh start provision takes precedent over §523(a)(8). The purpose of a fresh start policy is to allow debtors to afford the necessities of life at a quality and quantity expected within the mainstream American culture. It is consistent within the Bankruptcy Code and the fresh start policy for all debtors, including debtors with student loans, to have lifestyles approximating the middle class. The Bankruptcy Code legislative history supports this position. This is obvious if you review the impact bankruptcy has on debtors. Neither Chapter 13 nor Chapter 7 debtors are forced into poverty to achieve discharge of their loans.

But the history of debtors with student loans is different. With very few exceptions, debtors with student loans are unable to discharge their student loan debt unless they are at or below the Poverty Guidelines. The Bankruptcy Commission suggested that the undue hardship criterion meant debtors must observe a "minimal standard of living" during repayment. Does this require poverty levels of living? No. Poverty denotes "subminimal." When Congress and the Bankruptcy Commission spoke of minimal standard of living, they meant a level of living that brings debtors back into society at the lower ends of the middle class.

I need more information to prove this point. I request copies of any reports, memos, E-mail, reports to Congress, guidance to attorney, or any other correspondence was made by the Department of Education where the issue of the Bankruptcy Code "fresh start" policy is considered in relation to student loan dischargeability or adversary proceedings.

F. I believe Congress failed to clearly define "undue hardship" in §523(a)(8). As such, the Department of Education must have devised policy and defense strategies to uphold "undue hardship."

I need more information to prove this point. I request copies of any reports, memos, E-mail, reports to Congress, guidance to attorney, or any other correspondence made by the Department of Education where legal strategy was developed to interpret 11 US §523(a)(8).

G. I believe the Income Contingent Repayment (ICR) Plan is not appropriate for all persons with student loan debts. For certain classes of debtors, the income tax liability potential when the remaining debt is discharge poses a significant, if not impossible hardship. I believe the Department of Education fails to recognize the limitations of the ICR and fails to inform debtors of these limitations.

I need more information to prove this point. **I request** copies of any reports, memos, E-mail, analysis, reports to Congress, guidance to attorney, or any other correspondence made by the Department of Education that discusses the implementation of the ICR including advisement to debtors.

I look forward to receiving these documents before my trial date.

Sincerely,

Your name.

Stipulation (Sample)

```
                      SAMPLE — Stipulation

 1   Name 1
     United States Attorney
 2   Name 2
     Assistant United States Attorney
 3   Chief, Civil Division
      Name 3
 4   Assistant United States Attorney

 5       Address 1
         Address 2
 6       City, State Zip
         Telephone
 7       Fax
     Attorneys for Defendant
 8   United States Department of Education

 9
                UNITED STATES BANKRUPTCY COURT
10
          FOR THE CENTRAL DISTRICT OF CALIFORNIA
11
                  LOS ANGELES DIVISION
12

13   In re:                    Case No.   XX-XX-XXXXX-XX

14     Debtor Name,            Chapter 7

15         Debtor.             Adv. No.   XX-XX-XXXXX-XX

16     Debtor Name,            STIPULATION RE SETTLEMENT
                               AND DISMISSAL WITH
17         Plaintiff,          PREJUDICE; ORDER THEREON

18   vs.                       Pre-trial Conference:
                               Date:  XX XX, 20XX
19   UNITED STATES DEPARTMENT OF   Time:  XX AM/PM
     EDUCATION,                 Courtroom: Address
20                                         City
           Defendant.
21                             Hon.  Name
                               Bankruptcy Judge
22

23      This Stipulation is entered into by and between  Debtor Name

24         ("Plaintiff") and the United States Department of Education

25   ("Education"), to settle Plaintiff's Complaint To Determine

26

27                              1
```

1 Dischargeability of Debt Pursuant to 11 U.S.C. § 523(a)(8) filed on

2 DATE   .

3   Plaintiff is indebted to Education, as of   DATE   , in the

4 total amount of $(TOTAL DEBT)($ XX.00   in principal, and $ XX.00

5 in interest as of (Date Filed Adversary), as the result of a William D.

6 Ford Federal Direct Loan made to Plaintiff by Education in   DATE

7   ("Debt").

8   Plaintiff and Education desire to resolve this dispute and

9 terminate this adversary proceeding. The settlement memorialized by

10 this Stipulation will allow Plaintiff to retire the Debt, by paying

11 a reduced amount, if he abides by the terms herein.

12   Therefore, in consideration of the mutual covenants and

13 conditions herein, the parties agree as follows:

14   1.   Plaintiff shall pay Education $ XX.00 per month for X

15 years (for a total of $ XXX.00). Payments shall be due by the end

16 of each month, and they shall begin, at the latest, by   DATE   .

17   Plaintiff intends to set up a monthly electronic funds

18 transfer to Education. In the event that Plaintiff does not make

19 payments by way of electronic funds transfers, he should send

20 payments, in the form of cashier's checks or money orders, to

21 Education at the following address:

22   U. S. Department of Education
              Payment Center
23   P. O. Box 53260
              Atlanta, GA 30353-0260
24

25   Plaintiff must put his social security number on the face

26 of all checks and money orders.

27   2

1   2.   If Plaintiff makes the payments required under Paragraph 1

2   above (a total of $ XX.00), the remaining amounts of the Debt will

3   be considered by Education as discharged through Plaintiff's

4   bankruptcy.

5   3.   Plaintiff may pre-pay the $ XX.00   required under

6   Paragraph 1 above, without penalty, and receive an earlier

7   discharge, through bankruptcy, of the remaining amounts of the Debt.

8   4.   If Plaintiff does not make the payments required under

9   Paragraph 1 above, the remaining amounts of the Debt will not be

10 considered as having been discharged through bankruptcy, and

11 Education may use all available remedies to collect the remaining

12 amounts of the Debt.

13   5.   This Stipulation shall not affect Education's rights (or

14 any other part of the federal government's rights) as to any other

15 debts owed by Plaintiff, other than the Debt.

16   6.   Except to the extent this Stipulation directly conflicts

17 with the terms and conditions of the loan documents applicable to

18 the Debt, the terms and conditions of the underlying loan documents

19 remain unaffected.

20   7.   The parties agree that this adversary proceeding be

21 dismissed, with prejudice to refiling.

22   8.   The parties shall bear their own costs.

23 ///

24 ///

25 ///

26 ///

27   3

1   9.   No modification of this Stipulation shall be effective

2 unless made in writing and signed by the authorized representatives

3 of the parties.

4   Respectfully submitted,

5 Dated: _____   Name 1
                               United States Attorney

6   Name 2
                               Assistant United States Attorney

7   Chief, Civil Division

8

9   _____
                               Name 3
                               Assistant United States Attorney

10

11   Attorneys for the United States
                               Department of Education

12

13 Dated: _____   _____
                               (Debtor's Name)

14   ORDER

15   Based on the foregoing Stipulation and for cause shown,

16   **IT IS SO ORDERED** and the parties shall abide by this

17 Stipulation. Adversary Proceeding No. XX-XX-XXXXX-XX is hereby

18 dismissed, with prejudice.

19

20 Dated: _____
                             HON. Name
                             UNITED STATES BANKRUPTCY JUDGE

21 ///

22 ///

23 ///

24 ///

25 ///

26 ///

27   4

This section includes:

<u>Blank Legal (Pleading) Paper</u>

    Your Local Rules will specify the maximum number of lines for the documents to be submitted. Most courts specify not more than 28 lines per page. The enclosed blank is for 28 lines. Although you are welcome to make copies of this paper for typing your own pleading, we recommend that you buy some at your local stationery store. This is because when you photocopy pages, they usually shrink by 2% or more each time, thereby making it difficult for a typewriter to line up.

For all forms listed below, check with your court to verify its correctness. If the form is not correct, obtain the correct form from the court clerk:

<u>Adversary Proceeding Sheet (Cover)</u>

<u>Summons and Notice of Status Conference</u>

<u>Proof of Service</u>

<u>Joint Status Report</u>

1
2
3
4
5
6
7
8
9
10
11
12
13
14
15
16
17
18
19
20
21
22
23
24
25
26
27
28

B. 104 (Rev. 8/99)	**ADVERSARY PROCEEDING SHEET** (Instructions on Reverse)	ADVERSARY PROCEEDING NUMBER (For Court Use Only)

PLAINTIFFS Address	DEFENDANTS Address
ATTORNEYS (Firm Name, Address, and Telephone Number)	ATTORNEYS (if known)

PARTY (Check one box only)　☐　1 U.S. PLAINTIFF　☐　2 U.S. DEFENDANT　☐　3 U.S. NOT A PARTY

CAUSE OF ACTION (Write a brief statement of cause of action, including all U.S. statutes involved)

NATURE OF SUIT
(Check the one most appropriate box only)

☐　454 To recover money or property

☐　455 To revoke an order of confirmation of a Chapter 11 or Chapter 13 Plan

☐　456 To obtain a declaratory judgment relating to any of **the foregoing causes of action**

☐　435 To determine validity, priority, or extent of a lien or other interest in property

☐　426 To determine the dischargeability of a debt 11 U.S.C. § 523

☐　459 To determine a claim or cause of action removed to a bankruptcy court

☐　458 To obtain approval for the sale of both the interest of the estate and of a co-owner in property

☐　434 To obtain an injunction or other equitable relief

☐　498 Other (specify)

☐　424 To object or to revoke a discharge 11 U.S.C. § 727

☐　457 To subordinate any allowed claim or interest except where such subordination is provided in a Plan

ORIGIN OF PROCEEDING (Check one box only)　☐　1 Original Proceeding　☐　2 Removed Proceeding　☐　4 Reinstated or Reopened　☐　5 Transferred from Another Bankruptcy Court　☐ CHECK IF THIS IS A CLASS ACTION UNDER F.R.C.P. 23

DEMAND	NEAREST THOUSAND $	OTHER RELIEF SOUGHT	☐ JURY DEMAND

BANKRUPTCY CASE IN WHICH THIS ADVERSARY PROCEEDING ARISES

NAME OF DEBTOR	BANKRUPTCY CASE NUMBER
DISTRICT IN WHICH CASE IS PENDING	DIVISIONAL OFFICE	NAME OF JUDGE

RELATED ADVERSARY PROCEEDING (IF ANY)

PLAINTIFF	DEFENDANT	ADVERSARY PROCEEDING NUMBER
DISTRICT	DIVISIONAL OFFICE	NAME OF JUDGE

FILING FEE (Check one box only)　☐ FEE ATTACHED　☐ FEE NOT REQUIRED　☐ FEE IS DEFERRED

DATE	PRINT NAME	SIGNATURE OF ATTORNEY (OR PLAINTIFF)

Attorney or Party Name, Address, Telephone & FAX Numbers, and California State Bar Number	FOR COURT USE ONLY
Attorney for Plaintiff	

UNITED STATES BANKRUPTCY COURT
CENTRAL DISTRICT OF CALIFORNIA

In re:	CHAPTER _____
	CASE NUMBER
Debtor.	ADVERSARY NUMBER
Plaintiff(s).	*(The Boxes and Blank Lines below are for the Court's Use Only) (Do Not Fill Them In)*
vs.	**SUMMONS AND NOTICE OF STATUS CONFERENCE**
Defendant(s).	

TO THE DEFENDANT: A Complaint has been filed by the Plaintiff against you. If you wish to defend yourself, you must file with the Court a written pleading, in duplicate, in response to the Complaint. You must also send a copy of your written response to the party shown in the upper left-hand corner of this page. Unless you have filed in duplicate and served a responsive pleading by _____, the Court may enter a judgment by default against you for the relief demanded in the Complaint.

A Status Conference on the proceeding commenced by the Complaint has been set for:

Hearing Date:	Time:	Courtroom:	Floor:
❏ 255 East Temple Street, Los Angeles		❏ 411 West Fourth Street, Santa Ana	
❏ 21041 Burbank Boulevard, Woodland Hills		❏ 1415 State Street, Santa Barbara	
❏ 3420 Twelfth Street, Riverside			

PLEASE TAKE NOTICE that if the trial of the proceeding is anticipated to take less than two (2) hours, the parties may stipulate to conduct the trial of the case on the date specified, instead of holding a Status Conference. Such a stipulation must be lodged with the Court at least two (2) Court days before the date set forth above and is subject to Court approval. The Court may continue the trial to another date if necessary to accommodate the anticipated length of the trial.

Date of Issuance: _____

John Smith
Clerk of the Bankruptcy Court

By: _____
Deputy Clerk

This form is mandatory. It has been approved for use by the United States Bankruptcy Court for the Central District of California.

Revised December 1998 (COA-SA)

F 7004-1

In re	CHAPTER _____
Debtor.	CASE NUMBER

PROOF OF SERVICE

STATE OF CALIFORNIA, COUNTY OF _____

1. I am employed in the County of _____, State of California. I am over the age of 18 and not a party to the within action. My business address is as follows:

2. ❏ **Regular Mail Service:** On _____, I served the foregoing Summons and Notice of Status Conference (and any instructions attached thereto), together with the Complaint filed in this proceeding, on the Defendant(s) at the following address(es) by placing a true and correct copy thereof in a sealed envelope with postage thereon fully prepaid in the United States Mail at _____, California, addressed as set forth below.

3. ❏ **Personal Service:** On _____, personal service of the foregoing Summons and Notice of Status Conference (and any instructions attached thereto), together with the Complaint filed in this proceeding, was made on the Defendant(s) at the address(es) set forth below.

4. Defendant(s) and address(es) upon which service was made:

❏ Names and Addresses continued on attached page

I declare under penalty of perjury under the laws of the United States of America that the foregoing is true and correct.

Dated:

_____   _____
Type Name   *Signature*

This form is mandatory. It has been approved for use by the United States Bankruptcy Court for the Central District of California.

Revised December 1998 (COA-SA)

F 7004-1

Attorney for

UNITED STATES BANKRUPTCY COURT
CENTRAL DISTRICT OF CALIFORNIA

In re:

Debtor.

Plaintiff(s).

vs.

Defendant(s).

CHAPTER _____

CASE NUMBER

ADVERSARY NUMBER

DATE:
TIME:
PLACE:

JOINT STATUS REPORT
LOCAL BANKRUPTCY RULE 7016-1(a)(2)

TO THE HONORABLE UNITED STATES BANKRUPTCY JUDGE:

The parties submit the following JOINT STATUS REPORT in accordance with Local Bankruptcy Rule 7016-1(a)(2):

A.   PLEADINGS/SERVICE:

1.   Have all parties been served?   ❏   Yes   ❏   No

2.   Have all parties filed and served answers to the complaint/   ❏   Yes   ❏   No
counter-complaints/etc.?

3.   Have all motions addressed to the pleadings been resolved?   ❏   Yes   ❏   No

4.   Have counsel met and conferred in compliance with Local Bankruptcy   ❏   Yes   ❏   No
Rule 7026-1?

5.   If your answer to any of the four preceding questions is anything other than an unqualified "YES," then please explain below (or on attached page):

(Continued on next page)

In re		CHAPTER _____
	Debtor.	CASE NUMBER

B.   <u>READINESS FOR TRIAL</u>:

    1.   When will you be ready for trial in this case?

        <u>Plaintiff</u>   <u>Defendant</u>

    2.   If your answer to the above is more than four (4) months after the summons issued in this case, give reasons for further delay.

        <u>Plaintiff</u>   <u>Defendant</u>

    3.   When do you expect to complete <u>your</u> discovery efforts?

        <u>Plaintiff</u>   <u>Defendant</u>

    4.   What additional discovery do you require to prepare for trial?

        <u>Plaintiff</u>   <u>Defendant</u>

C.   <u>TRIAL TIME</u>:

    1.   What is your estimate of the time required to present <u>your side of the case</u> at trial (including rebuttal stage if applicable)?

        <u>Plaintiff</u>   <u>Defendant</u>

    2.   How many witnesses do you intend to call at trial (including opposing parties)?

        <u>Plaintiff</u>   <u>Defendant</u>

    3.   How many exhibits do you anticipate using at trial?

        <u>Plaintiff</u>   <u>Defendant</u>

(Continued on next page)

In re		CHAPTER _____
	Debtor.	CASE NUMBER

D.   **PRE-TRIAL CONFERENCE:**

A pre-trial conference is usually conducted between a week to a month before trial, at which time a pre-trial order will be signed by the court. [See Local Rule 7016-1.] If you believe that a pre-trial conference is not necessary or appropriate in this case, please so note below, stating your reasons:

<table>
<tr><td align="center"><u>Plaintiff</u></td><td align="center"><u>Defendant</u></td></tr>
<tr>
<td>Pre-trial conference ___ (is)/ ___ (is not) requested.
Reasons: _____
_____
_____
_____</td>
<td>Pre-trial conference ___ (is)/ ___ (is not) requested.
Reasons: _____
_____
_____
_____</td>
</tr>
<tr><td align="center"><u>Plaintiff</u></td><td align="center"><u>Defendant</u></td></tr>
<tr>
<td>Pre-trial conference should be set <u>after</u>:

(date) _____</td>
<td>Pre-trial conference should be set <u>after</u>:

(date) _____</td>
</tr>
</table>

E.   **SETTLEMENT:**

1.   What is the status of settlement efforts?

2.   Has this dispute been formally mediated?   ❏   Yes   ❏   No
     If so, when?

3.   Do you want this matter sent to mediation at this time?

Plaintiff		Defendant	
❏ Yes ❏ No		❏ Yes ❏ No	

(Continued on next page)

In re		CHAPTER _____
	Debtor.	CASE NUMBER

F. <u>**ADDITIONAL COMMENTS/RECOMMENDATIONS RE TRIAL**</u>**:** *(Use additional page if necessary.)*

Respectfully submitted,

Dated: _____   Dated: _____

_____   _____
Firm Name   *Firm Name*

By: _____   By: _____

Name: _____   Name: _____

Attorney for: _____   Attorney for: _____

The articles in this section are illustrative, not exhaustive. In general, you will need to research the factors influencing your case.

The articles include:

- Almost Two-Thirds of All Bankruptcies Due to Medical Bills
- The Consequences of Age on the Ability to Repay
- Discrimination Based on Age
- Discrimination Against the Highly Educated
- Discrimination Based on Sexual Orientation
- Reverse Discrimination Based on Gender or Race
- U.S. Economy (2005)
- Brunner Test Alternative

Almost Two-Thirds of All Bankruptcies Due to Medical Bills

Dr. David Himmelstein, associate professor of medicine at Harvard Medical School conducted research in 2004 into the relationship between medical problems and expenses, and bankruptcy. Reported in the journal of *Health Affairs*, Dr. Himmelstein found that almost two-thirds of all bankruptcies in the United States were caused by soaring medical bills. Most of those affected were middle-class workers with health insurance. Dr. Himmelstein stated, "Most of the medically bankrupt were average Americans who happened to get sick. Health insurance offered little protection."[1]

The researcher got permission from bankruptcy judges of five states (California, Illinois, Pennsylvania, Tennessee, and Texas) to survey 1,771 people who filed for bankruptcy. Sixty-two percent (931) cited medical causes for their bankruptcy, which affected 1.9 to 2.2 million Americans (filers plus dependents). Of those who went bankrupt due to illness, the average out-of-pocket expenses were $11,854 since the onset of the illness.

He found that in the two years prior to filing for bankruptcy:
- 54% went without needed doctor or dentist visits because of cost
- 43% did not fill prescriptions because of cost
- 40% lost telephone service
- 19% went without food
- 15% had taken out second or third mortgages to pay for medical expenses

Immediately after completing the bankruptcy, Dr. Himmelstein found debtors experienced continued problems, including:
- 33% continued to have problems paying their bills following bankruptcy, including paying their mortgage/rent and utility payments
- 9% were rejected for car loans
- 5% were turned away on apartment rentals
- 3.1% were turned down for jobs

Dr. Himmelstein stated, "Even good employment-based coverage sometimes fails to protect families, because illness may lead to job loss and the consequent loss of coverage . . . [especially] when they are financially most vulnerable."[2]

George Cauthen, lawyer for Nelson Mullins Riely & Scarborough LLP in Columbia, South Carolina, reviewed every bankruptcy petition filed in South Carolina from the years 1982 to 1989. He concluded that medical bills and divorce were the two leading causes of bankruptcy. He also found that less than 1% of all bankruptcy filings were due to credit card debt. Credit card debt causing bankruptcy is, "truly a myth."[3]

TO THE READER: If you want to present information like this in your court case, you will need to update it with current statistics and more. Do not copy the above article verbatim. Instead, paraphrase and update this article as needed.

---

[1] Gox, Maggie (Health and Science Correspondent.) (Feb 2, 2005). Half of bankruptcy due to medical bills. *Reuters*.

[2] Davis, Jeanie Lerche. (Feb. 2, 2005). Medical bills can lead to bankruptcy. *WebMD Medical News*.

[3] Gox, Maggie (Health and Science Correspondent.) (Feb 2, 2005). Half of bankruptcy due to medical bills. *Reuters*.

The Consequences of Age on the Ability to Repay

Often times, the Department of Education seems to act as though persons with student loan debts can always find employment— regardless of age. This article presents some of the research showing the relationship between ageing and the ability to work and, hence, make student loan payments.

As common sense tells us, there is a direct correlation between a persons age and need for living assistance. Here are some numbers:

Social Security Benefits[1]—
- 91% of people age 65 or over received SSI benefits in 2004
- For 34% of all SSI recipients, the SSI benefits represented 90% or more of their total income.
- For 31% of all SSI recipients, the SSI benefits represented 50-80% of their total income.
- For 21% of all SSI recipients, the SSI benefits represented 100% of their total income.
- Overall, almost 2/3 of all persons over age 65 and over depend on SSI benefits for most or all of their income.

Obviously, the older the debtor, the more likely he or she is dependent upon SSI benefits to live and generally have little discretionary income.

Disability[2]—
- 16.1% of men and 14.7% of women ages 62-64 are severely disabled and unable to work.
- 22-31% of men age 62-67 have disabilities that limit their ability to work.

Again, it is obvious that older people have greater instances of disabilities that affect their ability to work and make income.

Participation in the Workforce by Age[3]—
- Men 65 to 74 comprise 3.2% of the labor force.
- Men 75 and over, comprise 0.6% of the labor force.

Since the downturn of the economy, there have been many articles about the difficulties older workers have finding employment. For example, see Tiffany Hsu, April 10 2009, "Job Market is Especially Cruel for Older Workers," *Los Angeles Times*; "Older Workers Need Not Apply," April 12, 2009, *New York Times*; or Michael Luo, April 12, 2009, "Longer Unemployment for Those 45 and Older," *New York Times*.

Obviously, the older a person is, the less likely he or she works.

The purpose of the information is to show that reaching age 65 is a milestone in many ways. Financially, most people over age 65 are dependent upon SSI benefits, and are unable to secure additional income through work due to disability, discrimination, and other reasons. As such, payment plans through the Department of Education for outstanding student loans need to be structured to end by the time the debtor begins to receive SSI—around age 65.

In reality, the Department of Education recovers very little from outstanding student loans from debtors over age 65. Poverty, disability and other factors make it impossible for older debtors to pay towards old student loans. Plus, for persons on SSI who live at the poverty level, the loans are generally uncollectible. As the baby-boomers reach retirement, this issue will become more common and a plan should be developed by the Department of Education to address the problem.

Forcing older debtors into the Income Contingent Repayment (ICR) Plan is non-productive and causes an undue hardship. The Department of Education needs to consider some realistic percentage-on-the-dollar settlement during the years in which older workers are employed.

TO THE READER: If you want to present information like this in your court case, you will need to update it with current statistics and more. <u>Do not copy the above article verbatim. Instead, paraphrase and update this article as needed.</u>

---

[1] All statistics taken from the *SSA's FY 2004 Performance and Accountability Report.*

[2] All statistics are from the National Bipartisan Commission on the Future of Medicare, *Increasing the Medicare Eligibility Age,* 1998.

[3] Statistics from the Bureau of Labor Statistics, Office of Occupational Statistics and Employment Projections, *Table 11 — Distribution of the population and labor force by age and sex, 1980, 1990, 2000, and projected 2010.*

Discrimination Based on Age

Ageism is such an onerous problem in the American workplace that Congress passed the Age Discrimination Employment Act (ADEA) in 1967. Every state in the Union has a Department on Aging providing information, referral, and more, to persons over age 50. Most major cities also have social services aimed particularly for older workers. Despite all these efforts, "age discriminatory practices are thought to be so widespread in business that enforcement is difficult although not impossible"[1].

How bad is age discrimination in the workplace? "Age discrimination cases filed with the Equal Employment Opportunity Commission hit 19,921 [in fiscal year 2001]" – a more than 41% jump from 14,141 in 1999[2]. In 2002, age discrimination cases jumped another14.5% from the previous year (EEOC, 2003). Workplace age discrimination "complaints make up one of the fastest-growing categories of workplace bias"[3].

Discrimination complaints actually filed are just the tip of the iceberg. Most workers or job applicants who experience age discrimination do not file formal complaints. Also, businesses have "gotten a lot smarter about how they [discriminate]"[4].

"In the past decade, downsizings, job insecurity, increased use of part-time and contract employees and greater reliance on automation have created what some researchers call a 'corporate culture of expendability' among older workers, the Administration on Aging says"[5]. "Employers know the law. They do not any longer mention age in their ads. But they have other ways of getting the message across. The ad that begins 'Young, aggressive company' seeks 'bright, energetic' office manager, purchasing agent, engineer or secretary is sending a clear signal. Many companies, particularly in high technology, specify years of experience as a way of indicating what they want. It's usually two-three or three-five years, sometimes as many as ten-fifteen for executive spots. The implication is that no one with a twenty-five year employment record need apply"[6].

Some companies have an acronym to sum up their view of older workers "like TFO (for Too F****** Old). If you're over 50, or even over 45, and looking for a job, the attitude is all too familiar, and the fact that age discrimination is illegal doesn't matter"[7] (Fisher, 2004). A survey of members of ExecuNet (www.execunet.com) "found that 82% consider age bias a 'serious problem' in today's workplace, up from 78% in 2001" (Fisher, 2004). Of those members who were managers, "a startling 94%, almost all in their 40s and 50s, said that they believed their age had resulted in their being cut out of the running for a particular job"[8].

How bad is it for workers in their fifties once they have been laid off? Only one-half of men ages 55-61 found new jobs after being laid off[9]. In most cases, it was part-time employment. Further, "After being laid off, the older worker [over 50] has a 50 percent probability of taking a pay cut in future jobs"[10] and this pay cut may be as much as 39%[11]. Realize, this means that half of older workers NEVER find any kind of employment again for the **rest of their lives**. "Once an older worker is out of the labor force for a full year, the probability of working the next year is minuscule"[12].

"It is difficult for many older workers to find a new job and many become discouraged"[13]. In fact, the term 'discouraged' is an official designation when used to count the number of persons unemployed (discussed in a later article). Discouragement comes not only from lack of landing a job, but also from the societal condemnation toward the older unemployed worker. "To the public in general, and even to older people who aren't job hunting, the unemployed older worker evokes stereotyped reactions: If they had been any good to begin with they wouldn't be out of a job. They must be slowing down, out of date. Or, if it has been established that the older worker is the victim of a mass layoff or merger, they aren't looking hard enough; don't know how to present themselves (they oversell, undersell); or are too fussy. They want too much money, or they won't consider changing fields. They won't or can't develop new skills. Maybe they're unwilling to relocate"[14]. Many older workers give up looking for work.

Some older workers try a number of coping mechanisms to overcome job application discrimination. "Candidates are omitting dates or work experience from their resume. Others are taking more drastic steps, such as coloring their hair or getting plastic surgery"[15]. Yet these strategies can backfire. " Scott Testa, chief operating officer at Mindbridge Software, stated, "We are seeing more and more prospective employees trying to hide their ages on resumes. That's one more reason to delete the resume from the pile. If they hide that, what else are they hiding?"[16].

The problem with age discrimination in California mirrors those of the nation. "The California Employment Development Department showed in a 1998 report that while 82% of laid-off workers ages 25-54 landed new jobs, only 60% of those ages 55-64 secured new employment"[17]. Likewise, unemployed workers 45 years of age and over averaged more than "twice the time to procure new employment [for those who landed a job] [as] their younger counterparts"[18].

No industry is immune from the problem of age discrimination. You would think engineering, the sciences, teaching, and similar fields would have less age bias considering that we constantly hear of shortages of scientists, engineers, and teachers. Yet, "age discrimination seems to be endemic to the entire aerospace industry"[19]. The recent Shuttle disasters have called into question the loss of older, experienced personnel at NASA. Yet, NASA "fills out its positions with people who are 'fresh out,' meaning fresh out of college. In other words, the agency wasn't going to consider anyone who was middle aged"[20].

What about job placement agencies? Few fee-charging agencies will represent older workers. These agencies are not in the do-good business, but rather must make a profit by placing workers— and they know older workers are a liability. As one representative reported, "[Employers] want young people . . . We'd get job requisitions from well-know high tech companies saying no one over 40"[21]. As such, these agencies rarely make the effort to represent older workers.

The non-profit and free job-placement agencies are mostly supported through government programs. "Most clients who apply to these agencies are referred to openings that pay less than $6.00 an hour, many of them part time"[22]. Further, authors Brudney & Scott, in their research on job-placement agencies, found job fairs targeting older workers to "never succeed." There is a lot of hope, but significant job placement of older workers never happens.

The American Dream "promises that if you work hard, show initiative, don't make too many waves, and save your money, you will progress up the ladder and spend your latter years in security. . . yet [older workers] experiences tell us that it's time to stop dreaming"[23].

This article is a short overview of the problem of age discrimination in the workplace. There are thousands of books and articles on the subject. Federal and state aging agencies have produced thousands of pamphlets, opinion papers, and more. The problem is real and not going away.

TO THE READER: If you want to present information like this in your court case, you will need to update it with current statistics and more. <u>Do not copy the above article verbatim. Instead, paraphrase and update this article as needed.</u>

---

[1] Johnson, Elizabeth & Williamson, John. (1980). *Growing old: The social problems of aging.* New York: Holt, Rinehart and Winston.

[2] Fisher, Anne, (2004, February 9). Workplace: Older, wiser, job-hunting. *Fortune*.; Cohen, Adam. (2003, March 2). Too old to work? *New York Times*.

[3] Marshall, Samantha, (2003, May 12-18). Age bias complaints rise as the workforce grays. *Crain's New York Business*.

[4] Mille, Margaret. (2003, August 24). Ageism in the workplace. *Sarasota Herald-Tribune*.

[5] Ibid.

[6] Brudney, Juliet & Scott, Hilda. (1987). *Forced out*. New York: Simon & Schuster, Inc.

[7] Fisher, Anne. (2004, February 9). Workplace: Older, wiser, job-hunting. *Fortune*.; Cohen, Adam. (2003, March 2). Too old to work? *New York Times*.

[8] Ibid.

[9] Administration on Aging. (2002, January 17). *Age discrimination: A pervasive and damaging influence*. [On-line]. Available: http://www.aoa.gov/factsheets/ageism.html [2002, October 15]

[10] Cohen, S. (2002, March 7). *How to fight age discrimination*. [On-line]. Available: http://ww.kiplinger.com [2002].

[11] Joyce, E. (1999, March). *Age bias may thwart boomers*. [On-line]. Available: http://www.ncoa.org/news/archives/abe_bias.htm [2002, November 13].

[12] Berkowitz et al. (1998). The older worker. *Industrial Relations Research Association*.

[13] Crampton, Suzanne & Hodge, John. (2003). *The aging workforce and age discrimination*. Hawaii International Conference on Business, June 18 -21, 2003. Sheraton Waikiki Hotel, Honolulu, Hawaii, USA

[14] Brudney, Juliet & Scott, Hilda. (1987). *Forced out*. New York: Simon & Schuster, Inc.

[15] Armour, Stephanie, (2003, July 20). More job seekers try to hide their ages. *Money*.

[16] Ibid.

[17] Kleyman, Paul. (2004). Options needed for aging workers. *Aging Today*. [report available online at www.cchi.org.

[18] Ibid.

[19] Khol, Ronald. (December 18, 2003). NASA gets away with blatant age discrimination. *Machine Design*.

[20] Ibid.

[21] Brudney, Juliet and Scott, Hilda. (1987). *Forced out*. New York: Simon & Schuster, Inc.

[22] Ibid.

[23] Ibid.

Discrimination Against the Highly Educated

Many believe that a person with a Master's degree, and in particular, a Doctorate should 'absolutely' be able to find a job. It is not true. Often a higher degree acts as an impenetrable wall against employment. This section reviews the research on the effect of higher education on employment.

The Effect of Higher Education on Employment:

It is a myth that a Ph.D. 'guarantees' employment. In a study done by the American Institute of Physics, one-third of its members who received their Ph.D. were unable to find permanent employment within the first year after graduation[1]. Even in the long run, some Ph.D.s are not able to find employment. The University of Washington Graduate School reports the rate of unemployment among Ph.D.s in 2001 to be 1.5%[2]; this is the unemployment rate within the first 10 years after obtaining the degree. Thus, a small number of Ph.D.s looking for work are still not able to land a job after 10 years of effort. These findings are similar to an earlier study done by the National Science Foundation. It, too, found that 1.5% of Ph.D.s were unemployed in 1995[3].

Even Ph.D.s in Computer Sciences face a difficult future. "As of 1997, 6.1 percent of new computer science Ph.D.'s could not find stable, full-time employment. The rate was significantly higher than the jobless rate for the entire American workforce"[4].

Our society promotes education as the road to success. It is often reported that college educated workers make significantly more income than non-college educated—referred to as an education "income gap." "In June 2003, an estimated 1,286,000 Bachelor's degrees were conferred, along with 436,000 Master's, 80,400 First Professional, and 46,700 Doctoral degrees, as well as 633,000 Associates degrees. Degrees in all these categories are up substantially since the mid-1980s, as young people have heeded the advice given them to acquire more education"[5]. But has all this effort and expense paid off? The income gap "has been shrinking since 1989, not growing. . . .[Further] between 1979 and 1992, the percentage of U.S. men holding B.A. degrees but earning poverty-level wages (about $13,000 per year) doubled, to 6 percent. A recent MacArthur Foundation study found that in Chicago, fully 9.2 percent of the working poor hold B.A.'s"[6]. In January 2004, it was reported that "there were more unemployed workers 25 years or older with college degrees than there were unemployed workers without high school diplomas"[7]. Any level of college education affords, on the average, greater lifetime income over those with no college education. But, a college education does not automatically translate into higher levels of employment or greater financial prosperity.

The National Science Foundation study found a number of other correlates between obtaining a doctorate and employment. "Disruptions in full-time employment subsequent to receiving a doctorate" and working part-time prior to receiving the Ph.D. were associated with significantly higher unemployment rates[8].

Another correlate was the age of the recipient at the time the doctorate was awarded. As the National Science Foundation reported, "Age at completing the doctorate is strongly associated with unemployment. When controlling for other relevant variables, the unemployment rate ranged from 0.6 percent for those who received doctorates before age 26 to 5.8 percent for those who received doctorates at age 40 or older"[9]. Shockingly, the unemployment rate for computer programmers over the age of 50 was an astounding 17 percent"[10]. Thus, even those with higher college degrees and/or who work in technical fields are not sheltered from age discrimination.

The current official unemployment rate in the United States is about 5.6%. Notice that the unemployment rate for Ph.D.s over 40 years of age is similar or higher. This would indicate that, contrary to popular opinion, <u>there</u>

is very little difference in employment rates related to level of education. It is a myth that a doctorate 'guarantees' life-long highly paid employment.

TO THE READER: If you want to present information like this in your court case, you will need to update it with current statistics and more. Do not copy the above article verbatim. Instead, paraphrase and update this article as needed.

---

[1] Chu, Raymond & Curtin, Jean. (1996, September). Underemployment among post doctorates 1994 Society Membership Survey. *American Institute of Physics* (AIP).

[2] The Graduate School, University of Washington. (2001, May). PhD career paths at UW—An update. *Notes on Graduate Education*.

[3] Shettle, Carolyn F. (1997). *Who is unemployed? Factors affecting unemployment among individuals with doctoral degrees in science and engineering.* National Science Foundation, Division of Science Resources Studies, Special Report, NSF 97-336.

[4] Tonelson, Alan. (2000). *The race to the bottom: Why a worldwide worker surplus and uncontrolled free trade are sinking American living standards.* Boulder, Colo: Westview Press.

[5] Almeida, Paul. (2003, June 18). *On the globalization of white-collar jobs.* Testimony before the U.S. House of Representatives Committee on Small Business.

[6] Ibid.

[7] Gongloff, Mark. (2004, March 1). Outsourcing: what to do? *CNN/Money*.

[8] Shettle, Carolyn F. (1997). *Who is unemployed? Factors affecting unemployment among individuals with doctoral degrees in science and engineering.* National Science Foundation, Division of Science Resources Studies, Special Report, NSF 97-336.

[9] Ibid.

[10] Tonelson (2000).

Discrimination Based on Sexual Orientation

Although there has been progress in civil rights for lesbians and gay men, the United States is still a dangerous place for those who are open about their homosexuality or who are perceived to be lesbian or gay. One measure of this is antigay violence, which has increased steadily every year, and now is the number one hate crime reported to police each year[1]. Similarly, the numbers of antigay employment claims are increasing. Another measure is the firestorm consuming U.S. media and governmental meetings over the prospect of gay marriage. Antigay sentiments impact the work environment.

Contrary to public belief, lesbians and gay men have lower incomes than the general population. Lee Badgett has conducted the most accurate research on the economic discrimination lesbians and gay men experience. Besides many other correlations, she discovered "men with male partners earned 26% less than married men with the same education, location, race, age, number of children, and disability status did"[2]. She states, "The findings for gay men strongly suggests the influence of workplace discrimination"[3].

TO THE READER: If you want to present information like this in your court case, you will need to update it with current statistics and more. Do not copy the above article verbatim. Instead, paraphrase and update this article as needed.

---

[1] Stewart, Chuck. (2003). *Gay and lesbian issues: A contemporary resource.* Boulder, CO: ABC-CLIO Publishers, p. 48.
[2] Badgett, M.V. Lee (1998). *Income inflation: The myth of affluence among gay, lesbian, and bisexual Americans.* Washington, D.C.: NGLTF Policy Institute.
[3] Ibid.

Reverse Discrimination Based on Gender or Race

This article is a true example of reverse discrimination based on gender or race; names have been changed to ensure confidentiality.

Dr. Smith received his Ph.D. in Women's Studies with an outside emphasis on Gay Studies. He applied for hundreds of jobs with universities throughout the world as either a Director of Women's Studies or Director of Lesbian and Gay Student Support. In his 9 years of applying for work, he was never granted an interview. Upon investigation, he found that out of 671 departments[1] (NWSA, 2002) of Women Studies, only 7 had male directors. That means that women head 99% of Women's Studies Departments. Academically, both men and women may qualify as director of such departments since Gender and Women's Studies are fields of knowledge either gender may learn. But the reality is that men are almost never hired for these positions. Similarly, Dr. Smith applied for every LGBT Resource Directorship. He was never granted an interview. According to the Lesbian, gay, bisexual, transgender Resource Directory (2004) found on the web, there are 2 1/4 times as many women directors as there are men[2]. Men are rarely hired to head these departments.

Dr. Smith's degrees and professional writings qualify him to teach multicultural courses, and work in or be the director of Affirmative Action offices. He applied for hundreds of such positions over the years and never received a job. He is a member of the American Association of Affirmative Action (AAAA) and has presented at their conferences. AAAA is overwhelming non-white whereas Dr. Smith is Caucasian. In reality, college Affirmative Action offices only hire non-white directors and usually women. Dr. Smith has experienced reverse discrimination to such a significant degree that employment in his chosen field has not materialized.

TO THE READER: If you want to present information like this in your court case, you will need to update it with current statistics and more. Do not copy the above article verbatim. Instead, paraphrase and update this article as needed.

---

[1] *NWSA 2002 Updated Directory of Women's Studies Programs.* (2002). NWSA Women's Center, Georgia Institute of Technology, Rm 216, Student Services Building, 404-385-1563, yvette.upton@vpss.gatech.edu.

[2] *Lesbian, gay, bisexual, transgender Resource Directory.* (2004). www.lgbtcampus.org/cirectory.htm

U.S. Economy (2009)

The U.S. economy performance over the next ten years affects the borrowers' ability to repay on student loans. Professional economists have not been able to make long-range predictions regarding the U.S. economy. In fact, economists have been grossly incorrect about predicting the job growth rate since the official end of the recession in 2001. As stated in *CNN/Money*, "it's important to remember that economists have done a lousy job of predicting job growth lately; the consensus forecast for payroll growth has been overly optimistic in 9 out of the past 14 months"[1].

With the current economic downtrend, unemployment is rising monthly and approaches or exceeds 10% nationwide. However, this number represents only those who have made claims with unemployment. The actual number of unemployed is estimated to be almost double the official number.

Because of the glut of qualified professionals on the market, "companies are being incredibly restrictive in how they look at people [for job openings]"[2]. This means that many highly educated and experienced workers cannot find employment.

Two governmental policies are having a strong impact on the U.S. job market—"guest workers" (H1-B and L-1 visa) and "outsourcing." These policies have greatest impact on the highly educated. The <u>H1-B and L-1 visa programs</u> allow foreigners to enter the U.S. to legally work. The rationale behind the program is the claim made by some businesses that there is a shortage of U.S. talent in particular industries and that foreign workers are needed to fill the gap. Within the last five years, over a million foreigners have entered the U.S. as guest workers[3]. The computer, engineering and medical industries have been the primary users of the program. Initially, it was claimed that the programs would not take jobs away from U.S. citizens and not depress wages within the respective industries. After many years of implementation, the U.S. Department of Labor reported in April 1996, "We found the program does not protect U.S. worker's jobs; instead, it allows aliens to immigrate . . . and then shop their services in competition with equally or more qualified U.S. workers without regard to prevailing wage . . . [and] the prevailing wage may be eroded over time."[4] Two recent private studies have confirmed the U.S. Department of Labor report, which states, "Heavy use of these H1-B workers is reducing the wages of computer and software workers in particular."[5] Thus, the guest worker program is reducing many jobs in the United States, particularly jobs requiring specialized education and training, and has impacted (depressed) the wages for those jobs.

Also related to the guest worker program is the problem of "<u>outsourcing</u>" jobs to foreign workers. Here, U.S. companies find workers in other countries to fill jobs that otherwise would be performed in the U.S. (sometimes referred to as "offshoring"). As Paul Almeida (2003) discusses in his article, *On the Globalization of White-Collar Jobs*, "When manufacturing jobs started moving offshore, we were told not to worry, that the U.S. comparative advantage was in services and high technology. We were assured that the new global division of labor was both natural and benign: we would keep the high-paying, high-skilled jobs, while the developing countries would do the actual work of making things. For decades, American workers were told to simply acquire more skills and education in order to succeed in the U.S. job market. Now engineers with Ph.D.s and recent college graduates alike are hearing that they are too expensive, that their job can be done more cheaply abroad. Meanwhile, the U.S. trade picture is also shifting in ominous ways."

A survey conducted by Deloitte Research found that the 100 largest financial services firms expected to "shift $356 billion worth of operations and about two million jobs [out of the U.S.] to low-wage countries over the next five years"[6]. Not only financial services, but other kinds of white-collar work—computer programming, "patent research, credit checks, tax return preparation, insurance claim processing, even the reading of CAT scans"[7]— (which use the telephone and Internet communication systems) are being transferred to low-cost countries. There is an "apparent wholesale flight of technology jobs like computer programming and technical support to lower-cost nations, led by India"[8]. As a result, "The number of computer jobs in the United States dropped 10 percent in the past two years"[9] further impacting college enrollment in these fields. "The Computing Research Association's annual survey of more than 200 universities in the United States and Canada found that undergraduate enrollments in computer science and computer engineering programs were down 23 percent this year"[10].

Bill Gates of Microsoft Corporation recently went on a speaking tour to encourage young people into computer programming and computer education programs[11]. Gates is aware of the negative sentiments which outsourcing has created for his business in the United States. Yet, Microsoft is one of the primary users of computer programmers in India. This schizophrenic behavior— moving highly skilled jobs out of the United States while at the same time publicly telling people they should seek higher education for jobs that are no longer in the United States— is not lost on students entering college. Students are voting with their feet by choosing other fields; obtaining college degrees in fields exposed to outsourcing is a dead end.

"Alan Greenspan and President Bush believe the best response to the movement of U.S. jobs offshore is the same thing it's always been: educating U.S. workers so they can get better-paying jobs. But some economists doubt education will fully ease the pain."[12] Talent pools in other countries are "massive"[13] and highly educated. Both Indian and Chinese cultures highly value education and have large numbers of highly skilled and educated workers. For example, India graduates more Ph.D.s in computer science each year than the United States. Many economists believe higher education is not the solution to lack of jobs caused by outsourcing[14].

Outsourcing to foreign workers has become a major political issue in the United States. Severe negative reactions by citizens recently occurred when a few government departments began outsourcing jobs that could be done locally. "The political reaction in the United States against such outsourcing has built rapidly in the last year; nearly two dozen states have voted on legislation to ban government work from being contacted to non-Americans. . . More recently, the United States Senate approved a bill aimed at restricting outsourcing of contracts from two federal departments"[15]. Several major political figures are challenging the outsourcing threat while other politicians within the Bush administration are embracing outsourcing. On March 16, 2004 in New Delhi, India, Secretary of State Colin L. Powell "sought to assure Indians that the Bush administration would not try to halt the outsourcing of high-technology jobs to their country"[16]. Earlier in 2004, Gregory Mankiw, chairman of the White House Council of Economic Advisors called outsourcing a "long-term plus for the economy".[17] A great political outcry was stirred and the Bush administration claimed that it would work to train people for new jobs.

Many manufacturing jobs having moved overseas and now high-technology white collar jobs are also moving; the only jobs left are waiters, teachers, plumbers, electricians, construction workers, physicians, nurses, dentists, real estate, food service, auto repair and other skilled by labor-intensive jobs that require a live person to perform. These are the jobs of the future. "This is shattering news to the waiters, cashiers, home and health care workers, and tens of millions of other Americans toiling at jobs which often pay minimum wage or slightly higher— the very Americans being urged into all the reeducation and retraining programs that the optimists have promised the government or business one day will adequately fund and get right. No matter what careers they prepare themselves for, they will remain trapped in the race to the bottom."[18] Many economists believe the "trend is real, irreversible and another step in the globalization of the American economy."[19]

Conclusion: The United States has been caught in a "no job growth" recovery from the recession of 2000-2001 and has seen a major crash since the severe economic slump since 2008. Economists are perplexed by the situation and have been consistently wrong in predicting new job growth. Both the guest worker programs and outsourcing of jobs to foreign workers are contributing to the problem— and mostly for the highly educated. As stated above, engineers with Ph.D.s and recent college graduates alike are hearing that they are too expensive and their jobs are being transferred to India or other low-cost country. This means that increasingly more highly educated people will not be able to find appropriate employment in the United States, and will not be able to service their student loans.

TO THE READER: If you want to present information like this in your court case, you will need to update it with current statistics and more. <u>Do not copy the above article verbatim. Instead, paraphrase and update this article as needed.</u>

---

[1] Gongloff, Mark. (2004, March 4). Job boom still a hope, not a fact. *CNN/Money*.

[2] Ibid.

[3] Almeida, Paul. (2003, June 18). *On the globalization of white-collar jobs*. Testimony before the U.S. House of Representatives Committee on Small Business.

[4] Tonelson, Alan. (2000). *The race to the bottom: Why a worldwide worker surplus and uncontrolled free trade are sinking American living standards*. Boulder, Colo: Westview Press.

[5] Ibid

[6] Almeida (2003, June 18).

[7] Donnelly, Francis & Ramirez, Charles. (2003, August 10). Michigan loses as tech jobs slip overseas. *The Detroit New Technology*.

[8] Lohr, Steve. (2004, March 1). Microsoft, amid dwindling interest, talks up computing as a career. *The New York Times*.

[9] Donnelly and Ramirez. (2003, August 10).

[10] Lohr. (2003, December 22).

[11] Ibid.

[12] Gongloff. (2004, March 4).

[13] Donnelly and Ramirez. (2003, August 10).

[14] Gongloff. (2004, March 4).

[15] Rai, Saritha. (2004, February 9). Indians fearing repercussions of U.S. technology outsourcing. *New York Times*.

[16] Weisman, Steven. (2004, March 17). Powell reassures India on technology jobs. *The New York Times*.

[17] Ibid.

[18] Tonelson. (2000).

[19] Lohr. (2003, December 22).

Congress should rescind §523(a)(8). If undue hardship tests are to continue, we suggest a comprehensive alternative to the Brunner test, which would include:

1. Good Faith Analysis —
   a. Length of Time—Courts should examine when the petition was filed. If it is soon after graduation, there should be the presumption of abuse by the debtor. If it is more than 7 years since graduation, it should be concluded the debtor failed to gain any financial rewards from the education and honestly needs to discharge his or her student loan.
   b. Traditional Meaning of Good Faith under the Bankruptcy Code
      i. Efforts to Attain Employment— The court should expect out-of-work debtors to aggressively seek work—perhaps a couple of hundred applications per year. However, this effort to find employment must be tempered with consideration of the size of the loan. If a debtor owes $50,000 or more, it makes no sense for the debtor to seek minimum wage jobs because such jobs will never provide the income necessary to make loan payments. High loan debtors need to seek higher paying jobs—but these are fewer in numbers so the court should expect fewer job application attempts.
      ii. Efforts to make payments toward the loans— If the debtor made payments whenever income allowed, and filed the necessary deferments or forbearances during low-income periods, the debtor should be considered to be acting in good faith.

2. Living Standard of Debtor — The court needs to evaluate the overall living situation of the debtor and dependents. The court should make an overall analysis to determine that the debtor is not living an extravagant life, i.e., incurring unnecessary and frivolous expenses, and/or sitting on comfortable income or assets. The Bankruptcy Code does not mandate the debtor to live at or below the poverty level to be entitled to a "fresh start." Quite the opposite; the bankruptcy systems was designed to help prevent individuals with massive debts from falling into an oppressive lifestyle. Similarly, §523(a)(8) makes no mention about the standard of living of the debtor and it should not be construed that the debtor must be impoverished to be granted a "fresh start."
   A word of caution concerning the analysis of "frivolous" expenses; some bankruptcy decisions have shown the extreme unreasonableness of the Department of Education. For example, an AIDS patient living on SSI was asked to get rid of his cat so he could pay an additional $20 each month on his student loans. Courts need to keep in mind what a minimum living standard really entails and not allow such extreme interpretation force debtors into oppressive lifestyles.

3. Debtor's Potential Ability to Repay Loan— The harsh interpretation of the second prong of the Brunner test relates to the debtor's potential ability to repay the loan and has resulted in many absurd court decisions. The court first needs to accept that it is <u>impossible to absolutely determine the future ability of a debtor to repay loans</u>. Even the Brunner court recognized this limitation, yet it ignored its own understanding and made a decision as if it could make an absolute determination. Second, the court needs to accept the <u>myth that higher education guarantees higher standards of living</u>. If courts fail to accept these two truths, extreme and nonsensical decisions will continue to be made by bankruptcy courts.
   a. <u>Length of Loan</u>— If a debtor has been unable to repay his or her loan during the original loan term length and there is no evidence of fraud, the loan should be discharged. Although the 7-year limit was removed from §523(a)(8) in 1998, the rationale for this time limit has not

changed. A debtor who has aggressively sought work, lived modestly, and made loan payments when possible but was never lucky enough to land appropriate employment for more than 7 years, is not attempting to defraud the government; it is called life. The student loans should be discharged.

Further, a debtor who has been unable to repay his or her student loans for more than 7 years is giving the strongest possible evidence that there are factors surrounding the debtors life that preclude increased future income. Past employment histories should be used as evidence to predict future employment opportunities.

b. <u>Factors Affecting Future Employment</u>— A common sense approach to determine future ability to repay student loans is to examine the factors that affect employment opportunities for the specific debtor. Some of these <u>factors</u> include:

    i. <u>Age / Race / Religion / Gender / Sexual Orientation Discrimination</u>—

        • The U.S. has a long history of <u>prejudice</u> and <u>discrimination</u>. Many laws have been passed at the federal and state level to address some of these problems. Governmental agencies have been formed and funded to help fight discrimination. Despite these efforts, discrimination is rampant in the U.S. and this affects debtors in their efforts to seek employment. Courts need to be realistic about the problems of discrimination in employment and not act as though it does not exist.

        • <u>Ageism</u>: The U.S. is extremely ageist. Every state and the federal government have departments devoted to helping older citizens, including employment. Laws have been passed to outlaw discrimination based upon age, but they are toothless. A 26 year old with a Ph.D. is much more likely to gain employment than a Ph.D. who is 50 years old. In fact, 50-year or older workers who loose their jobs, have a 50% chance of NEVER working again at ANY job, at any hourly rate, for the rest of their lives. Similarly, a 50-year or older worker who is out of work for a year or longer, has a near zero chance of getting ANY job ever for the <u>rest of his or her life</u>. Ageism is <u>real</u> and bankruptcy courts need to consider this in their decisions.

    ii. <u>Education Level</u>: Contrary to common belief, higher levels of education do not automatically equate to better employment opportunities. Over the past 20 years, colleges have pumped out millions of graduates. Of the totality of jobs in the U.S., few require higher education degrees. College graduates are competing for a scarce number of high-paying jobs. Further, employers are hesitant to hire people with college degrees for low-level jobs. There is rampant discrimination against the highly educated by employers claiming the applicant is "over-qualified." Bankruptcy courts need to realistically overcome the presumption that educated debtors "should" be able to find high-paying jobs.

    iii. <u>Degrees and Certificates</u>: Some students fail to complete school and obtain a degree. Some students obtain a degree but fail to obtain a state certificate required to work in their field. The lack of degree or certificate will impact the debtor's ability to obtain appropriate employment. For example, physicians and attorneys who finish school but fail to obtain a state license will be blocked from practicing and, thus, cannot be hired in their chosen field. In each of these cases, the lack of degree and/or certificate impacts future ability to obtain employment.

    iv. <u>Past Employment Record</u>: It is important for courts to review past employment records of debtors. Employers review these records while evaluating workers to hire and rightly or wrongly, make conclusions about the desirability of the applicant. Perhaps a debtor was a whistleblower or filed antidiscrimination claims against his or her employer, future employers may decide the applicant is a "trouble-maker" and reject his or her application.

    v.   Economy: The health of the economy directly impacts the debtors' ability to obtain employment. Courts need to look not only at the employment picture for the economy as a whole, but the dynamics within particular segments of the economy. For example, because of outsourcing, many areas of the computer industry are collapsing; registration in college computer programs has dropped by more than 25% in just one year (2004). Courts need to get past the idea that "since you are educated, you can get a job" and understand that many factors beyond the control of the debtor impact the ability to obtain work, and in particular, high-paying work.

    vi.   Debtor Health: Debtors declared permanently disabled are able to have their student loan debt discharged through a disability discharge. However, many debtors find themselves trapped because they are partially disabled. The Department of Education treats partially disabled debtors the same as fully-abled workers. Courts need take into consideration the health of the debtor, and realistically evaluate the potential for employment and income for the partially disabled.

    vii.   Debtor Dependents: Caring for others impacts the ability of debtors to service student loans. Courts should examine the anticipated length of time the debtor will be responsible for the care of dependents. For example, the length of care for a teenage child is generally shorter than for a permanently disabled child, spouse or partner.

  c. Size of Loan: The size of the loan has direct impact on the ability of the debtor to service the loan.

    i.   Debt/Earning Ratio: At one time, student loans represented a small percentage of a debtor's total income. Increasing numbers of students are obtaining loans for future employment in their chosen field but which will never generate income sufficient to repay the entire loan. Courts need to consider the ratio between the loan size and the ability to repay; the greater this disparity, the greater the necessity to discharge the loan.

    ii.   Loan Terms: One method used by the Department of Education to reduce debtor loan monthly payments is to renegotiate the loan terms. For some debtors this is successful. The most extreme plan is the Income Contingent Repayment (ICR) Plan. Under an ICR, when a debtor's income exceeds a set level, payments are to be made on the loan. When the debtor's income drops below this level, no payment is made. Interest accrues whether payments are made or not. It is possible for debtors to face a lifetime of payments under the ICR. For debtors with little prospect of improving their future income, the ICR serves no purpose, and, in fact, violates the "fresh start" core concept underlying the Bankruptcy Code. If it is determined there is little or no prospect for the debtor to improve future employment or income, and there is no fraud involved, the court should reject the Department of Education's attempt to place the debtor on the Income Contingency Plan and discharge the loan.

It is important for the court to question, at each step along the analysis, if the debtor is engaging in fraud. If the answer is no, the common sense approach would be to allow the discharge of the loan. The main purpose of §523(a)(8) is to eliminate fraud from the student loan repayment program.

APPENDIX G
Resources

U.S. Bankruptcy Court Contacts

Alabama (11th Circuit)

Northern Districts
Counties: Bibb, Blount, Calhoun, Cherokee, Clay,
Cleburne, Colbert, Culman, DeKalb, Etowah, Fayette,
Franklin, Greene, Jackson, Jefferson, Lamar, Lauderdale,
Lawrence, Limestone, Madison, Marion, Marshall,
Morgan, Pickens, Saint Claire, Shelby, Sumter,
Talladega, Tuscaloosa, Walker, Winston • (The Court
meets in Anniston, Birmingham, Decatur, Florence,
Gadsden, Huntsville, Jasper, Talladega, Tuscaloosa)

Northern District of Alabama
Eastern Division
103 Federal Court House
12th and Noble Streets
Anniston, AL 36202
256-741-1500 (v)
www.alnb.uscourts.gov

Northern District of Alabama
Birmingham Division
1800 5th Avenue North, Room 120
Birmingham, AL 35203-2111
205-714-4000
www.alnb.uscourts.gov

Northern District of Alabama
Northern Division
P.O. Box 2748
Decatur, AL 35602
256-353-2817 (v)
www.alnb,uscourts.gov

Northern District of Alabama
Western Division
1118 Greensboro Avenue
P.O. Box 3226
Tuscaloosa, AL 35401
205-752-0426 (v)
205-752-6468 (f)
www.alnb.uscourts.gov

Southern District of Alabama
Counties: Baldwin, Choctaw, Clarke, Conecuh, Dallas,
Escambia, Hale, Marengo, Mobile, Monroe, Perry,
Washington, Wilcox • (The Court meets in Mobile and
Selma)
201 St. Louis Street
Mobile, AL 36602
334-441-5391 (v)
334-441-5612 (f)
www.alsb.uscourts.gov

Middle District of Alabama
Counties: Autauga, Barbour, Bullock, Butler, Chambers,
Chilton, Coffee, Coosa, Convington, Crenshaw, Dale,
Elmore, Geneva, Henry, Houston, Lee, Lowndes,
Macon, Montgomery, Pike, Randolph, Russell,
Tallapoosa • (The Court meets in Dotham, Montgomery,
Opelika)
Montgomery Division
One Court Square, Room 127
Montgomery, AL 36102
334-206-6300 (v)
334-206-6374 (f)
www.almb.uscourts.gov

Alaska (9th Circuit)

District of Alaska • (The Court meets in Anchorage,
Fairbanks, Juneau, Ketchikan, Nome) Historical
Courthouse

District of Alaska
605 West Fourth Avenue, Room 138
Anchorage, AK 99501-2296
907-271-2655 (v)
907-271-2645 (f)
www.akb.uscourts.gov

District of Alaska
U.S. Courthouse
101 12th Avenue, Room 370
Fairbanks, AK
907-456-0349
www.akb.uscourts.gov

District of Alaska
U.S. District Court
709 W. 9th Avenue, Room 979
Juneau, AK 99802
907-586-7458
www.akb.uscourts.gov

District of Alaska
648 Mission Street, Room 507
Ketchikan, AK 99901
907-247-7576
www.akb.uscourts.gov

District of Alaska
U.S. District Court
Front Street
P.O. Box 130
Nome, AK 99762
907-443-5216 (v)
www.akb.uscourts.gov

Arizona (9th Circuit)

One District • (The Court meets in Phoenix, Prescott, Yuma)

District of Arizona
Phoenix Division
2929 North Central Avenue
Ninth Floor
P.O. Box 34151
Phoenix, AZ 85067-4151
602-640-5800 (v)
602-640-5846 (f)
www.azb.uscourts.gov

District of Arizona
Tucson Division
110 South Church Street
Room 8-112
Tucson, AZ 85702
520-620-7500 (v)
520-620-7457 (f)
www.azb.uscourts.gov

District of Arizona
Yuma Division
325 W. 19th St., Suite D
Yuma, AZ 85364
520-783-2288
www.azb.uscourts.gov

Arkansas (8th Circuit)

Eastern District
Counties: Arkansas, Chicoat, Clay, Cleburne, Cleveland, Conway, Craighead, Crittenden, Cross, Dallas, Desha, Drew, Faulkner, Fulton, Grant, Greene, Independence, Izard, Jackson, Jefferson, Lawrence, Lee, Lincoln, Lonoke, Mississippi, Monroe, Perry, Phillips, Poinsett, Pope, Prairie, Pulaski, Randolph, Saint Francis, Saline, Sharp, Stone, Van Buren, White, Woodruff, Yell • (The Court meets in Batesville, Helena, Jonesboro, Little Rock, Pine Bluff)

Western District
Counties: Ashley, Baxter, Benton, Boone, Bradley, Calhoun, Carroll, Columbia, Clark, Crawford, Franklin, Garland, Hempstead, Hot Springs, Howard, Johnson, Lafayette, Little River, Logan, Madison, Marion, Miller, Montgomery, Nevada, Newton, Ouachita, Pike, Polk, Scott, Searcy, Sebastian, Sevier, Union, Washington • (The Court meets in El Dorado, Fayetteville, Fort Smith, Harrison, Hot Springs, Little Rock, Texarkana)

Western and Eastern Districts
300 West 2nd Street
P.O. Box 3777
Little Rock, AR 72201
501-918-5500
www.arb.uscourts.gov

California (9th Circuit)

Eastern District
Counties: Alpine, Amador, Butte, Calaveras, Colusa, El Dorado, Fresno, Glenn, Inyo, Kern, Kings, Lassen, Madera, Mariposa, Merced, Modoc, Mono, Nevada, Placer, Plumas, Sacramento, San Joaquin, Shasta, Sierra, Siskiyou, Solano, Stanislaus, Sutter, Tehama, Trinity, Tulare, Tuolomne, Yolo, Yuba • (The Court meets in Bakersfield, Fresno, Modesto, Sacramento)

Eastern District of California
Fresno Division
1130 0 Street, Suite 2656
Fresno, CA 93721
559-498-7217 (v)
www.caeb.uscourts.gov

Eastern District of California
Modesto Division
1130 Twelfth Street, Room C
Modesto, CA 95352
209-521-5160 (v)
www.caeb.uscourts.gov

Eastern District of California
Sacramento Division
501 I Street, Suite 3-200
Sacramento, CA 95814
916-930-4400 (v)
916-498-5469 (f)
www.caeb.uscourts.gov

Central District
Counties: Counties: Los Angeles, Orange, Riverside, San
Luis Obispo, Santa Barbara, and Ventura Hills.) • (The
Court meets in Los Angeles, Riverside, San Fernando
Valley, Santa Ana, Santa Barbara.)

Central District of California
Los Angeles Division
Federal Building
300 N. Los Angeles Street
Los Angeles, CA 90012
213-894-3118 (v)
213-894-0225 (f)
www.cacb.uscourts.gov

Central District of California
Santa Ana Division
U.S. Courthouse
411 West Fourth Street
Santa Ana, CA 92701
714-338-5300 (v)
www.cacb.uscourts.gov

Central District of California
Santa Barbara Division
1415 State Street
Santa Barbara, CA 93 101
805-884-4800 (v)
www.cacb.uscourts.gov

Central District of California
San Bernardino Division
3420 12th Street
Riverside, CA 92501-3819
909-774-1000 (v)
www.cacb.uscourts.gov

Central District of California
San Fernando Division
21041 Burbank Boulevard
Woodland Hills, CA 91367
818-587-2900 (v)
www.cacb.uscourts.gov

Northern District
Counties: Alameda, Contra Costa, Del Norte, Humboldt,
Lake Martin, Mendocino, Monterey, Napa, San Benito,
Santa Clara, Santa Cruz, San Francisco, San Mateo,
Sonoma, Santa Rosa • (The Court meets in Eureka,
Oakland, Salinas, San Francisco, San Jose, Santa Rosa)

Northern District of California
Oakland Division
P.O. Box 2070
Oakland, CA 94604-2070
510-879-3600 (v)
www.canb.uscourts.gov

Northern District of California
San Francisco Division
P.O. Box 7341
235 Pine Street, 19th Floor
San Francisco, CA 94120-7341
415-268-2300 (v)
www.canb.uscourts.gov

Northern District of California
San Jose Division
280 South First Street, Room 3035
San Jose, CA 95113-3099
408-535-5118 (v)
www.canb.uscourts.gov

Northern District of California
Santa Rosa Division
99 South E Street
Santa Rosa, CA 95404
707-525-8539 (v)
www.canb.uscourts.gov

Southern District
Counties: Imperial, San Diego • (The Court meets in San Diego)

Southern District of California
325 West "F" Street
San Diego, CA 92101-6998
619-557-5620 (v)
619-557-2646 (f)
www.casb.uscourts.gov

Colorado (10th Circuit)

One District • (The Court meets in Denver, Grand Junction, Pueblo)

District of Colorado
U.S. Customs House
721 - 19th Street
Denver, CO 80202-2508
303-844-4045 (v)
888-213-4715 (toll free)
www.cob.uscourts.gov/bindex.htm

Connecticut (2nd Circuit)

One District • (The Court meets in Bridgeport, Hartford, New Haven)

District of Connecticut
915 Lafayette Boulevard
Bridgeport, CT 06604
203-579-5808 (v)
www.ctb.uscourts.gov

District of Connecticut
Hartford Division
450 Main Street
Hartford, CT 06103
860-240-3675 (v)
www.ctb.uscourts.gov

District of Connecticut
157 Church Street
New Haven, CT 06510
203-773-2009 (v)

Delaware (3rd Circuit)

District of Delaware
824 Market Street, Fifth Floor
Wilmington, DE 19801
302-252-2900 (v)
www.deb.uscourts.gov/general.htm

District of Columbia (DC Circuit)

(The District of Columbia is in its own circuit, the District of Columbia Circuit, and its own district, the District of Columbia District.)

District of Columbia
D.C. Division
333 Constitution Avenue, NW
Washington, DC 20001
202-273-0042 (v)
www.dcb.uscourts.gov

Florida (11th Circuit)

Middle District
Counties: Baker, Bradford, Brevard, Charlotte, Citrus, Clay, Collier, Columbia, De Soto, Duval, Flagler, Glades, Hamilton, Hardee, Hendry, Hernando, Hillsborough, Lake, Lee, Manatee, Marion, Nassau, Osceola, Orange, Pasco, Pinellas, Polk, Putnam, Sarasota, Seminole, St. John's, Sumter, Suwannee, Union, Volusia • (The Court meets in Fort Meyers, Orlando, Jacksonville, Tampa)

Middle District
2110 First Street
Fort Myers, FL 33901
www.flmb.uscourts.gov

Middle District of Florida
Jacksonville Division
311 West Monroe Street, Room 206
Jacksonville, FL 32202
904-232-2852 (v)
www.flmb.uscourts.gov

Middle District of Florida
Orlando Division
135 West Central Boulevard, Room 960
Orlando, FL 32801
407-648-6365 (v)
www.flmb.uscourts.gov

Middle District of Florida
801 N. Florida Avenue
Tampa, FL 33602
613-301-5134 (v)
www.flmb.uscourts.gov

Southern District
Counties: Broward, Dade, Highlands, Indian River,
Martin, Monroe, Okeechobee, Palm Beach County, St.
Lucie, Palm Beach County, St. Lucie • (The Court meets
in Ft. Lauderdale, Miami, West Palm Beach)

Southern District of Florida
Miami Division
51 Southwest First Avenue, Room 1517
Miami, FL 33130
305-536-5216 (v)

Southern District of Florida
West Palm Beach Division
701 Clematis Street, Room 202
West Palm Beach, FL 33401
561-665-6774 (v)

Northern District
Counties: Alachua, Bay, Calhoun, Dixie, Escambia,
Franklin, Gadsden, Gilchrist, Gulf, Holmes, Jackson,
Jefferson, Lafayette, Leon, Levy, Liberty, Madison,
Okaloosa, Santa Rosa, Taylor, Wakulla, Walton,
Washington • (The Court meets in Gainesville, Panama
City, Pensacola, Tallahassee)

Northern District of Florida
227 North Bronough Street
Suite 3120
Tallahassee, FL 32301-1378
850-942-8933 (v)

Georgia (11th Circuit)

Northern District
Counties: Banks, Barrow, Bartow, Carroll, Catoosa,
Chattooga, Cherokee, Clayton, Cobb, Coweta, Dade,
Dawson, Dekalb, Douglas, Fannin, Fayette, Floyd,
Forsyth, Fulton, Gilmer, Gordon, Gwinnett, Habersham,
Hall, Haralson, Heard, Henry, Jackson, Lumpkin,
Meriwether, Murray, Newton, Paulding, Pickens, Pike,
Polk, Rabun, Rockdale, Spalding, Stephens, Towns,
Troup, Union, Walker, White, Whitfield • (The Court
meets in Atlanta, Gainesville, Newnan, Rome)

Northern District of Georgia
75 Spring Street Southwest, Room 1340
Atlanta, GA 30303
404-215-1000 (v)
404-730-2216 (f)
www.ganb.uscourts.gov

Northern District of Georgia
Newnan Division
18 Greenville Street
Newnan, GA 30264
770-251-5583 (v)
www.ganb.uscourts.gov

Northern District of Georgia
Rome Division
600 E. First Street
Rome, GA 30161-3187
706-291-5639 (v)
www.ganb.uscourts.gov

Southern District
Counties: Appling, Atkinson. Bacon, Brantley, Bryan,
Bulloch, Burke, Camden, Candler, Charlton, Chatham,
Coffee, Columbia, Dodge, Effingham, Emanuel, Evans,
Glascock, Glynn, Jeff Davis, Jefferson, Jenkins, Johnson,
Laurens, Liberty, Lincoln, Long, McDuffie, McIntosh,
Montgomery, Pierce, Richmond, Screven, Taliaferro,
Tatnall, Telfair, Toombs, Treutlen, Ware, Warren,
Wayne, Wheeler, Wilkes • (The Court meets in Augusta,
Brunswick, Dublin, Savannah, Statesboro, Waycoss)

Southern District of Georgia
Augusta Division
500 Ford St.
Augusta, GA 30901
706-724-2421 (v)

Southern District of Georgia
125 Bull Street
Savannah, GA 31401
912-650-4100 (v)
www.gasb.uscourts.gov

Middle District
Counties: Baker, Baldwin, Ben Hill, Berrien, Bibb,
Bleckley, Brooks, Butts, Calhoun, Chattahoochee,
Clarke, Clay, Clinch, Colquitt, Cook, Crawford, Crisp,
Decatur, Dooley, Dougherty, Early, Echols, Elbert,
Franklin, Grady, Greene, Hancock, Harris, Hart,
Houston, Irwin, Jasper, Jones, Lamar, Lanier, Lee,
Lowndes, Macon, Madison, Marion, Miller, Mitchell,

Monroe, Morgan, Oconee, Ogelthorpe, Peach, Pulaski, Putnam, Quitman, Randolph, Seminole, Stewart, Talbot, Taylor, Thomas, Tift, Turner, Twiggs, Upson, Walton, Washington, Webster, Wilcox, Wilkinson, Worth • (The Court meets in Albany, Athens, Columbus, Macon, Thomasville, Valdosta)

Middle District of Georgia
P.O. Box 1957
433 Cherry Street
Macon, GA 31202
912-752-3506 (v)
912-752-8157 (f)
www.gamb.uscourts.gov

Hawaii (9th Circuit)

One District • (The Court meets in Hilo, Honolulu, Lihue, Wailuku)

1132 Bishop Street, Suite 250-L
Honolulu, HI 96813
808-522-8100 (v)
808-522-8120 (f)
www.hib.uscourts.gov

Idaho (9th Circuit)

One District • (The Court meets in Boise, Coeur d'Alene, Jerome, Moscow, Pocatello)

District of Idaho
550 West Fort Street MSC 042
Boise, ID 83724
208-334-1074 (v)
208-334-1361 (f)
www.id.uscourts.gov

Northern Division
205 North 4th Street, Room 202
Coeur d'Alene, ID 83814
208-664-4925 (v)
208-765-0270 (f)
www.id.uscourts.gov

Northern Division
220 E. 5th Street, Room 304
Moscow, ID 83843
208-882-7612 (v)
208-883-1576 (f)
www.id.uscourts.gov

Eastern Division
801 E. Sherman St.
Pocatello, ID 83201
208-478-4123 (v)
208-478-4106 (f)
www.id.uscourts.gov

Illinois (7th Circuit)

Northern District
Counties: Boone, Carroll, Cook, Dekalb, Du Page, Grundy, Jo Daviess, Kane, Kendall, Lake, La Salle, Lee, McHenry, Ogle, Stephenson, Whiteside, Will, Winnebago • (The Court meets in Chicagoe, Joliet, North Aurora, Rockford, Waukegam, Wheaton)

Northern District of Illinois Eastern Division
219 South Dearborn Street
Chicago, IL 60604
312-435-5694 (v)
312-408-7750 (f)
www.ilnb.uscourts.gov

Northern District of Illinois
Western Division
211 South Court Street, Room 110
Rockford, IL 61101
815-987-4350 (v)
815-987-4205 (f)
www.ilnb.uscourts,gov

Central District
Counties: Adams, Brown, Bureau, Cass, Champaign, Christian, Coles, De Witt, Douglas, Edgar, Ford, Fulton, Greene, Hancock, Henderson, Henry, Iroquois, Kankakee, Knox, Livingston, Logan, Macon, Macoupin, Marshall, Mason, McDonough, Mclean, Menard, Mercer, Montgomery, Morgan, Moultrie, Peoria, Piatt, Pike, Putnam, Rock Island, Sangamon, Schuyler, Scott, Shelby, Stark, Tazewell, Vermilion, Warren, Woodford • (The Court meets in Bloomington, Dansville, Decatur, Galesburg, Kankakee, Paris, Peoria, Quincy, Rock Island, Springfield)

Central District of Illinois Danville Division
201 N. Vermillion Street
Danville, IL 61832
217-431-4820 (v)
217-431-2694 (f)
www.ilcb.uscourts.gov

Central District of Illinois
Peoria Division
100 Northeast Monroe Street
1st Floor, Room 131
Peoria, IL 61602
309-671-7035 (v)
309-671-7076 (f)
www.ilcb.uscourts.gov

Central District of Illinois
600 East Monroe Street, Room 226
Springfield, IL 62701
217-492-4551 (v)
www.ilcb.uscourts.gov

Southern District
Counties: Alexander, Bond, Calhoun, Clark, Clay,
Clinton, Crawford, Cumberland, Edwards, Effingham,
Fayette, Franklin, Gallatin, Hamilton, Hardin, Jackson,
Jasper, Jefferson, Jersey, Johnson, Lawrence, Madison,
Marion, Massac, Monroe, Perry, Pope, Pulaski,
Randolph, Richland, St. Claire, Saline, Union, Wabash,
Washington, Wayne, White, Williamson
(The Court meets in Alton, Benton, East St. Louis,
Effingham, Mt. Vernon)

Southern District of Illinois
750 Missouri Avenue, 1st Floor
East St. Louis, IL 62201
618-482-9400 (v)
www.ilsb.uscourts.gov

Indiana (7th Circuit)

Southern District
Counties: Bartholomew, Boone, Brown, Clark, Clay,
Clinton, Crawford, Davies, Dearborn, Decatur,
Delaware, Dubois, Fayette, Floyd, Fountain, Franklin,
Green, Gibson, Hamilton, Hancock, Harrison, Howard,
Jackson, Jefferson, Jennings, Knox, Lawrence, Madison,
Marion, Martin, Monroe, Montgomery, Morgan, Ohio,
Orange, Owen, Parke, Perry, Pike, Posey, Putnam,
Randolph, Ripley, Rush, Scott, Shelby, Spencer,
Sullivan, Switzerland, Tipton, Union, Vanderburgh,
Vermillion, Vigo, Warrick, Washington, Wayne • (The
Court meets in Evansville, Indianapolis, New Albany,
Richmond)

Southern District of Indiana
Evansville Division
352 Federal Building
101 NW MLK Boulevard
Evansville, IN 47708
812-465-6440 (v)
812-465-6453 (f)
www.insb.uscourts.gov

Southern District of Indiana
Indianapolis Division
116 U.S. Courthouse
46 East Ohio Street
Indianapolis, IN 46204
317-229-3800 (v)
317-229-3801 (f)
www.insb.uscourts.gov

Southern District of Indiana
New Albany Division
110 U.S. Courthouse
121 West Spring Street
New Albany, IN 47150
812-948-5254 (v)
812-948-5262 (f)
www.insb.uscourts.gov

Northern District
Counties: Adams, Allen, Benton, Blackford, Carroll,
Cass, De Kalb, Elkhart, Fulton, Grant, Huntington,
Jasper, Jay, Kosciusko, La Porte, Lagrange, Lake,
Marshall, Miami, Newton, Nobel, Porter, Pulaski, Starke,
Steuben, St. Joseph, Tippecanoe, Wabash, Warren,
Wells, White, Whitley • (The Court meets in Fort
Wayne, Gary, Lafayette. South Bend)

Northern District of Indiana
Fort Wayne Division
1300 South Harrison Street
Fort Wayne, IN 46802
Mailing Address
P.O. Box 2547
Fort Wayne, IN 46801-2547
260-420-5100 (v)
260-422-1668 (f)
www.innb.uscourts.gov

Northern District of Indiana
Gary Division
610 Connecticut Street
Gary, IN 46402-2595
219-881-3335 (v)
219-881-3307 (f)
www.innb.uscourts.gov

Northern District of Indiana
South Bend Division
401 South Michigan Street
South Bend, IN 46601
Mailing Address
P.O. Box 7003
South Bend, IN 46634-7003
574-968-2100 (v)
574-968-2205 (f)
www.innb.uscourts.gov

Iowa (8th Circuit)

Northern District
Counties: Allamakee, Benton, Black Hawk, Bremer,
Buchanan, Buena Vista, Butler, Calhoun, Carroll, Cedar,
Cerro Gordo, Cherokee, Chickasaw, Clay, Clayton,
Crawford, Delaware, Dickinson, Dubuque, Emmet,
Fayette, Floyd, Franklin, Grundy, Hamilton, Hancock,
Hardin, Howard, Humboldt, Ida, Iowa, Jackson, Jones,
Kossuth, Linn, Lyon, Mitchell, Monona, Osceola,
O'Brien, Palo Alto, Plymouth, Pocahontas, Sac, Sioux,
Tama, Webster, Winnbago, Winneshiek, Woodbury,
Worth, Wright • (The Court meets in Cedar Rapids.
Dubuque, Fort Dodge, Mason City)

Northern District of Iowa
P.O. Box 74890
425 Second Street, Southeast
Cedar Rapids, IA 52407
319-286-2200 (v)
319-286-2280 (f)
www.ianb.uscourts.gov/index.asp

Northern District of Iowa
Sioux City Division
Federal Building
320 Sixth Street, Room 117
Sioux City, IA 51101
Mailing Address
P.O. Box 3857
Sioux City, IA 51102-3857
712-233-3939 (v)
712-233-3942 (f)
www.ianb.uscourts.gov/index.asp

Southern District
Counties: Adair, Adams, Appanoose, Audubon, Boone,
Cass, Clarke, Clinton, Dallas, Davis, Decatur, Des
Moines, Fremont, Greene, Guthrie, Harrison, Henry,
Jasper, Jefferson, Johnson, Keokuk, Lee, Louisa, Lucas,
Madison, Mahaska, Marion, Marshall, Mills, Monroe,
Montgomery, Muscatine, Page, Polk Pottawattamie,
Powshiek, Ringgold, Scott, Shelby, Story, Taylor, Union,
Van Buren, Wapello, Warren, Washington, Wayne •
(The Court meets in Council Bluffs, Davenport, Des
Moines)

Southern District of Iowa
P.O. Box 9264
Des Moines, IA 50306
515-284-6230 (v)
515-284-6418 (f)
www.iasb.uscourts.gov/asp/home/default.asp

Kansas (10th Circuit)

One District • (The Court meets in Kansas City, Topeka,
Wichita)

District of Kansas
Kansas City Division
161 U.S. Courthouse
500 State Avenue
Kansas City, KS 66101
913-551-6732 (v)
www.ksb.uscourts.gov

District of Kansas
Topeka Division
240 U.S. Courthouse
444 Southeast Quincy Street
Topeka, KS 66683
785-295-2750 (v)
www.ksb.uscourts.gov

District of Kansas
Wichita Division
167 U.S. Courthouse
401 North Market Street
Wichita, KS 67202
316-269-6486 (v)
316-269-6181 (f)

Kentucky (6th Circuit)

Eastern District
Counties: Anderson, Bath, Bell, Boone, Bourbon, Boyd, Boyle, Bracken, Breathitt, Campbell, Carroll, Carter, Clark, Clay, Elliot, Estill, Fayette, Fleming, Floyd, Franklin, Gallatin, Garrard, Grant, Greenup, Harlan, Harrison, Henry, Jackson, Jessamine, Johnson, Kenton, Knott, Knox, Laurel, Lawrence, Lee, Leslie, Letcher, Lewis, Lincoln, McCreary, Madison, Magoffin, Martin, Mason, Menifee, Mercer, Montgomery, Morgan, Nicholas, Owen, Owsley, Pendleton, Perry, Pike, Powell, Pulaski, Robertson, Rockcastle, Rowan, Scott, Shelby, Trimble, Wayne, Whitley, Wolfe, Woodford • (The Court meets in Ashland, Corbin, Covington, Frankfurt, Lexington, Pikeville)

Eastern District of Kentucky
100 East Vine Street, Suite 200
Lexington, KY 40507
Mailing Address
Box 1111
Lexington, KY 40588-1111
859-233-2608 (v)
www.kyeb.uscourts.gov

Western District
Counties: Adair, Allen, Ballard, Breckinridge, Bullit, Butler, Caldwell, Calloway, Carlisle, Casey, Christian, Hart, Henderson, Hickma, Hopkins, Jefferson, Larue, Livingston, Logan, Lyron, McCracken, McClean, Marion, Marshall, Meade, Metcalfe, Monroe, Muhlenberg, Nelson, Ohio, Oldham, Russell, Simpson, Spencer, Taylor, Todd, Trigg, Union, Warren, Washington, Webster • (The Court meets in Bowling Green, Louisville, Owensboro, Paducah)

Western District of Kentucky
601 W. Broadway, Suite 546
Snyder Courthouse
Louisville, KY 40202
502-627-5700 (v)
502-627-5710 (f)
www.kywb.uscourts.gov/fpweb/louisville.htm

Louisiana (5th Circuit)

Western District
Parishes: Acadia, Allen, Avoyelles, Beauregard, Bienvile, Bossier, Caddo, Calcasieu, Caldwell, Cameron, Catahoule, Claiborne, Concordia, De Sota, East Carroll, Evangeline, Franklin, Grant, Iberia, Jackson, Jefferson Davis, La Salle, Lafayette, Lincoln, Madison,
Morehouse, Natchitoches, Ouachita, Rapides, Red River, Richland, Sabine, Saint Landry, Saint Martin, Saint Mary, Tensas, Union, Vermilion, Vernon, Webster, West Carroll, Winn • (The Court meets in Alexandria, Lake Charles, Monroe, Opelousas, Shreveport)

Western District of Louisiana
Alexandria Division
300 Jackson Street, Suite 116
Alexandria, LA 71301
318-445-1890 (v)
www.lawb.uscourts.gov

Western District of Louisiana
Lafayette-Opelousas Division
231 South Union Street, 2nd Floor
Opelousas, LA 70570
337-948-3451 (v)
www.lawb.uscourts.gov

Western District of Louisiana
300 Fannin Street, Suite 2201
Shreveport, LA 71101
318-676-4267 (v)
www.lawb.uscourts.gov

Middle District
Parishes: Ascension, East Baton Rouge, East Feliciana, Iberville, Livingston, Pointe Coupee, Saint Helena, West Baton Rouge, West Feliciana • (The Court meets in Baton Rouge)

Middle District of Louisiana
707 Florida Street, Suite 119
Baton Rouge, LA 70801
225-389-0211 (v)
225-389-3501 (f)
www.lamb.uscourts.gov

Eastern District
Parishes: Assumption, Jefferson, Lafourche, Orleans, Plaquemines, Saint Bernard, Saint Charles, Saint James, Saint John the Baptist, Saint Tammany, Tangipahoa, Terrebonne, Washington • (The Court meets in New Orleans)

Eastern District of Louisiana
501 Magazine Street, Room 601
New Orleans, LA 70130
504-589-7878 (v)
504-589-2076 (f)
www.laeb.uscourts.gov

Maine (1st Circuit)

One District • (The Court meets in Augusta, Bangor, Portland, Presque Isle)

District of Maine
P.O. Box 1109
300 U.S. Courthouse
202 Harlow Street, 3rd Floor
Bangor, ME 04401-1109
207-945-0348 (v)
207-945-0304 (f)
www.meb.uscourts.gov

District of Maine
537 Congress Street, Second Floor
Portland, ME 04101-0048
Mailing Address
P.O. Box 17575
Portland, ME 04112-8575
207-780-3482 (v)
207-780-3679 (f)
www.meb.uscourts.gov

Maryland (4th Circuit)

One District • (The Court meets in Baltimore, Greenbelt, LaPlata, Salisbury)

District of Maryland Baltimore Division
U.S. Courthouse
101 West Lombard Street, Suite 8308
Baltimore, MD 21201
410-962-2688 (v)
410-942-9319 (f)
www.mdb.uscourts.gov

District of Maryland
6500 Cherry Wood Lane. Room 300
Greenbelt, MD 20770
301-344-8018 (v)
301-344-0415 (f)
www.mdb.uscourts.gov

Massachusetts (1st Circuit)

One District • (The Court meets in Boston, Springfield, Worcester)

District of Massachusetts Eastern Division
1101 Thomas P. O'Neill Federal Building
10 Causeway Street
Boston, MA 02222
617-565-8950 (v)
617-565-6650 (f)
www.mab.uscourts.gov

District of Massachusetts
Barnstable Town Hall
376 Main Street
Hyannis, MA 02601-3917
617-565-6073 (v)
www.mab.uscourts.gov

District of Massachusetts
Federal Building and Courthouse
1550 Main Street
Springfield, MA 01103
508-770-8936 (v)
www.mab.uscourts.gov

District of Massachusetts Western Division
Harold Donahue Federal Building
595 Main Street, Second Floor
Worcester, MA 01608-2076
508-770-8900 (v)
508-793-0189 (f)
www.mab.uscourts.gov

Michigan (6th Circuit)

Eastern District
Counties: Alcona, Alpena, Arenac, Bay, Cheboygan, Clare, Crawford, Genesee, Gladwin, Gratiot, Huron, Iosco, Isabella, Jackson, Lapeer, Lenawee, Livingston, Macomb, Midland, Monroe, Montgomery, Oakland, Ogemaw, Oscoda, Otsego, Presque Isle, Roscommon, Saginaw, Saint Clair, Sanilac, Shiawassee, Tuscola, Washtenaw, Wayne • (The Court meets in Bay City, Detroit, Flint)

Eastern District of Michigan
Bay City Division
111 First Street
Bay City, MI 48707
989-894-8840 (v)
Www.mieb.uscourts.gov/indexl.html

Eastern District of Michigan
1060 Federal Building
211 West Fort Street
Detroit, MI 48226
313-234-0065 (v)
313-234-5399 (f)
www.mieb.uscourts.gov/index1.html

Eastern District of Michigan
Flint Division
226 West Second Street
Flint, MI 48502
810-235-4126 (v)
www.mieb.uscourts.gov/index1.html

Western District
Counties: Alger, Allegan, Antrim, Baraga, Barry,
Benzie, Berrien, Branch, Calhoun, Cass, Charlevoix,
Chippewa, Clinton, Delta, Dickinson, Eaton, Emmet,
Gogebic, Grand Traverse, Hillsdale, Houghton, Ingham,
Ionia, Iron, Kalamazoo, Kalkaska, Kent, Keweenaw,
Lake, Leelanau, Luce, Mackinac, Manistee, Marquette,
Mason, Mecosta, Menominee, Missaukee, Montcalm,
Muskegon, Newaygo, Oceana, Ontonagon, Osceola,
Ottawa, Saint Joseph, Schoolcraft, Van Buren, Wexford
• (The Court meets in Grand Rapids, Kalamazoo,
Lansing, Marquette, Traverse City)

Western District of Michigan
Southern Division
Ford Federal Building
110 Michigan Street Northwest, Room 299
Grand Rapids, MI 49501
Mailing Address
P.O. Box 3310
Grand Rapids, MI 49501
616-456-2693 (v)
www.miwb.uscourts.gov

Western District of Michigan
Marquette Division 202
West Washington Street 3rd Floor
Marquette, MI 49855
Mailing Address
P.O. Box 909
Marquette, MI 49855
906-226-2117 (v)
ww.miw.uscourts.gov

Minnesota (8th Circuit)

One District • (The Court meets in Duluth, Fergus Falls,
Minneapolis, St. Paul)

District of Minnesota
Duluth Division
416 U.S. Courthouse
515 West First Street
Duluth, MN 55802
218-529-3600 (v)
www.mnb.uscourts.gov

District of Minnesota
Fergus Falls Office
204 U.S. Courthouse
118 South Mill Street
Fergus Falls, MN 56537
218-739-4671 (v)
www.mnb.uscourts.gov

District of Minnesota
301 U.S. Courthouse
300 South Fourth Street
Minneapolis, MN 55415
612-664-5200 (v)
612-664-5303 (f)
612-664-5301 (TTY)
www.mnb.uscourts.gov

District of Minnesota
St. Paul Division
200 U.S. Courthouse
316 North Robert Street
St. Paul, MN 55101
651-848-1000 (v)
www.mnb.uscourts.gov

Mississippi (5th Circuit)

Northern District
Counties: Alcorn, Attala, Benton, Bolivar, Calhoun,
Carroll, Chickasaw, Choctaw, Clay, Coahoma, De Soto,
Grenada, Humphreys, Itawamba, Lafayette, Lee, Leflore,
Lowndes, Marshall, Monroe, Montgomery, Oktibbeha,
Panola, Pontotoc, Prentiss, Quitman, Sunflower,
Tallahtchie, Tate, Tippah, Tishomingo, Tunica, Union,
Washington, Webster, Winston, Yalobusha • (The Court
meets in Aberdeen, Greenville, Oxford)

Northern District of Mississippi
P.O. Drawer 867
205 Federal Building
301 W. Commerce Building
Aberdeen, MS 39730-0867
662-369-2596 (v)
www.msnb.uscourts.gov

Southern District
Counties: Adams, Amite, Clarke, Copiah, Covington,
Davis, Forrest, Franklin, George, Greene, Hancock,
Harrison, Hinds, Holmes, Issaquena, Jackson, Jasper,
Jefferson, Jefferson Davis, Jones, Kemper, Lamar,
Lauderdale, Lawrence, Leake, Lincoln, Madison,
Marion, Neshoba, Newton, Noxubee, Pearl River, Perry,
Pike, Rankin, Scott, Sharkey, Simpson, Smith, Stone,
Walthall, Warren, Wilkinson, Yazoo) • (The Court meets
in Biloxi, Gulfport, Hattiesburg, Jackson, Meriden,
Natchez, Vicksburg)

Southern District of Mississippi
725 Lashington Loop, Suite 117
Biloxi, MS 39530
601-432-5542 (v)

Southern District of Mississippi
100 E. Capital Street
Jackson, MS 39201
Mailing Address
P.O. Drawer 2448
Jackson, MS 39225
601-965-5301 (v)

Missouri (8th Circuit)

Western District
Counties: Andrew, Atchison, Barry, Barton, Bates,
Benton, Boone, Buchanan, Callaway, Camden, Carroll,
Cass, Cedar, Christian, Clay, Clinton, Cole, Cooper,
Dade, Dallas, DeKalb, Douglas, Gentry, Green, Grundy,
Harrison, Henry, Hickory, Holt, Howard, Howell,
Jackson, Jasper, Johnson, Laciede, Lafayette, Lawrence,
Livingston, McDonald, Mercer, Miller, Moniteau,
Morgan, Newton, Nodaway, Oregon, Osage, Ozark,
Pettis, Platte, Polk, Pulaski, Putnam, Ray, Saint Clair,
Saline, Stone, Sullivan, Taney, Texas, Vernon, Webster,
Worth, Wright • (The Court meets in Jefferson City,
Joplin, Kansas City, Springfield, St. Joseph)

Western District of Missouri
400 E. 9th Street, Room 1800
Kansas city, MO 64106
816-512-1800 (v)

Eastern District
Counties: Adair, Audrain, Bollinger, Butler, Cape
Girardeau, Carter, Chariton, City of St. Louis, Clark,
Crawford, Dent, Dunklin, Franklin, Gasconade, Iron,
Jefferson, Knox, Lewis, Lincoln, Linn, Macon, Madison,
Maries, Marion, Mississippi, Monroe, Montgomery,
New Madrid, Pemiscot, Perry, Phelps, Pike, Ralls,
Randolph, Reynolds, Ripley, Saint Charles, Saint
Francois, Saint Genevieve, Schuyler, Scotland, Scott,
Shannon, Shelby, Stoddard, St. Louis, Warren,
Washington, Wayne • (The Court meets in Cape
Girardeau, Hannibal, St. Louis)

Eastern District of Missouri
Thomas F. Eagleton U.S. Courthouse
111 South 10th St., Fourth Floor
St. Louis, MO 63102
314-244-4500 (v)
314-244-4990 (f)
www.moeb.uscourts.gov

Montana (9th Circuit)

One District • (The Court meets in Billings, Butte, Great
Falls, Missoula)

District of Montana
400 North Main Street
Butte, MT 59701
406-782-9878 (v)
406-782-0537 (f)
www.mtb.uscourts.gov

Nebraska (8th Circuit)

One District • (The Court meets in Lincoln, North Platte,
Omaha)

District of Nebraska
111 South 18th Plaza, Suite 1125
Omaha, NE 68102
402-661-7444 (v)
402-661-7441 (f)
www.neb.uscourts.gov

District of Nebraska
460 Federal Building
100 Centennial Mall North
Lincoln, NE 68508
402-437-5100 (v)
402-437-5454 (f)

Nevada (9th Circuit)

One District • (The Court meets in Elko, Ely, Las Vegas, Reno)

District of Nevada
300 Las Vegas Boulevard South
Room 2130
Las Vegas, NV 89101
702-388-6257 (v)
www.nvb.uscourts.gov

District of Nevada
300 Booth Street, Room 1109
Reno, NV 89509
702-784-5559 (v)
www.nvb.uscourts.gov

New Hampshire (1st Circuit)

One District • (The Court meets in Manchester)

District of New Hampshire
275 Chestnut Street, Room 404
Manchester, NH 03101
603-222-2600 (v)
603-666-7408 (f)
www.nhb.uscourts.gov

New Jersey (3rd Circuit)

One District • (The Court meets in Camden, Newark, Trenton)

District of New Jersey
Camden Division
401 Market Street, Second Floor
Camden, NJ 08102-1104
856-757-5485 (v)
www.njb.uscourts.gov

District of New Jersey
Newark Division
50 Walnut Street
Newark, NJ 07102
973-645-4764 (v)
www.njb.uscourts.gov

District of New Jersey
Trenton Division
U.S. Courthouse
402 East State Street
Trenton, NJ 08608
609-989-2129 (v)
609-989-0580 (f)
www.njb.uscourts.gov

New Mexico (10th Circuit)

One District • (The Court meets in Albuquerque, Las Cruses, Roswell)

District of New Mexico
421 Gold Avenue Southwest, Room 316
Albuquerque, NM 87102
Mailing Address
P.O. Box 546
Albuquerque, NM 87103
505-348-2500 (v)
505-348-6521 (f)
www.nmcourt.fed.us/bkdocs

New York (2nd Circuit)

Northern District
Counties: Albany, Broome, Cayuga, Chenango, Clinton, Columbia, Cortland, Delaware, Essex, Franklin, Fulton, Greene, Hamilton, Herkimer, Jefferson, Lewis, Madison, Montgomery, Oneida, Onondaga, Oswego, Otsego, Rensselaer, Saint Lawrence, Saratoga, Schenctedy, Schoharie, Tioga, Tompkins, Ulster, Warren, Washington • (The Court meets in Albany, Syracuse, Utica)

Northern District of New York
445 Broadway, Suite 330
James T. Foley Courthouse
Albany, NY 12207
518-257-1661 (v)
www.nynb.uscourts.gov

Northern District of New York
Utica Division
Alexander Pirnie U.S. Court House
10 Broad Street, Room 230
Utica, NY 13502
315-793-8101 (v)
www.nynb.uscourts.gov

Eastern District
Counties: Counties: Kings, Nassau, Queens, Richmond, Suffolk. Waters within the counties of Bronx and New York are shared with the Southern District • (The Court meets in Brooklyn, Hauppauge, Westbury)

Eastern District of New York
U.S. Courthouse
225 Cadman Plaza East
Brooklyn, NY 11201
718-330-2188 (v)
718-330-2833 (f)

Western District
Counties: Allegheny, Cattaraugus, Chautauqua, Chemug, Erie, Genesee, Livingston, Monroe, Niagara, Ontario, Orleans, Schuyler, Seneca, Steuben, Wayne, Wyoming, Yates • (The Court meets in Batavia, Buffalo, Mayville, Niagara Falls, Olean, Rochester, Watkins Glenn)

Western District of New York
Rochester Division
1220 U.S. Courthouse
100 State Street
Rochester, NY 14614
716-263-3148 (v)

Western District of New York
Olympic Towers
300 Pearl Street, Suite 250
Buffalo, NY 14202-2501
716-551-4130 (v)
www.nywb.uscourts.gov

Southern District
Counties: Bronx, Dutchess, New York, Orange, Putnam, Rockland, Sullivan, Westchester, Waters within the counties of Kings, Nassau, Queens, Richmond and Suffolk • (The Court meets in New York, Poughkeepsie, White Plains)

Southern District of New York
White Plains Division
300 Quarropas Street
White Plains, NY 10601-4150
914-390-4100 (v)
www.nysb.uscourts.gov

Southern District of New York
Alexander Hamilton Custom House
One Bowling Green
New York, NY 10004-1408
212-668-2870 (v)
www.nysb.uscourts.gov

North Carolina (4th Circuit)

Western District
Counties: Alexander, Allegheny, Anson, Ashe, Avery, Burncombe, Burke, Caldwell, Catawba, Cherokee, Clay, Gaston, Graham, Haywood, Henderson, Iredell, Jackson, Lincoln, Macon, Madison, McDowell, Mecklenburg, Mithchell, Polk, Rutherford, Swain, Transylvania, Union, Watauga, Wilkes, Yancey • (The Court meets in Ashville, Charlotte, Shelby, Statesville)

Western District of North Carolina
Jonas Federal Building
401 West Trade Street, Room 111
Charlotte, NC 28202
Mailing Address
P.O. Box 34189
Charlotte, NC 28234-4189
704-350-7500 (v)
704-344-6403 (f)
www.ncwb.uscourts.gov

Middle District
Counties: Alamance, Cabburus, Caswell, Chatham, Davidson, Davie, Durham, Forsyth, Guilford, Hoke, Lee, Montgomery, Moore, Orange, Person, Randolph, Richmond, Rockingham, Rowan, Scotland, Stanley, Stokes, Surry, Yadkin • (The Court meets in Durham, Greensboro, Winston-Salem)

Middle District of North Carolina
101 S. Edgeworth Street
Greensboro, NC 27401
Mailing Address
P.O. Box 26100
Greensboro, NC 27420-6100
336-333-5647 (v)
www.ncmb.uscourts.gov

Eastern District
Counties: Beaufort, Bertie, Bladen, Brunswick, Camden, Carteret, Chowan, Columbus, Craven, Cumberland, Currituck, Dare, Duplin, Edgecombe, Franklin, Gates, Granville, Greene, Halifax, Harnett, Hertford, Hyde, Johnston, Jones, Lenoir, Martin, Nash, New Hanover, Northhampton, Onslow, Pamlico, Pasquotank, Pender,

Perquimans, Pitt, Robeson, Sampson, Tyrrell, Vance, Wake, Warren, Washington, Wayne, Wilson • (The Court meets in Elizabeth City, Fayetteville, New Bern, Raleigh, Wilmington, Wilson)

Eastern District of North Carolina
P.O. Box 2807
1760 Parkwood Boulevard
Wilson, NC 27894-2807
252-237-0248 (v)
www.nceb.uscourts.gov

North Dakota (8th Circuit)

One District • (The Court meets in Bismark, Fargo, Grand Forks, Minot)

District of North Dakota
655 First Avenue North, Suite 210
Fargo, ND 58102-4932
701-297-7100 (v)
701-297-7105 (f)
www.ndb.uscourts.gov

Ohio (6th Circuit)

Northern District
Counties: Allen, Ashland, Ashtabula, Auglaize, Carroll, Columbiana, Crawford, Cuyahoga, Defiance, Erie, Fulton, Geauga, Hanckock, Hardin, Henry, Holmes, Huron, Lake, Lorain, Lucas, Mahoning, Marion, Medina, Mercer, Ottawa, Paulding, Portage, Putnam, Richland, Sandusky, Seneca, Stark, Summit, Trumbull, Tuscarawas, Van Wert, Wayne, Williams, Woods, Wyandot • (The Court meets in Akron, Canton, Cleveland, Jefferson, Masnfield, Toledo, Youngstown)

Northern District of Ohio
Akron Division
455 U.S. Courthouse
Two South Main Street
Akron, OH 44308
330-375-5840 (v)
www.ohnb.uscourts.gov

Northern District of Ohio
Canton Division
107 Frank T. Bow Federal Building
201 Cleveland Avenue Southwest
Canton, OH 44702-1929
330-489-4426 (v)
www.ohnb.uscourts.gov

Northern District of Ohio
Key Tower, Room 3001
127 Public Square
Cleveland, OH 44114-1309
216-522-4373 (v)
www.ohnb.uscourts.gov

Northern District of Ohio
Toledo Division
411 U.S. Courthouse
1716 Spielbusch Avenue
Toledo, OH 43624
419-259-6440 (v)
www.ohnb.uscourts.gov

Northern District of Ohio
Youngstown Division
Federal Building
125 Market Street
Youngstown, OH 44501
330-746-7027 (v)
www.ohnb.uscourts.gov

Southern District
Counties: Adams, Athens, Belmont, Brown, Butler, Champaign, Clark, Clermont, Clinton, Coschocton, Darke, Delaware, Fairfield, Fayette, Franklin, Gallia, Greene, Guernsy, Hamilton, Harrison, Highland, Hocking, Jackson, Jefferson, Knox, Lawrence, Licking, Logan, Madison, Meigs, Miami, Monroe, Montgomery, Morgan, Morrow, Muskingum, Noble, Perry, Pickaway, Pike, Preble, Ross, Scioto, Shelby, Union, Vinton, Warren, Washington • (The Court meets in meets in Cincinnati, Columbus, Dayton, Portsmouth, Steubenville, Zanesville)

Southern District of Ohio
Western Division
Atrium Two, Room 800
221 East Fourth Street
Cincinnati, OH 45202
513-684-2572 (v)
www.ohsb.uscourts.gov

Southern District of Ohio
Eastern Division
170 N. High Street
Columbus, OH 43215
614-469-6638 (v)

Southern District of Ohio
Western Division
120 W. Third Street
Dayton, OH 45402
937-225-2516 (v)
937-225-2954 (v)

Oklahoma (10th Circuit)

Western District
Counties: Alfalfa, Beaver, Beckham, Blaine, Caddo,
Canadian, Cimarron, Cleveland, Comanche, Cotton,
Custer, Dewey, Ellis, Garfield, Garvin, Grady, Grant,
Greer, Harmon, Harper, Jackson, Jefferson, Kay,
Kingfisher, Kiowa, Lincoln, Logan, Major, McClain,
Noble, Oklahoma, Payne, Pottawatomie, Roger Mills,
Stephens, Texas, Tillman, Washita, Woods, Woodward •
(The Court meets in Lawton, Oklahoma City)

Western District of Oklahoma
Old Post Office Building
Seventh Floor
215 Dean A. McGee Avenue
Oklahoma City, OK 73102
405-231-5642 (v)

Eastern District
Counties: Adar, Atoka, Bryan, Carter, Cherokee,
Choctoaw, Coal, Heskell, Hughes, Johnston, Latimer, Le
Flore, Love, McCurtin, Marshall, Murray, Muskogee,
Ofkuskee, Okmulgee, Pittsbug, Pontotoc, Seminole,
Sequoyah, Wagoneer • (The Court meets in Okmulgee)

Eastern District of Oklahoma
P.O. Box 1347
111 West 4th Street
Okmulgee, OK 74446
918-758-0127 (v)
918-756-9248 (f)
www.okeb.uscourts.gov

Northern District
Counties: Craig, Creek, Delaware, Mayes, Nowata,
Osage, Ottawa, Pawnee, Rogers, Tulsa, Washington •
(The Court meets in meets in Tulsa)

Northern District of Oklahoma
224 S. Boulder, Room 122
Tulsa, OK 74103-4217
918-581-7181 (v)
www.oknb.uscourts.gov

Oregon (9th Circuit)

One District • (The Court meets in Bend, Coos Bay, The
Dalles, Eugene, Klamath Falls, Medford, Pendleton,
Portland, Roseburg, Seaside)

District of Oregon
1001 Southwest Fifth Avenue
Room 700
Portland, OR 97204
503-326-2231 (v)
www.orb.uscourts.gov

Pennsylvania (3rd Circuit)

Middle District
Counties: Adams, Bradford, Cameron, Carbon, Centre,
Columbia, Cumberland, Dauphin, Franklin, Fulton,
Huntington, Juanita, Lacawanna, Lebanon, Luzerne,
Lycoming, Mifflin, Monroe, Montour, Nothumberland,
Perry, Pike, Potter, Snyder, Sullivan, Susquehanna,
Tioga, Union, Wayne, Wyoming, York • (The Court
meets in Harrisburg, Scranton, Wilke-Barre,
Williamsport)

Middle District of Pennsylvania
Harrisburg Division
P.O. Box 908
320 Federal Bldg.
228 Walnut Street
Harrisburg, PA 17101-0908
717-901-2800 (v)
717-901-2822 (f)
www.pamb.uscourts.gov

Middle District of Pennsylvania
Wilkes-Barre Division
Federal Building
197 South Main Street, Suite 161
Wilkes-Barre, PA 18701
570-826-6450 (v)
www.pamb.uscourts.gov

Eastern District
Counties: Berks, Bucks, Chester, Delaware, Lancaster,
Lehigh, Montgomery, Northampton, Philadelphia,
Schuykill • (The Court meets in Allentown, Doylestown,
Lancaster, Philadelphia, Reading)

Eastern District of Pennsylvania
900 Market Street, Suite 400
Philadelphia, PA 19107
215-408-2800 (v)
www.paeb.uscourts.gov

Eastern District of Pennsylvania
Reading Division
The Madison Building, Suite 300
400 Washington Street
Reading, PA 19601-3915
610-320-5255 (v)
www.paeb.uscourts.gov

Western District
Counties: Allegheny, Armstrong, Beaver, Bedford, Blair,
Butler, Cambria, Clarion, Clearfield, Elk, Fayette, Forest,
Green, Indiana, Jefferson, Lawrence, McKean, Mercer,
Somerset, Venango, Warren, Washington, Westmoreland
• (The Court meets in Erie, Johnston, Meadville, Mercer,
Pittsburgh, Warren)

Western District of Pennsylvania
5414 U.S. Tower
600 Grant Street
Pittsburgh, PA 15219
412-644-2700 (v)
412-644-6512 (f)
www.pawb.uscourts.gov

Western District of Pennsylvania
Erie Division
717 State Street, Suite 501
Erie, PA 16501
814-453-7580 (v)
814-453-3795 (f)
www.pawb.uscourts.gov

Rhode Island (1st Circuit)

One District • (The Court meets in Providence)

District of Rhode Island
380 Westminster Street, 6th Floor
Providence, RI 02903
401-528-4477 (v)
401-528-4089 (f)
www.rib.uscourts.gov

South Carolina (4th Circuit)

One District • (The Court meets in Charleston,
Columbia, Spartanburg)

District of South Carolina
P.O. Box 1448
1100 Laurel Street
Columbia, SC 29202
803-765-5436 (v)
www.scb.uscourts.gov

South Dakota (8th Circuit)

One District • (The Court meets in Aberdeen, Pierre,
Rapid City, Sioux Falls)

District of South Dakota
Central Division
Federal Building
225 South Pierre Street, Room 210
Pierre, SD 57501
605-224-6013 (v)
605-224-9808 (f)
www.sdb.uscourts.gov

District of South Dakota
Western Division
515 9th Street, Room 318
Rapid City, SD 57701
605-343-6335 (v)
605-343-4367 (f)
www.sdb.uscourts.gov

District of South Dakota
Southern Division
U.S. Courthouse
400 South Phillips Avenue
Room 104
P.O. Box 5060
Sioux Falls, SD 57117-5060
605-330-4541 (v)
605-330-4548 (f)
www.sdb.uscourts.gov

Tennessee (6th Circuit)

Eastern District
Counties: Anderson, Bedford, Bledsoe, Blount, Bradley,
Campbell, Carter, Claiborne, Cocke, Coffee, Franklin,
Grainger, Greene, Grundy, Hamblen, Hamilton,
Hancock, Hawkins, Jefferson, Johnson, Knox, Lincoln,
Loudon, Marion, McMinn, Meigs, Monroe, Moore,

Morgan, Polk, Rhea, Roane, Scott, Sequatchie, Sevier, Sullivan, Unicoi, Union, Van Buren, Warren, Washington

Eastern District of Tennessee
Southern Division
Historic U.S. Courthouse 361
31 East 11th Street
Chattanooga, TN 37402-2722
423-752-5163 (v)
www.tneb.uscourts.gov

Eastern District of Tennessee
Knoxville Division
U.S. Courthouse
800 Market Street, Suite 330
Knoxville, TN 37902
865-545-4279 (v)
www.tneb.uscourts.gov

Western District
Counties: Benton, Carroll, Chester, Crockett, Decatur, Dyer. Fayette, Gibson, Hardeman, Hardin, Haywood, Henderson, Henry, Lake, Lauderdale, McNairy, Madison, Obion, Perry, Shelby, Tipton, Weakley • (The Court meets in Jackson, Memphis)

Western District of Tennessee
Eastern Division
111 South Highland, Room 107
Jackson, TN 38301
901-421-9300 (v)
www.tnwb.uscourts.gov

Western District of Tennessee
Western Division
200 Jefferson Avenue, Suite 413
Memphis, TN 38103
901-328-3500 (v)
www.tnwb.uscourts.gov

Middle District
Counties: Cannon, Cheatham, Clay, Cumberland, Davidson, DeKalb, Dickson, Fentress, Giles, Hickman, Houston, Humphreys, Jackson, Lawrence, Lewis, Macon, Marshall, Maury, Montgomery, Overton, Pickett, Putnam, Robertson, Rutherford, Smith, Stewart, Sumner, Trousdale, Wayne, White, Williamson, Wilson • (The Court meets in Columbia, Cookeville, Nashville)

Middle District of Tennessee
701 Broadway
P.O. Box 24890
Nashville, TN 37203
615-736-5584 (v)
615-736-2305 (f)
www.tnmb.uscourts.gov
Texas (5th Circuit)

Western District
Counties: Andrews, Atascosa, Bandera, Bastrop, Bell, Bexar, Blanco, Bosque, Brewster, Burleson, Burnet, Caldwell, Comal, Coryell, Crane, Culberson, Dimmit, Ector, Edwards, El Paso, Falls, Freestone, Frio, Gillespie, Gonzales, Guadaloupe, Hamilton, Hays, Hill, Hudspeth, Jeff Davis, Karnes, Kendall, Kerr, Kimble, Kinney, Lampasas, Lee, Leon, Limestone, Llano, Loving, Martin, Mason, Maverick, McCulloch, McLennan, Median, Midland, Milam, Pecos, Presidio, Preal, Reeves, Robertson, San Saba, Somervell, Terrell, Travis, Upton, Uvalde, Val Verde, Ward, Washington, Williamson, Wilson, Winkler, Zavalla • (The Court meets in Austin, El Paso, Midland, San Antonio, Waco)

Western District of Texas
Austin Division
903 San Jacinto Boulevard, Suite 322
Austin, TX 78701
512-916-5248
512-916-5278 (f)
www.txwb.uscourts.gov

Western District of Texas
Post Office Building Alamo Plaza
615 East Houston Street
P.O. Box 1439
San Antonio, TX 78295-1439
210-472-6720, ext. 228 (v)
210-472-5196 (f)
www.txwb.uscourts.gov

Northern District
Counties: Archer, Armstrong, Bailey, Baylor, Borden, Brisco, Brown, Callahan, Carson, Castro, Childres, Clay, Cochran, Coke, Coleman, Collingsworth, Comanche, Concho, Cottle, Crockett, Crosby, Dallam, Dallas, Dawson, Deaf Smith, Dickens, Donley, Eastland, Ellis, Erath, Fisher, Floyd, Foard, Gaines, Garza, Glasscock, Gray, Hale, Hall, Hansford, Hardeman, Hartley, Haskell, Hemphill, Hockley, Hood, Howard, Hunt, Hutchison, Irion, Jack, Johnson, Jones, Kaufman, Kent, King, Knox, Lamb, Lipscomb, Lubbock, Lynn, Menard, Mills, Mitchell, Montaque, Moore, Motley, Navarro, Nolan,

Ochiltree, Oldham, Palo, Parker, Parmer, Pinto, Potter, Randall, Reagan, Roberts, Rockwall, Runnels, Schleicher, Scurry, Shackleford, Sherman, Stephens, Sterling, Stonewall, Sutton, Swisher, Tarrant, Taylor, Terry, Throckmorton, Tom Green, Wheeler, Wichita, Wilbarger, Wise, Yoakum, Young • (The Court meets in Albilene, Amarillo, Dallas, Fort Worth, Lubbock, San Angelo, Wichita Falls)

Northern District of Texas
U.S. Courthouse, 12th Floor
1100 Commerce Street
Dallas, TX 75242
214-753-2000 (v)
214-767-3588 (f)
www.txnb.uscourts.gov

Northern District of Texas
Fort Worth Division
501 West 10th Street, Room 147
Fort Worth, TX 76102
817-333-6000 (v)
www.txnb.uscourts.gov

Northern District of Texas
306 Federal Building
1205 Texas Avenue
Lubbock, TX 79401
806-472-5000 (v)
www.txnb.uscourts.gov

Southern District
Counties: Aransas, Austin, Bee, Brazoria, Brazos, Brooks, Calhoun, Cameron, Chambers, Colorado, De Witt, Duval, Fayette, Fort Bend, Galveston, Goliad, Grimes, Harris, Hidalgo, Jackson, Jim Wells, Jim Hogg, Kenedy, Kleberg, LaSalle, Lavaca, Live Oak, Madison, Matagorda, McMullen, Montgomery, Nueces, Refugio, San Jacinto, San Patricio, Starr, Victoria, Walker, Aaller, Webb, Wharton, Willacy, Zapata • (The Court meets in Brownsville, Corpus Christi, Houston, McAllen, Laredo, Victoria)

Southern District of Texas
Corpus Christi Division
1133 N. Shoreline Blvd.
Corpus Christi, TX 78401
361-888-3483 (v)
www.txsb.uscourts.gov

Southern District of Texas
P.O. Box 61010
Federal Building
515 Rusk Avenue
Houston, TX 77208-1010
713-250-5500 (v)
713-250-5550 (f)
www.txsb.uscourts.gov

Eastern District
Counties: Anderson, Angelina, Bowie, Camp, Cass, Cherokee, Collin, Cook, Delta, Denton, Fannin, Franklin, Grayson, Gregg, Hardin, Harrison, Henderson, Hopkins, Houston, Jasper, Jefferson, Lamar, Liberty, Marion, Morris, Nacogdoches, Newton, Orange, Panola, Polk, Rains, Red River, Rusk, Sabine, San Augustine, Shelby, Smith, Titus Trinity, Tyler, Upshur, Van Zandt • (The meets in Beaumont, Lufkin, Sherman, Tyler)

Eastern District of Texas
200 East Ferguson Street, Room 200
Tyler, TX 75702
903-590-1212 (v)
www.txeb.uscourts.gov

Utah (10th Circuit)

One District • (The Court meets in Ogden, Salt Lake City)

District of Utah
U.S. Courthouse
350 South Main Street, Suite 301
Salt Lake City, UT 84101
801-524-6687 (v)
801-524-4409 (f)
www.utb.uscourts.gov

Vermont (2nd Circuit)

One District • (The Court meets in Montpelier, Rutland)

District of Vermont
Opera House, Second Floor
67 Merchants Row
P.O. Box 6648
Rutland, VT 05702-6648
802-776-2000 (v)
802-776-2020 (f)
ww.vtb.uscourts.gov

Virginia (4th Circuit)

Eastern District
Counties: Accomack, Amelia, Arlington, Brunswick, Caroline, Charles, City, Chesterfield, Culpeper, Dinwiddie, Essex, Fairfax, Fauquier, Gloucester, Goochland, Greensville, Hanover, Henrico, Isle of Wight, James City, King and Queen, King George, King, William, Lancaster, Loudoun, Louisa, Lunenberg, Mathews, Mecklenberg, Middlesex, New Kent, Northampton, Northumberland, Nottoway, Orange, Powhatan, Prince Edward, Prince George, Prince William, Richmond, Southampton, Spotsylvania, Stafford, Surry, Sussex, Westmoreland, York • (The Court meets in Alexandria, Newport News, Norfolk, Richmond)

Eastern District of Virginia
Alexandria Division
200 South Washington Street
P.O. Box 19247
Alexandria, VA 22320-0247
703-258-1200 (v)
www.vaeb.uscourts.gov

Eastern District of Virginia
Newport News Division
101 25th Street
P.O. Box 1938
Newport News, VA 23607
757-222-7500 (v)
www.vaeb.uscourts.gov

Eastern District of Virginia
Norfolk Division
600 Granby Street, 4th Floor
Norfolk, VA 23510
757-222-7500 (v)
www.vaeb.uscourts.gov

Eastern District of Virginia
Richmond Division
1100 East Main Street
Room 301
Richmond, VA 23219
804-916-2400 (v)
www.vaeb.uscourts.gov

Western District
Counties: Albermarle, Allegheny, Amherst, Appomattox, Augusta, Bath, Bedford, Bland, Botecourt, Buchanan, Buckingham, Campbell, Carroll, Charlotte, Clarke, Craig, Cumberland, Dickenson, Floyd, Fluvanna,

Franklin, Frederick, Giles, Grayson, Greene, Halifax, Henry, Highland, Lee, Madison, Montgomery, Nelson, Page, Patrick, Pitsylvania, Pulaski, Rappahannoc, Roanoke, Rockbridge, Rockingham, Russell, Scott, Shenandoa, Smith, Tazewell, Warrenm Washingon, Wise, Wythe • (The Court meets in Abington, Big Stone Gap, Charlottesville, Danville, Harrisonburg, Lynchburg, Roanoke, Staunton)

Western District of Virginia
Harrisonburg Division
223 Federal Building
116 North Main Street
Harrisonburg, VA 22801
540-434-8327 (v)
www.vawb.uscourts.gov

Western District of Virginia
Lynchburg Division
P.O. Box 6400
1100 Main Street, Room 226
Lynchburg, VA 24504
804-845-0317 (v)
804-845-1801 (f)
www.vawb.uscourts.gov

Western District of Virginia
Roanoke Division
210 Church Avenue, Southwest
Room 200
Roanoke, VA 24011
540-857-2391 (v)
540-857-2873 (f)
www.vawb.uscourts.gov

Washington (9th Circuit)

Western District
Counties: Clallam, Clark, Cowlitz, Grays Harbor, Island, Jefferson, King, Kitsap, Lewis, Mason, Pacific, Pierce, Skagit, Skamania, Snohomish, Thurston, Whakiakum, Whatcom • (The Court meets in Bremerton, Everett, Kelso, Seattle, Tacoma, Vancouver)

Western District of Washington
Park Place Building
1200 Sixth Avenue, Room 315
Seattle, WA 98101
206-55-7545 (v)
206-553-0187 (f)
www.wawb.uscourts.gov

Western District of Washington
Tacoma Division
1717 Pacific Avenue, Room 2100
Tacoma, WA 98402-3233
253-593-6310 (v)
www.wawb.uscourts.gov

Eastern District
Counties: Adams, Asotin, Benton, Chelan, Columbia,
Douglas, Ferry. Franklin, Garfield, Grant, Kittitas,
Klickitat, Lincoln, Okanogan, Pend Oreille, Spokane,
Stevens, Walla Walla, Whitman, Yakima • (The meets in
Ephrata, Richland, Spokane, Yakima)

Eastern District of Washington
P.O. Box 2164
904 West Riverside Avenue, Suite 304
Spokane, WA 92210-2164
509-353-2404 (v)
509-353-2448 (f)
www.waeb.uscourts.gov

West Virginia (4th Circuit)

Southern District
Counties: Boone, Cabell, Clay, Fayette, Greenbrier,
Jackson, Kanawha, Lincoln, Logan, Mason, McDowell,
Mercer, Mingo, Monroe, Nicholas, Putnam, Raleigh,
Roane, Summers, Wayne, Webster, Wirt, Wood,
Wyoming • (The Court meets in Beckley, Bluefield,
Charleston, Huntington, Parkersburg)

Southern District of West Virginia
P.O. Box 3924
Charleston, WV 25339
304-347-3000 (v)
www.wvsd.uscourts.gov/bankruptcy/index.htm

Northern District
Counties: Brown, Calumet, Dodge, Door, Florence, Fond
du Lac, Forest, Green Lake, Kenosha, Kewaunee,
Langlade, Manitowoc, Marinette, Marquette,
Menominee, Milwaukee, Oconto, Outagamie, Ozaukee,
Racine, Shawano, Sheboygan, Walworth, Washington,
Waukesha, Waupaca, Waushara, Winnebago • (The
Court meets in Green Bay, Kenosha, Manitowoc,
Milwaukee, Oshkosh, Racine)

Northern District of West Virginia
U.S. Post Office and Courthouse Bldg.
Twelfth and Chapline Streets, Room 300
P.O. Box 70
Wheeling, WV 26003
304-233-1655 (v)
304-233-0185 (f)
www.wvnb.uscourts.gov

Wisconsin (7th Circuit)

Western District
Counties: Adams, Ashland, Barron, Bayfield, Buffalo,
Burnett, Chippewa, Clark, Columbia, Crawford, Dane,
Douglas, Dunn, Eau Claire, Grant, Green, Iowa, Iron,
Jackson, Jefferson, Juneau, La Crosse, Lafayette,
Lincoln, Marathon, Monroe, Oneida, Pepin, Pierce, Polk,
Portage, Price, Richland, Rock, Rusk, Saint Croix, Sauk,
Sawyer, Taylor, Trempe-aleau, Vernon, Vilas,
Washburn, Wood • (The Court meets in Eau Claire, La
Crosse, Madison, Wausau)

Western District of Wisconsin
Eau Claire Division
500 South Barstow Street
P.O. Box 5009
Eau Claire, WI 54702
715-839-2980 (v)
715-839-2996 (f)
www.wiw.uscourts.gov/bankruptcy

Western District of Wisconsin
P.O. Box 548
120 North Henry Street, Room 340
Madison, WI 53703
608-264-5178 (v)
608-264-5105 (f)

Eastern District
Counties: Brown, Calumet, Dodge, Door, Florence, Fond
du Lac, Forest, Green Lake, Kenosha, Kewaunee,
Langlade, Manitowoc, Marinette, Marquette,
Menominee, Milwaukee, Oconto, Outagamie, Ozaukee,
Racine, Shawano, Sheboygan, Walworth, Washington,
Waukesha, Waupaca, Waushara, Winnebago • (The
Court meets in Green Bay, Kenosha, Manitowoc,
Milwaukee, Oshkosh, Racine)

Eastern District of Wisconsin
Milwaukee Division
126 U.S. Courthouse
517 East Wisconsin Avenue, Suite 126
Milwaukee, WI 53202
414-297-3291(v)
www.wieb.uscourts.gov

Wyoming (10th Circuit)

One District • (The Court meets in Casper, Cheyenne)

District of Wyoming
111 South Wolcott Street
Casper, WY 82601
www.wyb.uscourts.gov
307-261-5444 (v)

District of Wyoming
P.O. Box 1107
2120 Capitol Avenue
Cheyenne, WY 82001-1107
307-772-2191 (v)
307-772-2298 (f)
www.wyb.uscourts.go

Glossary

Adversary proceeding: An additional lawsuit filed in conjunction with a bankruptcy. Adversary proceedings often ask the court to determine the dischargeability of a debt that is typically nondischargeable (such as student loans).

Bankruptcy Code: Title 11 of the United States Code (often abbreviated as 11 U.S.C) governs bankruptcy proceedings. Bankruptcy is a matter of federal law and is similar in every state.

Chapter 7: Is the most common form of bankruptcy and is available to individuals, married couples, corporations, and partnerships. It provides a quick discharge of debt.

Compromise: Policy of the Department of Education that accepts less than the total amount due on student loans to fully satisfy the conditions of the loan.

Consolidation: Combines a number of student loans into one loan.

Debtor: Person, partnership or corporation (legal entity) that is liable for debts and who is the subject of a bankruptcy.

Deferment: Postponement of student loan repayment under various, specific circumstances during which interest are not charged.

Deposition: Testimony that is given under oath, especially a statement given by a witness that is read out in court in the witness's absence

Discharge: The legal elimination of debt through bankruptcy.

Dischargeable: Debts that can be eliminated through bankruptcy. In general, student loans cannot be discharged through bankruptcy unless an adversary proceeding is launched and the court determines repaying the loans would cause an "undue hardship."

Dismissal: The termination of a lawsuit without either entry or judgment, i.e., the court does not record a discharge or denial of discharge.

Federal Poverty Guideline: The Social Security Administration developed the guidelines in 1964 by guessing the average family's total expenditure for food and multiplying it by a factor three.

FFEL: Federal Family Education Loan

Forbearance: Payments of student loans are temporarily postponed or reduced while interest is still charged.

Fresh start: A core feature of the U.S. Bankruptcy Code that acknowledges one of the primary reasons for bankruptcy is to allow debtors to wipe out most all debt to "freshly" start over.

Income Contingent Repayment (ICR) Plan: Plans that base monthly payments on the ability of the debtor to pay. It is the most flexible repayment plan offered by the Department of Education for Direct Loans. A complicated formula is used to calculate how much a debtor should be able to afford to make toward loan repayments (see Appendix A). If a debtor experiences hard times and his or her income drops, payments drops accordingly— sometimes to zero. The plan last for 25 years and any outstanding debt remaining at the end of the plan is discharged. However, debtors are liable for the taxes (income) on the discharged amount.

Interrogatories: Forms used by attorneys to gather information from witnesses.

Mediation: Informal meeting between the plaintiff and defendant before a trial to try and come to some mutually agreed solution, thereby negating the need to go to trial.

Meeting of the creditors: The one and only bankruptcy court meeting where creditors may challenge debts held by the plaintiff.

NELRP: Nursing Education Loan Repayment Program

Non-dischargeable: Debts that cannot be discharged through bankruptcy. The Bankruptcy Code list of non-dischargeable debts is found at 11 U.S.C.A. 523.

Offset: Taking some of your federal benefits to satisfy government debt.

Partial discharge: Some courts have approved discharging a portion of a student loan instead of taking an "all or nothing " approach.

Precedent: Court rulings that establish points of law. For example, when preparing your own case, you may want to find other similar cases that ruled a particular way so you can cite them as evidence of how your court should rule.

Trustee: A person appointed by the bankruptcy court to review debtor's schedules and to represent the interests of creditors in the bankruptcy proceedings.

Undue hardship: Congress did not clarify in §523(a)(8) the meaning of "undue hardship." Many courts have harshly and narrowly ruled that debtors cannot discharge educational loans unless they can demonstrate "a certainty of hopelessness" about their long-term financial condition.

Write-Off: Policy of the Department of Education to allow debtors who are unable to repay their student loans to completely eliminate their student loan debt.

Index

11 USC § 523. **Exceptions to discharge**, 158

A

Administrative Offset of Federal Benefits, 130
Adversary Complaint, 83
adversary proceeding, 73, 79
    Complaint, 195
    Complaint to Determine Dischargeability, 81
    filing fee, 81
    going forward, 17
    impossible to win, 2
    Proceeding Sheet (cover) instruction and form, 192
    time frame, 80
    who qualifies, 3
Adversary Proceeding Complaint (Sample), 210
Adversary Proceeding Sheet, 80, 83
Adversary Proceeding Sheet (Cover) (Sample), 209
age
    impact on ability to repay, 239
ageism, 57, 239, 241
Aid to Families with Dependent Children, 64
Amend Bankruptcy Forms, 6
Amendment to Schedule F, 172
Amendment to Schedule F Sample, 170
AmeriCorps Program, 13
Andrew M. Campbell, 123

B

bad faith, 56
bankruptcy
    annual rate, 54
    caused by medical bills, 238
    Chapter 13, 25
    Chapter 7, 25
    debt ratio, 55
    fresh start, 25, 59
    number of, 19
Bankruptcy Act (1898), 25, 30, 59
Bankruptcy Code, 25, 58, 63
Bankruptcy Code (2005), 66
Bankruptcy Commission (1978), 61
Bankruptcy Reform Act (1978), 22, 25, 38
Bankruptcy Reform Act (1998), 25, 30, 53
Bankruptcy Review Commission (1973), 20, 21
Black Lung, 15
BLS. *See* Bureau of Labor Statistics
Blue Back, 83, 84, 191
Brunner Test, 26, 28, 30, 87, 101
    alternative, 237, 251
    first prong, 29

second prong, 29
    third prong, 29
Brunner v. New York State Higher Education Services Corp, 28
Bryant Poverty Test, 26, 27, 30
Bryant v. Pennsylvania Higher Education Assistance Agency, 27
Bureau of Labor Statistics, 64

C

certainty of hopelessness, 26, 28, 54, 61, 65
Chapter 13, 25, 66, 73
Chapter 7, 25, 73, 79, 85
    Business Income and Expense Form, 165
    Form B6F-Creditors Holding Unsecured Nonpriority Claims Form, 166
    Schedule I-Current Income Form, 163
    Schedule J-Current Expenditure Form, 164
Cheesman v. Tennessee Student Assistance Corp, 41
children, 35
Civil Union, 36
Collection Financial Standards, 75, 94, 143
    Food, Clothing and Other Items, 144
    Housing and Utilities, 146
        California Example, 147
    Transportation Standards (2005), 149
Committee on the Judiciary, 22
Complaint to Determine Dischargeability, 81
Compromise, 93, 99
    authority, 13
    guidelines, 13
    letter of authority, 133
    who qualifies, 3
Congressional Bankruptcy Commission (1978), 65
Conner v. Illinois State Scholarship Comm'n, 42
Consolidation, 10
    interest rate, 109
    repayment options, 110
    repayment period, 110
Cornell, 20
Courtney v. Gainer Bank, 42
crime, 59
Current Living Condition, 34

D

DCIA. *See* Debt Collection Improvement Act
debt
    collection, 53
    partial discharge, 62
    priority, 60

Debt Collection Improvement Act, 15
debtor
    African American, 58, 59
    American Indians, 59
    independent students, 58
    minorities, 58
    partially disabled, 58
    single parents, 58
    white, 58
Default, 14, 22, 121
    consequences, 121
    defined, 121
Deferment, 9, 107
defrauded. *See* fraud
Department of Housing and Urban Development, 64
    Lower Income Families, 64
    median income, 64
    Very Low-Income Families, 64
Department of Labor, 64
dependents, 35, 56
deposition, 91
<u>diligence</u>, 38
Direct Consolidation Loan Program, 10, 118
Direct Stafford Loans, 107
disability, 12, 66
Discharge Options, 12, 118
    Direct Loan and FFEL, 118
    disability, 12
    military, 13
    other, 120
    teacher low-income, 12
discovery, 91
discrimination, 36
    ageism, 37, 241
    disability, 37
    ethnicity, 37
    gender, 37
    highly educated, 36, 37, 57, 244
    income, 58
    past terminations, 38
    physical characteristics, 37
    race, 37
    religion, 37
    reverse, 38, 247
    sexual orientation, 37, 246
    whistleblower, 38
divorce, 59
DOL. *See* Department of Labor
domestic partner, 36

E

Earned Income Tax Credits, 64
economy, 248
educational value, 64
Edward York, 21
EEOC. *See* Equal Employment Opportunity Commission
Eighth Circuit Court in Andrews v. South Dakota Student Loan
    Assistance Corp, 28

Equal Employment Opportunity Commission, 37
Equal Protection Clause, 56
equitable powers, 62
Ertel, Rep. Allen, 20, 21
exceptional, 29, 34, 36
Exceptions to Discharge, 158
Extended Repayment Plan, 11, 112
external factors, 36, 76, 95
extraordinary circumstances, 28, 61

F

Federal Benefits, 15
    garnish, 53
    seize, 53
    types, 15
Federal Family Education Loan, 10
    consolidation, 109
    discharge, 118
Federal Poverty Guidelines, 26, 27, 28, 30, 34, 38, 56, 58, 60,
    61, 63, 65, 66, 75, 77, 94, 96
    description, 153
    development, 64
Federal Student Aid Information Center, 13
FFEL. *See* Federal Family Education Loan
fixed income, 66
Forbearance, 10, 108
Ford v. Tennessee Student Assistance Corp, 43
forum shopping, 63
fraud, 38, 56
fresh start, 25, 30, 59, 60, 66
furlough, 88

G

GAO. *See* General Accounting Office
garden variety hardship, 61
garnish federal benefits, 53
General Accounting Office, 55
General Accounting Office Study (1976), 20
good faith, 27, 38, 56, 77, 96
    analysis, 30
Goulet v. Educational Credit Management Corp, 43
Graduated Repayment Plan, 11, 112
Gravante, 44
GSLP. *See* Guaranteed Student Loan Program
Guaranteed Student Loan Program, 19, 22

H

Half of All Bankruptcies Due to Medical Bills, 237, 238
Healey v. Massachusetts Higher Education, 44
Higher Education Act, 21, 22
House Report on the Bankruptcy Law Revision (1977), 20
HUD. *See* Department of Housing and Urban Development

I

ICR. *See* Income Contingent Repayment (ICR) Plan
Income Contingent Repayment (ICR) Plan, 81, 86, 101, 113
   challenges, 65
   description, 11
   formula, 113
   preparing response, 77, 96
   tax consequence, 12, 66
Infancy, 16
Innes v. Kansas State Univ, 45
interest rate, 109
Interrogatories, 73, 91, 136

J

Johnson court, 61
Johnson Test, 26, 30
   good faith, 27
   mechanical analysis, 26
   policy analysis, 27
Joint Status Report, 80
Joint Status Report (Sample), 217
judicial lawmaking, 62, 65

K

Kraft v. New York State Higher Educ. Servs. Corp, 47

L

Laches, 16
Lack of Useable Job Skills, 36
Legal Service Corporation, 64
Lehman v. New York Higher Educ. Servs. Corp, 47
Loan Discharge, 118
Local Bankruptcy Rules, 80
Lower Income Families, 64

M

Mail Matrix, 84, 203
Mail Matrix (Sample), 215
Maxine Waters, 59
mechanical analysis, 26, 30
median income, 64
Mediation, 86
mediator, 90
medical condition, 34, 57
Middle Income Student Assistance Act, 19
minimal standard of living, 60, 61
minimized expenses, 34
Modified Repayment Plans, 62, 65

Motion to Reopen Bankruptcy, 6, 7, 168, 169, 170
Motion to Reopen Bankruptcy Sample, 168
Myers v. Pennsylvania Higher Education Assistance Agency, 48

N

National Bankruptcy Review Commission Report (1997), 55
National Community Service Trust Act, 10, 108
National Defense Education Act (NDEA), 19
National Defense Student Loan, 19
NDSL. *See* National Defense Student Loan
nondischargeable debt, 21, 22, 59, 65
non-disclosure, 89
Nursing Education Loan Repayment Program, 13

O

Order, 84
overturn law, 54

P

parents, 36
pariah, 38
partial discharge, 34, 62, 65
past terminations, 38
Pena v. United Student Aid Funds, 48
Pennsylvania Higher Education Assistance Agency v. Johnson, 26
Perkins Loans, 12, 19, 107, 109
   discharge, 119
personal limitations, 34, 76, 95
Playing the Game, 86
policy analysis, 27, 30
Postponement, 9, 107
poverty, 64
   defined by AFDC, 64
   defined by Bureau of Labor Statistics, 64
   defined by Department of Education, 64
   defined by Legal Service Corporation, 64
   defined by Social Security Administration, 64
   guidelines Dept. Education, 117
   sociological definition, 64
precedent, 92, 123
Pretrial Hearing, 91
Pretrial Order, 92
principle of uniformity, 63
Proof of Service, 80, 84, 203
Proof of Service (Sample), 214
Proof of Service Cover, 84
Proof of Service Cover (Sample), 216
proprietary schools, 58

R

Railroad Retirement Benefits, 15
Reopening a Bankruptcy, 6
Repayment Options, 9, 107
Repayment Plans, 111
    constant multiplier, 115
    Extended, 112
    Graduated, 112
    Income Contingent, 113
    Standard, 111
representing yourself, 3
reverse discrimination, 38
Rivers v. United Student Aid Funds, 49
Roberson, 49

S

seize federal benefits, 53
Senate Permanent Subcommittee on Investigations (1993), 59
service of process, 83
Sheldon Steinbach, 21
siblings, 36
Skaggs v. Great Lakes Higher Educ. Corp, 49
Social Security, 66
Social Security Disability, 15
Social Security Retirement, 15
sociological definitions of poverty, 64
spouse, 36
Stafford Loan Program, 19
Stafford Loans, 107
Standard Repayment Plan, 11, 111
Status Hearing, 85
statute of limitations, 16
Stebbins-Hopf v. Texas Guaranteed Student Loan Corp, 50
stereotype debtor, 58
stipulation, 90
Stipulation (Sample), 224
Student Loan
    amount, 20
    bankruptcy
        consequence of age, 239
        rate, 55
        success, 54
        threat, 55
    cancellation. *See* Student Loan: discharge
    Consolidation, 10
    debt level, 23
    default
        consequences, 121
        increase, 20
        number, 20, 22
        rate, 55
    Deferment, 9, 107
    discharge
        bankruptcy, 12
        disability, 12

loans less than 10 years old, 15
loans more than 10 years old, 15
options, 12
Perkins, 119
rate, 20
teacher, 12
Extended Repayment Plan, 11
Forbearance, 10, 108
fraud, 56
Graduated Repayment Plan, 11
history, 19
how soon trying to bankrupt, 38
Income Contingent Repayment (ICR) Plan, 11, 113
infancy, 16
laches, 16
media hype, 20
Postponement, 9, 107
ratio to total debt, 38
Repayment Options, 9, 111
    Extended Plan, 112
    Graduated Plan, 112
    ICR Plan, 113
    Standard Plan, 111
spending increase, 22
Standard Repayment Plan, 11
statute of limitations, 16
subminimal living, 60
subpoena, 91
subsistence or poverty level, 61
suicide, 59
Summons, 80, 83, 201
Summons (Sample), 213
Supplemental Security Income, 15

T

teacher low-income, 12
Totality of the Circumstances Test, 26, 28, 30
    certainty of hopelessness, 28
    external factors, 37
Trial, 91
trustee, 81
Truth-in-Lending, 17
typical debtor, 58

U

U.S. Economy, 37, 248
U.S. trustee, 81
U.S.C. 31 §3716(e), 131
U.S.C. Chapter 11 §523(a)(8), 22
undue hardship, 22, 25, 30, 87, 101
    ageism, 37
    Civil Union, 36
    dependents, 35
    Domestic Partnet, 36
    exceptional circumstances, 34
    external factors, 36

extraordinary circumstances, 28
failed to define, 61
good faith, 27
job terminated, 36
lack of useable job skills, 36
mechanical analysis, 26
medical condition, 34
parents, 36
personal limitations, 34
policy analysis, 27
siblings, 36
spouse, 36
U.S. Economy, 37
whistleblower, 36
undue hardship tests
Brunner Test, 26, 28
Bryant Poverty Test, 26, 27
Johnson Test, 26
Totality of the Circumstances, 26, 28
wide variance, 63
unique, 29, 34, 36, 61
United States Attorney, 80

unpleasantness, 28
unscrupulous recruiters, 59

V

Value of the Education, 65
Very Low-Income Families, 64

W

Walcott v. USA Funds, Inc, 50
Wegfehrt, 28
Wetzel v. New York State Higher Educ. Servs. Corp, 50
whistleblower, 36, 38
Write-Off, 14, 93, 99, 100
guidelines, 14
letter of authority, 133
who qualifies, 3

Notes

PURCHASER INFORMATION (PRINT OR TYPE)

NAME _____

Mailing Address 1 _____

Mailing Address 2 _____

City _____ State _____

Country _____ Zip _____

Telephone _____

E-mail _____

SHIP TO: (IF DIFFERENT THAN PURCHASER)

NAME _____

Mailing Address 1 _____

Mailing Address 2 _____

City _____ State _____

Country _____ Zip _____

Telephone _____

E-mail _____

Quantity	Description	Unit Price	Total
	Bankrupt Your Student Loans and Other Discharge Strategies (3rd Edition) By Chuck Stewart, Ph.D. 2009 (over 300 pages) You will be guided, step-by-step, in the process of filing an adversary proceeding to discharge your student loans or negotiate a Compromise or Write-Off. Perfect binding. ISBN 9781425928551 www.Authorhouse.com Also available through www.BankruptYourStudentLoans.com.	$34.95	
	Lead Hazards in Residential Real Estate By Chuck Stewart, Ph.D. 2005 (516 pages) This is the most comprehensive book ever written on the problem of LEAD in residential real estate. ISBN 0-9764154-3-7	$89.95	
	Lead Hazards Teaching Packages (contains two complete packages) By Chuck Stewart, Ph.D. 2005 Contains both the OWNER Package and WORKER Package. Both packages contain color-coded curriculum, set of handouts, slide presentation on DVD, and 60-minute action DVD with English, Spanish and Chinese subtitles.	$119.95	
	Mold Hazards in Residential Real Estate By Chuck Stewart, Ph.D. 2005 (140 pages) The most comprehensive book ever written on the problem of MOLD in residential real estate. ISBN 0-9764154-4-5	$29.95	
	Mold Hazards Teaching Package (for Mold Hazards in Residential Real Estate) By Chuck Stewart, Ph.D. 2005 The package contains: • color-coded curriculum • set of handouts • slide presentation on DVD • 15-minute action DVD with English, Spanish and Chinese subtitles.	$79.95	
		Subtotal	
	PROMOTIONAL DISCOUNTS: Enter Code here _____ **Example:** If you received a flyer offering a discount toward purchase of these books, write the code on the line above, and then calculate the discount. Attach the promotional flyer to this invoice. For example, if the discount is 10%, calculate 10% of the Subtotal, write it in the right-hand column and subtract to get a New Subtotal.	(subtract)	
		New Subtotal	
	California Residents add 9.25% Sales Tax	Sales Tax	
	Shipping Notes: All books are mailed in the US by US Mail Book Rate unless special arrangements are made. For 1-5 books, include $5.90. For 6-10 books, include $9.70. All orders over $120.00, shipping is free. Contact us for rushed and International rates.	Shipping and Handling	
		Total	

Make checks payable to Stewart Education Services.
Send completed Invoice with payment to:
Stewart Education Services, 3722 Bagley Ave. #19, Los Angeles, CA 90034-4113
Personal checks, money orders, cashier's checks, Pay-Pal accepted.
No cash or credit cards. Allow 4-6 weeks for delivery.
Questions? E-mail to: contact@BankruptYourStudentLoans.com

Stewart Education Services
www.StewartEducationServices.com

I N V O I C E

PURCHASER INFORMATION (PRINT OR TYPE)

NAME _____

Mailing Address 1 _____

Mailing Address 2 _____

City _____ State _____

Country _____ Zip _____

Telephone _____

E-mail _____

SHIP TO: (IF DIFFERENT THAN PURCHASER)

NAME _____

Mailing Address 1 _____

Mailing Address 2 _____

City _____ State _____

Country _____ Zip _____

Telephone _____

E-mail _____

Quantity	Description	Unit Price	Total
	Bankrupt Your Student Loans and Other Discharge Strategies (3rd Edition) By Chuck Stewart, Ph.D. 2009 (over 300 pages) You will be guided, step-by-step, in the process of filing an adversary proceeding to discharge your student loans or negotiate a Compromise or Write-Off. Perfect binding. ISBN 9781425928551 www.Authorhouse.com Also available through www.BankruptYourStudentLoans.com.	$34.95	
	Lead Hazards in Residential Real Estate By Chuck Stewart, Ph.D. 2005 (516 pages) This is the most comprehensive book ever written on the problem of LEAD in residential real estate. ISBN 0-9764154-3-7	$89.95	
	Lead Hazards Teaching Packages (contains two complete packages) By Chuck Stewart, Ph.D. 2005 Contains both the OWNER Package and WORKER Package. Both packages contain color-coded curriculum, set of handouts, slide presentation on DVD, and 60-minute action DVD with English, Spanish and Chinese subtitles.	$119.95	
	Mold Hazards in Residential Real Estate By Chuck Stewart, Ph.D. 2005 (140 pages) The most comprehensive book ever written on the problem of MOLD in residential real estate. ISBN 0-9764154-4-5	$29.95	
	Mold Hazards Teaching Package (for Mold Hazards in Residential Real Estate) By Chuck Stewart, Ph.D. 2005 The package contains: • color-coded curriculum • set of handouts • slide presentation on DVD • 15-minute action DVD with English, Spanish and Chinese subtitles.	$79.95	
		Subtotal	
	PROMOTIONAL DISCOUNTS: Enter Code here _____ **Example:** If you received a flyer offering a discount toward purchase of these books, write the code on the line above, and then calculate the discount. Attach the promotional flyer to this invoice. For example, if the discount is 10%, calculate 10% of the Subtotal, write it in the right-hand column and subtract to get a New Subtotal.	(subtract)	
		New Subtotal	
	California Residents add 9.25% Sales Tax	Sales Tax	
	Shipping Notes: All books are mailed in the US by US Mail Book Rate unless special arrangements are made. For 1-5 books, include $5.90. For 6-10 books, include $9.70. All orders over $120.00, shipping is free. Contact us for rushed and International rates.	Shipping and Handling	
		Total	

Make checks payable to Stewart Education Services.
Send completed Invoice with payment to:
Stewart Education Services, 3722 Bagley Ave. #19, Los Angeles, CA 90034-4113
Personal checks, money orders, cashier's checks, Pay-Pal accepted.
No cash or credit cards. Allow 4-6 weeks for delivery.
Questions? E-mail to: contact@BankruptYourStudentLoans.com

Breinigsville, PA USA
19 October 2009
226009BV00007B/2/P